CONFESSIONS OF A PARISH PRIEST

AN AUTOBIOGRAPHY

Andrew M. Greeley

SIMON AND SCHUSTER
New York

Copyright © 1986 by Andrew M. Greeley
All rights reserved
including the right of reproduction
in whole or in part in any form
Published by Simon and Schuster
A Division of Simon & Schuster, Inc.
Simon & Schuster Building
Rockefeller Center
1230 Avenue of the Americas
New York, New York 10020

SIMON AND SCHUSTER and colophon are registered
trademarks of Simon & Schuster, Inc.

Designed by Irving Perkins Associates

Manufactured in the United States of America

1   3   5   7   9   10   8   6   4   2

Library of Congress Cataloging in Publication Data

Greeley, Andrew M.
    Confessions of a parish priest.
    1. Greeley, Andrew M., date–   . 2. Catholic Church—
United States—Clergy—Biography.   I. Title.
BX4705.G6185A3   1986   282′.092′4 [B]   86-13090
            ISBN: 0-671-61084-8

This memoir is dedicated to six of my fellow priests
whose friendship and loyalty have never wavered.

In Chicago
RICHARD DEMPSEY
JOHN KRUMP
LEO MAHON
JOHN SHEA

In Tucson
ROBERT BURNS
TOMAS O'CALAHANE

It may well be true that most of us love ourselves too well to be autobiographers.

—A. O. J. Cockshut,
The Art of Autobiography

The labyrinth is in fact the image par excellence of initiation ... every human existence consists of a series of initiatory ordeals or trials; man creates himself by a series of unconscious or conscious initiations.

—Mircea Eliade

The core of the Greeley novels is a mythology in which the fire of sexual passion, diffused into all aspects of human emotional experience, lights the way to a grail of upbeat grace ... he has found his mythology, ready to wear, on the racks of Irish Catholicism ... the characters live simultaneously in Chicago and *in illo tempore* ... millions of people respond to the mythology of the Greeley novels, in part because he touches on a mythology they already have and in part because he presents them with a mythology they want to have.

—Wendy Doniger O'Flaherty, from the preface to
Eros and the Womanliness of God by Ingrid Shafer

For hours I read the letters. Andrew Greeley is right. He is a parish priest. His parish is in his mailbox.

—Mark Harris,
The New York Times

PRAYER TO ST. BRIGID

Brigid chaigh, Cille Dara
Mo bhamogh, mo bhamchara
Go dti fam chli'na crios te
Go dti dom fhios an taoidhe

(Ah, Holy Brigid of Kildare
Gentle lady of springtime air
With your power ever guard me
And my tender love always be)

CONTENTS

PROLOGUE

TWIN LAKES

A sad bell clangs that suppertime is near
And the fat man with his dizzy jokes
Feet still dangling from the dark wooden pier
A castle hidden among the giant oaks
Enchanted wonder, great endless silver sheet
Smooth waters sliced by darting speedboat wakes
Gravel path and joyous sands beneath my feet
Faces of lost friends—summertime at Twin Lakes
Wonder, surprise, joy, magic do not last;
Weep little boy for Youth and What Might Have Been
Search not for sad sweet relics of the past
It's too late, you can't go home again
Old friends, dark castle, and magic silver lake
Oft found in dreams but lost when I awake

"You are going deeper and deeper and deeper," Erika Fromm's rich, Middle European voice said reassuringly, "you are climbing back down the ladder of your life and you are feeling very happy, oh, so very happy, deeper and deeper and deeper, you are filled with happiness. Now mentally you open your eyes and look around at this time of your life when you were so very, very happy. Where do you find yourself?"

I was three years old and standing on a green, sun-drenched hill, looking at the lawns rolling down to the dull silver platter of a lake. Behind me was a big stately Victorian mansion with turrets and porches, a magic castle perhaps. On either side were wooden buildings painted white with green trim surrounded by screened-in porches. In front of me a bed of thick red flowers surrounded a brilliant reflecting globe, a giant ball bearing; at the side of the lake a dark stone platform covered with a peaked roof and on the lake itself speedboats (Hunter Deluxe Specials!) and sailboats puttered about. Children and adults sat on a quaint wooden pier which jutted into the lake and kids my age were frolicking on a great slide which sloped into the warm, comforting waters. I rushed quickly down the slope of the hill and into the lake to join them.

Dr. Fromm's age regression had brought me back to ecstatically happy experiences at the outer fringe of my conscious memory. Here was where it all started. Commodore Barry Knights of Columbus Country Club, a magical place with a vast lake, towering jungle-covered hills, lawns and gravel-covered paths on which to run (and make shambles of one's knees), a dining hall with real mashed potatoes, gleaming corn on the cob, thick gravy, an endless supply of roast beef, crowds spread out on the lawn on a Sunday morning in front of the pergola following the progress of the Mass, a distant drama marked by a tinkling of a bell, barely to be heard over the summer sounds of the lake.

In the dining hall men wore ties though air conditioning was unknown; and at Mass on Sundays, they put on coats and even carried their straw hats in their hands (many of them, my father included, were in "plus four" knickers instead of long trousers and carried caps instead of hats). The priests who said the Mass lived in a secluded wooden house at the fringe of the country club, and enjoyed their quiet vacations, discreetly separated but not completely isolated from the laity.

My reexperienced happiness in Erika Fromm's hypnotic trance was generalized and unspecific. *Everything* about Twin Lakes made me happy. The lake, the jungle-covered hill, the lawns, the boats, the club-

14

house (as my magic castle was called) with its slot machines, my friends running down the hill and jumping into the water, the lurking mystery of the pergola at night. The fat man who was in charge of the club and told jokes in the dining hall, the limitless supply of food, chasing my father on the golf course, dreaming about the possibility that we would have a house of our own on the lake, looking through the thick overgrowth on the hill behind the club, excursions to Lake Geneva and the Fox Lake chain during which we actually were permitted to ride in Hunter Deluxe speedboats instead of gazing wistfully at them. There, at Twin Lakes, the early and middle 1930s was the matrix of my childhood and the matrix of my life.

There were some unpleasant memories: the smell of the outdoor toilets, the death during the winter of a dearly loved Twin Lakes friend (tonsil infection, poor radiant little girl), the day that my father, weary, worn and tired, came to Twin Lakes to tell my mother his business had been wiped out by the advancing Great Depression. Somehow Twin Lakes was never quite the same after that.

The images which had surfaced when Erika was teaching me the age-regression technique of self-hypnosis exploded out of my brain for weeks thereafter. First in my own self-hypnotic exercises, then in ordinary waking consciousness, the whole world of Twin Lakes in the 1930s recreated itself, benignly, vividly, overwhelmingly in my imagination. It was not that I was unaware of the Commodore Barry Country Club's role in my life before Erika had taught me (I was helping her design a questionnaire for a study she was doing on techniques of self-hypnosis in psychoanalytic therapy and she offered to teach me the technique). In the fragment of a memoir I wrote for Gregory Baum's book *Journeys*, published in the early 1970s, I mentioned the Twin Lakes phenomenon. John Kotre in his "intellectual biography" also cites the Twin Lakes experience in my life. The hypnotic interludes, however, revealed to me the critical influence Twin Lakes still is on my imagination.

The sheer raw vividness and power of the memories constrained me to turn to fiction writing. What until then had been a pipe dream became an obligation, a necessity. In most of my novels the experience of summer and summer resorts while growing up is important not merely as background against which the stories unfold, but as integral parts of the novel's structure.

The "Lake" in *The Cardinal Sins* is a rather more spectacular version

15

of Twin Lakes. Lake Geneva becomes the site for the first love affair of Hugh Donlon and the magic Maria in *Ascent into Hell*. Later Twin Lakes itself appears, notably in *The Angels of September* and *The Patience of a Saint*. The Grand Beach/Long Beach area on the southeast shore of Lake Michigan, which my sister Mary Jule insists is the locus of my attempt to recreate Twin Lakes for my adulthood, becomes the bastion of the Ryan family who people many of my novels. When my preconscious is unleashed in storytelling, summer symbolism seems automatically to appear.

I am summer people, surf, sand, water, thunderstorms, dense humidity, teenagers at night roaring down the dark resort streets, the tug of wind and water on a sailboat or wind surfer, the lake, sometimes lapping the beach, sometimes pounding furiously against it—these are the natural high points of my life. I dread the end of summer and despise the first signs of fall in the beginning of pro-football practice and the back-to-school ads in the Sunday papers. An even more dastardly erosion of summer is the conspiracy of professional educators to drag my teenage water-skiing friends to the classroom in the middle of August. To endeavor to end summer before Labor Day, indeed before Columbus Day, is a crime against nature. I am dangerously close to tears when the village is emptied and I must also abandon it to return to the city, a city I love, but a city for autumn rather than summer (we don't have spring in Chicago).

As O'Connor the Cat, the Grand Beach lifeguard who appears in various of my stories, most notably *Happy Are the Meek*, remarks, "Summer is over, but life goes on."

O'Connor the Cat can afford to say that because she's sixteen going on seventeen. At my age each passing summer, each passing day of summer, is to be grievously mourned.

I am always deeply moved by the summer scenes in poems and novels and films. The summer interlude in Ingmar Bergman's *Wild Strawberries* is one of the most powerful dramatic passages I've ever experienced. Stories of young love in the summer (most recently in the not terribly distinguished film *Flamingo Kid*) twist at my heart, not because I spent my teen years at a summer resort (alas, I did not) nor because I was ever in love as a young man during the summer (perhaps alas, I was not), but because there is something so terribly vulnerable about young men and women in summer-resort love. I feel a prodigious responsibility to protect

16

them from hurt and cynicism and disillusion—a foolish and absurd responsibility because the best I can do is to persuade them that disillusion if persisted in (*pace* T. S. Eliot) is the ultimate illusion.

I don't cry much, but I did when I read James Farrell's story of the summer romance of Studs Lonigan and Lucy Scanlan, one of the most touching accounts of young love ever written—and unlike the harsh realism of most of Farrell's fiction. I had the same reaction both times I saw the TV miniseries based on the Lonigan Trilogy. If ever there were a vivid portrait of what happens when grace is refused...

Ah, but was there a Lucy Scanlan in my life?

No, I was destined for the seminary and the priesthood. By my own choice, a choice I don't regret.

When he was still archbishop of Cincinnati, Joseph Bernardin asked me apropos of *The Cardinal Sins*, first of all, whether Patrick Donahue was based on him. I assured the archbishop he was not the model for Patrick, unless he had been a lot busier than I thought he had.

"What about the other people?" he asked.

"You mean Ellen, Joe?"

"Yes, of course. Ellen."

"No," I said. "There was never anyone like Ellen Foley in my life."

The archbishop shook his head sadly. "That's too bad."

Perhaps it is. Perhaps it isn't. One does not, I have learned through the years, fight the Holy Spirit. If there had been, somewhere, a woman in my life that I loved as intensely as Kevin Brennan loved Ellen Foley, she would present a real problem for this memoir. Probably I would not write the memoir. But, for weal or woe, there isn't any Ellen Foley in my past, although the storyteller in me realizes that a real-life counterpart of Lucy Scanlan or Ellen Foley would make it a far more interesting tale.

Someone who might have been?

Ah, that would be telling, now wouldn't it?

And do I feel sad that my Lucy Scanlan never really became my Lucy Scanlan? Or that my Ellen Foley never really became my Ellen Foley?

I never said there was any such person in the first place, did I now? Anyway, I am well aware that young love in summertime is ephemeral. If it is to survive, it must develop into something much different, stronger, more mature, more resilient, wiser. But this part of my story is not about such rational propositions and conclusions or even about my own summer

17

experiences and fantasies as an adolescent. Somehow in my instinct to reassert the mythological truth and the paradigmatic wisdom of the appealing vulnerabilities of summer love, deeply rooted in my Twin Lakes experience, is the core of my vocation to the priesthood and much of everything else in my life.

God, to use language it took me decades to discover, is the only lover who possesses the perfection of passion and excitement of first love in summer. S/He lurked, alluring and deceptive, on the pier at Twin Lakes.

Romantic? As you should have discovered even at this early stage of the book, I am an incorrigible romantic, so incorrigible that I believe God is one too.

My friend Father Roland Murphy, the distinguished Carmelite scholar and specialist on the Wisdom Literature in the Jewish Scriptures, points out that Wisdom in the Scripture is always described as feminine. He calls her Lady Wisdom and from a very careful analysis concludes that She is God's attractive charm as revealed in the order and the beauty and the graciousness of the creative world.

'Twas Herself, Lady Wisdom, I think who beckoned me from the pier at Twin Lakes. As I will record later in this book, my own image of God is that She is a Comedienne—and an Irish one at that. Life is finally either Comedy or Absurdity and I opt for the former alternative.

Hence occasionally in this book I will record an observation from Lady Wisdom, who for the purposes of this story must be imagined as speaking with a West of Ireland brogue (none of your elite Dublin accents, mind you!)

Why my paradigmatic responsibility to protect summer love, or more specifically, summer lovers, through encouragement and reassurance, to salvage innocence and hope, to be priest especially for young people in the summertime? I can only point to Twin Lakes and say I learned it there. "Learned" not in the sense of being taught it but in the sense of absorbing it from the physical and social and interpersonal environment (words which I didn't know in those days).

Why would I absorb this—what should I call it—Twin Lakes "mystique"? I think I've finally figured it out. I have thin boundaries; poignancies slip into my personality through an osmosis so subtle I'm not even aware it is happening. Even at seventeen, on a rare revisit to Twin Lakes, I found myself caught up in the confusion and agony of a young couple. The boy had just returned from Europe riddled with wounds suffered in

18

the Hürtgen Forest. I was a year or two younger than they and did not know experientially what time can do to innocence and hope. Still, I wanted to help them.

There was nothing I could or did do for them. The point, however, is that I *wanted* to help them. God knows the two of them—they soon broke up—could have used a priest's help, a wise and experienced priest, not a well-meaning seminarian with a crooked lance in his hand and a horse nearby named Rosinante.

More recently, after forty years, I have rediscovered friends from my grammar school days. Slowly and piecemeal they tell me what has happened in their lives since 1946 when they graduated from high school. They are young lovers again for me. I have the irrational urge to go back to the bad times in their lives and help them through those interludes.

Nonsense in both cases? Certainly. In 1945 and 1985 I knew it was nonsense. I didn't act on the instinct. I am not prone to the destructive pity of Graham Greene's tragic heroes, though I understand the nature of the temptation. You cannot finally make other people's decisions for them. You cannot protect them from the tragedies of their own mistakes. My altruistic instinct, formed at Twin Lakes and crucial to my priestly vocation, was at work. It would always be at work.

Summer has become, no, it always was for me, the time when the mysteries of life and death, good and evil, love and hate, are most sharply and clearly delineated. At the core of my summer personality, I am convinced, there lurks the most basic, the most fundamental, the most instinctual question that I can ask myself: is summer a delusion or is it a sacrament? My life is about the search for an answer to that question. In this memoir I wrestle explicitly and implicitly with that issue. Is summer a trick, a deception, is it the hint of an explanation, a rumor of angels, a splendidly tricky gift from a splendidly tricky God?

O'Connor the Cat is right: summer ends, and life goes on. There is life after summer, doubtless. But what is the answer to the question which is perhaps implicit in the Cat's dictum: is life a preparation for summertime?

I watch old movies of early childhood at Twin Lakes—now, such are the wonders of technology, transferred to videotape. They confirm the vivid images from my self-hypnotic sessions. The background is not as rich as I had pictured it, but the high-spirited little boy who dashes madly down the hill is a TV ad for "happy little boy."

Ha, you little brat, I say to myself, you don't know that you have permeable boundaries, do you? You're not aware of all the joy and the pain you are absorbing, all the hope and the cynicism, all the responsibility and poignancy, are you?

Nor do you realize, poor happy little boy, that you'll never feel quite so happy again. Later on you'll have memories of that happiness as though it was something that happened to someone else. You don't understand that the rest of your life will be a search to rediscover the origins of your childish high spirits.

The high spirits ceased. Abruptly? I think so. There was the small matter of the Great Depression, which wiped out my father's business and burdened the rest of his life with a terrible conviction that he had failed. Youthful joys would have stopped anyway. We all grow up. The issue is whether we write off childhood happiness as a deception or remember it as a sacrament. Maybe if childhood joys end abruptly, the passion of one's search for the sacramental in childhood happiness becomes even more implacable.

Dr. Ingrid Shafer, a scholar at the University of Arts and Sciences of Oklahoma, who has studied my novels, contends, not unreasonably, that they are all varieties of the search for the Holy Grail, for the magic cup (to use the name of my first novel) and the magic princess. My protagonists, heroes or heroines, are all searching for the secret of happiness rediscovered and for the tender and affectionate source of such happiness. Herself.

Professor Shafer suggests that in this respect I am like my characters, a kind of latter-day Art MacConn (Cormac MacDermot in my story) searching for the magic cup and the magic princess, a faintly comic Celtic Lancelot. Well, better a Celt than that creepy Victorian heavy breather L. du Lac, God knows. My Cormac MacDermot is even more comic than Art MacConn in the legend. I'll concede to Professor Shafer the validity of her model as literary analysis.

But the image I find more consoling is that of the man on Rosinante, battling windmills. Art MacConn was altogether too wise and Cormac MacDermot altogether too strong for me to be at ease with them.

Quixote. Keep that picture in your mind as you experience this story. A passionate quester, but a comic one too.

How important was my Twin Lakes experience? Many of us have

overarching symbols which play crucial roles in the structures of our imaginative life. Mircea Eliade returns repeatedly to the image of the labyrinth. My most important symbol is the lake.

When I consider my principal efforts, I see them all converging back to the Twin Lakes memory and the lake image. As a sociologist, my most important contribution is work on the religious imagination. As a commentator on American Catholicism, I have emphasized the ability of the community and the heritage to survive cheerfully, ignoring the lunacies of the institution because of the power of religious imagery. As a religious scholar, my critical work has been on Mary as the sacrament of the womanliness of God. And finally, in my latter days, as a storyteller, all these combine in tales of a quest for a magic cup and a magic princess who, it turns out, is also passionately searching for us.

Okay, Greels, as the kids call me, is funny, a laughable character, often even when he does not intend to be, maybe especially when he does not intend to be, like Don Quixote. They call me that too, or usually Quixots —"key-HOTES." There is comedy in this story of a priest-turned-writer-of-comedy, especially unintentional comedy.

(Oh, boy, how's that for giving a lead to reviewers! I'll provide them with two other clichés so they won't have to read beyond this prologue: my memoir is "self-serving and narcissistic"—as though any autobiography is not a consideration of the self in search of greater understanding of the self. Put that way, it doesn't make for a good smear, however. Another great line which I will offer for hostile reviewers, totally free of charge, is "When the reader is finished with this book he'll know more about Andrew Greeley than he could possibly want to know!")

But Quixote (the original one, that is) is a comic figure not because of his quest but because of the misperceptions in his quest. Life, if it is anything at all, is a quest for a Grail, an end of a rainbow, a leprechaun with a pot of gold, a Bali Ha'i in the South Pacific.

As I wrote this book and pondered my life and its matrix in Twin Lakes, I found myself more and more in agreement with Professor Shafer. Twin Lakes represents the tenderness of the cosmos, the tenderness of God of which the Lake was one of my early sacraments, and the tender dimensions of the self (Jung's anima without all the ideological overtones he puts on it) for which my life story is a quest (perhaps the life story of all of us). Curiously, writing this book about my quest has actually furthered the quest. What started out as an exercise in self-explanation and self-understanding intensified a critical segment of my pilgrimage towards the tenderness of God.

Robertson Davies in his recent quest novel *Bred in the Bone* suggests that the Grail for which we seek is the whole self, that which we consider "male" and that which we consider "female" (for lack of more powerful terms) combined. Jung would perhaps say the union between animus and anima. Others would call it personal integration. Yet others would see the androgynous personality as the goal of the inner quest.

The "tender self" and the "tender God" are correlates, each revealing the other. The girl is the Grail and the Grail is the girl and both are God in the Celtic version of the legend. Reading Davies's book, pondering Professor Shafer's analysis of my novels, and reflecting on the spiritual exercise this memoir turned out to be, I was led to the conclusion (as I revised for the penultimate time) that, quite simply, the quest is always for Gentle Love and for the gentle lover in oneself.

Back in the middle seventies when, as the first fruit of my sessions with Erika, I turned to poetry, I dredged up from my preconscious an image which I called "A Childhood Dream, Perhaps" and which hinted, without my being aware of it, the direction my spirituality (quest for God, quest for the total self) was taking at the time. It was a critical turning point of the later years of my life during which, as we shall see in a later chapter, I realized that the sociological function of Mary the Mother of Jesus was to reflect the womanliness of God. It therefore seemed that not only sexuality, but more precisely sexual differentiation and integration was a sacrament of enormous revelatory power both of the nature of God and the nature of the self. My cognitive and scholarly reflections were catching up with my deepest personal images:

Naked shoulders seen briefly through the branches
Brown body fleeing down the forest path
Girl, imp, sylvan, spinning her misty dance
What spirit is she? Never time to ask.
Slender arms and legs among the trees
She runs away but pleads with me to chase
Long brown hair flowing in the summer breeze
Unveils her girlish breasts but hides her face

22

Too playful innocent to be from hell
Angels in summer even wear more clothes
Stop flighty lass, your face I want to see
Gleaming skin, flying feet, why won't you tell?
Let me hug you, nature and name disclose,
Are you someone real or only part of me?

I take it that for all men, celibate and married, priest and lay, the quest for the warm and cherishing God and the warm and cherishing self (both of which are sacraments of each other) is the essence of spirituality. In my life the warm and cherishing lake is a sacrament of both. The Grail is God is the lake, each telling me something about the other (and water is the universal symbol of lifegiving energies, which may be why my daily exercise has become a mile swim—the warmer the water the better!).

There are many different paths on the quest. All involve women in some fashion, but not necessarily as bed partners. (More about that later.) Marriage is no guarantee that you'll find the magic princess; in fact it may turn out to be a situation in which you lose h(H)er.

Is there a cognate quest for women? Of course. What is the cherishing grail for which they must search? What for them is the sacrament which correlates with a passionately captivated God? (For God is, unaccountably, captivated by us even more than the most totally enravished human lover.)

You don't think I'm crazy enough to try to answer that question in the present context, do you?

(Lady Wisdom: Well, I should certainly hope not!)

Instead I will be content with the observation that the little boy running down the hill towards the lake (already a comic figure) is even at three a quester.

Watch the little boy run toward the lake. See him become Don Quixote on his battered old plug. Watch how he waves his crooked and decrepit lance. See him fall off his horse and tumble into the waters of the lake. Oh, look! He's the little boy again!

Right.

I have come to realize as a priest and a social scientist and a storyteller that we shape our lives to fit the experiences we have had, the images which record those experiences and the stories we share with one another about them. Our philosophy and theology and ideology are the superstructure which builds on our imaginative infrastructure. They are the rational reflection on and the articulation of our experiences, images and stories. They are important and essential, but we kid ourselves if we think they are the only or even the most powerful energies that drive our behavior. The imagination comes before the intellect, the image before the proposition, the story before the ideology.

Stated that way, my conviction seems fair enough, even obvious (especially since I'm not rejecting the intellect, only putting it in its place, so to speak, as partner to the imagination). Nonetheless, academic theology, academic social science, classroom religious education and classroom training in the fine and lively arts all begin from the opposite direction. Despite Aristotle and Thomas and William James, we pretend we are angels and organize systematically, aprioristically, and logically our lives and the accounts we present to ourselves and others about them. Then we subsume the images and the stories as an afterthought and if we have time.

We reflect and then we feel.

That is nonsense. No one lives that way. We all feel and then reflect. But, post-Cartesian people we are, we conspire in the pretense that it is the other way around.

How odd of God to have given us bodies.

I shall try to resist the archangelic temptation in this story, though Quixote-like I'm not all that good at resisting temptation. Nonetheless I begin with Twin Lakes: that experience, the images which survive from it, and the story of the quest to recreate it are the matrix of my life.

Now to be a bit more the social scientist. After my consciousness recreated the Twin Lakes experience under Erika Fromm's direction, I visited the present-day Twin Lakes, which was not nearly so splendid as my memories. Like everything else in childhood memories the scenes were much smaller and much less splendid. Commodore Barry Country Club had vanished; only the caretaker's house—now a real estate office— and a short road called Barry Road remained. The jungle-covered hill turned out to be a tiny rise in the ground and the enormous glittering lake an oversized pond. The land of my youth was now a pleasant, if slightly overcrowded middle-class resort with modern cottages jammed together where the country club once had been. Across the road were the remains of the Barry Subdivision, a collection of cottages built by the West Side Irish who viewed the "country club" as a center for vacation enjoyment but who preferred the privacy of their own homes. The houses were so tiny, only a little bit bigger, in fact, than the cottages in the Methodist camp grounds I once visited in New England and hardly as picturesque. The outhouses, I noted, had long since disappeared. If the lake at which Kevin Brennan, Ellen Foley, Maureen Cunningham and Patrick Donahue (characters in *The Cardinal Sins*) enjoyed their summer vacations was more splendid than the real Twin Lakes, the reason, I suspect, is that I was tipping my hat to the mythical memories of my past.

Our family owned a lot in the Barry Subdivision, but our plans to build a house there were aborted by the Great Depression. In my dreams, however, as far back as I can remember, I imagined we did own a house on the lake—a house threatened by great waves which crept up from the shore into the house and across the floor to where I was sitting. Somehow in the dreams the wall of water always retreated; the house survived. In real life I did finally buy a house on the shore of a lake, a much more dangerous and unruly inland sea than Twin Lakes. The dreams returned and in 1972 (one of the two or three most terrible years of my life) during a Lake Michigan St. Patrick's Day storm (nice irony, that) the lake swept away the beach, the boathouse, concrete stairs and walk, the landscaped lawn, the tree-covered dune—virtually everything up to within ten feet of the house. At the same time, we were blissfully adding to the other side of the house.

The house survived and so did I. The dreams stopped after I had started to write novels, perhaps because the fiction gave some sort of permanence to the Twin Lakes matrix of my life.

The Commodore Barry Country Club was in fact a summer camp, purchased by one of the largest Knights of Columbus councils on the West Side in the early 1920s. It flourished for perhaps eight years until the Great Depression wiped out the dreams of prosperity that possessed so many of the American Irish during the 1920s. It struggled through the thirties, slowly sinking under the weight of financial problems. It disappeared after the Second World War to be replaced by a subdivision. In the two brief decades it had passed from being an ambitious and at times pretentious dream of the newly middle-class Irish to a low-status resort not nearly comfortable or convenient enough for the now-affluent Irish. Its quarter-century history stood between two turning points in the acculturation of the Chicago Irish: the end of the First World War and

25

the false prosperity of the twenties and the end of the Second World War and the real prosperity of the forties and fifties. In the path of its history, two tragedies intervened—the Great Depression and the Second World War.

It was, in retrospect, not much—a summer estate of a Milwaukee beer baron, some rough-and-ready wooden structures built around the baron's home named most inaccurately after Chicago hotels like the Drake and the Blackstone and the Commodore. It seemed enormous and affluent and luxurious to me because that was all I knew in my life, and of transcending importance because so many of the people I knew were there in the summertime. I suppose for most of the young people of my generation even in my neighborhood it existed as little more than a name. For me and my family it was the world. My mother and father had met and courted there, my father was one of its founders and was always a senior, if behind-the-scenes, power in the club's policy decisions. We would ride to Twin Lakes in those days, a tortuous ride on the Northwestern railroad, stopping at Lake Zurich, Crystal Lake and Fox Lake before arriving at Genoa City. There we transferred to the country club "bus," a 1930-style pickup truck with a wooden roof and dark brown curtains, and bumped over the Wisconsin road to the beginning of another summer of enjoyment.

Looking back on Commodore Barry Country Club, it was uncomfortable and inconvenient. There were no showers or air conditioning. It was plagued by uncomfortable beds, rickety chairs and gaping holes in the screens. Barry was rustic living pretending to elegance with a country club name, but, in fact, representing a first-generation attempt of an immigrant group to carve out for itself an enclave of summer recreation—not so much an imitation of elite country resorts but an aspiration to an American Dream that was now almost within its grasp.

The Knights of Columbus were an important part of the life of young Catholic men and women in the Chicago of the early part of the twentieth century. The K.C. clubhouse was a social and recreational center, readily accessible by streetcar (no one owned automobiles) on weeknights and the dating/mating market at Sunday-afternoon dances. One could find a hundred young men on the clubhouse premises almost any night of the week. The K.C.'s secret ceremony was a promise of fraternal help in the business and professional world and a Catholic response to the Masons. They were also an independent Catholic lay organization, closely tied to

26

the Church, hardly rebelling against it, but still run by laymen and not by priests.

Situated on the near West Side of Chicago, Barry attracted on the north the Irish first- and second-generation lower-middle-class young men from such parishes as St. Malachy's, St. Columcile and Our Lady of Sorrows, and on the south from the Bohemian district called Pilsen. It also drew young Czechs who wanted identification with the Church but outside of the Czech ethnic community. So the Commodore Barry Indoor Baseball Team, which my father managed and which won several national championships, drew a considerable number of Irish names and three distinctively Czech names—Halas, Halas and Halas.

The most important of the Halases on the indoor team was the pitcher, a big hulking young man named George S. Halas. My family were Chicago Bear fans before we were a family and before there were the Bears. My sisters and I watched them from the press box during the late thirties and early forties when they were the Mighty Monsters of Wrigley Field if not of the Midway (a title which was inappropriately transferred to them when the University of Chicago—about which more, perhaps ad nauseam, later—abandoned football). I will confess that I was an obnoxious Bear fan all through grammar school and the seminary and ever since. Now that, in a time warp which seems almost impossible, I have something to be obnoxious about again in this year (1986) of Rozelle headbands on Jim McMahon and "Refrigerator" Perry, a defensive tackle scoring touchdowns, as the Bears blow out the league, on the subject of the Bears I suspect that I have become truly insufferable. Too bad. Go Fridge!

My father was a two-year public high school graduate (valedictorian in eighth grade at St. Michael's Grammar School—perhaps in the German language—as were two of his granddaughters, Eileen and Elizabeth at Marillac High School). My mother went to work for Sears, Roebuck and Company when she was fifteen years old after two years of St. Mary's High School. She operated an Elliott Fisher billing machine ten hours a day, five and a half days a week, for the princely wage of five dollars and fifty cents a week. My father's mother was a widowed schoolteacher and hence his family had a little bit more money than my mother's. In the first two decades of this century the Chicago Irish were still, on the whole, poor, not perhaps quite as poor as they'd been in the world of Mr. Dooley's Bridgeport recorded by Finley Peter Dunne at the end of the nineteenth century but not yet quite as affluent and respectable as the painting contractor who was the father of James Farrell's Studs Lonigan. By the end of the First World War, the Irish had maneuvered their way sufficiently into the mainstream of the middle class to begin to think about summer vacations with an occasional trip across the lake to Saugatuck in Michigan. It was but a step to plan their own resort, a major turning point which represented dramatically the expansion of the expectations of these children of the immigrants.

My father was as committed to the Commodore Barry Council as he was to the Democratic Party and the Catholic faith. My mother used to joke that if it came to a choice between the family and the Barry Council, she wasn't sure who would win. His work was behind the scenes, poring over the accounting books and straightening out the organizational and administrative messes his more boisterous and politically ambitious friends had created. Early in the short history of the country club he chose to exercise his influence behind the scenes too, standing for moderation, responsibility and good sense—to hear my mother tell it—against the flamboyant characters with imaginations untrammeled by any realism about paying bills.

Both my parents were teetotalers (alcoholism was rampant among males on both sides of the family), and when the noble experiment of Prohibition was ended, they opposed a plan to open a "tavern" on the golf course owned by Commodore Barry to be called the Red Barn. The supporters of "the Barn" had the not unrealistic expectation that the club could climb out of its financial problems with the income from alcohol consumption. My parents feared wild crowds, adolescent drinkers, and the deterioration of the family atmosphere. They were overruled and my father withdrew from active involvement in the club. My mother always insisted the Red Barn destroyed Commodore Barry. She frequently told a terrible story of an automobile accident in which a number of young people were killed at night driving away from the tavern. A young priest anointed them, tears running down his face, only fifteen minutes after he had warned one of the women who was killed that she ought to go a little easy on the drinking.

Yet Commodore Barry was not only the matrix for my youthful imagination, it was also a symbol of the great historical development that would later occupy my concern as a priest and a sociologist and a novelist—the story of the immigrants and their descendants, of the Irish

28

Americans' successful struggle to become thoroughly and successfully American while remaining Irish and Catholic.

The memories of Twin Lakes endure in my preconscious. But the real Twin Lakes as a social symbol and not a personal one was necessarily transitory, a way station on the pilgrimage to Long Beach/Grand Beach and other such posh places, a temporary layover on a rapid journey to acceptance (more or less) and affluence. As a person, I note that Twin Lakes was crucial in my life. As a sociologist, I am constrained to say it was an interesting but ephemeral transitional phenomenon, one at which none of my teenage friends from Grand Beach today would be caught dead.

It was part of the Old, not of the New. Later prosperity enabled the Irish to build real country clubs, not screened-in-porch imitations.

The glacial shift, from slum to suburb as I called it, would be joined by a second transitional phenomenon: the end of the Counter-Reformation at the Second Vatican Council and the beginning of the ecumenical age. The Catholicism of the Knights of Columbus at Twin Lakes would endure, we thought then; to use the title of one of Mark Harris's novels, "It looked like forever."

My current teenage buddies, being good Catholics (in their own way), would not walk out on the distant, silent, tinkling bell-on-the-pergola liturgy of my childhood. But they would think, should they stumble into it through some science fiction time warp, that it was "like, totally geeky, right?"

Right.

Liz Durkin (youngest niece): You mean, Uncle, you really *had* to say Mass in Latin when you were a young priest? Really?

Me: Really.

Success in the New World might have been expected by the children of the Irish immigrants—by people like my mother and father, for example—but they would not have anticipated the extent of the next generation's success. They took it for granted my two sisters and I would go to college, but I don't think they would have expected, not even in their fondest dreams, that two of their three children would earn doctorates from the University of Chicago.

After thousands of years as peasant farmers, and half a millennium of oppression by English rule, the Irish were finally achieving prosperity in massive numbers (to be followed quickly by the Italians and the Poles).

Moreover, after fifteen hundred years of Latin liturgy and four hundred years of rigid, defensive and static Catholicism, the fathers of the Vatican Council, by overwhelming votes and not fully realizing what they were doing, restored the pluralism of the medieval Catholic Church and almost as an afterthought put the Mass into English.

Prosperity was something the Catholic immigrants and their offspring might have expected, but pluralism in the Church was something they/ we never dreamed. Yet in fact, the changes of the Vatican Council, dramatic and eventually traumatic as they may have been, were an enormous blessing for American Catholicism. If the Church had not become more relaxed and open and more pluralistic in the early 1960s, then it would face an even worse crisis today as educated and successful third and fourth generations struggle for their own independence. The battle combining freedom and loyalty, emerging as I wrote the first draft of this chapter, between Geraldine Ferraro and Mario Cuomo, on the one hand, and Archbishop John O'Connor of New York, on the other, would have been even more violent and destructive. The Vatican Council, it has always seemed to me, enabled American Catholicism more easily to make the transition from uneducated immigrant to college-educated professional.

I went through these changes, became part of them, suffered because of them (though not much); I have rejoiced in them, studied them, written about them, analyzed them sociologically, spun stories around them—they are the warp and the woof of my life. One of my stories in this book is about the tumultuous era from the thirties to the eighties, surely one of the most fascinating periods in the whole history of Catholicism. I tell the story, first of all, for myself, as a spiritual exercise to straighten out the trajectories and the dimensions of my own life. I also tell it for whatever illumination it might afford others, present and future, trying to understand these incredible times—*The Best of Times, the Worst of Times*, as John Kotre called them in his intellectual biography of me a decade ago.

The story of these fifty years in my life and the life of American Catholicism is a strange mixture of comedy and tragedy. Yet all things considered, we made the major transitions with extraordinary vigor, balance and success. No one could have anticipated that American Catholicism could have survived nearly as well as it has.

On the other hand there have been casualties, particularly among the clergy and among women religious, and senseless and unnecessary personal suffering for many Catholics, both lay and clergy. Many of the losses were and are unnecessary, and much of the suffering could have been avoided. Worse yet, tremendous opportunities of the 1960s after the Vatican Council were mindlessly wasted, as the opportunities of the present moment are also, in substantial part, being wasted.

Catholicism in the United States was not ready either for the professional suburb or for the ecumenical age. I wrote my first book in 1958, warning of the problems and the possibilities in the professional-class suburbs (problems and possibilities which were vigorously denied by many of my clerical colleagues at the time). With my new sociology degree in hand, I wrote a number of books, most notably *The Hesitant Pilgrim*, in the wake of the Second Vatican Council, warning of the problems and the possibilities of the ecumenical age—warnings which were also discounted, particularly by the leadership of the American Church.

I am not happy that my predictions were accurate. Yet even today it seems to me that much of the hierarchy and many of the clergy are unaware of the extent and the importance of the changes that have occurred since Pope John was elected in the Sistine Chapel and John Kennedy in the electoral college. They still live in a nostalgia for the past, which they do their best to recreate while they parrot post-Conciliar terms.

The Church was unprepared to be faced with a college-educated Catholic population. (This change, incidentally, is not finished. In fact, the pace of Catholic movement into the professional class will *accelerate* for the rest of this century.) It was totally unprepared to cope with the resurgence of the Church's ancient pluralisms. Hence, we made a hash of the transitional era, ruining many people and blowing many opportunities. We continue to hurt people and we continue to blow the opportunities. We commit both these sins because of deficiencies of scholarship and leadership. Catholic liberals as well as Catholic conservatives were for the most part, and are for the most part, innocent of the scholarly depth in the social and theological sciences required to stay above the treacherous and unknown reefs of a transitional era. With a few notable exceptions, the hierarchic leadership exists on a spectrum running from mediocre to psychopathic. As one of my classmates in the seminary remarked, they misunderstood the vow of St. Louis Grignon DeMontfort to do always the more perfect thing and took instead the vow to do always the more stupid thing.

So my story, of pilgrimage on these two transitions, is a story of the triumph and disaster, tragedy and comedy, death and rebirth in American Catholicism. And in my own life. It is also a story of the vigor and creativity now to be found in the laity rather than in the clergy and the hierarchy.

It is therefore a story of surprises. My own priestly work is something I would never have imagined in the seminary—the result of chance and choice run together in an intricate path I still cannot fully comprehend. A number of the surprises have been acutely unpleasant; others have been challenging and exciting and rewarding. My father believed, and I still do believe, in seizing opportunities, a characteristic which, it turns out, is helpful in keeping one in the priesthood during a time of transition.

I'm a priest. Not a priest-sociologist or a priest-journalist, or a priest-novelist, or any multiple variation of those hyphenates. I'm a priest, a parish priest. The other things I do in life: sociological research, journalistic writing, storytelling, are merely ways of being a priest. I decided I wanted to be a priest in second grade, have never changed my mind, and have never had any doubts.

In its deepest meaning my life now seems to me to be a pilgrimage from Paradise Lost toward Paradise Found. It was God whom I encountered at the shore of Twin Lakes, God revealed through the happiness of childhood and God revealing through the sacraments of nature. It is God for whom I seek, often ineptly, sometimes stupidly. My friend Father John Shea, one of the best of the contemporary Catholic theologians, says the God for our time is not the God who creates but the God who calls. I have tried to answer the invitations of the calling God, sometimes without even realizing I was hearing Her/His voice. Grace, I have learned, lurks everywhere, even, perhaps especially, in disappointments and failures. As I have stumbled down the labyrinthine ways of my life, I have heard the voice—though not always recognized it—in my parishes, "St. Ursula" and "St. Praxides," in the dramatic changes of the Second Vatican Council, in the University of Chicago, in the pain of being a square peg in the Church and the priesthood, in my discovery of the importance of the religious imagination, and finally in my stories. Especially in my stories. I came to understand as I worked on this memoir that I was

32

writing my novels for myself more than for anyone else. They are an enterprise of self-discovery and exploration, an arena where, more vividly I think than any experience since Twin Lakes, I hear the voice, experience the grace, and try with diminishing success to escape the footfalls of the Hound of Heaven.

Have I found Paradise Regained? Discovered definitively the tender self? Caught up with Lady Wisdom?

Not yet, not even in the sense that we can discover Lady Wisdom in this world. But as I write my stories, I have the feeling I'm getting closer.

The man in the late middle years of life standing on the dune at Grand Beach reflecting back on the little boy dashing down the hill at Twin Lakes has a considerable advantage over the sawed-off punk of fifty years ago, for he has acquired technical skills, experience and, perhaps intermittently, some touches of wisdom. Hence, it is permissible, if not admirable, if he feels superior to his predecessor and allows himself sometimes the indulgence of thinking the little boy would have copped out of the agonies and the ecstasies, the frustrations and the successes, the failures and the accomplishments, the loyalties and the betrayal, that would cover the years from 1934 to 1984. And yet, if the older man watching the lake pound against the shore permits himself to feel superior to the boy, he is missing the point entirely. The little boy at Twin Lakes did not walk down the hill, he did not approach the lake calmly, coolly, rationally. He charged it with reckless, manic enthusiasm, and too bad for the lake if it didn't approve.

Go get 'em, Quixote. Whatever discontinuities may exist between 1934 and 1984, that characteristic of the little boy has proved remarkably durable. His successor a half-century later still charges—often joyously, sometimes imprudently, on occasion ingeniously—and if the little boy could speak to the older man he might well say, "Whaddya mean I wouldn't do it all over again if I knew what it was gonna be like? I could no more turn away from the opportunities and the challenges of the next fifty years than I could at this moment rest my pell-mell assault on Twin Lakes. You are charging life like I charged the lake because you are me and I am you and 1984 at Grand Beach is 1934 at Twin Lakes. Now is no time to stop racing."

For that choice I have no regrets.

PART ONE

Twin Lakes
to
Grand Beach

ECHOES

Tinkling cattle bells
Called down the candy clouds
So I could walk the hills
Along a singing forest road
To the marble city wall
By a large and quiet lake.
A beach ball, ten feet high,
Colored like a loony rainbow
Chased me to the shore
Agfa colored sails lightly stirred
As the ships rocked gently
Near the castle lawn
Pink straps confined
Pale white shoulders
And tender ivory throat

Framed in satin blond
And velvet Haydn strings.
The great jack pine
Stood astride the path
Reaching to the stars
Wild cactus plants
Exploded like apaches
And swarmed upon the town.
A hand reached out
Split the darkness open
Offering a tad of light
Illumined cold brown hills
Rumbled out the fog
And chased away the night.
Flower blossom tang
And sweet soprano songs
Routed me out of bed
Into the raging storm.
Silver olive branches
Bent lightly in the breeze
And snow white window panes
Green surf foaming bubbles
Teased champagne bellies
Touched skim milk bosoms
Eager on the strand.
Sullenly the sun went home
In a flaming snit
So envious of the moon
A stained glass afterglow
Hints of flaming passion
Soaking the bloodied sky
Anxious coyote laughs
On the shadowed desert floor
Scorpions crawl slowly home
And the puma prowls the ruined walls
Searching for his brief encountered mate
One by one the window lighted hills
Blink discreetly out

Andrew M. Greeley

Screen lovers quick falling veils
And deftly merging needs
While aimless ghosts glide by
With their hint of fearsome death.
Sparkling like Wisconsin Lakes
Laughing blue eyes
Tear apart the gloom.
Clown grinning little girl
Spins her giddy swing
To sky and back
While her cowboy brother
Plunges down the slippery slide
And in the splashing lake.
The fine salt laced air
Savored of strong red wine
In a slender chalice.
Mint flavored ice tea
As clean-earth rain
Soaking thirsty sands
Licked hot and weary skin
In the cemetery silence
Soft footfalls, uncanny words
The dark shapes cringed
Under quickly scudding clouds.
A drag and dusty day
Harried by darting demons
Turned sweet in tasting
Raspberry delicious lips.
Drained thick whipped cream
At lavender languid dawn
From flowing fountains
Of chocolate malted breasts.
Heels clicking on concrete walks
Stabbed the quiet spring
And urged the trees to bloom
In distant humid August
Hard running thighs crash
Against lace light curtains

37

And thunderheaded noon.
A haze of golden smoke
Bathes burgundy quiet ponds
Tinged with silken silver
And barbecue tainted mists.
The zither mocking Bach
Dancing behind the scenes
Or Mozart on the run.
Voices floated in the wind
Chiming on the thin night glow
And invited all to come.
Captured by lilac light
Modest in citrus scent
And half a light blue slip
She leaned at an open window
Discreetly sipping moonbeams.

CHAPTER
1
The Train to Biloxi

My second-oldest memory is of the Panama Limited.

The year must have been 1930, the month March. I was two; my sister Grace would not arrive for five more months. Another sister had died the week after her birth of spina bifida, the kind of problem which would be no great problem to doctors today. My parents and I were traveling to Biloxi, Mississippi, for a brief winter holiday.

Family mythology, confirmed by jerky "Cine-Kodak" films, said Biloxi was bitter cold that March, sunny but cold.

However, there were no pictures taken on the train. Yet, my memory of the dining car on the Panama Limited is clear and vivid, like a film I might have seen on a VCR last night. I recall the thick curtains and the blue-and-white pillows of our compartment, my mother's brown dress, the semidarkness of the dining car, the gleaming silver, white linen and sparkling plates on the table and the kindly man to whom I was introduced —Bob Switzer, a Chicago political power of some sort.

I often wondered whether a memory can survive so vividly from the age of two. And why did the dining car seem so dark? What were the strange circular lights on its walls, glowing dimly like oversized silver dollars?

No great issue, merely idle questions about one's beginnings. Yet intriguing for all that. In the autumn of 1984 I rode the Orient Express from London to Milano. When I walked into the dining car, faintly sleepy from the scopolamine patch which had protected me from the rigors of the English Channel, I walked back more than a half century. I was on the Panama Limited once again.

It was not retrocognition of the sort my hero Brendan Ryan experiences in *Rite of Spring* (a rare form of ESP) but the perfectly ordinary experience of entering a luxury dining car from the first decades of this century. Complete with the half-light and the circular lamps glowing on the walls.

So, for what little it is worth, my memory of the Panama Limited is valid.

My oldest memory is of a crib on the back porch of a yellow brick three-flat on Austin Boulevard with sunlight coming through the slats on the crib and creating bars of light and shadow on the white blanket. I am able to stand, but not to walk, less than one year old, so before February of 1929. I feel happy about something, whether it be the new crib or the sunlight or the fascinating ladder of light and shadow or being able to stand up, I don't know.

Again, although it doesn't much matter, I wonder whether it's an authentic memory. I have even visited the porch, which is, somehow, much as I remembered it.

For the purposes of this book, both memories are pertinent in two respects: they recall interludes of contentment and happiness, perhaps in the case of the Panama Limited an interlude of adventure. (Why not use Dr. Fromm's self-hypnosis to explore those interludes in greater detail? I have done so, but I don't trust my imagination's restraint. It could easily make up memories for the pure fun of it.) They also indicate that in the years after my birth my family was still at the upper end of the socio-economic ladder. Only financially comfortable couples lived in that building on Austin, and only the affluent took the Panama Limited to New Orleans and Biloxi. Not wealthy, not rich, but well-off, even six months after the collapse of the stock market in October of 1929. As I can best recall, my father's financial security lasted into the summer of 1931, a year after my sister Grace was born.

I have no recollection of what happened or how it happened, but I do sense, intuit, feel, whatever, that the happiness of the train to Biloxi and the hill at Twin Lakes came to an abrupt end. The love I experienced as unconditional before the change no longer existed. Obviously we must learn about limitations as we grow older; the pure bliss of being an adored firstborn son and only child cannot go on forever. Whether the change for me was any more sudden or traumatic than it is for any little boy is a question I can hardly answer with any confidence.

I kind of think it was, however. I know from later discussions with my mother and overheard conversations that "we lost everything in the Crash." Everything may not be all that much by present standards, but it did mean trips to Biloxi on the Panama Limited. I also sense that my mother was as devastated as my father by the loss—even more so perhaps—because she could not understand what had happened or how she should respond in support of my father.

A successful professional woman in her own right, she had given up her career to marry a man who seemed to promise permanent comfort and security as well as affection and amusement, a man of unquestioned probity and integrity. Now all was suddenly and insanely swept away. Was she going to be returned again to the dismal girlhood poverty of Western Avenue near Roosevelt Road?

A child doesn't understand the nuances of these questions. He merely perceives that something terrible has happened to those he loves and assumes responsibility for it.

I must not exaggerate. I don't think my self-acceptance is particularly low in comparison with most people's. To do all the crazy things I've tried to do in my life one must have a certain tenacity at the core of one's personality. As I'll try to explain in the next chapter, the relationship between vulnerability and toughness in my character is an intricate one.

I know, however, in the innermost parts of my being that there was a time that I liked myself a lot more than I do now—the comparison then is not with others, but with me at an earlier time.

Before, I suspect, the Crash.

I find it hard to read novels or biographies about the Great Depression. I am angered at films like *The Sting* which gloss it over with a patina of sepia nostalgia. Pictures or newsreels of the actual events make me turn away. I want to punch out the smart-mouth sixties intellectuals who condemn their parents and their predecessors without comprehending what the Great Depression meant to a couple of generations of Americans. I am sickened by the slick TV journalists who compare our current recessions, however unpleasant and disruptive, to the troubles of the 1930s. Do men who are the Eric Sevareids of our time, I feel like asking them, have to become hobos because there are no jobs for them?

I want to fight with the know-it-all writers of feature articles who decry the "complacency" of the fifties without realizing that we were more than halfway into that decade (just about the time I was ordained) before anyone over twenty-five was sure the Depression would not return.

The Great Depression was one of the three worst disasters of American history, the other two being the Civil War and the Spanish influenza of 1918-1919. My poor mother suffered through two of the three. As Caroline Ware said in the title of her book many years ago, it is the "invisible scar" on American society, a memory of a severe wound from which we have not yet completely recovered and the pain of which we have not yet honestly faced.

The Depression was a massive influence in my early years. If I am asked what my most powerful childhood memories are, I have to say they are memories of silence—my father's silent shock at what had happened in his life and my mother's silent inability to comprehend and respond.

They had married in 1927. My mother was thirty-two years old, my

42

father thirty-nine. Such late ages at marriage were not unusual among the second-generation Irish, who had brought the custom with them from the old country. All my mother's sisters married relatively late in life. The custom had disappeared by my generation, just as it would shortly disappear in the old country with the coming of modest prosperity. In both grandparental families there was tragedy, a not infrequent price paid by the immigrants for the success and affluence of their children and grandchildren. My mother's parents both died in their early fifties, her father in an accident in the sewers (the death certificates of both my grandfathers gave "chronic alcoholism" as the cause of death) where he worked, and her mother a few months earlier of the flu, leaving the seven children, ranging in age from the early twenties to under ten, to raise themselves, which, amazingly enough, they did, in the process achieving modest success. My mother worked at Sears for eighteen years, rising from a billing-machine operator to an executive secretary by the time she was married.

The pictures we have of my mother and her sisters, taken during the teens and the twenties, reveal them as chic, attractive women betraying no hint, in their style or posture, of the poverty in which they were raised at the turn of the century.

My father's father was a laborer and an occasional teamster—that is to say, he drove a team of horses for a delivery company. He died like my mother's father in his early fifties, perhaps after having deserted his wife and sons. His wife was a schoolteacher, born in London of County Mayo parents (all the other three grandparents were from Mayo and from towns only a few miles apart).

Mary Laura (Reynolds) and Thomas McNichols had seven children. Anne and Andrew Greeley had two sons who lived to adulthood (out of five births). One, Bill, the youngest, was a ne'er-do-well and an alcoholic who never married (two of my mother's three brothers were also alcoholics). My father, however, was just the opposite—a steady, reliable, sternly responsible young man. He began his career after high school graduation as the clerk and confidential secretary of an affluent businessman (Protestant) named H. B. Houston. While continuing his association with Houston, he went into business on his own, trading in stocks and bonds during the roaring twenties. By the time he married my mother, his capital was thirty-seven thousand dollars, and he planned to retire when it reached a hundred thousand—modest success and modest expectations, but still substantial enough for him to be thought of as affluent. Three and a half years later, it would all vanish.

In the worldview of my father and mother as they struggled up the economic and social ladder in the first three decades of this century there was an orientation towards excellence which they must have absorbed from their parents, who in turn probably brought it with them from Ireland and stuck to it despite the agonies of the immigrant experience, just as my mother and father would stick to it through the Depression years. I suspect that the principal source of this respect for quality was Grandma Greeley, who was, to judge from her picture, a tough little sparrowlike schoolteacher.

You respected excellence, perhaps not always the man who was excellent, but the excellence he possessed. The priest, businessman, political leader, engineer, athlete who was good at what he did, we were taught, deserved our admiration. Moreover, we were to use the talents God had given to us in pursuit of similar excellence ourselves. There was no point in comparing ourselves with others—we'd never be able to sing like Bing Crosby ("fer sure," as the teenagers of today would note)— but only with what we might become by using the gifts God had given us. You evaluated yourself only against yourself and not against others.

Such a set of values, pushed too far, could produce an adult who did nothing but work, a temptation from which I've never been free. On the other hand, the most positive result of learning these values early in life— more from example and attitude than from frequent explicit teaching— is that I am free to enjoy the excellence of others without making invidious comparisons or resenting their excellence.

Among my friends there is at least one person who is better than I am at everything I do—not all that great a feat, it seems to me. But why should I compare myself with Jack Shea as a storyteller, Pat Moynihan as a writer, James Coleman, Dudley Duncan, Stanley Lieberson, Norman Nie, Michael Hout as a data analyst, Pastora Cafferty as a student of urban social structure, Heidi Hornaday as a swimmer, Michele Brennan as a water-skier?

Or more precisely, why should I worry that in any such comparison they are better than I am (in the last, like *totally* better)? Why should I resent their superior talents and abilities? Why not instead enjoy their talents, learn from them, perhaps bask a bit in their reflected glory? Where was it ever written that their excellence should be a threat to me?

This value orientation seemed to me as a boy to be simple common sense and simple Christianity. I am subject to the temptation of envy, as is anyone. But because my parents taught me to admire quality and avoid comparisons with others, I was never caught in the terrible mixture of repressed envy, invidious comparison, and self-contempt that the German writer Max Scheler calls ressentiment; I am not a victim of the free-floating rage which would force me to hate those whose excellence threatens me.

At first I could hardly believe that such pathology existed, so foreign was it to my own childhood experience—even when I was the target of ressentiment's hateful rage. Now I know that it exists and is deadly dangerous, but it still seems silly.

In the seminary we were instructed in a different wisdom, the exact opposite of what I learned from my mother and father: we should repress and suppress our talents and abilities for reasons of obedience and humility and concern for the feelings of others who might not be so gifted. I listened and nodded, but never took such nonsense seriously. What an awful fool God would have been to make us who we are if S/He did not want us to use the gifts we had been given (I would not have added the S in those days). Any reading of the parable of the talents should have made it clear, I thought, that we do not bury our God-given (as I write this sentence I can almost hear my mother's voice saying) talents in the ground.

So I have reacted during my life when, for example, I was told that I should not write so much because it offended and threatened many other priests. But why? I asked (and I still ask, though now I understand the psychological dynamics).

Respect for excellence and its pursuit did not mean that you had to be excellent. You did your reasonable best. You didn't quit ("Greeleys don't quit," my mother insisted). If you failed, that was all right too, so long as you didn't quit. To perform well was better than not to perform well, but approval was not conditioned on performance, it was conditioned rather, not unreasonably it has always seemed to me, on trying.

Or as G. K. Chesterton remarked in a paradox which fit perfectly with my family experience, "What is worth doing at all is worth doing badly." You know you'll never be a great or even an especially good water-skier? It doesn't matter, so long as you don't give up. Does it take you a solid week of trying? Do you finally get up when teenagers from your parish pull up in a mega Chris Craft and your reputation for all eternity depends on it? It doesn't matter: you did it and you didn't quit.

So at the age of fifty-seven do you take up windsurfing (or board sailing as we initiates call it)? You learn how to do it and enjoy it even if you make a fool out of yourself—much to the amusement of another generation of teenagers—in the process.

A respect for excellence and a dedication to the development of the talents God has given could, if combined with perfectionism, drive a person mad. Fortunately for me, my parents' emphasis on effort rather than outcome—and powerful praise for effort—dispensed me permanently from the obligation to be perfect.

So I was freed by my parents, to a considerable extent anyway, of the need of perfectionism and of envious resentment of those who were better than I was—wonderful blessings because they have made it easy to distinguish between myself and my work. If your ego's basic existence is not identified with what you do, then you are free to play, to experiment, to take risks, to innovate. If the work fails, you don't fail. Were you afraid to turn to the writing of novels? What if you failed?

I figured I probably would. So what? It was fun to try.

When people attack your novels, does it hurt? Well, chocolate malts are more fun, but my novels aren't me—even if some of the Catholic critics are aiming at me more than at my work.

To tell the truth, neither question computes on my personal fear processor. My parents equipped me well to be a risk taker. I can't even understand from the inside the mentality that assumes a writer's integrity and worth as a person depends on the perfection of and approval for his writing.

Several Catholic critics, especially a woman who writes regularly for *Commonweal* (a magazine whose lifeblood is envy) and who makes kind of a career of attacking me, cheerfully announce to their readers that I am not Greene or Waugh or Mauriac or Undset or Michelangelo or Dante. Such comments are supposed to devastate me and warn off readers.

Well, patently, I am not any of those folk. Moreover I am not James Joyce, Agatha Christie, Marcel Proust or Flann O'Brien either. In fact, one could fill the pages of a book with a list of authors and artists that I am not.

46

But so what? Why need I be any of those people? And more to the point, why should my work be evaluated against theirs?

I write the kind of stories I can write and that I like to write, stories which I design to be comedies of grace (romances of renewal, according to Professor Ingrid Shafer). A lot of people enjoy these stories (most of the readers, as my research reveals) and also understand the religious themes and symbols. Why is it necessary that I be Graham Greene or James Joyce? Why isn't it enough to be me?

Some readers may think that it is an absurd position to take. The point here is that I was raised to think that way. My parents were content with me if I tried to do as well as I could what I was able to do. I wasn't compared with others whether they were more gifted than I or less gifted. I am, heaven help me perhaps, content with the same judgment as contented them. Again I must say from my stretch of the beach that seems like sound common sense, sound psychology and sound Christianity.

Nor did my parents have much respect for ideologues. The word would not have been used in that day, but religious or political enthusiasts turned them off. They thought the world was complicated and that those who had simple answers were not to be trusted. They were particularly offended by those who paraded their piety as a chip to be played in the business or professional world. Religious devotion, my mother repeatedly insisted (quoting my father), did not make up for not knowing what you were doing; nor did it permit you to cut moral corners.

I suspect that such values have made me perennially skeptical of the taut muscles, the shining face, the hard eyes of the enthusiast, whether it be a nun telling me about private revelations in grammar school, the priest quoting Padre Pio's prediction of the end of the world at a high school retreat, the radical leftists (preaching Marx but never reading him) who prattle about the "preferential option for the poor" without ever listening to the poor, the single-issue pro-life militants who disrupt my lectures, or the man-hating wing of the feminist movement. If I'm both a pragmatist, a pluralist, and an empiricist who prefers facts to mystiques and ideologies, the reason is that I am what my parents made me. I was a disciple of William James before I could read and write.

Hence I cannot abide gurus or those who would make someone a guru. My gut reaction to such abusive hero worship is that it is healthy for neither the worshiped nor the worshiper. Others may well disagree, which is their right, but I found the cult of the Berrigans in the late sixties and early seventies offensive, as much as I admired Daniel Berrigan personally. The cultists helped neither Dan, nor themselves, nor, finally, the cause of peace.

As I try to probe beyond my memories of my mother's and father's later years and beyond the anguish of the Crash, I see both my parents as intelligent, active, vigorous people. In her early twenties, my mother rode a burro down the side of the Grand Canyon, flew in a fabric-covered biplane, crossed Lake Michigan in a fragile sailboat, and traveled each summer to California or through the Canadian or American Rockies (I only made it to the Grand Canyon and to Lake Louise in my fifties, and did not ride down the side of one or hike on the trails of the other). My father, whose work for Mr. Houston required frequent trips to Mississippi, hunted on muleback and paddled in backwater bayous in a canoe (where, perhaps, he contracted malaria, from which he almost died when I was five years old and from which, my mother used to say, he never completely recovered).

They were both devout in their Catholicism if not altogether conventional in their relationship to the parish. Neither wore their piety on their sleeves and both were skeptical of those who did—knowing too much perhaps of the business and/or family life of some "active" Catholics.

My mother, like most Irish women of her generation, was a firm believer in what we used to call "sacramentals"—May altars, palm fronds brought home from church on Palm Sunday, candles, holy water, blessing of throats on St. Blaise's day, and, most important, ashes on Ash Wednesday, that symbolically powerful if liturgically underappreciated feast. She would light candles and sprinkle holy water about the house during particularly fierce thunderstorms which terrified us children—and her, too, presumably. Once, when I was a little older, I asked her whether the holy water really protected us.

Water jar (with a little silver nozzle) in hand, she paused. "Well, no, not the water; it's just a way of praying for God's protection. He made the holy water and He makes the storm too."

A better theory of the sacramentality of creation I would not find. Those "modern" Catholic liturgists who find the candle and the water "irrelevant" and poke fun at the "superstition" of "blessed" candles and "holy" water miss the point entirely. Moreover, the sexual symbolism of candle and water—explicitly alluded to in the blessing of the Easter

Water by the Easter Candle (before it was bowdlerized by the liturgists)—seems to have escaped them completely. When the candle was plunged into the water three times and the prayer was said, "May this candle fructify [*fructificare* is the verb in Latin] these waters," the meaning—to the fourth-century Romans who made the ceremony part of Holy Saturday—was obvious: the Resurrection of Jesus was the consummation of His nuptials with his spouse the Church. We who are baptized with the water are the first fruits of this passionate love affair.

My parents were both readers of newspapers and magazines and occasional books and both leprechaun comedians with wit and flair and energy. My father was short, only five-eight, slender, and balding even at the time of marriage. My mother was attractive and obviously both personable and competent. She was plagued by bad teeth and bad feet as a result of poor medical care in her youth and, also, barely escaped death during the Spanish influenza epidemic. She often described riding home on the Jackson Boulevard bus and seeing four or five houses in every block hung with black crepe marking the progress of that most deadly plague of modern times, a plague the memory of which has been repressed almost as completely as the memory of the Great Depression.

I suspect my parents married because they both thought it was time, because they were available to each other at Twin Lakes, and because they were fond of each other—not necessarily in that order. How passionate their love was is beyond my comprehension because they were, essentially, quiet, private, undemonstrative people (the comic flair was real enough, but it also often served as a mask). They certainly cared deeply about one another: my mother was devastated when my father died, and I can never remember his saying a harsh or unkind word to her, not even about some of her relatives who repeatedly sponged off us, not that we had all that much money to support sponging. The promise and the possibility in their life was blighted by "the Crash." Through the years when my consciousness was beginning to form, they were both suffering that anguish.

I was born in 1928, before the Crash, my sister Grace in 1930, only a few months before the bottom finally fell out of my father's stocks-and-bonds business, and my sister Mary Jule, a delightful afterthought, appeared on the scene with a smile in 1934. The Great Depression had its most powerful effect on the first two of us. By the middle 1930s, tragedy and disaster had become commonplace. We were living with it, and living better than many Americans, but we had not recovered from it and, as it turned out, we never would.

Mary Jule (for reasons now obscure, often called Juice, even by her husband, the incomparable Jack Durkin, one of the most "fun" human beings I have ever been privileged to know) and I became buddies almost from the day she came home from the hospital. She insists her version of life in St. Angela is a much younger version than mine, because she is a much younger person.

Grace and I were and are not so close, natural enough in the sibling pattern of a three-child family. In addition her life has been plagued by chronic ill health. Both she and Mary Jule insist that as the oldest and the boy and the future priest, I was the favored child and never had to dry the dishes—sheer calumny, or selective misperception. I dried the dishes lots of times. And cut the lawn. And went to the store. And put up the storm windows. And vacuumed the carpets. And washed the kitchen floor.

Sisters: (in unison) Martyr!

Me: Well...

My father was a man of extraordinary integrity. He once refused an opportunity to make several million dollars in a tax warrant transaction because Anton Cermak, then mayor of Chicago, demanded a half-million-dollar cut of the profits. In my early years of parish work an occasional old-timer would come up to me and ask if I was "Andy's son" and then invariably say something about his integrity and "fairness." He was a political liberal and a New Deal Democrat, and, despite Cermak, he was a loyal member of the Cook County organization. He wrote for the Knights of Columbus journals, something which excited me and made me proud of him, even as a little boy.

He did not drink but smoked far, far too much, doubtless one of the factors contributing to his early death. I have never smoked and did not touch the Creature until Rome and John Hotchkin corrupted me with wine in 1964. Even now, a glass of wine, a sip of Bailey's Irish Cream after dinner and, when in Tucson, one margarita—*only* one—are as far as I will go in downing the Creature.

Like Kevin Brennan and Blackie Ryan and Hugh Donlon in my stories, I was destined to go to a regular Catholic high school, either Fenwick or St. Mel's, and not to Quigley Seminary. Both my parents felt that fourteen was "too young" to know one's own mind about a vocation. My father, I suspect, knew too many unhappy priests to want me to risk the same fate.

The last part of seventh grade and the first months of eighth grade were a strange interlude in my maturation. St. Mel's was cheaper than Fenwick (seventy-five dollars a year as opposed to a hundred and fifty!), and my mother worried about the money. My father, more realistic about finances, thought that the ROTC training at St. Mel's (the only Catholic high school in the country with such a program; an influential Chicago congressman obtained the program as a price for his vote) would be useful for me as a preparation for the military service he saw as inevitable. Moreover, Fenwick (Dominicans) was thought of as a "rich kids'" school, St. Philip's (Servites) as a "poor kids'" school and St. Mel's (Christian Brothers) as somewhere in between. It seemed that I kind of belonged at St. Mel's.

Somehow, the Jesuits at St. Ignatius did not enter into the race, though as I would later learn they ran (and still run) the best high school in Chicago. I was not interested in going anywhere near the Jesuits because I heard they would try to make me one and because a number of the nuns had already urged me in that direction.

No way, guys. I want to be a parish priest.

I couldn't see myself toting a rifle at St. Mel's and I was wary of the alleged wealth of the Oak Park and River Forest kids at Fenwick, but those weren't the real issues.

I wanted to go to Quigley. Why not? As Sister Augustine, my eighth-grade teacher, put it, if you are going to be a priest why waste time fooling around with something else? My every instinct said I would be happy at Quigley and nowhere else. I didn't want to cause my parents any more worry than they already had, but I had made up my mind.

My bedroom was off the living room. One night in early autumn they were sitting in the living room listening, perhaps, to the Kraft Music Hall with Bing Crosby (one of my father's favorites).

"I'm going to take the Quigley admissions tests next week," I called, over the sound of our console Philco (Dad loved good radios).

Silence.

"Monsignor Gorman"—his closest friend in the priesthood—"said that I should last summer when I visited him out at St. Columbanus."

(True enough, but the monsignor did not realize I would use his advice against my parents.)

51

More silence.

"Fine," from my father, "if that's what you want to do. Don't feel you have to stay if you want to leave."

"No, I won't."

"How much does it cost?" My mother.

"About as much as Fenwick."

"That doesn't matter." My father.

(I was wrong. Quigley was the least expensive of the Catholic high schools in the city.)

That was that.

Weird?

I guess so. Why not just walk into the living room and tell them?

I don't know. I was certain they would go along, even be proud of me by the next morning. I had not the slightest doubt they would celebrate my vocation to the priesthood in the years ahead. I suppose it was the first time in my life I was prepared to act against their judgment. Perhaps the long silences in our family life made it hard to face them with such a decision. Whatever it was, I was sensitive to nuances to which I could not then give a name.

My father talked on the phone the next day to Bill Gorman, who told him the same thing Sister Augustine had told me and assured him my motives were responsible and mature. That settled it.

One of my father's close colleagues at work was an engineer named Torrey O'Brien, a charming and gifted man with a degree from MIT and, alas, a bit of a problem with the Drink Being Taken. I shared my dad's fondness for Torrey and was attracted by his suggestion that I too should go to MIT. Torrey was an active alumnus and spoke of the possibility of scholarship for someone as bright as I was supposed to be.

It was an intriguing possibility. It would please my father and I found it easy to identify with Torrey and what he did. But, intriguing or not, the possibility existed in the same unreal world as Fenwick and St. Mel's. Just as I knew I wasn't going to either high school, I knew I would never go to MIT. I had other fish to fry, other drummers to march to.

And the Lord God, She did a wonderful favor not only to Lucy Scanlan/ Ellen Foley, but to the engineering profession. I would have been one of the worst engineers in the history of humankind.

As it was, I took the Quigley exams, and the next autumn, as American marines battled in the mud on Guadalcanal, rode off on the red Chicago

Avenue streetcar to Quigley Seminary, a gray gothic building a block in from Michigan Avenue, which had yet to become the Magnificent Mile. (Cardinal Stritch was offered the land between Quigley and the Avenue for a hundred thousand dollars. The Archdiocese, the poor man claimed, didn't have the money. A block of the Magnificent Mile! Right next to the Water Tower!)

It was Quigley I wanted and it was Quigley I got.

No Lucy Scanlan!

I think I understand my parents' fears. In those days I thought that stories about men becoming priests because of parental pressures were fairy tales. You only became a priest because you wanted to, right?

My father knew better, and how he knew says a good deal more about him than I am able to explain even today.

He had a strange relationship with priests. Not only was he a close friend to many of them. He was the kind of man priests came to when they needed advice. In an era when such familiarity was practically unthinkable, he was on a first-name basis with many of them, including Monsignor Gorman, who had been a lifelong friend and who officiated at their marriage and twenty years later said my father's funeral mass. Moreover he was involved, through the Knights of Columbus, in helping alcoholic priests. He had no illusions about the sanctity of the priesthood. He was far more aware than most laymen of his generation of the problems priests encountered. I learned from him, somehow, to be much more realistic about my vocation than were many of my classmates. Some priests were compelled by their unhappiness to drink, and other priests would always be unhappy because their parents drove them to the priesthood. Neither my father nor I would have imagined that a little more than ten years after I was ordained the Church would in effect and perhaps unintentionally and certainly not as a formal and explicit policy declare an amnesty for such priests. An amnesty which John Paul II would abruptly end, after it was too late to try to end it.

Dad and our pastor, Monsignor Daniel F. "Diggy" Cunningham, were such great friends that he called him Diggy to his face in the front of church on Sunday, much to Diggy's amusement and the horror of my mother and sisters. When my mother tried to apologize to Diggy, his response was "I wouldn't let him call me anything else!"

Looking back, I see my father as a remarkable man. I knew it because I was told so often by my mother and by his friends and by priests I admired, like Cunningham and Gorman, yet often he did not seem extraordinary but only silent and withdrawn. I have to probe my memory back to the beginnings of the 1930s and remember standing in front of our apartment building on Austin Boulevard, just south of the Lake Street L tracks, waiting for him to get off the double-deck Washington Boulevard bus, walk towards me briskly and cheerfully and sweep me up in his arms with a laugh and a comic remark.

"Partner" was what he called me, the junior colleague in the business, God help us all. I loved it and so did he.

I was much closer to my mother, Grace Anne, or, as she was baptized, Annie Grace McNichols, than I was to my father. As I look over the letters we wrote when I was in the seminary, I realize we had become good friends. Even during the worst times of the Depression, her spirit of fun and laughter survived better than my father's. If my dedication to work is more tempered and finally less self-destructive than my father's, I'm sure she deserves the credit. I think, also, that I learned from her how to interact maturely and respectfully with women, something many priests never achieve. My mother was singularly unpossessive with her children, and almost never engaged in manipulative behavior. Perhaps that's why I'm shocked by and quite unable to cope with possessive or weeping or manipulative women.

My vivid memories of sickness and death and my powerful, somber recollections of the Depression-imposed silences stand as obstacles to other and happier memories of family life. Last year, I was invited to have dinner one night at the home of Mrs. Daley (the widow of the mayor), an honor awarded few folks in Chicago. The purpose of the dinner is beyond the scope of this book, but it was a fascinating and delightful evening. The meal was a perfect recreation of the pot roast dinners my mother used to make on Sunday afternoons.

Me: This food makes me feel like I'm a little boy and we're eating pot roast and noodles and listening to Father Coughlin or Monsignor Sheen on the radio. Using our good china too.

Mrs. Daley: (with a laugh) We only use the best china for priests.

(Dad did not buy Coughlin's anti-Semitism, by the way, not one bit.)

There were many other such family events, Christmas, Easter, Thanksgiving, First Communion breakfasts, that were filled with laughter and fun, conversation and celebration, good times and happiness.

What did we talk about?

That is terribly hard to recall. Politics, sports, music, the Church, the specifics elude me, as do the memories themselves until I'm forced back to them by something like the dinner at 32d and Lowe.

The conversations which do come back are insignificant. Or maybe not. My handwriting was always a problem, made so by the many nuns at St. Angela who complained about my penmanship—and ignored all the things I did well.

Mom: Your father has wonderful handwriting. Sister says you should go to summer school if you don't do better. She says you won't be able to write a decent Mass card when you're a priest.

(A totally accurate prediction, by the way.)

Dad: (irrelevantly) Did she ever notice Thomas Jefferson's handwriting on the Declaration of Independence or Abraham Lincoln's on the Emancipation Proclamation?

Mom: (pleased but still dogged) They didn't have to make out Baptismal certificates.

Dad: Monsignor O'Brien's penmanship isn't all that good.

Mom: He's an old man.

Dad: When those who get A's in penmanship get as many A's in other subjects as he does, we will begin to worry.

I know marriages well enough to know that many men and women survive crises, pull themselves together, and continue living. They carve out happiness for themselves regardless of particular traumas. It seems clear to me now my mother and father did just that, and did it rather well, all things considered. In truth, however, it dawns on me only as I write these words (type them on the word processor—that will show Sister!) that this is what happened. They went beyond 1931 because they had no choice. The Crash killed them, in a way, but they chose not to die, to go on, however difficult the living. In some deep inner corner of my memory 1931 is still more alive for me than it was for them by 1945.

I remember them, at the end of many, many days, sitting in the kitchen over a cup of coffee, talking contentedly to one another. Sometimes I would wake up at one or two o'clock and they would still be chatting happily. How reconcile this memory with the silence of Depression gloom?

I can only respond that I must have absorbed everything they said and repressed the memories out of a delicacy which refuses to intrude into their privacy. Such conversations, however, were good times for them.

Or maybe I don't want to think about their good times because they seem so precious and so short-lived in the face of all they had to suffer.

During the war and after, my father, now the vice-president of an aluminum-forging company, began a financial and personal recovery and my mother seemed to take a new lease on life. But the forging company was on the far South Side; my father rode to and from work almost every day on the streetcar, since he had never bought a car in the twenties, could not afford one in the thirties, and now, in the middle forties, seemed reluctant to experiment. The strain of the daily streetcar ride, long hours at the plant during the war, and the worry and the disappointments of the thirties would ultimately take their toll.

In March of 1947 I had a minor role in the seminary's production of *The Bat*. I was in fact the Bat, or rather the stand-in who played the criminal in Mary Roberts Rinehart's thoroughly unfair mystery so that the audience would not guess who the real criminal was. It must have been the ideal role for me because the audience hissed whenever I swept onto the stage with my black hat and black cape. My parents planned to attend the last night. I was wiped out in the afternoon by a virulent bug (flu it was always called; my mother did not forget 1919). They went anyway, at my insistence, but came home early. My father did not feel well. Pains in his arms and chest.

He recovered from this first heart attack and seemed spry and fit and enjoyed immensely the Quigley graduation reception I hosted (and paid for myself out of the money I had earned in summer jobs, despite the myth of my classmates that the party proved the family was wealthy) at the Lake Shore Athletic Club. In 1947 such elaborate graduation parties for a Quigley grad, even a *summa cum laude* grad (we received crosses, not diplomas, would you believe?), were unusual.

The party was not in my honor but his. We all knew that.

The following September, ten days after I had arrived at the seminary at Mundelein for my first year, Ed Fitzgerald, the "prefect of discipline" (dean of students to you post-Vatican types) pulled me out of line after breakfast.

"Tom Hosty called a few minutes ago. He anointed your father this morning. He's at St. Anne's Hospital. You'd better go in."

Poor Fitz was almost as shaken as I was.

"How bad?"

"A stroke, not good."

56

I rode in on the North Shore, took an L to North Avenue (got all confused by the trains, or is that a nightmare?), and then a cab, something I had never done before, to the hospital. He was unconscious and nearly dead. We watched for the next two days as the rest of life slipped away. Then late in the afternoon, there again, the hacking stopped, his eyes opened, his chest stopped moving, and peace slipped over his face like a gentle mask. Mom kissed him tenderly and we left.

The irrepressible Hosty had us laughing in the car as he drove us home. That's the way we Irish deal with death.

It was the first death I'd ever seen. Oddly enough it was not terrible. The loneliness afterwards was. We buried him at Queen of Heaven Cemetery, where someday I too will be buried, opened the safe deposit box, found that there was almost no money and no farewell letter, and tried to pull life together again. His company, of which he'd been corporate vice-president, would not even pay his last month's salary. He had been off too long after his first heart attack, the boss said.

Capitalist.

I went back to the seminary two days after the funeral. What else? Mom went back to work, Grace to high school, Mary Jule to eighth grade at St. Angela. We made do.

It was never the same.

Especially for my mother. I'm not quite sure how my mother managed to pull her life together, though my mother had been prepared by the tragic death of her own father. After the mourning, she took a position with one of the men for whom she'd worked at Sears twenty years before and continued to work all through my seminary years and into the late fifties, when the combination of diabetes and Alzheimer's disease slowed her down and she was forced to retire and move in with Jack and Mary Jule. We sold the bungalow and cut our ties with St. Angela after three decades. The last couple of years of her life were years of confusion, uncertainty and anguish, relieved, somewhat, by her pride in her children, her son the priest and her grandchildren, who, during her most confused time, sometimes were her own children once again.

Mom deteriorated, at first slowly, then rapidly. She was no longer the person we had known. Then Mary Jule called me one evening at Christ the King. Mom was in Resurrection Hospital. Diabetic reaction and possible bowel obstruction. I drove up to the hospital to anoint her before possible surgery. She barely recognized me. I barely recognized her.

"We can't let her die of diabetes," the doctor said after he told us that he planned to remove a cancerous section of the lower bowel.

"Why not?" I demanded hotly.

It did not become an issue. The next day, Easter Sunday, Mary Jule and Grace walked into the hospital room to find her dead. She had gone home so quietly that those in charge of the floor had hardly noticed. A quiet, if ugly, death, for the girl who had walked through the snow and wind to St. Charles Borromeo Grammar School with paper in her shoes to protect her feet from the ice which probed the holes in the soles of her shoes—for the young woman who went to work at fifteen (after deciding she didn't want to be a nun after all) for five dollars a week, for the professional woman who rode down the side of the Grand Canyon on a burro, for the mother who brought me into the world on a cloudy February morning in 1928 and who held the family together as I returned to the seminary to continue my pursuit of the priesthood.

Death isn't good to any of us.

In the funeral home before the Mass, the undertaker said to the three of us, "Now would be the time for you children to spend a few last moments with your mother before we close the casket."

We all looked at the poor man as though he had three heads and walked out into the sunshine.

"That's not Mom," Juice said to me through her tears.

"Damn right," I agreed through mine.

"Irish," Grace added to the chorus.

She was right. That's the way we Irish are about death.

From my father I drew my ease with the Catholic Church, my intellectual curiosity, my political convictions and commitments, the intensity of my work style, a leprechaun strain, driving energy, and a proclivity to dig in my heels when I'm pushed too far. The older I get the more I see myself in the "Old Fella" when he told off Anton Cermak.

From my mother I inherited whatever inclination to playfulness I possess, my feminism, my skepticism about pompous Catholics, lay and clerical, my intermittent (and often ill-advised) tendency to wander about the world. I certainly did not inherit her ability to visit strange places and do strange things and show no physical ill effects.

"What would your poor mother think if she read your novels?" I am occasionally asked by an older or old-fashioned Catholic.

My answer is unequivocal. "She would have loved them." She liked to read stories, she was not particularly prudish, and if her son wrote them, that was enough and more than enough to mean that they were good.

From the two of them I inherit, as did my sister Mary Jule, and heaven forgive us both for it too, my father's and mother's incorrigible flair. When presented with alternative courses of action, one quiet and inconspicuous and the other spectacular, my sister and I aren't really free to make a choice.

You can take risks and push yourself to your limits easily enough when you know what the ground is on which you stand; you can afford to gamble for high stakes.

God knows, our parents taught us what was the ground on which we stand.

Portrait of the Artist

SUMMER DREAM

Summers were hotter then, it seems to me.
Courting couples walk arm-linked down my street
Sure that the Depression would always be
Stockyard smell at night . . . how I loved the heat!
I dreamed often of a house by the lake
And caressing waters in sunset glow
Then cruel, wrenching waves break through the windows
Clutching, dragging all happiness below.
I still yearn for humid summer days
And revel in each thick and steamy night
In dreams still see the harsh, shattering waves
Crashing through the house, blotting out the light
Yet, oddly, I know not why, things have changed
Now the waves fall back and the house remains.

Let us pause again for images and pictures, this time images and pictures which tell about personality and character.

We begin with dreams. One dream and four nightmares.

In the dream I imagine, with such persuasive vividness that I am totally convinced it is true when I awake, that I can fly. Without the help of either airplane or wings. Usually I am running down a stairway, often as a young man at Quigley with a crowd of seminarians; my feet move so rapidly, I leave the stairs and soar, first down the corridors of whatever building I am in and then into the sky. Those who observe this unprecedented behavior strive to pretend it is not happening. Never do I fear that Icarus-like I will plummet to earth.

The second dream is clearly a nightmare but of a special variety. I am protecting myself and a group for whom I am responsible against invaders—insect creatures from outer space, enemy troops coming down a jungle river, most recently a group of armed terrorists from New Zealand (I had read a book about the Maoris that day) attacking a hospital. At the last minute my weapon jams or I run out of ammunition and ... nothing. But then I either awake or another part of my brain/self takes over and I go back to the dream with efficient weapons and rout the enemy.

What kind of a character is it that forces his preconscious to add happy endings to nightmares?

As I mentioned in the prologue, I used to dream about the house at Twin Lakes. The lake, as mild a body of water in real life as one can imagine, is furiously angry in the kind of storm which makes Joseph Conrad's *Typhoon* seem a spring shower. The waves wash across the highway, up the cliff (of which there were none at Twin Lakes) and into the living room, battering the furniture and threatening to sweep all of us away. Just as the water overcomes me, I wake up.

Sometimes I go back to sleep and rout the storm.

The other two dreams are less clear in waking consciousness. In one, a parent is still alive and I am charged with preventing an ugly death. I almost but not quite fail and awaken, powerless, while the parent lingers between life and death. It takes me some time to realize it is only a dream. Occasionally I'll turn on the light in my room to be sure.

The final dream is the least specific. I am charged with an important task; the last time it was bringing a message to the cardinal about the dangers of the Special Synod of Bishops in the fall of 1985. It is essential

62

I get to him in time, but the train won't start or the plane won't take off or I can't make any progress through the swamp in which, with the marvelous logic of dreams, I happen to be walking. I wake up angry, frustrated, guilty for failing, and terrified. These dreams probably don't need much exegesis.

My nightmares are frightening, but no more so than particularly well-done horror films or stories; they rarely reach the level of terror of *The Haunting of Hill House* or *Pet Sematary* or *Halloween*. Moreover, when I wake up and ponder them, the feeling is not unlike that of analyzing a horror film after one has left the theater. (Need I say that I enjoy such films?) Night terrors, which continue after one is awake, are quite another matter. Of these, thank God, I've never had a single one.

How often do I have such dreams? Every week, or at least two or three times a month. Doesn't everyone?

In December of 1984, I read in the *New York Times* (so it must be true) that researchers had reported that the average person has only one nightmare a year, and that only one in five hundred has them every week. I'm in the latter category. The investigators found a connection between frequent nightmares and creativity, a link perhaps attributable to a "genetic susceptibility to experience in general."

While "these subjects were not particularly neurotic and not particularly anxious, they are markedly open and defenseless, not having developed the psychological protections most people have. . . . they have . . . 'thin boundaries,' they 'let things through.'"

Most of the people in the study described themselves as unusually sensitive since childhood, easily hurt, particularly responsive to atmospheres and the feelings of others, unhappy as children, even though there were no overt family problems.

The scholars observed that the frequent nightmare types put their sensitivity, openness and vulnerability to positive use. "One important aspect of what makes a person an artist is having a psychological makeup of thin boundaries, which includes the ability to experience and take in a great deal from inside and outside, to experience one's own inner life in a very direct fashion and sometimes an unwanted ability to experience the world more directly, more painfully than others."

Much of the *Times* story was based on a book by Dr. Ernest Hartmann. As soon as his *The Nightmare* appeared in January of 1985, I devoured it at a single sitting.

63

"The most striking finding," Hartmann writes, "is . . . the openness and defenselessness of almost all the nightmare sufferers. They have not developed the usual defenses and protections most people have. They are not 'armored'; they are vulnerable in many respects . . . they were often over-trusting in relationships . . . very sensitive to the feelings of others, knowing when others are hurting . . . sometimes they react [to hurt] by forming temporary and very primitively hard boundaries . . . they are not [however] persons with an excess of aggressive drive or of hostility, but rather persons with thin boundaries such that normal fears and angers 'get through' to them and become more frightening for them than for most of us" (pp. 103 to 105).

I am not happy with Hartmann's use of the word "sufferer" because it implies the opposite to what his data suggest—the nightmare is more fascinating than terrifying.

Not neurotic—"open or willing to admit to problems, to quirks, to unusual experiences . . . in this sense the nightmare subjects are as a group 'unusual,' more open to suffering, more willing to admit to problems" (p. 85)—and not angry or hostile, the nightmare person may have schizophrenia in his family background (I don't, but perhaps alcoholism is the Irish schizophrenia) but is normally not psychotic either. God knows I don't retreat from reality. Charging it may be the other side of the coin, but a much healthier response. The person realizes that s/he is "different," "unusual," has excellent memories of the past, is not afraid to talk about himself (or write a memoir?) because while vulnerable he is not defensive—there's no payoff in it if your boundaries are so permeable. As one of Hartmann's subjects says, "If you remain alive and open the way I am, you eventually get hurt."

There is another aspect of the frequent-nightmare phenomenon, however. Hartmann notes several times that self-disclosure does not seem to be a problem for the nightmare personality. Boundaries being permeable, the person sees no reason in trying to hide. This may make him too trusting and overly vulnerable; it also gives him a certain kind of security and confidence.

Thus many people are afraid to write (even dissertations, to say nothing of articles or books) because of the self-disclosure required. The nightmare person knows he's an open book (as we all are; the others merely think they're not), so self-disclosure doesn't bother him.

So we worry less about being vulnerable. We take it as a given. We may get hurt more, but paradoxically, we don't care as much. Our awareness of vulnerability makes us, oddly, tougher.

Hartmann doesn't seem to understand that if one survives permeable boundaries, one must have developed a solid inner core—here the metaphor slips—which if not impermeable is nonetheless remarkably resilient.

He quite properly focuses on nightmares because that is his subject matter. In fact, however, the nightmare is the indicator; the thin boundary is the underlying personality disposition. How is it caused? Hartmann thinks it might be a genetic predisposition and also suggests that predisposition may interact with an interlude in early years when the mother was temporarily "not available" (worrying about the impact of the Great Depression on the father?). It doesn't sound unreasonable to me.

I don't fit all the symptoms of Hartmann's syndrome. My life is far too well organized, though God knows I can shift across the boundaries which structure my life with astonishing ease. I am neither mystic nor psychic, though I have engaged in sociological research on both phenomena. I've never experimented with drugs, but I have worked with self-hypnosis.

What happens when you join thin boundaries with my father's dominant characteristics of personal integrity and responsibility, with the leprechaun wit of both mother and father and considerable intellectual abilities? What do you get?

You get Quixots, that's who you get.

Quixots the priest and the storyteller.

Do I feel bad about being "strange" or "unusual" or "different" with my mixture of thin boundaries and heavy personal responsibility?

Lord, no.

There are assets and liabilities to every personality type. You take the good with the bad and understand you can't fight the Holy Spirit regardless. But I don't mind the way I am. At times my personality makes for a difficult life, but it also makes for one that is never dull.

I'm often told by priests that I am "sensitive," in a tone of voice that indicates it is a fault. Only after I read the piece in the *Times* did I realize that the opposite of "sensitive" is "insensitive," not an appealing characteristic unless you are committed to the thick-skinned machismo so admired in clerical culture.

What can I tell you about myself, filling in the spaces in Dr. Hartmann's paradigm (and doubtless proving my thin boundaries) so you'll know something more of the main character in the story?

Others might choose different traits, but, as I reflect on the face in the mirror, these are some about which you must be warned at the outset of the story. I am, like my father before me, a furiously hard worker. I don't think I'm a workaholic, as Eugene Kennedy once charged in *Time* magazine; I can goof off without much guilt. This last summer I water-skied almost every day (taking off one day a week so I could keep up with my teenage companions), scarcely the behavior of a workaholic. On the other hand, I am frantically efficient in my use of time. The first draft of this memoir is being dictated in Chicago and while traveling by ship and plane on a trip to Europe. *Markings*, the homiletic newsletter I wrote for the Thomas More Association for fifteen years, was, for the most part, dictated in the car as I drove back and forth to work, either in my office at NORC or at the University of Arizona. Even in my recreation I am compulsively efficient about time. Thus, often when I go to see a movie I arrange that it turns into a triple feature in order to save time riding back and forth to the theater complex or the shopping plaza (and in honor of the triple features at the Rockne Theater on Division Street where I spent legions of Saturday afternoons as a boy).

The propensity to overwork, which is certainly part of my personality, has become more serious since I turned to fiction, because the craft and art of storytelling is so demanding, so compelling, so enjoyable. But quite apart from this temptation, I must also admit that one of the major spiritual problems in my life, one against which I hope to struggle in whatever years God permits me, is my tendency to work too much: not to relax, reflect, think, pray, meditate as often as is possible and appropriate.

Many clerical readers of *The Cardinal Sins* proclaimed triumphantly that my narrator Kevin Brennan did not pray. As I will report later, in fact he prayed on twenty-three occasions in the story. I'm sure that the same reviewers will contend that I don't pray unless I state explicitly that I do. Indeed they may contend so anyway. For the record, however, I try to pray between forty-five minutes and an hour every day—reading from spiritual books, the Gospels and the Psalms. A detailed discussion of my prayer life is about as appropriate in this context as a detailed discussion of my romantic life. It suffices to say that a) my permeable boundaries make undistracted prayer impossible and b) God does mind distractions nearly as much as our seminary spiritual directors claimed He did.

(Lady Wisdom: Glory be to God, you should excuse the expression! If it was undistracted prayer I wanted, why would I be after creating anyone besides angels?)

In great part, I suspect, because of my receptive imagination, I am the victim of oscillating moods of euphoria and discouragement, with the ebb and flow of my moods especially volatile when I am worn out from travel or pressure or harassment by that instrument of the devil called the telephone.

Despite the Greeley Myth which flourishes in clerical culture, I do not particularly mind criticism. On the contrary, my social science works always appear only after rigorous criticism by professional colleagues. Moreover, publishers tell me I am the only novelist they know who has a board of readers, twenty in number, who read my novels and comment critically on them before I send them off to Warner Books. I will confess I do not like what passes for criticism in the Catholic community today because it is, in fact, not criticism but patronizing, name-calling, motive-questioning falsification of what a book or article says. However, long ago I gave up protesting the barbs of Catholic critics (because the protests only make the critics happy).

When I was writing a column, I engaged sometimes in bitter controversy. That's what column-writing, I thought, was supposed to be about. But I rarely felt personal animosity in such dialogue. I will, however, be candid and admit I rather enjoyed the exhilaration of the battle. One of the reasons, though not the principal one, for abandoning the column was that I had grown weary of the conflict, which, after a couple of decades, seemed a waste of time.

None of which is to deny that I have a fierce Irish temper, as well as a quick and ingenious Irish tongue. To make matters worse, I am not very good at expressing anger in interpersonal relationships, partly because I was raised that way, and partly because my training in the seminary and in the priesthood taught me to suppress anger completely instead of sharing it with others in a constructive and creative way. I'm just no good at confronting colleagues and coworkers who are not living up to their commitments. My anger and frustration builds up internally—then, when it explodes, if it explodes, it may well do so in such way as to cause grave harm to the relationship.

Need I say that I am well aware it's a characteristic which would not have made for a happy marriage unless I'd learned reasonably early in the game how to cope with it—not that all that many Irishmen with repressed tempers ever learn how to cope with it, in or out of marriage.

I remember once in my days as a young parish priest when a Hi Club dance on Friday night had been a particularly harrowing adventure with harassment from pastor, mother superior, janitor, head usher, invaders from Mt. Greenwood, freshman boys breaking Coke bottles, freshman girls giggling even more noisily than usual, more raiders from Mt. Greenwood, assorted drunks, and parental chaperons who thought they knew more about how to preside over the Friday-night rituals than I did. I was, through it all, your serene, smiling, happy, good-natured, cheerful Bing Crosby *Going My Way* type of young parish priest. Then, too late in the evening, two of my best friends in the senior class, Phil Doran and, I think, Bob Sullivan, showed up and began to hassle me: it was so late they didn't have to pay their fifty-cent admission, did they? Phil, who has since, as one might have expected, become a first-rate lawyer, made a particularly contentious case for the blatant injustice of charging them admission. So I hit the ceiling, told them off in rich, colorful and thoroughly unpriestly terms and banished them from the Hi Club for the rest of the year. They left the parish hall, two shocked and silent young men trying to figure out what in the hell had happened to their priest. Fortunately for me, I had enough sense to locate them ten minutes later, waiting in the parking lot for the end of the dance (and for the girls), and apologize. "Gee," said Phil (who now has teenagers of his own), "we didn't know what happened."

Much better, obviously, if I had blown up early at authentic offenders instead of late at relatively innocent targets (by definition, no teenager is ever completely innocent).

I don't know whether it could be said I bear grudges, but I certainly don't burn bridges that may be useful for reconciliation. Thus, while Morris Janowitz was one of my foes during the University of Chicago battles, I now pray for his health, at his request, every night. If anything, in the past I may have entered reconciliations too easily, without facing the original problems. A hasty and easy reconciliation, I have learned the hard way, is far worse than no reconciliation.

Criticism, then, I welcome; name-calling offends me, but I get over it. But there is another phenomenon which has happened often enough in my life (and inevitably, I suppose, given the kind of life I live) that I do not get over easily—betrayal by people I had thought were friends. In most such instances, reconciliation is hardly the issue because the betrayer is proud of what he or she has done. This sort of incident hurts and hurts terribly. I suspect one of the major spiritual problems for the rest of my life will be to learn how to avoid being consumed by bitterness over such incidents.

I am pathetically, perhaps pathologically, trusting. Many of the problems into which I have managed to fall in my life have been the result of giving trust too easily, too quickly, to the wrong people; of believing too readily that everyone with whom I deal is honorable and honest. At the present state of the game, I fear I may have swung too far in the opposite direction and grown suspicious of those I ought not to distrust. Eventually, perhaps, I will find the balance and sharpen my instinct about placing trust. I suspect, from stories my mother told me, and also from incidents I can remember myself, that one of my father's principal weaknesses as a businessman was his apparently incorrigible assumption that everyone had as much integrity as he did. In neither my father nor myself, however, is such naiveté a virtue.

Moreover, I give my loyalty almost as easily as I give my trust, and commit myself to friends and colleagues, sometimes passionately, without always asking myself whether such loyalty might not be both inappropriate and too hasty. "If you don't stand by your friends," said one of my young South Side Irish lawyer friends, "how can you possibly stand by an idea or an ideal?"

He was right, and, as I was later to find, he was not ready to stand by me when the lights in the room went out. Both loyalty and trust are important and admirable virtues, but when one errs by excess in the practice of such virtue, one needlessly and foolishly invites anger, disillusionment, bitterness. If I am frequently tempted to bitterness against the Archdiocese of Chicago, in substantial part the reason for that temptation is that I gave the Archdiocese and my fellow priests my loyalty and my trust too naively, far too easily, far too innocently. When friends ask me, "What did you expect to happen?" the question is a singularly appropriate rebuke. On balance, in matters of trust and loyalty and friendship, it is better to err by excess than by defect but it is even better not to err at all.

A penultimate vice/virtue is hard to name—"impishness," "flair," "leprechaun personality," "outrageous," even "loudmouthed" are words that have been used by various observers to describe this characteristic, which has created lots of trouble for me and also, to tell the truth, provided much amusement. It is an Irish trait and clearly a two-edged sword leading to accusations that I am not serious or am tart-tongued or irresponsible or frivolous or mean or nasty or am not concerned about the poor and the suffering. ("Mercurial" is the word that a certain prominent ecclesiastic from Chicago has used about me.) Most of the other traits described above represent characteristics which are both resource and temptation— personality propensities which, in my spiritual life, can go either way. To tell you the honest-to-God truth, however, I'm not ashamed of my leprechaun wit and have no intention of trying to restrain or control it in the years that may be left to me. When the laughter departs, so too does life.

There is another characteristic which I suppose I ought to mention, though it's hard to name it and even harder to describe it so I'll fall back on a character in my novel to explain what I mean. My sister Mary Jule Durkin claims that I am Kevin Brennan in *The Cardinal Sins* 20 percent of the time, and I would like to have been Kevin 40 percent of the time. However less spectacular my experiences might have been than Kevin's, we have this in common—both of us find it hard to acknowledge that we are admired and loved. We both, in horrible contravention of orthodox Christian doctrine, believe that we earn the love of God and of our fellow human beings by hard work and dedication, whereas, in fact, if love is earned, it is not love. As my colleague in Arizona Jim Harkin has remarked, Kevin is by far the more dangerous of the two priests. Pat Donahue can say, "Please help me." Kevin says, "I don't need anyone's help."

The love of God and of our fellow human beings is a given which we cannot possibly earn and to which we can only respond with love of our own. For different reasons, but with the same effect, Kevin and I have had to learn through the course of our lives that people do love us and expect from us, in some fundamental sense, only love in return. I don't think I'm as much of a stubborn, laconic, prickly hardhead as the narrator of *The Cardinal Sins*, but his flaw and mine are the same, even if mine is not quite so deep-seated or pervasive. It took me a long time in life to realize anyone loved me and even longer to comprehend that the only possible response to love is love in return. I suspect I'll spend the rest of my life trying to integrate and respond to these two phenomena.

70

Quixots, as is clear by now, is a priest—which may be a good thing for some poor woman. I will, God, She helping, always be a priest. I won't even leave if they try to throw me out.

What kind of priest, other than one with porous boundaries?

Canonically I am a priest in good standing at the Archdiocese of Chicago on an assignment made in the winter of 1965 by Cardinal Albert Gregory Meyer, through the agency of Cletus O'Donnell, who was his vicar general. Cardinal Meyer had assigned me to part-time university work in 1960. Four and a half years later, from what turned out to be his deathbed and his last assignment as far as I know, he released me from all regular parish responsibilities and assigned me full-time to academic and literary work at the National Opinion Research Center.

Bishop O'Donnell, in conveying the assignment, told me I could choose to live anywhere I wanted in the Archdiocese, not necessarily in a rectory. This is still my valid canonical assignment. It was confirmed, perhaps reluctantly, by Cardinal Cody and never revoked by him. And while Cardinal Bernardin has never confirmed it, save in response to a question on a radio program, neither has he made the slightest move to revoke it nor is he likely ever to do so.

What would you do, I am asked occasionally, if the cardinal told you to stop writing novels? The response is that it is not in the character of Joseph Louis Bernardin to order me to do that, as much as he would like to be freed from the pressure of those who complain about me. In the unlikely event that, under pressure from higher up, he should attempt it, I would respectfully invite him to walk east on Chicago Avenue until he arrived in Benton Harbor, Michigan. Freedom of expression is not a right the Church can bestow and take away. It's an inalienable right with which we are born. The Church does not grant it, the Church cannot revoke it, I cannot even in good conscience give it up because Church leaders demand I do. It is conceivable, though I think unlikely, that I could lose the canonical good standing which I now claim. If that happens, so be it. It is also possible, though unlikely, that ecclesiastical authority could laicize me. Both the cardinal and his Roman friends realize, however, that if they attempted to throw me out of the priesthood, I would simply not leave. I would continue to claim to be a priest theologically, if no longer in canonical good standing, and continue to do exactly the same work as I am presently doing.

I also define myself as a parish priest. "What do the priests out there

71

working in the trenches think of you?" demands Phil Donahue. Not much, I suspect, and not much if the data collected in a survey of their reaction are to be credited: one quarter strongly positive, one quarter strongly negative, one half indifferent or mildly negative. But the trenches are everywhere, including on the Phil Donahue show. The pertinent question is not what the ordinary priest in the parish thinks about me, but whether historically and theologically my work can be considered priestly. Only the innocent or the ignorant will deny that priests have been artists, scholars, storytellers, writers, journalists, tentmakers, fishermen, kings, generals, architects, stained-glass makers and virtually everything else that is human in the course of Christian history. No technique for preaching the good news of God's love has ever been rejected by the priesthood. Nor has the priesthood ever refused to permit the Holy Spirit to blow whither S/He will in moving priests to their own particular style of preaching the good news.

Donahue and most of my priestly colleagues may not see my work as parish ministry, but the non-Catholic writer Mark Harris in the *New York Times* perceived it as soon as he read my mail. So do the readers of my books, both in their letters and in the research which has been done on the readers. An unusual parish perhaps, but a parish still. It is part of the genius of Catholicism to make definitions as broad as possible and roles as encompassing as possible.

I also do weekend parish work in Tucson and love it. The charge that I do not do traditional parish work or do not like it is pure fiction.

A priest in good standing, a parish priest, and a square-peg priest. The priesthood is a narrowly bounded tribe; anyone who appears to have "gone off the reservation" will be subject to the same sort of sanctions. You will never be in trouble in the priesthood if your performance in the ministry is mediocre. No one will ever write letters about you to the archbishop if you sit peacefully in the rectory and do nothing; if you are not a good counselor or youth worker or liturgist, neither will any of your fellow priests create a mythology to dismiss you as a threat and a rival.

You begin to find yourself in trouble in the priesthood if you are able to do something reasonably well and with reasonable success. If you do a few things well and with a modest amount of success the letters of complaint begin to flow into the Chancery Office—your fellow priests begin to whisper in the bishop's ear. If you engage in many activities with what appears to be talent and skill and achieve what the world judges as considerable success, then you are finished. The outpouring of complaints gives you three choices: (a) you leave the priesthood; (b) you abandon your seemingly successful activities and return to the reservation; or (c) you settle down on the margins of the Church and the priesthood, prepared to be a square peg for the rest of your life. Letters of support from laity and testimonials of approval from some of your fellow priests make no difference because the bishop, in thrall like most of his colleagues to a tiny handful of complainers, knows the complaints are what count— even ten against a hundred positive remarks.

How can this be?

Maybe I should mention before I turn away from the mirror that no one should expect to find, with a couple of exceptions, any real-life counterparts of the people in my stories. I am none of my protagonists, though, obviously and inevitably, there is something of me in all my characters. Most of the people who come to life in my stories are creatures who spring into being in my imagination; doubtless composites of many people I have known but, normally, unself-conscious and unintentional composites (an exception is Noele Marie Brigid Farrell in *Lord of the Dance*, who is a deliberate composite of six Irish Catholic teenage women whom I have known through the years). On occasion some characters have been drawn from life, most notably Monsignor Mugsy Brannigan (the pastor of St. Ursula's), whose real-life counterpart is the still-flourishing Monsignor Daniel F. "Diggy" Cunningham, and Father Richard "Ace" McNamara of *Lord of the Dance*, whose real-life counterpart is Captain Richard Dempsey, Chaplain, United States Navy. In both cases, I might note, the real-life person is far more colorful than my pale fictional simulacrum. Larger-than-life people like Diggy and the Ace elude the storyteller's word processor.

A reader may find in this memoir the context, the setting, the matrix, the atmosphere, the environment, the worldview of my stories. St. Ursula is the St. Angela of my youth, and St. Praxides is the Christ the King of my young priesthood. I have tried to recreate these two magical communities as best I can. While the people who live in St. Praxides and St. Ursula are like the people who lived in Christ the King and St. Angela, they are not drawn directly from life, much as this may disappoint some of my old friends from St. Angela who insist, rather proudly I am told, that they are in one of my books. One exception: Maria Manfredy in *Ascent into Hell* looks physically like a young woman I knew long ago, but I did not know Maria's real-life counterpart well enough to say whether their personalities are similar, and when I wrote the book I had no idea what had happened to the real-life Maria in the last several decades. More recently I have discovered that my imagination was not completely inaccurate in its speculations. The real-life "Maria" is different in some respects from the fictional one, but equally impressive.

As a storyteller I am well aware that we organize, reflect, and shape reality through our stories. A story, be it in fiction or social science or theoretical physics or biblical exegesis, should be a chart which we use as a guide on our journey through complexity and mystery. The story is a model, a trajectory with a beginning and a middle—and if the story is as yet unfinished, as my life is, a line drawn toward a conclusion. A storyteller reorganizes, simplifies, eliminates, interprets, structures. I will not present in this memoir a videotape replay of my life thus far, both because I cannot and because, if I could, the result would be dull and uninteresting. I will rather organize my story around themes, plots and subplots, if you will. But I must acknowledge that another working with the same raw material might find different plots and subplots. Any memoirist imposes his own themes and subthemes on his story. I'm merely being up front about what is inevitable and necessary.

I must report that a number of friends who have read the manuscript of this book in its various drafts took strong exception to parts of it: Dick Dempsey, Nelson Callahan, and Jack Shea lamented that my usual state of enthusiasm and happiness does not come through. Rita Brown and Marilyn James from my St. Angela life thought I was much too hard on myself. Joan Anzia from my Christ the King life protested that there was no hint of how "attractive, funny, and tender" I am (God bless her!).

I record these reactions and note that I tried to take them into account in my revisions. Mostly, however, I am not the one to make judgments of that sort—as much as they please me.

There are doubtless many others who would disagree in the other direction. I'll give them a chance for their innings later on in the book.

As I read over this chapter and try to consider as objectively as I can the character I have presented in it, it occurs to me that from the beginning there was a strong possibility he would end up a square peg in his Archdiocese, his university and his city and the target of considerable dismay and dislike.

Contentious, pushy so-and-so. Indeed, the kind of fellow who could be described as "nothing but a loudmouthed Irish priest," who "never had an unpublished thought" and became the "company sociologist of the Catholic Church" and the "house intellectual of the Daley Machine."

(Only the first label is true, and I want it on my tombstone!)

However, a strong possibility does not mean an inevitability. What happens in a person's life is the result of individual moral choices he and others make. I did not have to write novels; it was a moral choice on my part to do so, made with some awareness of the risk involved. Nor was Cardinal Bernardin fated to inform me through an emissary that to be recognized again in the Archdiocese I would have to engage in public penance for the harm I had done those who had not read my novels but were shocked that I wrote them. That was a moral—and quite possibly politically astute—choice on his part.

In my relationships with Church, city, and university I could have elected to speak truth less bluntly and be less obviously a "loudmouthed Irish priest." On the other hand, those in positions of power and responsibility in the Church, the media, and the university in Chicago could have reasoned (as Cardinal Meyer once did and the *New York Times* and NBC's "Today Show" still do) that, after all, I did have some skills which might prove useful and that in any case I might be somewhat easier to "contain" on the inside than on the outside.

Would that have been morally and humanly better or worse?

The point here is not what is better or worse but that a human life is shaped by options—those that are offered and those that are not offered. The drama in any of our stories comes from the interaction of our own choices and the choices of those who create our interpersonal environment, the options exercised, the options not exercised, and the options denied. It is pop social science to reduce this interplay of choices to necessity. That things turn out the way they do does not mean they had to turn out that way. To confuse statistical probability with inevitability is not only a logical fallacy—it is a denial of the moral drama and the personal excitement of life.

That's what this story is about: choices, mine and other people's. Some of mine were not the choices that should have been. For that I am sorry. I am sorry for the mistakes I made out of ignorance or anger or stupidity or weariness or weakness or self-deception or inexperience or thoughtlessness or harshness or selfishness or insensitivity or haste—of which the last might be the most frequent if not the worst (and the cause of

75

many of the others). I'm especially sorry for those mistakes I made in the name of vincibly misconstrued virtue. I'm most sorry of all for the loves in my life at which I have blundered and for the opportunities of love that I have wasted.

There are, however, a lot of things for which I am totally unrepentant. Like writing stories of grace. If I should apologize for them, God, She would be upset with me, though not terribly upset because like all lovers, She is astonishingly patient. Especially with a lover, I would like to think, who She knows is kind of odd, different, strange, unusual. Permeable.

(Lady Wisdom: Sure, if I didn't want people to be different, would I have been after making them different!)

St. Ursula

CHILDHOOD LOVER

Children do not know their love is shallow
Fleeting as the April tulip blossom
"Cute" to their parents but transient, callow
A single wave on the sea of childhood calm
Her face, our words have long since faded
Yet we two felt love, knife sharp, for a while
Burned in my deepest self, now so jaded
The image of her slow and magic smile
We were eight, almost fifty years have gone—
Resigned, worn by life, is she haggard, spent?
Enduring years of nothing much worthwhile
Fearing each day's new pain, does she dread the dawn?
Or alive, is there still, spirit unbent,
Now and then at least a slow and magic smile?

RIVAL

A still life in my memory, aflame
As a Van Gogh blossom, radiantly fresh
Unfaded by the claims of age and pain,
And the first quiet hints of lurking death.
Girl and woman in delicate suspension,
Deft painting bathed in blue and golden glow
Perfection, promise in one dimension
And a self that has only begun to grow.
Now, wife, mother, widow, forty years have fled
Does your story, just begun, approach its end?
Are your bright grace and promise already dead?
Hope remains, distant rival, do not bend.
By God's love at fourteen you were not misled.
We shall be young once more, we shall laugh again.

"Where have you been for the last forty years?"

"I've been around."

Has it really been forty years and more since Roger Brown and I have spoken? Classmates, friends, at some deep level in both our personalities boys who understood one another, born on the same day, one the best athlete in the class, and the other the smartest—and perhaps the most obnoxious—boy in the class, we are talking on the phone again. Roger's son is in Billings Hospital for major surgery. He realizes that part of the year I'm on the staff at the University of Chicago, so he calls after forty years of silence and asks if I will visit the young man.

"Of course I will. His name is Pete? That was your brother's name, wasn't it? I'll be back in Chicago in a week, and when I arrive at NORC, the first thing I'll do is go over to Billings."

Pete was out of Billings by the time of my return and, thank God, recovering well. His interlude in the hospital, however, had been an occasion, which I can only call a grace, for his father and me to renew a friendship which lapsed because we were going different ways forty years ago. And with Roger and his wife, Rita (the girl who lived across the street from our house), I began to rediscover those who were friends, and classmates, and neighbors, and rivals in the world of St. Angela/St. Ursula when I was a little boy. This rediscovery is especially poignant and especially meaningful because when I turned to storytelling, under the influence of Erika Fromm's self-hypnosis, it was inevitable that all the vivid memories of those years and of that parish, which seems more remarkable to me now than it did even ten years ago, should surface with enormous vitality, power, and poignancy.

So, as a penalty for my sins, I was asked to lecture at the annual meeting of the Oak Park/River Forest Chamber of Commerce. It was not much of a meeting and the lecture was not all that effective (because, to tell the truth, the audience was more than mildly tuned-out), but I invited my new friends, the Brennans, and their late-teenaged children, Bob and Michele, as well as Roger and Rita to be my guests. I found myself at the table with Rita on one side of me and Michele on the other, caught, as they both quickly agreed, between two of the more vivid and powerful women in my life and caught, as most Irishmen are, between two women who see through him, like totally!

Right? Right.

It was a delightful evening, although it was necessary to restrain Mi-

hele and Bobby, who were fighting mad when a couple of drunks wanted
to challenge me about all the "dirt" in my novels. The past and the
present in my life merged smoothly and generously. Rita, in her early
fifties, seems even more attractive than she was in her middle teens, no
mean accomplishment, and Michele is, well, Michele—one of the real-
life counterparts of Noele Marie Brigid Farrell in *Lord of the Dance*.
Roger and I recounted all the nefarious things we did to torment our
teachers in grammar school. Well, Roger did them; I was far too well
behaved a young man to do anything but watch and silently applaud. As
the evening wore on, I enjoyed the presence of an old friend and two
lovely women and the amusement of Bob and Jeanine Brennan (a third
lovely woman I hasten to add if you like redheads, and I do) at this strange
turning point in my life. I realized that Bobby Brennan and Roger Brown,
Michele Brennan and Rita Brown, are not all that different and that the
world of St. Angela and River Forest, of La Follette Park and Grand
Beach, are much more similar than I would have thought and that the
continuities of life are, as my social science theory should have led me
to believe, much more powerful than the discontinuities.

In a way that I may never be able to sort out, my novels have brought
back the people from my past. Others began to appear out of what for
me has become the hazy twilight of the St. Angela years. Is it too early
to try to interpret this renewal of old relationships? As Rita Brown said,
"God must have had some purpose for drawing us all together again."

Lines of single-family brick bungalows, 1936 Fords puffing down the
street, red streetcars at Division Street and North Avenue, touch football
games in the street, the Austin bus and the Lake Street L downtown,
sitting on the front porch talking on hot summer evenings, Motto's Drug
Store, the local pool hall whose name I forget because I never went inside
(Fred's, Roger tells me, not unlike the Grand Beach rock group), shopping
for my mother in the presupermarket Jewel, making a mess out of model
airplanes and boats, hearing about the Pearl Harbor attack as the great
1941 Chicago Bears played the then Chicago Cardinals.

We were policemen and firemen, precinct captains and undertakers,
clerks and small businessmen, and a handful of managers, like my father,
and professionals. The Great Depression ground to a halt, World War II
ended in victory, but still we were cautiously conservative about our
personal lives. We were used to hard times and to a timeless Church.
The changes in our economic and social environment that were to begin

in 1947 and in the Church a decade later with the Vatican Council were beyond our wildest imaginings.

For most of us there was no need to imagine these things. Despite the hard times, the environment of the neighborhood was pleasant enough. Everyone knew everyone else, we all understood the tremendous importance of loyalty to one's friends, standing by one's "own kind." There were a few well-to-do among us and they were respected, but not envied, I think. Whatever had been our heady ambitions during the 1920s, they were gone by the 1940s—enough that we had made it into the middle class. No one expected much else, and what in the world was a Ph.D., anyway?

Even when you drive down the streets on a dark, rainy March evening, the old neighborhood still has the power to stir up memories so powerful the years slide away. It is a hot summer day, and you are trudging toward the grassy wooded playground that surrounds the tiny swimming pool. Somehow music from the Bing Crosby movie *Holiday Inn* sounds in the background.

You're standing on the street corner of Austin Boulevard in front of the Baptist church waiting for a bus to take you downtown to the insufferably dull summer job.

You're coming out of the smelly La Follette Park gym on a cold Thursday afternoon in midwinter with the other seminarians—cursed with a Thursday instead of a Saturday holiday—having run off vast amounts of animal energy on the basketball court.

You are sitting in the Rose Bowl, a dim ice cream parlor presided over by a suspicious-looking but attractive Greek, or waiting in line at the Jewel food store, daydreaming about a certain lovely blonde.

You are playing touch football with already badly scraped knees on the asphalt streets.

You are filing into the Catholic school in neat, orderly ranks while the sisters nervously jangle little bells. Occasionally the tall, gray-haired, beaming monsignor watches proudly.

You are kneeling in the back of church at six-thirty Mass in the morning barely able to stay awake.

You and your friends meet on the school playground for softball on a Saturday afternoon.

You are studying Latin to be an altar boy.

The girls from the class are in tears on grammar school graduation day

80

(a phenomenon which seems not to have declined appreciably in forty years).

You are coming back from the seminary, encountering grammar school classmates long unseen who are, in the late 1940s, confused about whether they made the right decision not to go to college.

You are walking home from church on Sunday morning, reading the headlines about the Korean War.

You are making your First Communion in the old wooden church.

Then it is your father's funeral in the basement church that replaced the wooden structure, a gym in the making.

And then the memories rush in—you are saying your first mass . . . your mother's funeral . . . the new, gleaming, white gothic postwar church. Time goes back even further, and the images become more jumbled, less defined: the WPA has a camp in the "prairie" (what we called vacant lots in those days) across the street from your house. The neighborhood streets are being reconstructed, and everybody jokes about how little the WPA people work—apparently they didn't understand then the connection between WPA and the battle against the Depression. You remember the Roosevelt for President posters on the side of the elevated tracks (Who will win? you ask your mother uncertainly. The answer is categoric: "Roosevelt, of course!"), the old open-air two-decker buses, the Century of Progress, Italo Balbo's seaplane flying over the city, the stockyards fire, the smell of the yards floating over the neighborhood on a hot, humid, stuffy, summer evening—and the yards were a long, long distance away. You remember little children tagging along to school, having no idea how long it would take them to walk the three blocks and dashing madly those last few moments, quite certain they were late and Sister would (horror of horrors!) keep them after school. And then, way, way back, you remember tricycles and Irish Mails rushing enthusiastically down the sidewalk on Augusta Boulevard, and baseball games in the alley, and horse-drawn garbage carts and milk trucks (Wanzer trucks were green, remember?).

And you remember people, people you haven't seen for forty years— grammar school teachers, some pleasant, others not, some saintly, some irrepressibly funny. You remember the old monsignor, Funeral Frank he was called, because he made every funeral in the Archdiocese. You remember John Hayes, the young curate who had you doing a dialogue Mass in the middle 1930s. You remember the "prominent" parishioners (mostly, if the truth be told, insufferable dullards); you remember the kids down the street or next door, the people with whom you played basketball on the driveway in front of the garage of your house—now some of them old enough to be pastors (though not monsignors yet).

You remember the smartest girl in the class, who was also the prettiest, too pretty ever to be teacher's pet. Your crush on her, as best as you can remember, began in third grade and was always enjoyed at a great and safe distance. You wonder what ever happened to her. Looking at the grammar school pictures, you decide that it was neither adolescent fantasy nor nostalgia for the 1940s that made her seem beautiful. She truly was gorgeous.

Rita Brown: Both you and Roger had a crush on her.

Me: (not too defensively) Who didn't?

And after we had dinner with her...

Rita: You stared at her all night.

Me: Do you blame me?

Rita: Not the first time.

You remember the troublemakers in the class who turned out to be policemen, social workers, and politicians. You remember them all as they were forty years ago, and you realize with a start that most of them probably have grandchildren now.

How odd that they have grown older when you haven't.

You remember the precinct captain who was also the undertaker. You remember the vast numbers of fellow seminarians. For a while the parish was producing more than a priest a year, though it was not doing nearly so well with nuns. You remember the parish saints—or at least everyone said they were. You remember the crowds in back of church on Sunday mornings. You remember the war veterans coming home in 1945 and 1946, swarming off to college determined to break the constraints of the Depression. You remember the crabs, the crazy people, the eccentrics, the haunted houses, the policemen at school crossings, the redheaded mailman, the athletic directors of the park, the courtly alderman, and even the voices of Norman Ross, Sr., and Clifton Utley on the radio at seven fifty-five in the morning. They all suddenly come alive again. The neighborhood streets are filled with memories, some of them sad, some painful, some poignant, but many of them glorious. They're alive again now both in novels and in rediscovered friends.

The "gathering in" of old relationships, initiated with Roger Brown's phone call, will be one of the agendas for the years I have left; some aspects of it, however, seem pertinent to this story. My friends from the St. Angela days seem to have worn well. Rita and Roger are, if anything, more in love with each other than they were when they were teenagers. Roger, a quarterback on a Fenwick city championship team and later at Notre Dame, may not have become a radical feminist but he prepares dinner often, and enjoys his status as a gourmet cook. They and the others like them that I'm meeting again concretize one of the fundamental plots of my sociology and my stories and my priestly ministry—the American Catholic population has survived, through no fault of their leaders or their scholars, extraordinarily well, the twin crises of prosperity and change in the Church.

As I listen to some of my rediscovered friends with a mixture of nostalgia and fascination at the story of their lives, I realize the Church has made them suffer. There are only hints, lightly touched and showing no bitterness, of agonized decisions. Once more I marvel at the faith of those who remain enthusiastically Catholic despite what their Church and their clergy have done to them.

Irish folk (the Irish Irish as opposed to the American Irish) tell me my novels display "sense of place," a characteristic which Seamus Heany calls a "feeling, assenting, equable marriage between the geographical country and the country of the mind." While I move now mostly in the world of what social scientists call "cosmopolitans" I am a confirmed "local," rooted in places and passionately loyal to them. I do impose on the geographical country my own spiritual and emotional and intellectual country in what I hope is an assenting and equable marriage. This is not a matter of choice on my part; it is programmed into me by my most fundamental values and my most powerful preconscious templates. My "places"—Twin Lakes, St. Ursula, St. Praxides, Grand Beach, Arizona— readily become sacraments, sacred and revelatory places. I don't apologize for this, by the way. I think it responds to the strong needs of our fundamental nature as creatures constituted in time and space.

Wandering is all right so long as you have a place to come home to.

There is a neat if often painful paradox in all this. Despite my passionate loyalty to my sacred places, what I do or perhaps more accurately who I am tends to make me unwelcome in the places which mean so much to me—university, Archdiocese and city. It is perhaps too bad for them that they are not flexible and open enough to accept my curious mixture

83

of dissidence (which is less serious in reality than it is in, often neurotic, mythology) and loyalty. It is also too bad for me.

I can understand why I was something of a square peg at St. Angela in the old days. I read too much, I thought too much, I talked too much. Yet I may exaggerate how much of an outsider I was or perhaps misperceived the possibilities even then. Roger and I were as different as two boys could be, yet somehow we shared a respect that went beyond our common birthday. I remember watching him on the football field at Notre Dame in 1946 and sensing for reasons I could not articulate that there would be something which would always bind us together.

"You were so quiet then," one of them says, tapping the pile of Hewlett-Packard output which was an earlier draft of this book. "Now I know much more about you than you do about me."

"Mnn..." I say for want of something better.

"It is good to know you again," she continues, "or maybe for the first time. Somehow, we knew that you would reappear."

I leave that alone.

Four years after I saw him on the field at Notre Dame, Roger Brown would be in the lines in Korea, Rita was at home with a baby son, and I was in the seminary at Mundelein. Their life has been tougher than mine and they have survived it with grace. I think of them as "wearing well." Maybe the question ought to be put the other way around. How well, after all, have I worn a life which has been, all things considered, relatively free of sickness, tragedy and death?

Is the priest the grace or are his lay friends? Increasingly I am persuaded that they are the grace for me.

It is curious, graceful, astonishing, that my stories have brought them back to me for the rest of my life. I never thought then I would write stories, but even then the religious power of story had been revealed to me.

I was in eighth grade, fourteen years old, when I read Lloyd Douglas's novel *The Robe*, a story about the Roman officer who crucified Jesus and won his seamless robe in a toss of the dice.

Douglas's tale of Marcellus the officer, Demetrius, his slave, and Diana, his love, had an enormous influence on me. I recently wrote an introduction to a new edition in part to discharge a long overdue debt to Lloyd C. Douglas.

The Robe was the first adult novel I had ever read; it changed my mind about religion, about fiction, and about the possible relationship between the two. Douglas was a transition between the adventure stories of childhood (including, I confess it, the Hardy Boys) and the classics of young adulthood (we didn't have teenagers in those days). I continued to reflect on the relationship between religion and fiction through the years, especially as I devoured in high school so-called Catholic novelists who were much discussed in the Catholic Church in my young adulthood — Graham Greene, Evelyn Waugh, François Mauriac, Georges Bernanos, Leon Bloy. Finally, almost forty years later, when I turned to storytelling of my own, it was a result of a long intellectual and imaginative process which started with reading *The Robe*.

I began Douglas's novel in the quiet of my room at the front of our house at Mayfield and Potomac on Chicago's West Side, with some hesitation and even guilt. On the one hand, the book was being read and discussed by many of my parents' friends, some loving it and some professing to be shocked by its approach to the Bible. On the other hand, it had been roundly denounced in the official Catholic press. The charge, as best as I can remember it, was that Douglas's work was "naturalist" and "rationalist" in its description of the miracles of Jesus, an allegation which in retrospect seems absurd.

I was already well on my way to becoming an obsessive reader: my mother would later tell stories about finding me in the basement, head at the bottom of the stairs, feet higher up, reading old newspapers. I came by that passion naturally enough since she and my father were also dedicated readers, though not of what we would now consider serious fiction. Despite my mother's comic stories, they were proud that their son liked to read (I played basketball too, enthusiastically and badly; they were also proud of the enthusiasm if not the ineptness).

In such a home environment it would have been unthinkable not to satisfy my curiosity about this controversial book—especially since one of the parish priests said he thought it was a great story, despite the Catholic press.

Douglas did perhaps find natural explanations for the changing of water into wine at Cana and for the multiplication of the loaves and fishes, but he certainly did not try to explain away most of the other miracles. Quite the contrary, Marcellus comes to believe finally because of the miracles he hears about from eye-witnesses.

It is a curious indication of the change in Catholicism that while forty years ago, Douglas was faulted for not being literal enough in his approach to the Bible, now he might be criticized, especially by Catholic biblical scholars, for being too literal.

Despite my mild fears that perhaps I was being disloyal to my Catholic heritage, I could not put the book down. For the first time in my life I was experiencing the power of a skilled storyteller to create a world of his own and characters of his own who compelled my attention and engaged my whole personality. So this is what a storyteller did and this is why people read stories!

Moreover, the world he created was a world I already knew from my religion classes in St. Angela Grammar School, the world of the time of Jesus, of Rome and Jerusalem, of Greece and Galilee in the first century A.D. (C.E. as we call it now, Common Era, afraid either of the Latin of *anno domini* or perhaps of offending unbelievers with a reference to the Lord). But, unlike my religion class in which Jesus and his contemporaries seemed part of another world and another species, the characters in *The Robe* were as real as my neighbors, my classmates, the girl down the street. (I imagined Diana looked like her. The same girl would emerge, relatively unchanged in my imagination, four decades later in my own *Ascent into Hell*.)

That was a powerful religious experience for me. The overlay of piety, sentimentality, and devotion which had been added to the Bible had somehow made it all, if not quite unreal, at least a world which existed in a different category of being. To meet Peter and John and Stephen and Paul and Bartholomew and to listen to real people who had really known the real Jesus changed the religious game, dramatically and definitively. The New Testament was, as I would say now, continuous with my world and not discontinuous.

Perhaps the way our teachers treat the Bible does not have the same effect on everyone, but I have learned through the years that by trying to make the biblical actors superhuman, we who teach often make them nonhuman and inhuman, and hence uninteresting, to those who are human. Such, of course, was not the intent of the Evangelists, but we often distort their intent to suit our purposes and our fears. A novel like *The Robe* revivifies the world of the Bible and reestablishes its contact with us and the relationship between the people who live in the Bible stories and our lives.

To make them appear like people we already know is no mean achievement. Jesus and his friends became real to me those late evenings in the quiet of my room in a way they had never been before. It was a turning point in my life.

Why, I wondered, are there not more stories like this? It is still, I think, a pertinent question. Later I would discover Sholem Asch (*The Nazarene* and *The Apostle*) and the wonderful Henry Sienkiewicz (*Quo Vadis*). And the question would broaden: why don't the churches use fiction to transmit their heritages? Jesus taught mostly through stories ("I will use parables to speak to them, I will tell them things unknown since the creation of the world." Matthew 13:35). Why don't we?

The question would become even more insistent when my sociological research persuaded me that religion finds its origin and its raw power in the imaginative dimension of the personality. In religion, experience, image (symbol or metaphor, if you will) and story precede propositional and theological reflection. Why then do we not more often use story (narrative as the newly emerging theologians of story call it) to transmit our religious heritages? Why not more religious novels, films, TV series?

The explanation is the same as that for the criticism of *The Robe* in the 1940s. Religious leaders, trained in dry, propositional theology, distrust story; they demand that the story be edifying (which the parables of Jesus were not), that the characters be saints, not sinners in need of salvation (as all the readers are), and that the storyteller offend not even the most timid of the "faithful" (a demand which would have put Jesus himself on the Index of Forbidden Storytellers).

But in St. Angela in 1942 with MacArthur fleeing the Philippine Islands and Bataan about to fall to the Japanese I wanted only to be a priest, not a storyteller. It would take many years before I would realize that the Lord who jumped vividly out of the pages of *The Robe* (though Douglas wisely kept him offstage) for me was also a storyteller.

St. Angela is on what we used to call the far West Side of Chicago, overlapping one block the other side of Austin Boulevard into Oak Park. The south boundary was halfway between Chicago Avenue and Augusta Boulevard; its north boundary, a mile away, one block north of North Avenue; and its eastern boundary a block east of Central Avenue. The Chancery Office had designed the boundaries of the parish with fine disregard for both the borders of the city and the principal east-west and north-south thoroughfares. Doubtless they were compromises between the founding pastor of St. Angela and the neighboring pastors from whom

87

territory was being taken. No pastor ever gives up territory readily. With the departing land, he also sees departing income. But the gerrymandered boundaries of St. Angela guaranteed that mothers on all sides of the parish would worry anxiously about their children crossing such main thoroughfares as Austin Boulevard, Augusta Boulevard, Central Avenue and North Avenue. Presumably, such thoughts did not trouble either the Chancery Office or the founding pastor, Father Fitzgerald.

St. Angela was at the north end of Austin, a once independent village annexed by the city at the turn of the century. The south end of the parish included several blocks of wooden homes that were part of the old village of Austin, built before the First World War. North of them were several blocks of apartment buildings, mostly two-flats constructed in the 1920s. The north end of the parish was part of the bungalow belt, the most distinctive contribution to domestic architecture in Chicago in the era between the two wars.

The wooden balloon houses of earlier eras were replaced with one-story brick homes solidly constructed and designed with some taste and elegance for habitation by the new members of the middle class during the misleading prosperity of the 1920s. The bungalow seemed to us then to be the ultimate in domestic architecture, not likely ever to be replaced, for it was solid, comfortable, imposing. Those who owned such homes, perhaps the first land that was really theirs in a thousand and more years of family history, kept them well painted and well landscaped (perhaps not quite as fanatically so as in the Polish neighborhoods) even through the "hard times" of the 1930s. Ours was a "substantial" neighborhood; while we were hit as hard as anyone else by the Depression, few of the men in the parish were "on relief" or working for the WPA. We struggled and survived and pretended we were better off than we really were— some of us to the extreme extent of voting Republican, although the Cook County regular Democratic organization of that day routinely delivered the 37th ward to the Democratic column on election day, especially on presidential election day.

I suspect the Chancery Office was not happy with Father Fitz because he did not expand the parish "plant" during the 1920s and early 1930s to respond to the rapidly growing population of St. Angela. The second pastor was Monsignor Francis O'Brien, who had already distinguished himself by building two parish plants and was clearly sent to St. Angela's with the mandate to catch up. The old wooden church, musty, dusty, tiny, quaint, crowded, hot, and to my young sensitivity wondrously sacred, was torn down in 1936. The school was expanded, the rectory was moved down the street and around the corner (with a new front end which included a two-story gallery room for the pastor). An addition to the school was built which included a large auditorium, half of it in a basement, that would serve as the parish church for almost twenty years and would be the church of my confirmation, grammar school graduation, and seminary days, to be replaced shortly before my first Mass with an attractive, vast gothic structure of white stone with stained-glass windows (in one window, at the insistence of Monsignor "Mugsy Brannigan" —as I would call Diggy Cunningham in my stories—there was depicted a Notre Dame football player).

The parish waited twenty years for its new church, in part because of the war and in part because Monsignor O'Brien's health failed. His final days were dramatic. In a strange, terrifying, sweltering week in summertime, Father Harry Lawlor, one of the curates, died, and then, a few days later, the monsignor died too, mourning the young priest, of whom he was fond; "My Harry and my God!" were reputed to be his last words. His successor, Father Thomas Hayes, was also in his grave a couple of years later. Incompetence, sickness, death plagued the parish then, until the coming of the vigorous and energetic Monsignor Daniel F. Cunningham, who had, among his other exploits, played shortstop for the Chicago White Sox for a few weeks in 1916 before going to the seminary.

All of this history existed only on the surface of parish life. We mourned our dead priests, we sensed the drift and confusion, we hailed the irrepressible Diggy (who so ably delegated responsibilities that he was able to administer the parish and the Catholic school system of the Archdiocese and at the same time play golf almost every day in the summertime and earned, with considerable merit, the title of the number one Notre Dame football fan in the country). But the slow and subtle rhythms of the parish life went on, maintained by the regular and loyal devotion of the laity and the efficient industry of the nuns. Boys and girls showed up for school in September, marched in orderly "ranks" into the buildings, worked and studied with silence and industry, and departed at three o'clock in the same orderly ranks in which they had entered. Their coming and going was supervised by efficient and normally responsible patrol boys (patrol girls would only come later, a delay for which God forgive us). And once a month the monsignor or one of the other priests would show up in the classroom, pass out the report cards, praise and admonish us, and then depart back to the rectory for whatever problems they might have to face in that sacred and mysterious house. First Communion, preceded by First Confession, occurred every year, Confirmation every other year, grammar school graduation in June with clocklike regularity, as did a novena to St. Anne in the summertime, a mission every other autumn, and the *Tre Ore* devotion for three hours from twelve to three on Good Friday. Sermons were preached, collections were taken, the sick visited, the dead buried, converts instructed, young people processed through the complex canonical requirements before marriage.

Some Catholics went to the public schools, though not many, and a few more to public high schools. They were, it must be confessed, treated like second-class citizens, but, in substantial part, it was a matter of their own choice or, rather, of their parents' choice, or so it seemed then. It mattered who the pastor was and who the priests were, but not all that much. The quality of sermons, sympathy in the confessional, interest in the grammar school kids and the teenagers—these varied, depending on who the priests were, but the essentials of the parish were so routinized and so totally accepted by the laity and so efficiently administered by the nuns (who were in those days the real strength of the immigrant and post-immigrant Church) that it was as unthinkable that the rhythms of parish life would change as it was that bungalows were not the ultimate in middle-class domestic architecture.

Mind you, priests were respected and admired and revered, and their failings—tardiness, irresponsibility, alcoholism, and in the case of an occasional "visiting priest," homosexuality—were ignored. The priest was the community's symbolic leader and, as such, important, but, as I would learn only much later, priests were not the ones who kept the parish community going.

There were five parish societies: the Holy Name for married men, the Altar and Rosary for married women, the St. Vincent de Paul Society to help the "poor of the parish," and variously named organizations for young men and young women, none of which, in my day at any rate, displayed much vigor or vitality. The Hi Club or the Teen Club, that marvelous and wonderful form of Catholic adolescent ministry, would only develop at St. Angela in the Diggy Cunningham years when I was away in the seminary at Mundelein (and hence I could tell my teenage charges at Christ the King that I had never been a teenager—not much of an exaggeration, come to think of it).

There were occasional study groups, and we recited the dialogue Mass between priests and people, in Latin, naturally. The latter two activities were the result of the efforts of Father John Hayes, a "labor priest" who taught at Quigley Seminary and who would later go on to the National Catholic Welfare Conference in Washington. Hayes, I would later learn, was one of the group of bright young priests trained by or gathered around Monsignor Reynold Hillenbrand, the rector of the seminary at Mundelein, a group of men who made Chicago one of the most interesting dioceses in the world in its experiments and innovation in the forties and fifties. If St. Angela was not as exciting as some of the other West Side parishes—St. Mel's, Resurrection, St. Catherine's—it was a more accurate harbinger of what was to come in the Church.

The parish of St. Angela meant and means much to me. It was the hard-rock ground of Midwestern, modestly liberal Irish Catholicism of the thirties and forties, on which I heard for the first time the stories which are the central message of the Catholic heritage and experienced the celebrations that are the heart of the Catholic religious sensibility. It is one of the points of orientation of my life. Why did it take forty years to explore, once again, the relationships of that crucial time?

I was marked (by myself) for the seminary and for the priesthood. That meant, according to guidance we received at the seminary, that we ought to end our relationships with the young men and young women we had known in grammar school. We were not to be part of a teenage culture (though the word "teenage" had yet to be invented). Our grammar school friends might contaminate us and cause us to lose our vocation. Therefore, we should avoid them as though they were occasions of sin or even the agents of Satan. It seemed to occur to no one that in a relatively short period of time we would be serving as priests, if not to exactly the same young people, then to our contemporaries, who had gone through the anguish and the anxieties of adolescence during the war and the postwar prosperity. Just at the time, then, when grammar school relationships might solidify into adolescent relationships that could, perhaps, endure for a lifetime, we were to be wrenched out of the possibility of such relationships. Dutiful and obedient seminarian that I was, I went along.

91

Nor, to tell the truth, was it particularly hard to go along, for my contemporaries were entering into their "wild" phase of the life cycle. Drink, sex (usually mild—necking, petting, dirty talk) and vandalism were what my contemporaries were most interested in—and I was not. With my new friends at the seminary I shared common goals and values. There was little hardship in relinquishing my grammar school mates. Perhaps, reflecting upon it, I missed them then more than I realized. When it came time to dredge my imagination for people and stories for my novels, their names and faces and experiences came back with extraordinary vividness.

The advice that one avoid one's contemporaries was, in retrospect, mindless, though not because we needed the teenage experience to understand teenagers. Most men and women promptly forget their teenage fears and problems and hopes as soon as they're married and do not recall them by the time they have teenagers of their own. Probably the best thing I do, even today, in the traditional pastoral ministry is relate to teenagers, because, as Michele Brennan remarked once, in a characteristic comment, "You've always been a teenager, Father Greeley. You just never grew up."

It was a compliment, by the way.

Nor is the objection to the old seminary isolation that it interfered with our chances to learn about women especially valid. The dating/mating game of adolescence is not designed to confer much knowledge of or understanding of or sympathy for the opposite sex. As for finding out whether I liked girls, I knew well I did. The reason seminarians ought to have, and now in great part do have, a "normal" adolescence is that it is part of the maturational experience of the men and women with whom they work and there's a chance that a priest who's had a teenage of his own (as I did not) will understand a little bit more about himself and about his people, whether they be adolescents or adults.

As a grammar school student in St. Angela I was on the fringes of the class. I was too smart, knew too many answers and received grades that were much too high; moreover, God forgive me for it again, I fear I was obnoxious about displaying my intelligence, annoying my fellow students and teachers alike. Someone in the class coined the term "walking encyclopedia" for me and, characteristically, I was proud of it. Moreover, as an athlete I didn't begin to exist, inheriting none of my father's indoor baseball—or any other—skills. This didn't prevent me from trying (then

92

and now), but I was laughably incompetent (then as now) too, as my teenage water-skiing companions will confirm.

Michele: You mean you were *never* any good at sports, Father Greeley? It's not just *old* age?

Me: Tell me about it.

I was a sports fan if not an athlete. I listened to Bob Elson broadcast the Cubs games even before I went to grammar school and the Bear games on Sunday afternoon. I was one of those who heard live the description of Gabby Hartnett hitting the home run into the "gloaming" to win the pennant in 1938. The Bears won every year. Dark times since then, till 1984, a year of limited triumph which my nieces and nephews celebrated by buying me for Christmas and birthday Cubs and Bears jackets so "Uncle will be the coolest priest in Tucson!"

And during the glorious 1985 season I would discover that one of the women from St. Angela had a stronger claim on Bear loyalty than I had—which somehow doesn't seem right! Lucy Scanlan at the Bear Games every Sunday!

After the games I tuned to "Tom Mix," "Orphan Annie," "Jack Armstrong" and "Don Winslow of the Navy." I learned soon that there were stories on the daytime programs too and became an early addict of the soaps. Even then, however, the appeal of stories to my porous personality was strong. I was a confirmed daydreamer even before I learned to read and write.

In school I became a studious dreamer, devouring books, mostly novels but really almost anything I could get my hands on. During junior high school years when the first signs of romance were stirring, I avoided such activities firmly and completely, if not so firmly or completely fantasies about them. (No post office or spin the bottle for me, no way!) Thus, I really didn't fit. By the time adolescence was upon me I knew it; and my classmates knew it. I was simply not part of the social life of seventh and eighth grade.

I'm afraid I was a trial to my teachers. Alas, I was too naive to realize that the best thing a bright little boy with encyclopedic knowledge can do is keep his big Irish mouth shut. The nuns got even with me by complaining about my handwriting. One kind nun commented that my brain went faster than my hands. Another, less kind, pounded my fingers with her ruler.

I didn't tell my father. When another nun hit my sister he descended on the convent with icy fury and warned her never to do it again. I felt I could take care of myself.

I'll admit I didn't like the nuns (with some exceptions). I thought they picked on me unnecessarily. Now I realize that I threatened and dismayed them. I was, you see, a little strange and incredibly naive about how teachers react to strange, bright students.

Yet to hit a little boy with a ruler because you don't like the way he is holding a pencil is an appalling action for a woman who claims to be a bride of Christ. Okay, I've done things as a priest of which I am heartily ashamed. I know that weariness and discouragement can make you forget who and what you are. Sister was an unhappy and troubled woman. Not all the nuns were that way, but too many were.

Even as a little boy, I knew instinctively that many of the sisters were not happy women, even though they told us that priests and nuns were the happiest people in the world. The religious orders of women are responsible for most of what is good in American Catholicism, yet there was something wrong in their internal structure and culture. As soon as the changes came, many of the younger women left en masse, right after they had won the battle for change. Now it would appear that the traditional orders are finished, a tragedy I wrestle with at great length in my story *Virgin and Martyr*. As best as I can discover the problem of the religious communities of women was that they did not have enough respect for the privacy, the dignity and the freedom of the individual woman member. But now that the problem has been corrected, the religious orders are dying out.

Often I ask myself if resentments from my grammar school experiences with the sisters and later unhappy contacts with domineering superiors at Christ the King and castrating ideologues in the various "movements" during the late sixties have biased me against religious women. Minimally I am suspicious. Nonetheless I respect what they have done and am impressed by the skill and commitment and professional competencies of many of them. I am appalled at the male chauvinist oppression which they have had to endure. Yet I am not at ease with nuns; the ruler against my fingers and the active dislike many of them felt for me in grammar school still linger in my memory.

But then so does the memory of Sister Augustine (now Sister Ciel McCormack), who taught me in eighth grade and was one of the finest women I have ever known. I have never had a nun as a close friend.

I don't rule out the possibility, but I continue to be wary of them.

In retrospect, I realize that perhaps marginality didn't enter my life with the coming of John Patrick Cody to Chicago, but was there all along. However, with even deeper reflection, I understand there was much affection and love for me at the the St. Angela of my youth—affection and love neither I nor my friends understood or were able to express. Not staying with them long enough to acquire the skill for such expression was a price I thought I had to pay to become a priest. I was simply wrong. I listened to false teachers and false prophets. If I had to do it again, I would certainly do it differently.

Was all this youthful marginality good or bad? Probably a mixture of both. I may have been deprived of some of the good times of adolescence and I certainly missed many of the bad. I lost a lot of people whom I would even then, if I were honest about it, rather not have lost. On the other hand, it is altogether possible I would have drifted away from them anyway, and sufficiently later in life there would be no possibility of a reconstruction of some of those friendships now occurring. You have to lose people, perhaps, before you find them. To end one's exploration of a place where one has begun and to recognize it for the first time, one has to set out on the exploration in the first place. I now recognize St. Angela not merely as a culture and a community of the past but also as a developing network of friends in the present. The latter I take as pure grace.

So, when did I decide I was to be a priest? In Sister Alma Frances's classroom, in second grade, in the late autumn of 1935 when she asked how many boys wanted to be priests. About half of us raised our hands, and Sister, God be good to her, said that perhaps one of us would make it. Actually two of us did, my close friend Lawrence McNamara, now bishop of Grand Island, Nebraska, being the other.

Larry left the Chicago Archdiocese when we graduated from Quigley in 1947. We stayed in touch through our years in the major seminary. I remember saying, at his First Mass banquet, that it was almost inevitable our paths would separate and we would see each other rarely in the years to come. The notion brought tears to the eyes of some of his family and made Larry look sadder than any priest should look on his First Mass day. The prediction was accurate enough, but that friendship was not ended, it was merely put on a back burner for a while. We see each other occasionally and chortle over the fact that I was such a model seminarian and preseminarian and he, frequently, was more relaxed with the rules than I, but went on to become the bishop and I became the perennial dissident priest.

Why did you want to be a priest? That question is a lot harder to answer. I can remember the day I decided, but I can no more articulate the reason for the decision today than I could then. I liked the priests, I respected them, I admired what they seemed to do—intervening some- how between God and humans—and I wanted to do the same thing. The impetus and the drive to the priesthood came not from the family, but from me, not exactly against their better judgment, but against some gently spoken reservations.

My response to the reservations was typical of the little boy who had raced down the hill at Twin Lakes. Why experiment with something else when you've made up your mind what you want to do? Why put off ordination for one more year? Why make the course thirteen years instead of twelve?

Even then time was crucial. Urgency had already intruded into my life. I could not have said it then but I was searching for my Grail, hunting for the God who lurked in the lake, pursuing Paradise Lost and (to change the metaphor) running from the Hound of Heaven.

Would I do it that way again? I think so. I suppose it sounds strange when I say I never changed my mind after that day in Sister Alma Frances's classroom. I sailed through the various decision points in the seminary without the slightest hesitation. The subdiaconate and the promise of celibacy (about which more later) was not a solemn or terrifying expe- rience. A day or two before ordination I had the strongest doubts I've ever had in my life, and they were pretty weak. (A girl, not a real one, but imaginary. She still appears in my dreams, like me—despite Michele Brennan—totally unaged.)

It was a priest I wanted to be; it was a priest I became; it's a priest I am; and it's a priest I intend to continue to be. I liked the priests, and I liked what priests do. I still admire those men who represent, in their daily lives, the finest of the pragmatic wisdom and the sensible dedication which seems to me to characterize the Catholic priesthood at its best, men who are represented in my books by the redoubtable Blackie Ryan. The men I knew at St. Angela, as a boy and a seminarian, had their faults and limitations—and some in later life would decide that I had been a terrible mistake—but they were, each one of them, good priests, more professionally responsible and dedicated than are some priests today. I wanted to do what they did and that I have done, though often in ways they and I would have then thought highly improbable. Improbable doesn't mean wrong.

In the thirty years that I have been a priest, St. Angela has changed dramatically. In the fifties and the sixties, under the leadership of Diggy Cunningham, it flourished and became *the* great Irish parish on the West Side. The school doubled in size. The big new church was filled every Sunday. The parish became a center for every imaginable form of Catholic activity. Roger and Rita and their kids were as involved in the all-purpose parish as were my friends in Christ the King. For a few years, I think, the only difference between the two parishes was size. And, critically, housing stock.

St. Angela's days were numbered. The bungalow turned out not to be the ultimate solution. The large post–World War II families needed larger homes. The success of many of the younger parishioners meant they wanted better homes in North Oak Park beyond the boundaries of St. Angela in St. Giles or in River Forest, Westchester, Oak Brook, Elmhurst, Park Ridge, Mount Prospect. Many young couples, who had lived for a while in an apartment building, chose to buy a bigger and newer home in the western suburbs instead of moving back into St. Angela. Rapidly it became a mission parish, maintaining an alternative school, as do so many other urban Catholic parishes, for inner-city minority students.

I do not want to romanticize St. Angela. I trust, in this account of it, I've made clear its limitations; yet, it was a place to grow in wisdom and age and grace before God and men, a ground on which to stand, a place where you knew who you were and where you were going, an ecclesiastical community where, despite the limitations of the clergy, there was probably better understanding between priests and people than there are in many of the post-Conciliar parishes where *a priori* authoritarian liberal pastors preach rotten sermons, ignore teenagers, and are in constant conflict with their parishioners. Bill McCready once remarked with whimsical exaggeration (half fun, in full earnest, as my mother would say) that the Irish were finished with their Church. "They don't expect much from the priests," he observed, "only a decent sermon, a smile in the back of church on Sunday and something like a Hi Club for the kids. If you get any of those things nowadays, the pastor acts like he's doing you a big favor."

97

The decent sermon, the smile in the back of church, and "something for the kids" was taken for granted in Diggy Cunningham's St. Angela. That it is no longer taken for granted is evidence of the deterioration of leadership of American Catholicism. At a meeting of the National Federation of Priest Councils (one of the worst collections of incompetent nitwits to whom it has ever been my displeasure to speak) a delegate took issue with my remarks on the importance of preaching—remarks which were not personal opinion, but merely a report of statistical evidence. "I am parish priest to the world," he said, "not just to my own parish."

How he was going to be a priest to the world when he was not concerned about the sermon to his own parish did not seem to him a matter for concern.

The challenge, it has always seemed to me, is not to "create communities" as the fashionable clerical cliché puts it. Rather it is to recognize their existence, then labor diligently to transform them from the inside into better and more open communities. St. Angela's cannot be born again, save in renewed friendships, but for American Catholicism to grow up, the worth of communities like St. Angela's must be recognized and respected.

And celebrated.

In one of her chapters in our book *How to Save the Catholic Church*, my sister speaks of a parish whose liturgical rhythm of weekly and daily Mass, Stations of the Cross in Lent, benediction on Sunday afternoon, Sorrowful Mother novena on Friday evening, special feasts like Thanksgiving and Christmas, ashes on Ash Wednesday, throat blessing on the Feast of St. Blaise, missions and novenas, First Communions, Confirmations and graduations, was more closely tied to the lives and the religious needs of its people than are many of the *a priori* liturgical practices of the post–Vatican Council era in which poorly trained "liturgists" impose their own historicist schemes on the lay people, without any sensitivity to their religious needs or aspirations.

Neither my sister nor I have ever been angry at the Church (as much as we may be offended by some of the idiots who hold positions of authority in it). We sympathize with those who have suffered from oppression by priests and nuns and continue to suffer from them. We sympathize with those whose religious education consisted mostly of rules and superstitious piety. But their experience is not ours; and we believe our experience more adequately resonates with the Catholic heritage. Moreover we feel that anger at the Church, while often understandable, is finally not a useful emotion.

So St. Angela in my imagination is alive and dead and alive again, the St. Ursula of my stories and the true story of lost and rediscovered friends—or perhaps discovered for the first time. They emerge out of the past to recollect, reflect, renew, make me feel young again. As June Rosner, who tries to keep me out of trouble with the media and has become my Jewish mother (everyone should have a Jewish mother!), tells me, this rebirth of old friendships and rediscovery of old friends is remarkable, almost incredible. Grace, pure and simple.

At supper with some of them I tell a woman whose grammar school persona lurks in my novels that I'm delighted she likes my novels. "I had no idea who you might have become. Perhaps you would not like them."

"We haven't changed. You have."

"You've changed too."

"Not as much as you."

I nod in agreement.

"Why did you change?" she continues.

A fair question from someone who remembers the studious, quiet little boy of the late 1930s and is trying to connect him with the author of novels like *Lord of the Dance*, to put into words what it is like to read a novel by a person you knew long ago.

I tell her about becoming an outcast when Cardinal Meyer died and Cardinal Cody came to Chicago. From one approved I became, without doing a thing, one disapproved. "When you have nothing left to lose, you become reckless."

Although it's a less than adequate answer, she accepts it. You don't push too hard on such delicate questions.

But how *should* I answer? It's a long story: Christ the King, the University of Chicago, the Vatican Council, my work on *The Mary Myth*, the decision to write novels—each one changing me a little bit more.

All tricks, or so it seems to me now, of a Graciousness that was determined to change me for Her own purposes, most ingenious of which was to continue the invitation which I heard obscurely at Twin Lakes and more clearly in Sister Alma Frances's classroom.

It was an invitation which led me to leave behind my friends in St.

Angela and board the Chicago Avenue streetcar for the daily trip to Quigley.

But now, it would seem, I left some of them behind only for a little while.

CHAPTER
4
Quigley

FRONT PORCH

Quiet were the streets, peaceful the summer nights
On tottering chairs youthful experts all
We solved for the world many ancient fights
Precisely which ones I cannot quite recall
With root beer we sipped, unread, Marx and Freud
We nibbled on law and love and God
And potato chips, our Catholic passions buoyed
We charged ahead youthful energy unawed
So easy 'tween two wars our youthful dreams
For those days, coming alive, memory sighs
Gone, driven on the wind, only nightmare screams
Noisy are the crickets under humid skies
The picture fades, I watch time's curtain fall
Who were they? Odd, I cannot quite recall

Quigley seminarians were forbidden to smoke, not only on the school premises and during school hours but also, in direct violation of basic human rights, when they were away from school or at home. Since I didn't smoke, I was not troubled by the rule save in principle: they had no right to control our personal lives. Normally I kept my rebellious thoughts to myself. I would for many more years play the system, until I found that Rome had turned the system over to lunatics.

The smoking rule, however, was rarely enforced. Between classes, the smokers would adjourn to the "blue room" (men's room—and there was, as you may well believe, no women's room) and puff away. Clouds of blueness would filter out into the corridor. The two prefects of discipline—Vince Casey, God be good to him, and Tom Grady, now bishop of Orlando—would wander by the various blue rooms apparently oblivious to the smoke.

Vince would even walk into the room in search of some offender on other grounds and not notice the smoke.

I asked Tom, in those days and for many years thereafter (until I began to write novels) a friend and hero, why the rule was on the books if it was not enforced.

"The question should be phrased the other way."

"Why it is not enforced, if it is on the books?"

"Right."

"Oh."

He didn't answer the question and I was no more enlightened than I had been. Now the answer is obvious: the uptight administration made the rule (doubtless at Cardinal Mundelein's insistence) and the laid-back faculty was not about to enforce it.

Quigley was a remarkably permissive high school for that or any time. The faculty apparently felt that since the school attracted relatively more peaceful and intelligent young men than most, they could be left to themselves as long as the property or the lives of the faculty were not put in serious jeopardy.

Sometimes even then.

As part of the "war effort" we were equipped by the Office of Civilian Defense with hand-pump fire extinguishers—the early-day equivalent in fatuousness to Jimmy Carter's gasoline allocations which created the long lines at the pumps. Just as there was no shortage of gasoline, there was no danger of the Germans or the Japanese dumping incendiary bombs on the roof of Quigley Preparatory Seminary; in both cases the bureaucrats were trying to educate us.

However, the seminarians found good use for the extinguishers, as one might imagine: they put out imaginary fires on one another. After lunch hour on the third floor the walls of the corridor would be dripping water.

"It must be raining," a priest would mutter with a barely suppressed grin as he walked through the drenched hallway.

Our class was deprived of its Greek teacher one day. Two of the more ingenious young men crept into the corridor, possessed themselves of the OCD equipment, swarmed back into the classroom and soaked all of us.

They retreated, amid curses (mild) and threats (deadly), to replenish their weapons. In the meantime an elderly Polish priest who taught classics came to replace our Greek prof. He was known as one who "taught the blackboard," that is, he focused his nose and a piece of chalk on the board and never turned away.

The raiders returned and with nary a glance at the front of the room doused us all a second time. Then they saw the new teacher, did a classic, horrified double take and fled for their lives.

The teacher went right on talking to the board. When the noise abated he added to his mumbled monotone a word of admonition: "Boys, control yourselves, please."

I never have been able to figure out whether he knew what had happened.

On other occasions, however, when faculty themselves happened to turn a corner on the third floor, encounter a band of OCD raiders, and find their cassocks drenched, there was no doubt they knew what was going on.

They laughed.

Only long after VJ day did the OCD equipment vanish from the third floor. RIP. Was I involved in any of the OCD battles? Certainly not! As I've said before, Quixots was a good boy in those days.

We were not supposed to date or even associate with our grammar school friends, a rule I took seriously. Many others did too; some did not. They were found out, often by Quigley faculty who lived at the local rectory. The priests reacted as did Xav Martin in *Ascent into Hell* when he encountered Hugh Donlon with Maria—they simply didn't notice. Not a few of the young women with whom my classmates were found were like Maria: hard not to notice. They still went unnoticed

103

even when they were formally introduced to the "arresting officer."

We experienced at Quigley, I am convinced in retrospect, the famed openness, tolerance and liberalism which had been a historical characteristic of the Chicago clergy for more than half a century and which had survived at Quigley (though not at the major seminary, St. Mary of the Lake at Mundelein) the authoritarianism of Cardinal Mundelein. This spirit would remain alive until it was strangled by Cardinal Cody.

As long as you did your homework and avoided too much trouble, as long as you didn't steal exams (as one cabal did in 1943), the faculty left you alone. Spiritual directors urged us to heights of generosity and commitment most of us did not understand, but no one checked up on us, not even to determine whether we were going to Mass every morning at our parishes.

You didn't have to learn to read and write and think at Quigley, but it was possible to do so. No one objected, and some of the faculty were intelligent enough and interested enough to help you. Quigley was, from the perspective of subsequent events, the better of the two seminaries. It was little more than a commuter high school for young men who were thinking about the priesthood, a reasonably good one presided over by priests, many of whom were good teachers and admirable role models. Thursday was our day off and we went to school on Saturday (a form of protecting us from our contemporaries, particularly contemporary young women).

Much of our education was rote memory. We learned all kinds of things about Greek and Latin, parsing, syntax, vocabulary, but we never did learn, despite five years of classical education, to read Greek or Latin, in retrospect an educational tragedy. Larry McNamara, John Ryan and I nevertheless enjoyed ourselves, riding down to Quigley on the bumpy old Chicago Avenue trolley, sometimes shivering at the street corner in subzero weather, waiting a quarter of an hour for the trolley to appear, and often running from State Street to Quigley when the trolley was tied up in front of Montgomery Ward by a freight train. We went to the movies on Wednesday night and/or Saturday night, played cards with our friends, listened to the 1947 World Series on the radio and passed through relatively trouble-free adolescences. The crisis of maturation was not eliminated by the seminary, only postponed. More of that later.

It was in Quigley that I first discovered the world of ideas. Theodore Maynard's *The Story of American Catholicism,* given to me as a prize at the end of my freshman year, opened up the world of history and of the incredible heritage of American Catholicism. I learned how to write sentences and paragraphs and to appreciate good literature. Newman, Chesterton, Dickens, Scott, Joseph Conrad, Francis Thompson, Gerard Manley Hopkins, Willa Cather, Sinclair Lewis, Thackeray, Wilkie Collins, Churchill, Hawthorne, Melville, Belloc, Dawson: such writers occupied most of my time when I was not at school, or not sleeping, or not playing basketball.

Through the years since then I have learned much about literature, particularly "Catholic" literature, from Bill Henkel whose parents and my parents were friends from Commodore Barry days and who was a close St. Angela friend till he was in sixth grade when his family disappeared to Homewood—a South Side suburb which might just as well have been in Bahia as in Cook County as far as I was concerned. Then he reappeared in my life at Quigley—stopping me in the corridor one day when I was in second year and he in first with the comment, "You didn't think you were going to get rid of me that easily, did you?"

He is my oldest friend—back to infancy—and one on whom I could always count. I've never had a conversation with him which has not been fun.

Bill and I learned a lot about literature in Quigley, accidental learning perhaps, but important nonetheless. The seminary happened to have on its staff a couple of priests, notably Tom Liske and Tom Grady, who had excellent literary taste and managed to communicate it to some of us who had antecedent interests in literature. While by chance I learned much about literature at Quigley, there was nothing in the program to teach me about the rest of culture, save for an occasional talk on art by Father Austin Graff. However, after seeing a film biography of George Gershwin, *Rhapsody in Blue,* I discovered the Grant Park symphony orchestra and spent many summer evenings under the moon with my sister Grace or an occasional unwary classmate becoming acquainted with classical music, a love which led to Orchestra Hall and Opera House and now more recently to season tickets and patronage of both institutions. My classmate John Finnegan and I went to the *Messiah* and *Hamlet* and *La Traviata* (with Tibbett) and to an address by Franklin Roosevelt in Soldier Field shortly before he died.

Slowly it dawned on me that the Church once was the matrix for all the arts. What ever happened? I began to wonder.

I suspect I learned more at Quigley than was intended. That gray building with its chapel, imitating the Sainte Chappelle in Paris on the Ile de la Cité, stands at the foot of the John Hancock Center, where I live some of the time. Occasionally I contemplate what I might have thought when I was a high school seminarian both of the John Hancock Center and of myself inside it.

And as I look down at the dirty gray gothic building, I discover again that of the people who taught there I have mostly fond memories.

During my years there I became interested in politics and social problems. My political orientations were liberal Democrat by inheritance, and there was nothing in my adolescent reflection on the subject to cause me to change my convictions. A reading of the social encyclicals when I was about fourteen persuaded me the social reforms of the New Deal were in harmony with the Catholic social tradition. At the same time the columns of the young George Higgins began to appear in the Catholic press. These articles had a great impact on me, because Higgins's pragmatic liberalism seemed to resonate so much with my own. He helped me to articulate my developing social convictions. George would later become a good friend and start me on my own column-writing career. He did so with the full awareness, I am sure, that I could easily emerge as a rival for the limited space in the Catholic press.

I came to Quigley with a religious faith as unexamined as it was intense. I learned during those years to examine it candidly and objectively without losing either the faith or its intensity. The pilgrimage from Paradise Lost (Twin Lakes) to Paradise Found is a going forth and a coming back, an exploration of new colored lands (Chesterton) and a return to the place from which we began only to know it once more for the first time (Chesterton first, then Eliot).

Paul Ricoeur calls such a pilgrimage the journey from the First Naiveté to the Second, from the uncritical acceptance of a religious symbol through a time of analysis and "unpacking" the symbols to a critical acceptance of and commitment to the symbols. For example, one says the Rosary before the statue of Mary, praying to her as the Mother of God. One analyzes the symbol, looking at both the theology which has grown up around Mary and the correlative symbols of woman in nature and world religions; one discovers that it has been Mary's role in the Catholic tradition to reflect, reveal, "sacramentalize" the womanliness of God, the tender, life-giving, nurturing affection of God, then one returns

106

to the statue to pray to and honor, through the Mother of Jesus, God as mother, Mary as the symbol of the tender God for whom even at Quigley I was searching, Lady Wisdom with whom I was trying to catch up.

(Herself: Faith, isn't it time you've learned that there's no catching up to do?)

Such a journey is essential to religious maturation. Education in the home and the school should be designed to facilitate such a pilgrimage. When I was in school and at Mundelein, however, every effort was made to keep us in the First Naiveté and equip us with answers to all the questions with which a threatening world might challenge that faith. Now, in effect, the opposite is the case. Much of what passes for Catholic education at all levels seems fixated at the "unpacking stage," critical of the symbols but unable to reintegrate them into the personality. Somehow it is thought that such irresolution is the proper posture of a mature man or woman, although in fact it is never mature to refuse to make your peace with the religious symbols of your childhood.

The reason for this fixation, I think, is that many religious educators, priests, nuns, laity, are themselves caught between the two naivetés and proud of that fixation. Having been tricked, as they see it, by the First Naiveté, they are not about to risk the Second. Theology and religious education have, as they see it, a destructive role, not a constructive, reintegrating, and synthesizing one.

Hence they turn to secular relevance for validation of their lives and especially to the "preferential option for the poor," one of the most immature and uneducated phrases to appear in the post-Conciliar faddisms. Surely we must be committed to the poor. But social activism is a *consequence* of religious faith, not a substitute for it. Nor does cant about the "preferential option" help the poor one bit, not without more professional knowledge and skills than most priests or nuns possess. In fact, the most significant contribution to the poor made by the Church in this country is the maintenance of alternative schools in the inner city, but they never are included in the exercise of the so-called "preferential option."

To paraphrase Thomas à Kempis (whom I never liked, mean-spirited, passive-aggressive little anti-intellectual that he was), it is enough to feel an option for the poor without defining it or without doing anything serious about it other than talking. Such is the adolescent behavior of those who are imprisoned between the two naivetés and refuse to budge.

107

(Nor are women included in it when bishops or the Vatican talk about "preferential option." If Church authority should denounce rape, child molestation, forced incest, and wife beating, women might get the idea that they could be priests. Or even altar girls.)

For some men and women the crisis of religious maturation is more painful than for others. I confess I have little sympathy for those whose crisis is marked by self-dramatization and self-pity—and *by no disciplined efforts to go beyond the crisis*—the kind of folk for whom complaints about what they were taught in grammar school by the nuns and nostalgic laments for what they have lost are a pose of religious maturity. Neither angry nostalgia nor angry social activism are by themselves an adequate response to history's richest and most powerful tradition of religious symbols.

My religious maturity pilgrimage started at Quigley as I worked at the integration of the religious symbol system I had absorbed from family and neighborhood (I wouldn't have used that model or those words then, but that was what was happening). "Worked at" is the wrong phrase. It didn't seem like work then and it doesn't seem so now. I read history and politics and economics and fiction and poetry and allowed the images and pictures from my reading to confront and interact with the experiences and images and pictures of my faith. The result was synthesis, not labored or protracted but instantaneous and effortless, already made before I had noticed it.

My porous boundaries seem to mean that I am equipped with a built-in synthesizer, a compiler utility (to use computer language) which eagerly devours new images and blends them with the old so that both become stronger in my memory. The images come first, then reflection on them and propositional articulation.

We all have such a dimension to our personality—call it the "creative imagination," the "agent intellect," the "preconscious," the "poetic faculty." For better or worse my thin boundaries give me easy access to mine.

You will not understand the rest of this story unless you realize that my preconscious (often unconscious) "compiler" is endlessly and restlessly and independently at work examining, rearranging, juxtaposing, integrating, pictures first, then stories and then ideas which are the articulation of the pictures and stories. It enables me to absorb Joseph Conrad's novels, retain the vivid images from his tales, see the latent Polish Catholic

108

influence in them, and revise and refine my own Catholic images and stories in light of his.

A gift, a blessing, a grace? Sure. And also a responsibility to use and share with others.

In my efforts to synthesize and to think responsibly about religion which began at Quigley, G. K. Chesterton was an enormous help, though not for the reasons he was read in those days by most Catholics. GKC was a brilliant controversialist, but his controversies and mine were and are not the same. It was his awe at and admiration for the sacredness and the wonder and the surprise of ordinary life and the sacramentality of the world which fascinated me. His book on St. Francis of Assisi was the first and still in many ways the most powerful explanation of the Catholic imagination to penetrate my own. "Aha," I found myself saying, "*That's* what it's about. Sure, it all figures. When God said the world was good, he really meant it was good.

"How come," I went on, "so many priests and nuns think it is bad?"

Chesterton had the answer: while St. Francis turned the tide against the Manichee temptation, the mopping-up wasn't over. Not by a long shot. Even today, Catholic bluenoses, whether they be the sexual bluenoses of the right or the social activist bluenoses of the left, are still on the Manichee side, still refusing to celebrate the epiphany of Being in beings, of God in creatures.

My religious pilgrimage, then, branched off from that of many of my contemporaries on the unheated Chicago Avenue "red rocket" as it plunged doggedly through the snow and the Polish neighborhoods every morning (except Thursday and Sunday) and even more wearily rumbled back at the end of the day. I was a sacramentalist, I suppose, since Twin Lakes. In my search for Paradise Found Again, I became a self-conscious sacramentalist in the Quigley years, poring over GKC and Newman on the "red rocket," talking over Cokes in the garage parkway with such seminary friends as Larry McNamara and Gene Faucher (a few years older than we and our hero, much to his embarrassment), walking through dark streets of Oak Park and River Forest on thick humid summer nights, arguing on the front porch with neighbors and friends till we all had to go to bed so we could be ready for the next day's dull summer jobs (stock boy at Carson's, clerk at the Pullman company). I knew beyond all question that Creation was a sacrament of God and I knew that such an image was at the core of the Catholic tradition.

109

Even today I am challenged when I express that insight, felt at Twin Lakes, articulated on summer nights in St. Angela. It is not what the priests and nuns, I am told, taught us in school. It is not a contribution to the cause of the poor. It is irrelevant.

Ah, I say, but it *is* Catholic.

I am sorry for the questioners, but I have to say that they ask the question out of ignorance of the Catholic heritage, an ignorance which in most cases is surely not their fault. I have on my side not only Newman and Chesterton and Dante and Belloc and Joseph Conrad and Hopkins (his "May Magnificat" is Chesterton's *St. Francis* in verse) and Michelangelo, but Thomas Aquinas and all the greats of the tradition. My position, I was to find much later when I read David Tracy, is the "classical" Catholic position.

Alas, on both the right and the left today, that and a dollar will get you a ride on Mayor Harold's subway. Neither cares anymore about what is classically Catholic, a terrible judgment on the failure of Catholic religious teaching when they were young. And now.

What about those sacraments par excellence of God's attractive love— women?

I had no adolescent loves. (Well, there was a beauteous redhead at Carson's one summer whom I worshiped from afar, very far, worse luck for me perhaps.) The seventh- and eighth-grade crushes faded in the all-male atmosphere of my Quigley commitment (though those women still flourish in my preconscious and always will, which is what the imagination is for). Other loves and other fallings in love would come later. (No love affairs, though that is hardly the point.) You hardly expect me to talk about them, do you? That would be telling, now wouldn't it?

And anyway if you're all that interested read the poems.

As one student of memoirs remarks, though the author "may equally be celibate or happily married or sexually promiscuous, there is something inherently virginal about his aim. He is retreating from life, temporarily, to find something in himself that the ordinary round of life, both domestic and professional, ignores or pushes to one side."

So, those of you who were expecting "kiss and tell," eat your hearts out!

Blackie Ryan, when asked how many women he happens to be in love with, sighs, "As many as possible."

110

The statement is a truism. We humans are designed to fall in love with, to be smitten by, to take delight in, to be painfully devastated at the sight of, and to enjoy ecstatically members of the opposite sex (as persons, I hasten to add to fend off the polemical feminist reviewer). The upper limit of the number of such persons who can affect us is not a matter of choice but is structured into our personality—which does not mean it becomes necessary to sleep with all or even any of them, as Blackie quickly qualifies his lament.

Women have had a profound influence on my life. Who and how and where and when and why need not, or in any case will not, detain us presently. On another occasion? Ah, that would be telling now, wouldn't it?

The faculty at Quigley was not actively hostile to women, as the faculty at Mundelein would later prove to be. Parish priests most of them, they could hardly pretend that half of the human race was not of the opposite sex. They did not accept the goal of Italian minor seminaries of creating a third sex. Such a congeries of attitudes constitutes Manicheeism, as Bruce Marshal called it, the strange heresy that God made an artistic mistake when He established the mechanics and dynamics of human procreation.

Or the equally strange notion that She made an aesthetic blunder in arranging for the organs by which human neonates are fed.

As Father Jaimie Keenan, priest in one of my short stories, remarks, "If Jesus did not admire the breasts of women, he was singularly ungrateful to his Heavenly Father who designed them to be attractive." It's a long way from St. Bonaventure who describes women as ordure and vomit to Jaimie Keenan, but in this respect the latter is orthodox and the former is not.

Whatever faults Quigley may have had, it was not, unlike Mundelein and most other seminaries of the time, prone to either heresy.

We used to sing at our basketball games, "Quigley will shine tonight!" It still shines in my memory.

I trust it is clear I don't regret the celibate commitment I made to the priesthood when I went to Quigley. I won't pretend I am indifferent to the loss of intimacy that commitment required. But Jesus promised those who followed Him a hundredfold. My life, despite its ups and downs, has been more happy than not by a considerable margin (this book has perhaps more of the downs than of the ups because that is the nature of storytelling). I do not want to trade places. I don't want to go back to the "red rocket" and change my mind.

By the time I graduated from Quigley in June of 1947 I had a clear if not yet detailed picture of my commitment, and I was well into critical analysis of the religious symbols of my childhood and beginning the Second Naiveté. I had a solid grasp of what the Catholic heritage was about.

And I was bound for a seminary, St. Mary of the Lake at Mundelein, where I would live for seven years in an intellectual and spiritual environment where the finest components of the Catholic tradition were not only considered worthless, but often actively condemned.

CHAPTER
5
Mundelein

THE FIFTH OF MAY—1954

The expected day was bitter cold
Warning us perhaps
Of what we'd have to face
But no hint of John
Or the unchanging changed
And the rock which came apart
Would that our hearts were warm
Ready for the frantic fray
Light and quick, dancing in youthful glee
But they gave us not the slightest hint
Unprepared, we were standing docile there
When the roof came tumbling in
A few escaped never to return.
Others ran for safe and quiet holes
Still others stood mute, the end accepting
Some, sensing fun, said let's begin to dance—
A blind leap long ago in the deeper dark
Do it again? I've already told you so

St. Mary of the Lake Seminary at Mundelein, Illinois, was only about forty-five minutes from Twin Lakes. Its red brick buildings, carefully barbered lawns, neatly arranged flower beds and blue lake at first made it seem deceptively like Paradise Found.

It was, however, a caricature of paradise, a sick institution, presided over by sick men and training priests many of whom would fit badly into the post–World War II society and even worse into the post–Vatican II world. Later they would leave the priesthood in droves.

Looking back, it is small wonder.

On a cold January night in 1950 the spiritual director came to the wind-rattled chapel of the Philosophy House to deliver his final fervent warning before we went home for vacation. We stayed at the seminary at Christmas because Cardinal Mundelein, who'd been dead for more than ten years now, didn't see why the young men in his seminary would want to go home at Christmas because the seminary was such a beautiful and splendid place. The ancient and intense Jesuit spiritual director, a somber, bald, wizened little gnome, harangued us about the need to avoid the "ballot," or so it seemed. Most of us sitting in the House Chapel had not the foggiest idea what he was talking about but we had learned to tune him out anyway. Finally I caught on and scratched on a piece of paper to Frank Gill who was sitting next to me, "ballet!"

Frank and I both doubled up laughing. We were being warned about the dangers of the ballet as though of the two hundred of us there might be more than one or two who even knew there *was* a ballet, much less how one sought out such immoral entertainment during a January vacation. Most of us didn't even know there was an Orchestra Hall or an Opera House or any of those other unfamiliar cultural buildings. The spiritual director's problem was a film called *The Red Danube* which we had seen a couple of weeks before and in which a then very young Janet Leigh played a ballerina and skipped about in moderately revealing ballerina costumes (much less revealing than what Ms. Leigh's daughter, Jamie Lee Curtis, frequently wears in contemporary films). Doubtless some of our number had run to the spiritual director to report that Ms. Leigh's costume had occasioned "dirty" thoughts. Suspicious of our animal energies and desires, the spiritual director was acting against imaginary conspiracies to ogle other women's bodies at ballet performances during the vacation.

I've often wondered how many clerical balletomanes were born that

114

night in the chapel, on the assumption that if "Skippy" thought we shouldn't go to the ballet, then that provided excellent reason for going.

As the rector of St. John's Seminary in Camarillo, California, used to say (many years after 1950), remember that every woman is a walking womb waiting to be fecundated!

Right.

My as yet inarticulate theory of sacramentality (as old as Catholicism, if not taught much at Mundelein) had not developed far enough at that time to enable me to refute intellectually the seminary's anti-woman animus (or to diagnose the latent homosexuality of the seminary's pervasive and perennial cronyism and favoritism). I did know, however, that they were wrong, dead wrong, about women. To suggest that the physical attractiveness of Ms. Leigh was evil or dangerous or anything else but admirable seemed to me utterly absurd.

God, not the devil, made women beautiful, appealing, attractive. Somehow the church then and now has not quite been able to cope with that unassailable doctrine.

God made them equal too, another doctrine which we have yet to assimilate.

At Mundelein, a sprawling, jerry-built, red-brick-and-white-window-framed Georgian museum piece, a shabby (by 1950) Disney World imitation of a great university, we were taught to fear and hate women, to think for ourselves as little as possible, and to cultivate mediocrity and envy.

Splendid preparation for a vocation which in the space of four years would put us in a world slightly more than half of which is made up of women and a substantial number of which women are not unattractive, even if they're wearing a good deal more than a tutu!

One of the more pleasant things about growing older is that the number of attractive women in the world seems to increase. I told Michele Brennan that when she informed me in Noele Farrell terms that I was *really* old.

She thought about it, nodded agreement and then, fitness buff and Irish late teen that she is, drew the moral. "So long as they take care of themselves, anyway."

The ballet story was hilarious on the occasion. Only in retrospect does it seem tragic. There are some happy memories too: red brick, greenery, blue lake and sky; writing letters and darning socks in scripture class, two precious hours of visiting on six Sundays a year. Parents were only tolerated, the implication being that we were permitted to see them only because we and they were weak. If we were real Christians we would cut ourselves off from our families. Making cocoa in the room between classes, walking around the lake during snowstorms and in the midst of budding spring greenery. John Courtney Murray telling us the World Series score in the middle of a retreat; *Time* magazine smuggled up and down the corridors, incessant sermons about obedience, the fierce clang of the bell at five twenty-five in the morning. And finally, ordination day, the coldest May 5 in history. (Ed Roche: "Did anyone say it would be a cold day in hell when you guys would be ordained?")

The trouble was no one knew what lay ahead. The seminary was rigid and timeless. It did not change; it did not have to because the Church would not change. The rules were strict; life was regimented. There was a time for everything and everything had its time and place. You memorized answers and turned in essays, listened to the lectures in Latin, were granted two weeks at home in the middle of the year plus the summertime, and did not have to make many decisions (once you made the one to be a priest), and the seminary life had to be endured— seemingly forever—as a necessary precondition.

It might have worked reasonably well were it not for the Vatican Council. For many priests who went through that system the answers they had memorized were no longer adequate, the rules they had kept no longer meant anything, the conformity imposed on them was collapsing all around. The external structures of the Church as an organization and the intellectual structures of apologetic Catholicism collapsed almost overnight, and we had the choice of either growing up or getting out. A lot got out. A few lucky ones like me were prepared and found the transition relatively easy and even enjoyable, but we were, I fear, the minority.

The ballet story illustrates one of the four ultimately inadequate guiding principles of our twelve years of seminary training—warn the seminarians about women and do everything in your power to keep them away from women. So intense was this paranoia that the prefect of discipline, a man with doubts of his own about the system, remarked ruefully that after a while you imagined you heard the click of high heels on the seminary's concrete sidewalks. The second purpose was to train us in obedience, which was hailed as not only the prince of virtues but the only one that mattered in a parish priest. The third, and much less important, goal was to teach us some of the theology and philosophy we would need in parish work—not enough to make us think seriously about such matters, but enough so that we would appear to know a little more than what was included in the catechism. Teach it to us in Latin, because that was the language of the Church wasn't it? Fourth, the seminary tried to develop in us, as a means of social control, a passive acceptance of mediocrity and the ability to use envy as a sanction against any among us who tried to be anything else but mediocre.

Heaven knows there was little if any effort expended on teaching us how to preach. You memorized theology texts so you could establish that you knew enough theology to walk up to the pulpit after reading the Gospel on Sunday morning, but it was never required of us to prove we could translate the theology we had memorized into language accessible to the laity.

Some sermons might just as well be preached in Latin.

For the laity, you see, were unimportant. The person that counted in our lives was to be our pastor. Few of us would ever be pastors (or so it seemed then—the class of 1949's motto was *numquam pastores*, never pastors). Therefore, since we were to be curates or assistant pastors for most if not all of our lives, we had to be trained not to communicate with the laity—a minor consideration—but to please our pastors. Hence obedience, absolute unquestioning obedience, to the pastor and the higher ecclesiastical authorities was the primary virtue. Charity and zeal, which had originally brought me to the seminary, were never mentioned. The object was to produce not competent priests, not zealous priests, not sensitive, charitable, sympathetic priests, but obedient and chaste priests.

The seminary system was a form of behavior modification, a total institution—relatively little concerned with our interior motivations, aspirations, hopes or fears—that demanded external conformity and watched us carefully to make sure we showed no signs of dangerous departures from that conformity. It kept us away from women as much as it could: only two weeks of vacation in January, assignments to work in orphanages or other such places in the summertime and then, the last three summers, sending us off to a "villa" in northern Wisconsin. The Mundelein authorities, some of them good and admirable men, argued that the system was what Cardinal Mundelein (the seminary's

117

founder) had wanted and it seemed in perfect keeping with the wishes of the Council of Trent.

In case you have forgotten, the Council of Trent was convened four hundred years ago.

Patently, it did not work: our wills and our hormones continued to function. Perhaps the training would have produced young men who would have stayed in the priesthood and did what they were told in the immigrant/Counter-Reformation Church. But among our predecessors in many cases, this desirable result was achieved at the price of turning a fair number of them into alcoholics, loafers or eccentrics. It was, however, no preparation for the exploding Church of Pope John XXIII and the Vatican Council. Once the rigid social controls of diocesan and rectory life were lifted, many of us revealed we had no idea of what a priest was, or what the content of the Catholic heritage was, and many of us left the priesthood to marry after all.

In a way, however, the "Behavior-Mod" seminary did work. It kept us emotional adolescents, who had never made a decision on our own and would not, and eventually could not, make decisions of our own in the parishes—until we became pastors and then were forced to make every-body's decisions for them.

Ecclesiastical authorities were pleased that our education was fourth-rate. We were, it was argued, even in the fifties, better educated than most of the people we would meet in our parish work (a monumental misreading of the signs of the times). Our allegedly high-quality education would protect us from the temptation of pride (almost as bad as "sen-suality"). Musical talent was to be cultivated because the seminary needed musicians to perform the sacred rituals properly and a cathedral often needed a musician to be responsible for its choir. So some musicians were selected for special treatment, though not necessarily the most tal-ented, probably because talented musicians might want to do something more ambitious than direct a choir. A few, because of administrative meticulousness or physical appearance, were chosen for canon law, Chan-cery Office work, and possible promotion to the hierarchy. Every other talent was to be ignored or suppressed because, as it was said not altogether facetiously, all a parish priest needed to be able to do was to say the Rosary and to call the Chancery for instruction. As far as I can determine, in the twenty years before my doctorate not a single priest of the Arch-diocese was assigned to Ph.D. graduate school work.

Andrew M. Greeley

Young people reading my novels like *The Cardinal Sins, Thy Brother's Wife* and *Ascent into Hell* often ask me if a seminary is really as bad as I describe it. The appropriate answer is "No, not anymore. That's what it used to be. Only worse." Whether the new seminary, which tends to be more like a psychiatric institution than the penal institution of old, is any more successful in producing mature, well-trained priests is an open question. At least, however, the new seminary is not committed to the notion that neither the world nor the Church ever changes.

A psychiatrist who often works with priests told me once that she knew a priest was beginning to mature when he stopped blaming the seminary for his problems and probed back into the conflicts of his family life. It is foolish and immature to fixate on the seminary of thirty years ago. It is dead, as are most of the men who presided over it. No useful purpose is served by being angry at history. However, those laity who have a hard time understanding priests, let us say, over forty-five ought to realize how ill equipped intellectually, emotionally, morally and spiritually we were for the post–Vatican Council Church, and how many of us were pressured by our families and by seminary authorities to make celibate commitments the nature of which we did not fully understand, and how many of us were trained in the fear and loathing of women.

In Umberto Eco's *The Name of the Rose* there are repeated references to women as swamps and traps designed to swallow up the souls of men. John Broomyard, an English Dominican of the same era, lifting a metaphor from scriptures, warned that women were a graveyard, well kept on the outside and filled inside with death and corruption, attitudes not all that different from that of the spiritual director who warned us of the dangers lurking in the splendid form of Janet Leigh. Women were portrayed as a threat to the virtue of celibates and the manliness of married men. They were, as one medieval saint put it, "vomit and ordure. . . . How then can we ever want to embrace what is merely a sack of rottenness." St. Jerome said woman was the door of the devil. St. Maximus said she was the shipwreck of man. St. Athanasius thought she was the clothed serpent.

And you wonder why the Church is hung up on sex!

How was this hatred for women reconciled with devotion to Mary the Mother of Jesus? And did Lady Wisdom even exist for such people?

The answer was that Mary (and Lady Wisdom to the extent that She was recognized at all) were utterly desexualized. The mother of Jesus was admirable not because she shared a common womanhood with all her sisters, but because she was radically different from them.

Again, how odd of God to create creatures so evil that the best of them is good precisely because she is denied those biological characteristics which constitute women as distinct from men.

The "distinguished" Jesuit faculty that was supposed to be teaching us was not distinguished. Despite their incredibly low course load (sometimes only one course a semester), virtually none of them published anything. A few, notably Thomas Motherway, Edward Brueggeman and Edward Reynolds, were gifted, hardworking men who had some respect for and appreciation of scholarship. The rest were misfits in the Jesuit order who were palmed off on us because the Jesuits never liked the Roman mandate which forced them to teach at Cardinal Mundelein's seminary and because, understandably enough, they saved their best men for their own institution. With some wonderful exceptions (like Ed Reynolds, who taught us about Shakespeare) the Jesuit faculty insisted we memorize our Latin texts and do precious little else. Of course, we could not read the philosophers and theologians who were our adversaries.

Read Kant or Hegel or Freud or Marx or Comte or even William James or John Dewey? Certainly not; they are on the Index, are they not, at least implicitly? Anyway, they don't matter because they're wrong.

As Jack Shea has remarked to me, at Quigley you sensed you were probably getting a better education than the guys at Fenwick and St. Ignatius (I'm not sure about that anymore). At Mundelein you knew your education was inferior to what your siblings and contemporaries were receiving at Catholic colleges and universities. If you were a naif like me and asked for lists of books for further reading, you were suspect. You were perhaps trying to curry favor. Maybe you were even, God save us, *ambitious.*

I don't know how we were expected to pass the time during the five hours each day we were confined to our rooms and charged to study. As one Jesuit told us, we should review our notes from previous years, reread our textbooks (which many of us could not understand because the Latin was so obscure) and study for our exams.

And after that?

Well, don't dwell on dirty thoughts or imagine you hear the seductive

120

click of heels on the sidewalks. Or make plans to go to the ballet. Or fantasize about Janet Leigh's breasts.

I realized even then that the emphasis on obedience in preference to zeal was a perversion, and sensed that the isolation from women simply would not work. Nonetheless, I kept my own counsel, honored all the rules (I was a great rule-keeper until well after my thirtieth birthday), and gave the proper responses to the prefects of discipline and the spiritual director and the rector when they asked me about my fitness for the priesthood. God knows those poor men, if they had the faintest idea of what I was to become, a fiction-writing, bishop-criticizing square peg, would never have let me be ordained. I couldn't foretell that future either, though I did know the seminary regime was foolishness incarnate and some of the men who administered it were fools.

However, as the reader of this memoir has probably decided by now, I am, to put the best possible face on it, single-minded (the reader may want to say driven or even monomaniacal). I wanted to be a priest. If you had to endure Mundelein's folly to be a priest, so be it. I would endure and make use of the five isolated hours a day to do all the reading I possibly could. I could read French, and even in the late forties and the early fifties I was fascinated by the great French postwar theologians, Jean Danielou, Henri de Lubac, and Yves Congar, who would later become a friend and colleague on the staff of the international Catholic journal *Concilium*.

The Second Vatican Council was shaped by the European theological faculties and their experiences during and immediately after World War II. Mostly by luck, I was prepared for those changes, because I had read all the available works of those European scholars. I was unprepared for the speed and the depth of the change, but I still count it as one of the fortunate breaks of my life that I *knew* the theology before it transformed the Church. (The second lucky break was the opportunity to test and mature my faith in the crucible of the University of Chicago, a couple of years before the winds of Pope John's open window swept through the Church.)

What about women during the seminary years? What can I tell you? Not much. Not because of reticence, but because there isn't much to tell.

As I remarked earlier, I learned a lot about the sensitivity and tenderness appropriate in man/woman relationships from my mother. There was not much chance to practice those skills either at the seminary or during my years at Christ the King (save with teenage young women). Since then, I am reasonably confident my sensitivity to and sympathy for women is comparable with that of married men, probably better than that of most married men. I wasn't permanently harmed by those twelve years of relative isolation. I didn't like it, to tell you the truth, but it was part of the game and I was prepared to play it.

Social research that I did much later would demonstrate that a confidant relationship between a woman and a sensitive, sympathetic parish priest enhances both the woman's and her husband's marital fulfillment. It also leads to sympathies among people in such confidant relationships, both toward the ordination of women and the continuation of celibacy— as though both husband and wife realize the payoff in the confidant relationship depends on the priest's celibacy. Additionally, it implies that men could profit equally from such confidant relationships with women priests.

The isolation from women did me no great harm, but I felt cheated then and still do. There was virtually no opportunity to mature and grow up with women of my own generation.

What, then, about celibacy? If I had it to do over again, would I become a celibate priest? Or if I was a young man with the option between celibate and married priesthood, would I choose celibate priesthood?

These are tricky questions. Obviously I didn't leave the priesthood when it was possible to do so and marry. I know now far better reasons for celibacy than were ever given us in the seminary. The priest is a specially trusted confidant. The priest is a sign of mystery and fascination, pointing to a world beyond himself (hence people's fascination with my novels about priests); the priest is perhaps the most fascinating man in the world, potentially at any rate. He has more freedom for more total commitment. Spare me any comparisons between celibate Catholic priests and married Orthodox priests or Protestant ministers or priests.

A zealous married man will accomplish a lot more than a lazy celibate, but just as obviously a zealous celibate has more time for more extensive and more intensive relationships than does a married clergyman with proper commitments to his wife and children. Finally, as Kevin Brennan says in *The Cardinal Sins*, it is a good thing to have some men in the

122

world live in a way that demonstrates that you can love women without having to jump into bed with them. There are risks a celibate can take—and even things he can say about marriage—that no married man would dare say, if only because having said it he would have to live up to it in his own marriage.

So, unlike many of my colleagues, I think celibacy is one of the treasures of the Western Church and I would hate to see it lost. Optional celibacy, at the present at any rate, would mean what it does to most of our separated brothers: compulsory marriage. The strength and the independence and the vigor of the celibate Catholic priesthood (when it is lived to the fullest and does not become an excuse for irresponsibility, insensitivity and laziness) is a strength and a glory of the Western Church, a strength and glory for which, unfortunately, the Western Church does not bother to make many theological or psychological arguments because for the last thousand years it has blindly enforced celibacy as a rule.

My own solution to the celibacy problem is a limited-term priesthood, a "Priest Corps," not unlike the Peace Corps. In the not too distant past, to be a priest forever meant to be a priest for ten years, because, on the average, priests died at about thirty-five (in nineteenth-century Chicago, from cholera epidemics). Can we not create an environment in which, after someone has fulfilled a commitment of five or ten years to the priestly ministry, he may go forth with dignity and honor and gratitude—still a priest but not in the active ministry save in times of emergency? Would not such a man be a special kind of husband and father in the world because of his years of service in the priesthood?

Given the fact that young men now become priests with far more awareness of the possibility of withdrawing from the ministry than we did, it would seem to me such a strategy would merely make a virtue of necessity, and would give us far more priests than we presently have.

Moreover, the demands made on a parish priest these days are so intense that many of us burn out by the time we're forty. There is no point in constraining someone to stay in the priesthood when he has given his best for a long time and really has little left to offer. If you're able to work with teenagers after forty, for example, it is a special grace of personality and biology, not something that can be routinely expected. It is a hideous mistake to keep men in the priesthood who are not happy with the work. They do enormous harm to the unfortunate lay people of God on whom they take out their frustrations and unhappiness. My limited-term "volunteer" priesthood would seem both to protect celibacy and to give those priests who want to marry an option of doing so with dignity and honor when their term of service is finished.

Our sociological research shows it would also solve the vocation shortage overnight.

Do I regret that I have never been married? Do I miss having children and grandchildren? Is there something absent in my life because there has never been a relationship of long-term sexual passion with a woman?

The answer to all those questions is yes. I'm well aware that priests tend to romanticize family and sex, and then to be disappointed after they marry at the burdens of family life and the erratic rhythms of sexual passion and fulfillment. Nonetheless it would have been wonderful to have a family. Still, I would do it all again, and feel now and have felt all through my priesthood more than compensated for those lacunae in my life which are the result of my commitment to service of God and Church.

Recently a woman who knows a lot about poetry told me that one of the sonnets I wrote in the middle seventies seemed to her to explain what it was like to be a celibate, a person who sublimates but does not repress (any more than we all repress). She even saw a phallic image in the third line, of which I am sure I was not aware when I wrote the poem:

Go away, ministering spirit, brown-eyed
Lithe-bodied sex object, shapely font of life
In the soggy thickness of our rugged ride
A quenching hint of mother, lover, wife.
Be not womanly, turn indifferent, hard
A plastic courtesy of the Friendly Skies
It is sexist to thirsty gulp your charm
And bask in the clear tropic light of your eyes.
You tempt us with your smile, our spirits grown
To violate the harsh fashion of unisex
Chauvinist we are coded in our bones
Hope and loving peace at a woman's breast.
In the cold, a girl's tenderness the sun.
Since we left the caves, a woman's warmth is home

Have I known women to whom I could have been happily married? You bet. I'm not sure how happy they would have been married to *me*. I've served them better as their priest than I would have as their husband.

As one of my sisters remarked when I had done something she found inept, "God was awfully good to some poor woman when He gave you a vocation."

"I'd be a priest again," one of my friends remarked recently, "but I wouldn't want to do it alone."

I don't think I've ever been alone in the priesthood. (To tell the truth, I might even have wished for more solitude rather than less.) But to view marriage as a companionship, it seems to me, is to trivialize it. In fact, marriage is designed to be a passionate friendship, a volatile if pleasurable claim on our ultimate resources and, therefore, an environment in which children can be reared.

If it's companionship you want, find a nice affectionate Irish wolf-hound.

Such observations are not to demean marriage but rather to argue that it is demeaned by those clerics who think that marriage will cure their inner pains. In fact, even if a marriage works reasonably well (and given the process of spouse selection in our society, that modest achievement requires considerable luck), it doesn't cure anything. Nor is it designed to slake the thirst for "self-fulfillment."

If celibacy was an option for Western Rite priests, as it is for priests in many of the Eastern Rite Churches, would I have exercised the option for marriage when I was a young man and did not understand, as well as I do now, the assets of celibacy and the payoffs in it? That is a tough question. If we could have married in our twenties, most of my contemporaries in the seminary would have done so. The reason would be that celibacy was presented to us as a rule and little else. If the rule was abandoned, why keep it?—save, perhaps, that we had been so rigidly indoctrinated in aversion to women. If the reasons for celibacy that I know today had been available to me in my twenties and I had had a choice I probably would still have chosen the celibate commitment.

Friendship was a rare commodity at Mundelein. We were supposed to be close to our classmates and went through the superficial motions. We were surely companions in adversity and we shared a common "enemy"—the authorities. Suspicion and rivalry, however, kept the level of mutual trust low. We rarely talked about ideas, so there was almost no intellectual sharing, and we rarely communicated about serious problems, so there was almost no personal sharing.

125

Class spirit was an illusion, one we tried to maintain for a few years after ordination and then gave up. I suppose that the seminary was like St. Angela's: there were many more who wanted to be friends. None of us knew how. We were young men, and young men do not know what to do with their emotions. Moreover the seminary wanted us to be suspicious of one another, lest too much trust provide the matrix for sedition.

I was often the object of such search for secret information by the authorities. They picked the wrong man. My father's son, I was far too honest to lie; and my mother's son, far too devious to tell them what they wanted to hear. I would not play God against my classmates.

Once they sought information on Jim Sweeney, who became our class's solitary saint. If I had told them what they wanted to know, Jim would never have been ordained. I evaded their probing with considerable skill and promptly told Jim what they were trying to find out about him.

While Jim and I were as unlike as two Chicago Irishmen could possibly be and while I suspect he never could figure me out, we had always liked one another, and that incident cemented our trust. After our ordination we always exchanged impish grins whenever we met.

We had beat the bastards.

I regret that time and our different work interfered with the development of that friendship. I think I was the first person he told that he had an incurable disease. Perhaps both of us wanted to be close friends and didn't know how.

Of all the class, only a few—John Krump, the Catholic chaplain at Northwestern, George Helfrich, and perhaps a few others—stand by me now. Yet a couple of true friends from the twelve years in the seminary are more than many can claim.

The night before complex open heart surgery, John called to ask me to administer the Sacrament of the Sick (I think that's what we call it now). "I don't have any oils," I confessed.

"Get them," he said.

So, after the Dave Baum show on WIND, at nine-thirty of a raw March night, I was driven in the block-long maroon limo which my publisher furnishes when I'm on promotion tours to the Olson Pavilion of Northwestern Hospitals, to anoint my closest friend from the old days. John, his sense of humor unaffected by the proximity of death, was upset

126

that the limo and its attractive blond woman driver had not been parked outside of his room. He recovered, thank God.

The best phrase I can use to describe the seminary's ambience is juvenile peevishness. Christmas seemed especially likely to bring that characteristic to the surface. Some of us, furious at the authorities for their policy of isolating us from our families at that holy time of the year, would arrange for the families to participate at Midnight Mass in the rear of the New England Congregational-style church which was our main chapel. Then we would duck around in back to exchange brief greetings. (My mother and sisters came occasionally, but stern keeper of the rules I was in those days, I went nowhere near them.) The powers that ruled us seemed to be aware of this violation and to wink at it. Then one year, without warning, they stopped winking and caught a crowd of seminarians *in flagrante delicto*—wishing their parents and siblings Merry Christmas, for which God forgive them.

Not only were they punished but the rest of the seminary was too— holidays, recreation periods, movies all canceled. The authorities, you see, believed in collective guilt and collective punishment.

When the authorities were offended they sulked like little children. In our deacon year, some of us were found committing the unspeakable crime of sneaking *Time* into the Sacred Orders building. The rector, whose intelligence never did permit him to get beyond the simple dichotomy of "good class"/"bad class," decided we were a bad class. He sulked for months. And we sulked back.

My feeling then and now was that it was all childish, both the Christmas rule and the ways of eluding it, both the isolation from the world in which we were going to work and the smuggling tactics that enabled us to find out about the Korean War and Senator McCarthy and the first Eisenhower/Stevenson race and the Chicago Bear scores—both the sulking and the counter-sulking.

What I didn't understand then was that the immaturity such an atmosphere of childish peevishness reinforced was precisely what the Church leadership wanted in its young priests.

No one warned them that a tidal wave was stirring.

I am a much harsher critic of the seminary now than I was then. The great clammy dead hand of the old seminary continues to blight the life of the Church. I was not unhappy at Mundelein because

I found it easy to make my peace with the system and exploit it.

What had begun at Quigley continued at the seminary, now almost entirely on my own. There I escaped the dullness and monotony of the philosophy and theology classes by reading social and labor history and economics. Not only did I discover the postwar theological ferment in Europe as I plowed through Congar, de Lubac, the younger Danielou, I then turned back to their predecessors Pierre Rousselot, Ambrose Gardeil, Maurice Blondel and, curiously enough, John Henry Newman, who may yet be recognized as the most important theological influence on the Second Vatican Council. There were five illuminations I experienced in reading these writers which would stand me in good stead in the years ahead as I continued my quest for the Grail, my pilgrimage from Paradise Lost to Paradise Found, my pursuit of the Hound of Heaven who was, like Brigid in *The Magic Cup* pursuing Cormac, chasing after me.

1. *History matters*. The most significant of the insights. The Church was shaped differently in the past than it is today. The essence of Catholicism ought not to be identified with the Counter-Reformation, late-nineteenth- and early-twentieth-century forms in which we find it. Later I would realize that the basic division in the post-Vatican church is between those who take history seriously and those who do not. History tells us of a far more pluralistic Church than do the catechisms or theology manuals. St. Gregory and St. Augustine of Canterbury, for example, exchanged correspondence on the dozen or so justifications for remarriage after divorce (none of which would be accepted as such today). In the nineteenth century, the Vatican resolutely refused to speak out explicitly on contraception, even though France was solving its population explosion by *coitus interruptus*. "Do not disturb the Faithful," the Holy Office warned, a position which was repeated in his conferences for confessors by St. John Vianney, the Curé d'Ars. Leo XIII wrote an encyclical at that time in which there was no mention of birth control. Many medieval theologians did not think fornication was a terribly serious sin. In the Diocese of Constance in the 1400s, priests were permitted to have concubines so long as they paid a tax—a fee for each wife and each child. The revenue from the tax constituted one third of the income of the diocese (an interesting idea but one which I suspect would have its drawbacks in this feminist age!).

I don't intend we should return to older policies, I merely cite them as evidence that the posture of a Church which never changes is unten-able.

I mentioned the Leo XIII encyclical to Jean Jadot when he was apostolic delegate to the United States. The archbishop's eyes twinkled. "Ah, you know about that, do you?"

I sure did, not that knowing about it made any difference in 1968 when *Humanae Vitae* was issued.

2. *Reality is dynamic and changing, not static and timeless as the watered-down Aristotelianism we were learning seemed to suggest.* You must change to remain the same. The Church remains the same not by immobility but by sensitivity to change.

3. *Faith is not merely an act of intellect but rather an act of love by which the whole personality commits itself to an already inviting Lover.*

4. *The Reformation is over; it is time to abandon the garrison posture of the Counter-Reformation Church and begin ecumenical dialogue with Protestants—and with all men and women of goodwill and good faith.*

5. *To adjust to these truths, the Church must be reformed.* Congar's *True and False Reform in the Church* described a breathtaking agenda for such reform. The book was suppressed (I read only excerpts in the Catholic magazine *Cross Currents*) and the author was sent into exile. Later we would realize it was little more than an agenda for Vatican II.

I was not threatened by any of these insights; they slipped into my personality and facilitated my journey from what I would later learn was the First Naiveté to the Second.

We were cut off completely from the world whose salvation was to be entrusted to us in a few years. No newspapers, no radios, and heaven help us no television. We found out about the world—ugly, evil place it was—from faculty comments and from reading the Jesuit magazine *America*. Sitting on a cushionless chair in my silent and unadorned room, not totally immune to the imagined sound of clicking high heels, I devoured its pages as soon as it came every week.

I learned about Catholic social theory and about Catholic literature. Spurred on by what I had read in *America*, during the summer months I devoured Greene and Waugh and Marshall and Mauriac and Bernanos and Undset and Bloy and Claudel. The arguments about "the Catholic

129

novel" which raged in its pages seemed to settle the questions about the novel as an art form and the novelist's freedom from the need to edify and preach. It seemed the Catholic novelist, about whom there were even then courses at many Catholic colleges, despite an occasional bishop's prohibition, could write about sex, even vividly, as part of his story about the meaning of life in the Catholic perspective. He did not have to experience sin to write about it, because, obviously it was said, fiction is a work of imagination, not experience. Nor was it appropriate to demand that the Catholic novelist write with fear that a young adolescent might be shocked by his book; fiction was for the mature adult reader, not the junior high school student (of whom many today are more sophisticated than the mature adults of the 1940s, but that's another matter). Greene was finally supported against his prudish critics.

At that time I was persuaded of both the concept of the Catholic novel and of its importance as a means of religious communication. Greene's *The Power and the Glory* was, despite an informal condemnation from Rome, the finest book ever written on the priesthood.

It was an idea, even without me as a storyteller, that I would not have mentioned to my seminary classmates. Had not fiction been dismissed as a waste of time by the authorities? Did not the rector condemn a lecture on Graham Greene presented at our pathetic "Bellarmine" literary society with quotes from St. Paul about "immorality"? Were not novels banned? Were we not discouraged from reading them on vacation? Did not we know that the ordinary "cap and sweater" Catholic lay person had little time or interest in fiction?

Our class arrived at the seminary at the height of its anti-intellectualism. Three years before, Monsignor Reynold Hillenbrand, the autocratic but theologically and politically liberal and intellectually sophisticated rector, had been replaced, at the instigation of the Jesuit faculty or the influential pastors of the city, depending on whose story you believed, because the young priests he had trained were too liberal or not obedient enough or, again depending on whose story you believed, because he had not been politic enough in dealing with the pastors.

Just before our arrival the young diocesan priest/professors were also purged, to be replaced by some of the worst dullards in the Chicago province of the Jesuits. The diocesan faculty was committed to various "movements": the Catholic Action groups inspired by the Belgian Canon (later Cardinal) Cardijn—Christian Family Movement, Young Christian

130

Students, Young Christian Workers, Cana Conference; the Liturgical Movement, which advocated more lay participation in the liturgy; the social action movement, which supported more justice, particularly for blacks; and new catechetical movements which argued for changes in the way the Faith was taught. Today all these efforts look pretty tame— merely a continuation of the Church's traditional social concerns and a recognition that there was a new kind of lay person abroad in the parishes. But in the late 1940s and the early 1950s they were considered ridiculous and perhaps dangerous.

At the same time I was thinking about the relationship between art, especially fiction, and religion and reading the theologians, I was encountering another sign of the time. Through the intervention of a friend and former fellow seminarian, John Crean, I made contact during the summer vacations with the extraordinary Catholic groups that flourished in the University of Chicago environment between the Second World War and the Korean War. They were veterans mostly, making it into the big-time academy on the strength of the GI Bill. Self-conscious intellectually because of their university experience and self-conscious religiously because of the YCS ferment on the Catholic undergraduate campuses of that time, these young men (and some young women) represented perhaps the most exciting Catholic presence the University of Chicago was ever to know.

Talking to them made it clear to me that the European theology was by no means irrelevant to the American situation. I remember standing on an L platform one night going home from Hyde Park and suddenly becoming aware that this was the first generation of Catholic intellectuals the United States had ever seen. There had been intellectuals before, but never in such large numbers and never as committed to the Church as these people were. I remember saying to myself that the Church would never be the same again.

In 1950, Pius XII, scenting the winds of change in the Church, did his best to anticipate the storm with the reactionary encyclical *Humanae Generis*. De Lubac and Danielou were silenced, Congar sent into exile in Africa, Teilhard died in an apartment hotel in New York City. The negativism of the encyclical and the harshness of Rome's treatment of some of its best thinkers at first seemed effective. Danielou went over to the other side, became a cardinal, argued later that the College of Cardinals was of divine institution, and died, poor man, in a Paris whore-

131

house. De Lubac ate humble pie and was also later rewarded with the red hat, though he never really did change his teaching. The winds seemed to die down.

In 1950, I was surprised and delighted to observe among the younger Catholic scholars around the University of Chicago that while *Humanae Generis* offended and infuriated them (because as they said quite properly it did not understand what they were about), it neither drove them from the Church nor turned them from their convictions and their research. The encyclical had failed and become counterproductive precisely because it did not listen, it did not understand.

I would discover later that the Church would be changed in the postwar years not merely by its first-generation intelligentsia but also by the first generation of successful upper-middle-class professionals, the people who were the targets of the despised "movements"—and changed far more rapidly than I would have imagined that night on the L platform. What *Humanae Generis* had done to the postwar intelligentsia, *Humanae Vitae* would do eighteen years later to the postwar professionals. And for the same reason. The second encyclical did not listen. It did not understand.

Sadly, most of those Catholic pioneers at the University of Chicago dropped from sight. They teach in colleges and universities around the country. They do not publish. One rarely hears of them. Somehow or other, the spark of the late 1940s went out.

The forces they represented did not go away. By 1954, at ordination, I realized in a way most of my classmates did not that we were going out into a world different from the one we had left seven years before. It was not merely that television had appeared in the intervening years. There were new ideas sweeping the Church from the European universities, and there were new people in the American Church filled with these ideas. In addition, while Monsignor Hillenbrand and his faculty had been removed from the seminary before my arrival, the Catholic Action movements they had launched in the United States were appealing to a new generation of well-educated lay professionals who, while they may not have been University of Chicago intellectuals, were still not like the people I knew at St. Angela.

My own generation at St. Angela, I would discover much later, was changing too.

Meanwhile, back at the seminary we rarely discussed anything of serious importance. Some of the older seminarians, product of the Hillenbrand era derivatively, were much more serious. Through my friend and coparishioner Gene Faucher (one of the finest priests in the world) I met Leo Mahon, like Dick Dempsey and in later years John Shea the son of a cop, and became fascinated by his charisma and insights. The first time we talked—on a car riding down 67th Street in 1947—we began to argue, and we have never stopped arguing. As G. K. Chesterton said of his brother, we have never once quarreled.

"Leo, you're wrong!" has been my favorite opening gambit through the years. However, he is rarely wrong (save when he disagrees with me). He has made an enormous and imaginative contribution to the work of the Church both in Chicago and in Central America, a contribution the Archdiocese has never recognized. In a properly run Church he should have been made a bishop long ago.

The worst effect of the seminary was that its exploitation of envy and mediocrity as instruments of social control deprived the Church of talent it would need desperately in the coming crisis. Long after the old seminary died, its lingering effects on clerical culture are still much with us.

One of the most destructive exercises of clerical envy I ever witnessed was the effort of a clique of priests to destroy one of their class who had become an officer in an early Chicago priest association. The man had not been part of their "in" group. It grated on their nerves, like a fingernail on a blackboard, when he emerged as a leader of younger priests. They set out to harass and torment him and succeeded in driving him out of the priesthood.

No one tried to stop them.

Not everyone in the priesthood acts like that, you say?

Almost everyone who knew of this situation was silent while this man was being wiped out. I pleaded that he be helped. The response was to admit the clique was envious and then to go on to discuss the useful points they had made against him—his stylistic mistakes and his weaknesses as a leader and a human being. Doubtless, like all of us, he had his weaknesses and made mistakes. Those who compromised with envy were almost as bad as the envious themselves. You do not compromise with such people, you do not negotiate with them, you do not "defend" their target against them. Rather you denounce envy for what it is in the most powerful language possible and then stomp on it, crush the life out of it. You dismiss the envious with the most appropriate scatological and obscene words at your command.

Otherwise you cooperate with them.

The laity must finally realize that much of the identity crisis which currently plagues their priests is based on the low esteem in which priests hold themselves. Research I would do in 1970 showed the average assistant pastor experienced less job satisfaction than an unskilled laborer—mostly because for all his educational years, he was in fact an unskilled laborer. It's hard to feel good about yourself when you believe you do nothing well. In the church of thirty years ago priests escaped that dilemma by finding satisfaction in their social status; but the changes in the Church and in the Catholic population have taken away most of that status (despite the often pathetic efforts of some middle-aged pastors to reassert their status by passive/aggressive authoritarianism and attempts to control who receives the sacraments and who does not—in direct violation of canon law, incidentally). Hence, as a veteran priest remarked to me recently, "We have no hope left."

Yet one cannot talk about "professionalizing" the clergy in the sense of developing internal standards of motivation and excellence of performance without being accused of desacralizing the role. "I became a priest," a certain bishop once thundered at me, "to serve Jesus Christ, not to be a professional."

I insisted I was using the word in opposition to "amateur," but he would have none of it. Apparently serving Jesus Christ somehow justified amateurism.

Hence priests "take courses" but often do not finish the papers or the dissertations necessary for degrees (less than half complete such work, according to one observer of advanced clerical education). You want to learn a little bit more, but not enough more to be really better than/different from "the rest of the guys."

Reading these pages and agreeing with me mostly, Leo Mahon argues that I should say priests have no monopoly on envy. I quite agree. I've had a chance in my life to study three professions closely as I worked in them. Academics are remarkably envious people. Journalists are even more so. And priests make professional journalists look envy-free.

Why?

134

The reward structure is limited in the priesthood. Spiritual motives ("humility," "resisting pride," "docility," "obedience," etc.) are used to reinforce envy. Priests are taught to be envious by their teachers and by their elder colleagues.

The priest in the next parish is building a reputation for running an interesting and exciting community. People are saying others might learn from him. Do you wander over to see what's happening? Chances are not only you won't do that, you'll cooperate in a campaign to vilify his efforts and question his motives. When your laity ask you about him, you'll have two or three acid observations to cut him to pieces.

Or a priest who was in the seminary in your time is being hailed as a great preacher. You rejoice in his accomplishments and urge people to listen to him? Fat chance. At every opportunity you will tell others what a dunce he was in the seminary and how he really ought not to be taken seriously. He is, you'll admit, not all that bad at holding an audience, but he doesn't have enough solid theological training to know what he is talking about. Right?

Right.

Not all priests are that way, you say?

Surely not. But let me propose as a small experiment that you find the local priest of your choice and praise in his presence something another priest has done or is doing. Listen to his reaction.

Even money you'll get an outburst of envy like the two I have just described. Observe too that he'll call the other priest by his first name, even though he has never met him—a hint that he's one of the brothers who has gone *off* the reservation.

If you try my experiments and if the priest rises to the bait, note how he can hardly help himself. He is driven almost by a compulsion to blacken the reputation of the other priest even though by so doing he makes himself look patronizing and demeaning. Envy is not an option for many of us. It has become a built-in character trait.

Most priests? A majority of priests? Many priests?

Enough so that mediocrity and envy permeate the clerical culture and no one dares to stand up and denounce them, save under pain of being driven off the reservation and, if it can be arranged, out of the priesthood.

Not much in the envious priest of the warmth or generosity of Jesus of Nazareth, who was put to death because of envy.

Envy will continue to be the besetting vice of the priesthood until bishops refuse to be intimidated by it, discontinue it as a guiding principle of their governance and denounce it loudly and often. Envy will not free the priesthood from its clammy hands until the leaders of the priests band together to destroy it. Leo Mahon thinks it's on the wane. Leo, you're wrong! It's worse than ever and you are one of its prime victims.

Michele Brennan: How did you put up with such a yucky place, anyway?

Me: Pure cussedness.

Then and now.

Why? I wanted to be a priest. My instincts told me there was more to the Church than the seminary. My reading of the new theologians confirmed those instincts.

Mundelein was and is a beautiful place physically; a cozy escape from the world. As ordination drew close I was reluctant to face the world, knowing, as many of my classmates did not, that I was utterly without the preparation or the maturity required to be a parish priest.

"Suppose the pastor wants me to work with teenagers?" I said to one of my classmates. "I haven't the foggiest idea how to do it."

"Teenagers can be ignored unless they're delinquents," my classmate replied. "Don't worry about it."

The teenagers with whom I would deal for ten years after ordination and intermittently for the rest of my life, even until this day, were neither delinquent nor spoiled (though their parents feared they would be), and I turned out—much to my astonishment—to be good with them. It was no fault of the seminary's, however.

Suddenly, the seemingly endless seven years at Mundelein were almost over. We began to parade around the seminary's lovely grounds, with our shiny new breviaries, reading in Latin some twenty-five psalms every day "under pain of mortal sin" even though we did not understand the Hebrew poetry in any language. We were told God didn't care if we knew what we were praying so long as we were praying "in the name of the Church." As though in the psalms themselves He didn't reject mindless "sacrifices and burnt offerings."

(Now I realize there is more richness of meaning in a single psalm than I can handle in a day. The breviary expired after it was permitted for us to say it in English. As Ernie Primeau, who taught me at Quigley and was one of the great bishops of the Council, for which he was left in Manchester, New Hampshire, as punishment by the vindictive Curia, put it, "That fellow David, he was no Christian." I still read psalms every day, but now because I can understand and appreciate their beauty, not because I am afraid God will send me to hell for missing a couple of them at the end of the day.)

We bought chalices, made plans for our first Mass, practiced Mass under the watchful eyes of classmates assigned to make sure we had learned to honor all the rubrics. My supervisor was as punctilious as a novice mistress, much to my impatience and eventual anger. God, I assumed even then, was not a rubricist. Finally I passed. My tormentor married a nun shortly after the changes and decamped. I suspect, however, that he is still a punctilious rubricist.

Then came May 5, 1954, the coldest fifth day of May in history, and my first day in the priesthood. Was it an anticlimax? I have often asked myself. Were not my emotions that day as cold as the weather?

I think now the answer is yes and no.

My mother and sisters, my family and friends, were ecstatic. I was worn out, going through the expected motions with little sense of personal joy—or anything else. A letdown, I suppose, after a buildup which no one day could sustain. I also had, how to put it, a deep sense that there would be difficult times ahead.

The parents and family and friends were then sent home and we were led off to a clerical banquet in the seminary dining hall. When Albert Meyer came to Chicago, he looked around the dining room and demanded, "Where are the parents?"

Rector: They've gone home.
Meyer: They should be here.
Rector: They've gone home.
Meyer: Why?
Rector: This is a dinner for priests.
Meyer: The parents should be here.
Rector: Cardinal Mundelein wanted it to be a dinner for priests.
Dead silence from Meyer.
Rector: The parents have gone home.
Meyer: I want them here next year.

I've always savored that conversation (reported by a member of the next ordination class, who was waiting on tables). The times, they were changing.

The anticlimax ended the next morning at my first private Mass in the St. Angela convent chapel with Diggy Cunningham, proud as punch, hovering around to make sure I did everything right. Then joy flooded every cell of my being, joy that I had anticipated since Sister Alma Frances's room in eighth grade, joy which, as the Scripture says, no one can ever take from me, joy which is still with me, joy which keeps me in the priesthood regardless of what happens.

Diggy: Not bad for a beginner. You did it pretty well.

Me: Thanks, I was unconscious.

Diggy: (catch in his voice, blue eyes watering behind his glasses) Your father would be proud.

Me: Thanks.

Diggy: So am I.

I should have hugged him. We didn't do things like that in 1954.

Thirty years later, when I send him the large-print editions of my stories in which Monsignor Mugsy Brannigan makes an occasional genial appearance, Diggy writes back to say I'm the greatest Catholic novelist in America and that he's still proud of me. I'm not, but I'm proud of him.

In 1954 I knew the times were changing. We were not going to be parish priests protecting the faith of the working-class immigrants in the comfortable static Counter-Reformation enclaves like St. Angela. French sociologists (notably unencumbered by data, as it turned out) were already buzzing around the United States, preaching that the old national parish was breaking up. They insisted the new generation of educated and successful Catholics would drift away from Catholicism, as had their European counterparts. These itinerant pseudo-scholars were serenely confident they understood our country at the end of the second week on our shores. They were, incidentally, obsessed by the automobile and compulsively asked every priest they met which kind of car he drove. In fact they missed the point completely. They did not perceive (nor did I then) that the new neighborhoods that formed in the suburbs would become even more enthusiastically Catholic than the old.

So I was intellectually prepared for change. I was not prepared to be actively involved in it, however, nor much affected by it. I did not have any idea how monumental and traumatic the change would be or what curious and lonely paths it would cause me to walk.

Nor was I ready for the two logical conclusions of the forces that I had observed beginning to work—Christ the King parish in Beverly and the Second Vatican Council.

St. Praxides

CHRIST THE KING—ALL HALLOWS EVE

The ghosts of yesteryear stir the fallen leaves
Alive and dancing in the autumn air
As in those gentle days for which my spirit grieves
When they were young and all our vision fair.
The leaves twist down the neatly curving street
By the handsome house o'er the fading lawn
Why did they run from such a promise sweet
Where, O good friends, have the bright young faces gone?
The leaves pursue their wild and drunken dance
To the music of a mournful wailing tune;
Now reeling blindly from their final chance
In the hazy sunlight, towards a smoking doom
Lives dimmed like golden leaves, tainted by winter frost
Young hope once dearly loved and now long lost

The Hound of Heaven, She threw me a fast pitch with Christ the King parish, to mix metaphors outrageously. I can only explain that phase of my life by piling metaphors on top of one another. CK (as the kids called it) is the love of my life, Twin Lakes and St. Angela combined, the most critical way station on my pilgrimage for that which was Lost to that which may yet be Found, the magic cave where the Grail remains hidden, a frequent setting for the nightmares my permeable boundaries let in.

It also represents quintessentially the challenges and the possibilities of "post-immigrant" Catholicism, a subject which would preoccupy me as a priest, a sociologist and a storyteller for the rest of my life.

Four stories set the context for Christ the King:

About ten years ago a new pastor came to a neighboring parish, a contemporary of mine. He called me after the first six months there and said, "Andy, you're right, this is a magic neighborhood just like you always used to say. Why don't you come out and have supper and tell me what to do."

Although I doubted he would do anything I said, I accepted the invitation. Supper was transferred from the rectory to the house of my colleague Bill McCready, because, I suspect, the pastor was afraid a report might go to the cardinal that he was entertaining me inside the rectory. Much of the evening was spent in listening to the pastor's complaints about teenagers: they played basketball in the courts across the street from the rectory every hour of the day or night in spring, summer and autumn, they drank, they broke windows, they were disrespectful, they even, God forgive them for it, sat on the rectory front lawn at two o'clock in the morning.

I observed that in most Catholic parishes in the world, that kind of geographical closeness of the teenagers would have been considered a monumental advantage.

"Yeah?" said the pastor dubiously. "Well, maybe I ought to tell the youth minister to come around to the rectory at two o'clock in the morning and talk to the kids on the lawn."

"With all respect for your youth minister, I don't think that's what they want. They want to talk to you or one of the other priests. Bring them into the house and feed 'em pizza and after a couple of nights they'll be on your side."

He didn't seem to understand what I was saying and went on to complain about the broken windows in the schoolyard (windows covered by insurance). Then he told me how a group of sophomore girls had descended on the rectory in high dudgeon to say they were tired of their boys being blamed for what the seventh-graders were doing (it is one of the iron laws of parish life that seventh-graders and sophomores are always the ones who break things). The pastor assured me he had had a pleasant conversation with these young women and that he really didn't blame them or their boys.

"You invited them to come back?"

The pastor admitted he had not. It had not even occurred to him.

"Well," I said, "if you'd asked them back, in a couple of weeks they would have brought their boys along and you would have the makings of a Young Christian Students group or whatever you wanted to call it— a group of teenagers on your side and not against you."

The pastor explained that life was so busy in his rectory there was little time for such things.

"Okay," I said, scarcely able to conceal my enthusiasm, "I'll do it for you."

He did not, to put it mildly, grab at my offer. After I left he asked Bill McCready, "Did Andy really mean that?"

"Oh yes," Bill replied, thinking of the responsibilities I had already piled on myself, "I'm afraid he did."

About the magic neighborhood I have never been reasonable or rational or sensible or prudent or discreet.

Another story:

The pastor came storming down to my room furious. "Mrs. Hack [not her name] was on the phone to me just a few moments ago about the cheerleaders you're organizing for the eighth-grade football team."

"I'm not organizing anything," I said, distastefully. "The eighth-grade girls are organizing it themselves."

"Do you think that's appropriate for children that age?" he thundered.

"I don't know," I said. "I think Mrs. Hack's girl didn't make the squad. If you want me to stop it, though, I'll tell the kids the monsignor says no eighth-grade cheerleaders."

"Don't do that," he said. "Now you've started it, it would be a mistake to stop it."

He meant that if I stopped it and blamed it on him then he would be inundated with phone calls from the mothers of those who *had* made the team. In fact, the whole conversation was designed so that he could tell complainers, either way, that it was my fault, not his. As an after-thought he added, "I don't suppose any of the other parishes have eighth-grade cheerleaders?"

"They all do." I turned back to my typewriter. "Still, if you want me to stop it, I will."

"No, if the other parishes have eighth-grade cheerleaders, I suppose we must permit it too."

He now had his final excuse. To those who objected he could blame all the other parishes and me—another marvelous pastoral finesse.

A third story. I was in the sacristy of the basement church at Christ the King (we had yet to move into the modern new church which was to be dedicated in a few months) preparing for my first Sunday Mass at my new assignment. One of my teenage allies—I'd made some already—whispered in my ear, "You watch, the pastor's going to stand right outside the door where he thinks you can't see him and listen to your sermon, then after Mass he'll complain about what a poor preacher you are. He always does it. It gives him one more advantage over you."

So I preached and so I saw the pastor lurking just outside where he thought he was invisible. I must have done pretty well, for he never complained about that or any of my subsequent sermons. Neither did he ever compliment any of them. As a matter of fact, in the ten years I was at the parish, I never heard a single word of approval. When the new church was opened, Carmelites from Mount Carmel High School were hired to do the eleven-fifteen and twelve-fifteen Masses on Sunday, masses which attracted well over half the parish. The pastor didn't mind visiting priests who were better preachers than he was. They came and went. They were no threat to his security in the parish.

A curate, he argued, must be kept away from the people. I was for-bidden even to stand in the back of the church on Sunday morning greeting parishioners, the exact opposite of Diggy Cunningham's insistence on everyone greeting the people at St. Angela. Rather, the other curate and I were banished to the rectory basement after our Masses, to count money. The pastor would greet the people because they were *his* people, and we would count the money because we were *his* priests. "I have to keep you away from them," he said. "Some of them have a lot of money and if I allow them to become close friends with you, they'll spoil you with all their money. Besides, there's a lot of drinking going on in the parish, and you should stay away from that."

For a while I would wearily explain in the face of this harangue that I didn't drink, had no intention of drinking, and that my family was upper-middle-class as well and that I doubted anyone in the parish could "spoil" me.

Did the pastor really believe that argument or was he rationalizing his own jealous attitudes toward the parish?

Both, I suppose. His health was poor, his hearing was failing, the parish was growing larger and more complicated, and the winds of change were already stirring. By reputation, he had been a fine teacher at Quigley Seminary and a wonderful young pastor. Later on, after he retired and continued to live at the parish, the curates worshiped him. It was just my misfortune to arrive at a bad time in his life and perhaps his misfortune to have to put up with me during that same period.

He counted the number of phone calls I received, forbade me to go out after supper, save for a Christian Family Movement meeting once every other week, and bowling every Thursday night. (Thursday was my day off. It didn't make any difference: it was still part of my obligation to the parish to bowl.) After nine o'clock almost every night he would come down and peer through the glass door of the rectory office to see to whom I was talking. "You should dismiss them at nine, nine-thirty at the latest," he insisted. When Father John McEvoy, who was to die at Christ the King, came to the parish, he was subjected to the same rigid controls, even though he was forty-two years old. To make matters worse, when John Hotchkin arrived after McEvoy's death, the pastor was told by the cardinal that he would have John for only a few years because he was destined for Chancery Office work. He also told him I would be going part-time to the University of Chicago. The pastor didn't like that, but dutifully obedient priest that he was, he cooperated even to the extent of hearing my Saturday-afternoon confessions so that I could study.

I fear the presence of Hotchkin and myself in the rectory was a heavy cross for him. Now he had two priests whom he did not understand, whom he could not control, and whom he greatly feared. Finally he got rid of both of us, but after that there was little time to enjoy Christ the King because Cardinal Cody arrived and began his purge of older pastors. The monsignor was not on the hit list, but the anxieties he felt every day expecting the cardinal to show up in a vast black limousine to demand his resignation finally got to him, and he resigned without being asked, convinced, wrongly, it turned out, that he was heading off the cardinal at the pass.

The last story. On a Christmas day in the late 1950s I received an obnoxious phone call at home from an obnoxious Jesuit who had read a paper of mine about "St. Praxides," a mythical suburban parish much like Christ the King. I had written it as a memo, mostly for myself, to articulate what I saw as the problems and the possibilities of the new quasi-suburban upper-middle-class Catholic parish (ours was one of the first; scores would follow). I had shown the memo to the pastor and to one or two people in the parish and a couple of my friends in the priesthood. Monsignor was upset. There were many things, he told me, I was too young to understand about the parish. I surely wasn't going to publish it, was I?

I wasn't going to publish it; it was just a memo I had written to clarify my own thoughts.

Well, George Higgins had passed his copy on to this obnoxious Jesuit, who called Christmas Day at Christ the King rectory looking for me and raved to the pastor about the wonderful paper I had written and how much they wanted to publish it in this particular Jesuit's magazine.

I was horrified by the call. In the late 1950s anyone with any sensitivity would have known that a pastor would not welcome the information that his curate was writing memos about *his* (the pastor's) parish. How dare the Jesuit intrude in my life on Christmas Day and create even more suspicion between me and the pastor? No, I said, I had no intention of publishing it.

It didn't ruin my Christmas day, but it sure ruined the pastor's. His family was celebrating in the monsignorial suite when I returned to the rectory, so I crept into my room. But he heard me, left his family behind, and harangued me because I had permitted the document to fall into the hands of a Jesuit journalist. I think, but I can't remember for sure, that I called Higgins and told him not to show the paper to anyone else.

It was later redone, with most of the local references taken out, and appeared as my first book, *The Church and the Suburbs,* but more about that later on. I always think with some glee of the pastor when I set a novel in St. Praxides.

(I have no idea who St. Praxides was, even what is the sex of the good saint. It was a name that stuck in my head from hearing the Roman

Martyrology read to us at lunch in the seminary. However, in my novels St. Prax has become the forester who built the boat in which St. Christopher crossed the river to pick up the Baby Jesus. Hence the glorious stained-glass window in the back of the real CK has been changed to a picture of the forester carrying his ax—called by the teenagers "Prax's Ax.")

Why did I put up with such oppression for ten years? For reasons not unlike those for which I put up with Mundelein and the isolation from my grammar school friends at Quigley: I had wanted to be a priest. Now I was a priest in a dream parish. I was mesmerized by the magic of Christ the King and especially by the charm and the promise of its teenagers. If I had to tolerate a suspicious and jealous pastor as the price to pay for continuing to work in that magic neighborhood, then I would certainly do so.

Whence comes the magic? Is it in the long line of "the ridge," the only appreciable elevation in Cook County and probably the dune line on the beaches of what was the remote ancestor of Lake Michigan? Is it in the curving streets, the woods (another geological relic), the charming old turn-of-the-century homes on the East Side? Or is it in the new, elegant just-after-the-war homes on the West Side? Is it in the compact, self-contained boundaries of the community, surrounded as it is by railroad tracks, forest preserves, and golf courses? Is it the small size—not really much bigger than a small town as far as its Catholic population goes? Is it the fact that the neighborhood has a history—unlike most postwar Catholic suburbs? Is it that virtually everybody came to the neighborhood at the same time as part of the massive move upward of the Catholic middle class after the war? Is it that so many of the older people are childhood friends and relatives who became successful at about the same time (to their own considerable surprise)? Is it in the two modern churches in the community and the long line of progressive clergy who set traditions well before I arrived?

All these influences are at work, and more too, I suppose. How do you explain magic?

A perfect neighborhood? Hardly, but still . . . still what?

If there was a tragic flaw among the South Side Irish, it was not conservatism or parochialism or racism or clericalism; it was the Irish passion for respectability—a passion which, among the upper middle class and well-to-do, deprived them of their flair and wit. Most could

147

not laugh at themselves; and when the Irish cannot laugh at themselves, they've got trouble.

They were great politicians and great drinkers, great storytellers and hard workers, occasionally some of them were great lovers; but they so wanted to be approved, they were so afraid of ridicule, so cautious in the face of the utterly damning "What will people say?" or "Who do you think you are?" And if the storytellers, playwrights, and bards, the great scholars and thinkers, the dreamers, visionaries, mystics, prophets and saints, did not grow up in that neighborhood, the ultimate reason was the fear of losing respectability. It was an attitude which, sad to say, was reinforced by most of the clergy who served them. (The clerics themselves were afraid of what others would say.) If that neighborhood slips out of existence and loses the opportunity to become a permanent, stable, integrated neighborhood (which I now doubt), the blame will lie not with the blockbusters, the redliners, the panic peddlers or the racists; it will be the misguided passion for respectability and all its resulting caution, narrowness and rigidity that will have destroyed the community.

It is still alive and well. The smiling children still pour out of the schools, the ice cream parlors are filled on Saturday afternoons, grammar school football games keep the parks crowded all day Saturday, the crowd mills around in the back of the church on Sunday, the teenagers hang around the basketball and volleyball courts, cars speed up and down Longwood Drive, the Rock Island pulls in at five twenty-five, kids sneak cigarettes and beer in the park at 100th Street (maybe a little pot nowadays), volleyball games continue in the Ridge Park field house, 95th and Western traffic jams are as bad as ever, the squirrels scurry up and down the fiery autumn trees, sophomores still slouch aimlessly down the street on the way home from school. The bells of the church no longer chime for weddings and funerals because a subsequent pastor overruled his parish council and decided not to spend twenty thousand dollars to tuck-point a bell tower that the architect said was one of his best designs. (I remember the first Christmas in the new church with the chimes ringing carols over the snow-clad neighborhood.)

However, you can still go to Irish wakes almost any night of the week at Lynch's or Heany's or Loughlin's or Donnellan's, as one by one that old generation goes to the reward which each has both feared and expected. The precinct captains still try to make the city bureaucracy work for you, and children can still play on the sidewalks without fear of being hassled. The neighborhood has changed subtly; it is now almost solidly Catholic (at one time, though it seemed all Catholic, it was only half). Large numbers of city employees have moved in, clinging to the only strip on the South Side left to white people; upper-middle-class blacks, even more cautious and respectable than the Irish, have joined the community; there are many more Ph.D.s than there used to be, and a much larger number of corporate transients who will only stay for a while before moving on. (In the old days nobody ever moved out—not until the kids were raised.)

So it is a more variegated, more differentiated, and perhaps less integrated neighborhood than it used to be. The old social controls have weakened both for weal and woe; the bonds are no longer as tight. Yet you still wonder, as you look at the faces, whether you might not be in the west of Ireland.

"Your name is Wright, isn't it, kid?" "Yes, Father, how did you know?" "Your mother's name is Mary Ellen, isn't it?" "Yes, Father, how did you know?" "Well, you go home and tell her that a funny old priest asked if she remembers the day when she was your age and she got 'lost.'" The kid looks at you as though you're absolutely crazy, and you remember the astonished seventh-grader who showed up in front of her parents' house at ten-thirty at night to find several squad cars and a substantial segment of the neighborhood just about ready to begin her wake. (Good God, Mary Ellen, you had better not have forgotten that day, because I think it was then your husband made up his mind to marry you.)

St. Angela was a "natural community" in the sense that as a second-generation parish it was an unself-conscious development of the immigrant neighborhoods. Most of the parishioners did not really have other options for their social and religious identification.

But CK was a self-conscious community. The people, mostly third- and fourth-generation, had other options for social location. They chose the parish as the community with which they identified because they wanted to keep alive the values and social support of the St. Angela–style parishes in which they grew up. It was a parish community created by free contract.

By the time the Irish moved to Christ the King parish in Beverly Hills, the neighborhood was strictly optional. They no longer needed the parish-neighborhood as a community in which they could huddle together in mutual support against a basically mysterious and hostile society. The neighborhood as an entry port for immigrants and as a base of operations for the second generation was obsolescent. And yet without any hesitation, the affluent third and fourth generation founded parishes which had a vigor and ingenuity that if anything made the neighborhood even more supportive, more rewarding, and a more influential part of their lives. For them the neighborhood was an option, one they both unquestioningly and enthusiastically chose.

I was given charge of the teenagers by the pastor because they were the only group in the community of whom he was not jealous. If I wanted to take the teenagers away from him, that was perfectly fine. And by giving me charge of the adolescents in the community he cut me off from everyone else. Thus, I had a rather strange ten years in a parish of which I was incorrigibly fond and in which I scarcely even met anybody over twenty-two.

I had no notion how to deal with adolescents, not the slightest, and I made only three rules for myself:

1. I would treat them like adults, an easy enough thing for me to do because I didn't have to live with them twenty-four hours a day like their parents.

2. I would protect their confidences. If I knew a bunch of freshman boys were drinking, I might kid them about it but I would not report them to their parents.

3. I would find out who their leaders were and quickly get them on my side. For a decade or so we had the most active and most enthusiastic high-school-age ministry in the city, mostly because once the teenagers realized I was serious about giving them responsibility they rose to the occasion—not all the time and not always with much durability but still, because it was *their* Hi Club, *their* plays, *their* Young Christian Students groups, not mine, they worked diligently and enthusiastically for their success. We fought off the pastor, the mother superior, the engineer and misguided parental chaperons for ten years, and then, as soon as Hotchkin and I were gone, our replacements, with the pastor's enthusiastic approval, killed the entire program. (Incidentally, both the Jesuit who called me on Christmas Day and the young priest who took the lead in destroying our teenage program have since left the priesthood and married.)

The success of the parish teen activities put the monsignor in an acutely embarrassing position. On the one hand, he was pleased when the pa-

150

rishioners complimented him on the work I was doing with the "kids."
On the other hand, the compliments were sufficiently generous as to
make him fear that I was becoming popular with the people through their
children.

Moreover, he didn't much like teenagers and the parish grounds were
becoming a hangout for them, not only the schoolyard ("the Courts" in
which, if one is to believe Noele Farrell in Lord of the Dance, God
especially dwells), where they played volleyball and basketball, but the
meeting hall and the rectory basement, the offices, the corridors and
even, he suspected (because his sister, who was the housekeeper, told
him), in the latter days his own suite when he was away on one of his
many vacations.

Everyone seemed to like this gathering of the teenage clans on parish
property—the kids who had a new excuse to get out of the house at night
("We're going over to the rectory!"—an excuse which was not always
true!) and the parents who liked to see their kids with the priests.

Thus the poor pastor was hard put to banish the adolescents. He insisted
that no one from outside the parish was to be permitted to participate—
the mission of the Church obviously stops at parish boundaries—and
then made an exception for the young people from St. Barnabas to the
south because he was told they accepted our young people. (The same
game was played in their rectory on occasion—successfully because
neighboring pastors did not communicate with one another. Thank God!)
We knew that if you excluded the friends of your own teens you wouldn't
get them. An awful lot of young people became honorary members of
St. Barnabas!

Moreover, he absolutely insisted that there be no Friday-night Hi Club
assemblies during Lent. It was wrong, he argued, to have dances during
Lent. The Hi Club gathering was hardly a dance (until the last desperate
five minutes), and the reasons for bringing the young people together on
parish grounds (to keep them out of worse trouble and to subtly influence
their lives—"Not drunk again, you idiot!")—were as valid in Lent as at
any other time. Nonetheless it gave him an excuse to get the teenagers
out of his hair for a few weeks and to provide an explanation parents
would accept, however skeptically.

So we began a Sunday-night lecture series—a Lenten service for teens
and young adults.

Another draw.

The battle over Lemuel X. Quicksilver was not a draw. The pastor was easily threatened by complaints, especially anonymous complaints, which could put him in a snit for two weeks (we often schemed about writing anonymous complaints about the way he treated his curates, but didn't have the nerve, for which God forgive us). In a curious division of labor he heard the complaints of the two or three people who wanted the air conditioner turned off in the summer, while we heard the complaints of the hundreds after it was turned off—the air conditioner, you see, was like the gym in many parishes: it was there to be there and not to be used.

Well, Hotchkin and I contrived a series of sermons for the children about some special people we knew—Lemuel X. Quicksilver, a Martian anthropologist who parked his flying saucer outside my window on Saturday nights, Maximilian the Mad Monk, who rang the chimes in our bell tower, and Max's brother, Erich the Eyrie Anchorite. The kids loved these characters (after twenty years many still remember them), and so did the adults. The second-grade girls even claimed to have seen them!

One man complained to the pastor, and we were forbidden to mention them again. One complainer. Naturally the rest of the people complained to us about the disappearance of Lem and Max and Erich.

I still am angry at myself, after all these years, for accepting that ukase. I should have told him that what I preached, as long as it was not heresy, was none of his damn business. But the seminary socialization experience had its impact even on those of us who didn't believe the theory.

Behavior mod.

The disastrous relationship with my pastor for ten years was not totally his fault. I'm sure I projected the image of the quick-witted, articulate intellectual, a threat in other words. In addition, some people seemed to like me. I did many things in the parish community without bothering to tell him. (As John Hotchkin would later remark, "We are obliged in charity to protect the pastor from undue worry. If he knew everything we were doing, he would certainly unduly worry!")

When the Vatican Council came along and most of the things I was pushing for in the Church became realities, I suspect this frightened the monsignor even more, for he saw Hotchkin and me as the wave of the future and his own grip on *his* parish slipping away. Hence we both had to go: Hotchkin back to Rome for his doctorate in ecumenical theology and I to the University of Chicago on an almost full-time basis. That was fine with the pastor. We could be New Wave clergy anyplace we wanted so long as it wasn't in *his* parish.

As I've said before, I'm not good at interpersonal conflict or at releasing anger. In retrospect, I can see why the pastor thought me potentially disloyal and a threat to *his* popularity, *his* parish. I was neither disloyal nor a threat, but we were never able to talk about that or anything else. Whatever responsibility for that was his, some of it was also mine because I was not mature enough or self-possessed enough to face him down. My ten years in Christ the King were spent in a rectory where I was good friends with the other curates (Tom Kaveney, Jake McEvoy and John Hotchkin), and lived in a perpetual state of armed neutrality with my pastor. He was not a bad man, he built a modern church, he had encouraged liturgical participation for a quarter century during a time when most pastors dismissed it as near heresy, he did not require that black-vestment "Masses for the dead" be said every day, he permitted Cana and CFM, YCS and YCW, all the new movements in the Church, to organize themselves in his parish.

My relationship with him was a mess, both our mutual fault and that of the system which tended to create a situation where, in the immortal words of J. F. Power, an assistant pastor was a mouse in training to be a rat.

Part of being a mouse was that you didn't have a car. Cardinal Mundelein, forty years before, had decreed that priests could not own a car during their first five years in the ministry. George Casey, the vicar general, in explaining this to us shortly before ordination admitted it was a "good question" whether the rule made sense any longer because the Archdiocese had changed so profoundly. Nonetheless, because "the cardinal" (Mundelein) wanted it, the rule would continue. "If you need a car," he said fatuously, "your pastor will buy you one."

Naturally the pastor would make the decision. My pastor didn't see why I needed a car. An hour and a half on foot in ten-below-zero weather bringing Communion to the elderly sick of the parish several mornings a week was good exercise, though not the sort in which a pastor ever engaged.

"Brisk morning," he would beam over the breakfast table after his eight-o'clock Mass (he always said the eight-o'clock) when I would trudge in purple from the cold (my first two years were marked by abnormally chilly winters).

"Yeah," I would agree with contemptuous lack of enthusiasm.

Bringing Communion to and visiting the sick was a responsibility that weighed heavily on me. We didn't do it nearly often enough. Yet there was so much else to do, I had to be in class by nine (teaching seventh- and eighth-grade religion—including on my technical "days off"), and you could cover just so many homes between seven and eight forty-five. Even today I have nightmares in which the sick are forgotten.

In St. Angela's it was possible to do all your work without a car. The community was compact and the hospitals and funeral homes were within easy walking or streetcar distance. But in the new postwar parishes, the situation was different. You could spend an hour and a half on public transportation, both ways, traveling to a wake or a hospital. I tried to make as many visits to the sick and the dead as I could, but time ran out. I would walk over to Little Company of Mary Hospital (perhaps a forty-minute walk) a couple of days a week to visit our sick there. The pastor protested one day.

"I don't know where you go when you're out in the afternoons."

"To the hospital, where I told you I go."

"How do I know that?"

"You could follow me in your car, I suppose."

I strode out of the room, violently angry. I should have confronted him on the spot.

He raised hell with me whenever I borrowed anyone's car to make a particularly long drive on a busy day to a distant hospital or wake. His position was that only the pastor needed to visit the sick or bury the dead.

Then Jake McAvoy arrived and on the first day he was in the rectory tossed me the keys of his Ford Fairlane.

I drove my new toy through the parish.

"Well," said Tom Kelly when I showed up at the basketball courts with the beautiful black car. "Now you're the equal of any sixteen-year-old male in the parish."

Not nearly so free, in truth.

I relate these stories neither because I am angry at the poor man, who is now dead and gone, nor to celebrate my own immaturity (of which I am ashamed—I should have either demanded he provide a parish car or bought one of my own regardless of what Cardinal Mundelein might have thought in whatever section of the Hereafter he may inhabit) but to record what it was like to be a young priest in those days.

154

Despite the endless difficulty with the monsignor, I loved the parish and the work. Gwendolyn Brooks, the poet laureate of Chicago, called Beverly the land of the golden garden. I didn't see the community quite that way, but I fell so in love with it that I would have stayed there forever if I had not been transferred.

Manicured lawns. The trees arching over the curving streets, shrubbery neatly arranged in front of each house—green everywhere, glistening in the warm summer sun as the newly ordained priest (me) set off down the street to take his first parish census (with the pastor's warning in his ears about staying away from drink). Georgian, Dutch Colonial, Early American, and an occasional imitation Frank Lloyd Wright home—comfortable, spacious, sometimes elegant. Swarming activity on the basketball and volleyball courts; unending streams of teenagers pouring into the Hi Club as the Melody Knights beat out into the night what must have been primordial rock and roll; YCS meetings in the rectory basement and CFM groups gathered around the coffee table; the great white brick modern church; picnics at Potawatami Park or in the Warren Dunes in Michigan; sophomores ambling down the street after school and college students pouring in at Christmastime; Gate 14 at the Notre Dame games; the annual Easter and Christmas plebiscite when the size of the collection was taken as a sign of the parish's continuing approval of the pastor's work (a sign always doubted but always given); a blanket of snow turning the golden gardens white.

I cannot even imagine who I would be or where I would be or what I'd be doing if July of 1954 had not found me riding with more than a little bit of awe down Hamilton Avenue (one of the loveliest streets in the city of Chicago) seeing the almost-finished new Christ the King Church, at that time, beyond all doubt, the most modern in the diocese. In my wildest dreams I could not have expected a first assignment quite like the one I got. For many priests, the first assignment is something like a first love—something you get over but never quite get out of your system. For me, the impact was much stronger: *I will never get over Christ the King.* It is still my parish, still my neighborhood, and always will be.

I knew theoretically that American Catholicism was changing in 1954, but I was totally unprepared to find myself dropped into the middle of what quite obviously was the parish of the future. Beverly, as one priest with an Irish gift for turning a phrase commented, was the upper crust of the Irish middle class. It represented one of the three or four places in the city where the Irish had made it big not merely as individuals but as a group. In Beverly we were no longer the poor immigrant or the honest "cap and sweater" crowd (as one priest proudly said of his parish), or the hardworking laborers or the responsible clerks, salespeople, and high school teachers. Here were the professionals, the managers, the successful small businessmen, the stockbrokers, the lawyers, the judges, the union leaders. Here it was not only possible for all the young to go to college, it was unthinkable that they should not. Here the American-ization of the Catholic immigrant groups was entering its final phase. The Irish had arrived.

Some of the adults, not all but some, were suspicious of me for two reasons. First of all, I did not display the humility of a priest from a poor family being graciously accepted into a well-to-do parish. The second or third question I was asked after an introduction was "What did your father do?"—an obvious attempt to position me socially.

My response was straightforward: he had been in stocks and bonds and then became a corporate executive. I could tell by their expressions that they really didn't believe me. It just was not possible a priest could be from their own social class.

Moreover, many of them did not like my preaching. It was not the first sermon the pastor monitored but one still in the old basement church which led one well-meaning man of the parish to recommend that I try not to preach so smoothly or confidently.

"You're a good preacher, Father, very good. But people don't like it when a young man seems effortlessly good at something. Maybe you should sort of struggle painfully to improve preaching instead of being so self-confidently skillful at it."

Or as Kathleen Connelly was to say many years later, "The first few weeks you got a reputation for being a smart-mouth."

Me: Wrong, Kathleen. Smart-ass.

In CK I experienced for the first time a phenomenon that would occur repeatedly for the rest of my life: I hardly needed to appear before people began to choose up sides. I was intelligent, self-confident (actually I was scared stiff for the first several years, but hid it well), energetic; therefore, I had to be up to something. It didn't take some of the CK people long to figure out what: I had been sent by the cardinal to integrate the neighborhood. Their confidence that the pastor would be able to stop me was not great.

I believed in racial integration and I also believed that Beverly could survive for decades as an integrated neighborhood (a prediction that thirty years later has proved remarkably accurate), but I did not think it was my job to impose integration on the community and certainly had not been assigned to do that.

The dogmatic certainties in the community about me (many from St. Barnabas parishioners who had never met me and never heard me preach) told more about the people who were captured by these certainties than they did about me.

Yet for a confused young priest, it was difficult to understand why so much falsehood and so much hatred would arise when you'd scarcely set foot on the premises.

Another, more amusing and perhaps more typical, dialogue, this time characteristic both of the neighborhood and of the new relationship between the clergy and the laity, was between me and Bob Podesta during my first year at CK.

Podesta: Father, this may seem impudent of me—and it may even be impudent—but I think if you work a little harder and practice, you might be able to sing better at Mass.

Me: Podesta, it isn't impudent. It's just wrong. Like Dick Roache, I'm a mental hummer.

Podesta: Just a little more effort...

Me: Bob, I practiced every day for two years just to get through my First Mass!

Podesta: Practice more.

Bob and his wife, Corrine, one of the smartest women I've ever known, are perhaps my most durable friends from CK days. We still fight about politics. He was head of the Economic Development Administration in Nixon's first term and was fired by the President after reelection because he was too close to too many Democrats. An EDA official called me once about a project and suggested I might want to meet his boss, who, he said, was one of the most skillful political operatives among the Nixon businessmen in Washington. "I was his confessor for ten years," I replied in one of those ripostes you dream about.

Bob voted for Nixon against John Kennedy, which led Jim Casey, voting in his first election, to stop by the rectory and say, "I just went over and canceled Podesta's vote."

My latest jibe is that he couldn't possibly vote against a fellow Italian

(Mario Cuomo) in 1988. He responds that after all he is *half* Irish.

A good investment broker, but wrong about politics and the possibility of improving my singing.

He almost ran for mayor of Chicago once—until his wife asked him what he would do if he won, a Republican mayor against a Democratic city council.

Podesta was not and is not parochial. He was born, I think, with a vision that goes beyond the local, though like me he is firmly rooted in the local. Hence his ability in Washington to deal and become friends with such men as William Fulbright, Hubert Humphrey, and, another great and good friend of mine, Daniel Patrick Moynihan. His breadth of vision, however, was not typical of the community. We were too new in the upper crust of the middle class to have a broad vision.

Racism was a problem only time and the mortality tables would cure. When I confidently and accurately predicted then that the parish would be majority white for at least three decades, the parish racists were not reassured; those who are still alive will not even today, I'm sure, give me any credit for being right. I did not insist on racial matters in my sermons, but I did not avoid them either.

One Sunday I read a quote from the *New York Times* about the shiftlessness of the blacks, which seemed to delight much of the congregation. Then I admitted I had made a mistake. It was from the nineteenth-century *New York Times* and it was not about the blacks but the Irish.

Judge Tom Donovan, sitting in the front pew and hardly a raving integrationist, broke up laughing.

The pastor was furious, but he could hardly take a stand against racial integration.

See what I mean? Smart-ass.

(Lady Wisdom: Sure, you were a terrible man altogether!)

While I was trying to figure out my parish and its people, I began to devour the work of David Riesman, who surely must be rated one of the most influential thinkers of our time. The problems of suburban leisure which concerned him in those days I had only to look out the rectory windows to see confounding the people of my parish. Later, I came to know David well. Like his Harvard colleague Robert Coles, Riesman is a secular saint, a man of immense personal concern and generosity with an unerring instinct for those who need his support and the invariable grace to offer it.

In my work and in the writing that was coming out of it I was relying more and more on sociological, psychological and psychoanalytic writings. Karen Horney, C. Wright Mills, and Erich Fromm were some of the people I devoured most eagerly because they seemed so pertinent to the work I was doing. I also became once more fascinated by American history and American Catholic history in particular, a subject I thought I had left behind in the minor seminary. If it was American my people were becoming, I had to figure out what that meant.

I also became one of the "Catholic action" clergy of the Archdiocese of Chicago. John Egan and Bill Quinn, in particular, but also Leo Mahon, Walter Imbiorski, Jake Kilgallon, Gerry Weber, John Hayes and, indirectly, Reynold Hillenbrand all had a profound influence on my thinking at this time. We met on Sunday evenings in Jake Kilgallon's room at Annunciation rectory, from which flowed a steady stream of innovative projects in the diocese. I was the youngest member of the group and terribly flattered by the attention and interest of the others. We had all said at the seminary that the Christian Family Movement was a great idea and it was too bad the pastors of the diocese would resist it. We could not have been more wrong. By the time we were ordained, CFM had become a worldwide phenomenon.

The Sunday Night Group was the matrix for much creative work. At one session Gerry Weber announced with ponderous Teutonic certainty that he could write a better catechism than any of those currently being produced. Leo Mahon, never one to let an opportunity for a challenge pass by, said (in effect and as I remember it), okay, why don't you write it and stop talking about it? The Weber Kilgallon/Life in Christ catechism series was born that night, a catechetical approach which was half a decade ahead of its time and a surefire market success in the post–Vatican Council Church.

The Sunday Night Group was a precious resource in the Chicago Church. It fell victim to many things, especially a mixture of the Conciliar revolution which went beyond any of our expectations and Monsignor Hillenbrand's dogmatic authoritarianism—a charismatic leader whose wit and brilliance had been dulled by persecution and bad health. There has never been anything like the group since, though I have tried a number of times to reproduce it. In a properly run Archdiocese the cardinal should have such a group meeting in his own parlor one Sunday night a month.

For me, the young and enthusiastic priest, the Sunday-night meeting was the pastoral educational experience I had missed at the seminary. My theoretical visions were concretized. I went back to CK after each meeting—careful to return before the eleven o'clock deadline the pastor and the dead Cardinal Mundelein had imposed on me—with a vast baggage of new ideas with which to experiment (and wonder that "Hilly," so dogmatic and insensitive, could be a charismatic leader to everyone but me, including even George Higgins on his occasional visit from Washington).

They're gone now, dead or in exile or retired or no longer part of my life, all but Leo Mahon, who in the priesthood is something of what Roger and Rita Brown are from my grammar school years—an old friend dramatically rediscovered or perhaps discovered for the first time.

The organizational structures—the so-called "specialized Catholic action movements," YCS, CFM, etc.—which drew the Sunday Night Group together were not unacceptable at Christ the King. To give the pastor his due honor, I did not start CFM in Christ the King, I was assigned to it. He did not fully understand what Hilly and Bill Quinn and Jack Egan were up to, but his instincts said that if they were doing it and some of his people wanted it, then CK would have it.

The problem with CFM was that its members came to see all too clearly what the challenge of the Christian life to risk-taking and generosity, particularly with one another, might mean. They endorsed a positive response to it in principle but were, understandably, frightened of it in practice. I was too naive to be sensitive to their fears and pushed ahead enthusiastically toward fuller and richer community life, instead of giving them time and reassurance when they needed it.

Eventually CFM in Christ the King fell apart, not without deserved blame for the heedlessly enthusiastic young priest.

My closest friends—and strongest dissenters—in CFM were Dick and Gerry Roache. We continued to be friends after CFM collapsed. When Gerry, one of the most remarkably witty and generous women I have ever known, found she was probably going to die from cancer, she summoned me to their home, far now from Beverly, so that I would be around at the end.

I doubt I made any difference in their life or the life of their family. But they made a difference in mine, particularly at the time of Gerry's brave death.

I was well aware even in those days that I was trading on enthusiasm with a thin depth of experience, and that I was making mistakes a more mature or less enthusiastic priest might not make. Many times I said to myself and to others that I was learning at the cost of my own mistakes, which were not hurting me, but might be hurting others.

The response was automatic: How else *do* you learn?

I felt you didn't let interns (which was what I in effect was) do heart surgery.

In retrospect, God's grace and the charity of the people seemed often, though not always, to make up for my mistakes. Some of them have more graceful memories of those years than I do.

Many things may have been forgiven my enthusiasm precisely because I was at least enthusiastic. That, God knows, has not changed.

At Christ the King, then, it was not necessary to talk the pastor into any organization. You name it, we had it. We also had bridge tournaments, a bowling league, parish drama groups and almost every form of parish activity that human ingenuity and/or compulsiveness has imagined. The pastor believed (shrewdly) that you gave the people everything they wanted—just so long as the clergy were back in the rectory by eleven o'clock at night.

Those were heady times. There were new ideas abroad in the Church. Through the Sunday Night Group I was tuned in to these ideas almost as they were evolving. It began to look like the challenge and the opportunity of the "embourgeoisement" of American Catholicism would be easily met. In retrospect our theories were dangerously shallow and our techniques naive. If we had had another generation, we might have been able to work it out, but that time was not given to us.

In retrospect I am appalled at my own audacity. John Egan, who may have had occasion many times since then to regret launching me into orbit, asked me to give a lecture to a study group of priests when I had been ordained about a year and a half. I can't believe he asked me and I can't believe I did it. Given the training I had received and the background I came from, I can't believe I was writing "authoritative" books and articles long before I had completed my fourth year in the priesthood, heedless of the envy such activity might provoke. (It took me a long time to catch on to that.) It would be, I suppose, both the humble and appropriate thing to say that when I reread those books I am impressed with how naive, unsophisticated and youthful their author was. But I won't say that. When I reread my books, my real reaction is that, dammit, I was right!

The Beverly Irish aren't all that great until you consider the alternatives. It is still my parish even twenty years after I was transferred to St. Thomas the Apostle in 1964 (as a favor to both the pastor and myself, it was explained). I'd still be at Christ the King now if I could, doing exactly the work I was doing a quarter century ago and now with a lot more freedom to become acquainted with the adults of the parish, many of whom, in a nice twist, are my former teenagers, now with teenagers of their own (whom they understand no better than they were understood by their own parents). Would I really go back there?

Once more I permit Bill McCready his quote: "I'm afraid he would."

Until then St. Praxides will continue to appear in my novels, a magic parish producing such wondrous characters as Noele Farrell and Blackie Ryan and O'Connor the Cat and Caitlin Murphy and George Quinn the Bean Counter.

The best experiences of my years at Christ the King were with the teenagers—as well, my failures with them are among my deepest regrets. I was warned by the older folks that the teenagers were "spoiled." Their parents, I was told, were trying to give them everything they (the parents) had lacked, and the result was selfish, inconsiderate, rude, and superficial young people.

This was calumny. They were poised, sophisticated, open, friendly, respectful of the clergy, polite, grateful for anything that was done for them. They were also, for the most part, smart, gifted, and, as it turned out, an anxious and troubled group.

I did not perceive until it was too late the most poignant truth about "my" teenagers: their vulnerability and fragility. They were under enormous pressure from their parents to be as successful as they were, and, normally, to do so by following a path toward career and family achievement that their parents had laid out for them even before they were conceived. "We made it because we were tough and could survive hard times," the parents would say. "You're not tough. You don't know the meaning of hard times. You'll never have to sacrifice like we did. You should appreciate how fortunate you are and work even harder so you won't be a disgrace to your family."

But to be comforted and reassured was far more consequential for them than to be challenged. I was correct in seeing them as the lay leaders in the future of the Church. Many of them have gone on to be influential professionals. Many of the women have survived the ambivalences about the role of women in the last twenty years and have not burned out in their early forties.

Nonetheless, an enormous amount of talent and energy and generosity and enthusiasm was ground up in the Christ the King of that era. My teenage friends of the years from 1954 to 1964 are, in a way, a lost generation: too late for the Korean War and a little too early to be part of the radical unrest of the late sixties. Those children of the first generation of newly affluent Chicago Catholics were caught in psychological and cultural minefields which, for most of them, it was impossible to negotiate, especially with an inept and enthusiastic but still insensitive young priest as the navigator.

The world has changed. The present generation of young Catholics in the Chicago area seems to me to be in general blessedly free of selfhatred and low self-esteem. Noele Marie Brigid Farrell in my novel *Lord of the Dance* is an imaginary Christ the King teenager composed from many real-life counterparts. Whatever her problems may be, low selfregard is not one of them.

Michele: She sure sounds like me, Father Greeley. Like totally.

Me: She has red hair, and you're from River Forest, not Beverly.

Michele: *Well,* I did borrow the Shannons' Hobie Cat, didn't I?

Me: And float it all the way down the beach beyond the harbor to Mr. Nie's house. And blame me.

Michele: What else are priests for? Anyway, (giggle) my mother *never* found out, not even when you put that story in the novel.

Despite my problems with the pastor, they were, perhaps, the days of my most uncomplicated happiness. I was a young man utterly involved— head over heels involved—with the kind of work I had wanted to do all my life. I loved every moment of it, the sick calls, the hospital visits, the confessional, the altar-boy practices, teaching in the school, the courts, the athletic contests, Sunday Mass, Holy Week, the Midnight Mass at Christmas, CFM meetings, Baptisms, First Communion, marriage preparation (the pastor always officiated at the wedding, since he was the pastor and "they expect it"), counseling in the rectory offices, wakes, funerals, convert instructions, sermon preparation, the return of college kids at Christmas, throughout the gentle turn of the liturgical year which ran from the opening of school in September to the culmination of parish life—graduation in early June. This was what my life was supposed to be about. I was on a ten-year high—a time missed even today, even a few minutes before I write this paragraph when I meet Tom Havey, an old parishioner, in a Michigan Avenue restaurant and regret once again that I ever left.

I did not leave parish work because I did not like it. On the contrary, I loved it and still do. One of the reasons for spending part of the year at the University of Arizona in Tucson is that I can do weekend parish work there, which I cannot do in Chicago. My intent was always to combine both. That my life did not develop in such a direction was the result of the decisions of others (decisions continuing to this minute) and not my own.

When I began graduate work at the University of Chicago in 1960, I was firmly convinced I could be a parish priest and a scholar (or more precisely a scholarly technician for the changing Church) at the same time. Both . . . and, not either . . . or, as Jack Hotchkin used to say. It was not to be.

Once I almost returned to Beverly to begin again. That too was not to be.

Why don't you give it all up now, an occasional pious (and patronizing) priest correspondent asks, and go back to real priestly work?

The answer is "Because there are too many priests like you who don't see that scholarship, journalism and storytelling are as much priestly work as parish ministry." To give them up now would be a sin of infidelity to my deepest convictions and a violation of the grace of the Spirit which has made possible my work in my third parish—the one Mark Harris says is in my mailbox. I will not go back onto the "reservation," either to keep patronizing and pious colleagues happy or even because I enjoy the work of the parish priest so much and miss it desperately.

Looking back on those years I must admit I charged CK with the same enthusiasm that I charged the lake at Commodore Barry twenty-two years before—and with about the same skill, wisdom, and maturity. All the pent-up creative energies of my twelve years in the seminaries exploded. Here was Paradise Found and I would assault it, capture the Grail and find God by sheer determination and persistence.

Twenty-two years later I am able to smile at that manic young priest. A small smile.

He had a lot to learn about loving. Zeal, enthusiasm and dedication

164

he had aplenty. Sensitivity and tenderness he had yet to learn. The Grail is not found by enthusiasm. Nor the magic princess either. Nor the tender God. Nor Lady Wisdom. One accepts the Gift instead of hunting it down. But if the tender God is not to be overtaken by enthusiasm (because S/He is already present) neither is Lady Wisdom to be found without enthusiasm. The hardworking young priest had half the truth. That was a lot better than not having any of it.

(Lady Wisdom: Some day you'll learn, *maybe*, that I don't have to be pursued. I am nearby, like the girl down the street.)

Most of what I tried at CK failed. A few years ago I would have said everything failed. But, just as the emergence from the mists of time of my grammar school classmates from St. Angela has forced me to rethink that segment of my life, so have hints of the same phenomena from the CK years led me to believe that maybe I have been too hard on myself and on God's grace.

"The greatest gift you gave me and others was creative thought," writes one of those shapes in the mist. "I always knew there were other ways of seeing, but you really brought it out of the closet and gave it credibility, validity, blessed encouragement."

Who, me?

A friend and colleague at the University of Chicago, Arthur Mann, says of this ambition of mine to return to my first love, "You can't go home again!"

The hell I can't.

I can always go back in the world of fiction if not in the world of fact. I can walk down Longwood Drive with Blackie Ryan (CK '58) and his half sisters, Chantal and Trish. I can visit Joe and Mary Kate Murphy in their old house and perhaps encounter Timmy and Pete and their respective young woman persons—Melissa Jean Ryan and Cindasoo McLeod (PO/2d USCG). I can pay my respects to old Ned Ryan and listen to his bittersweet memories of his first wife, Kate Collins the Communist, and share his recollection of the morning of October 22, 1944, off the coast of Samar Island, when a few destroyer and destroyer escort captains, left in an impossible position by inept admirals, chased away the main force of the Imperial Japanese Navy.

I can walk by the Courts and watch Noele Farrell and her father, Pulitzer Prize–winning novelist Danny Farrell, engage in a grudge match of "twenty-one." I can slip into St. Prax's (under Prax's Ax) with George the Bean Counter and Lisa Malone. If it's midnight Mass, maybe I'll encounter Brendan Ryan and his Ciara Kelly or Nick and Cathy Curran or even Mr. and Mrs. Redmond Peter Kane (he the prize-winning columnist, she the recently appointed federal judge). During my Christmas visit to St. Prax's I might bump into those transplanted West Siders from St. Ursula of my own generation, Mike Casey the Cop and Annie Reilly.

Oh, yes. I can go home again.

Whenever I want.

And bring millions of people with me.

CHAPTER 7

Portrait of the Artist: Another View

Thus far I have portrayed Greels/Quixots as a passionate if often inept quester for Lady Wisdom, a romantic if frequently naive pilgrim from Paradise Lost to Paradise Regained, a sometimes amiable, sometimes angry, always enthusiastic innocent with bright dreams and permeable boundaries, and as yet little sensitivity or tenderness.

There is, as you can learn from half the rectories in the country, another view, one that I have promised if not exactly equal time, at least an opportunity to make its case. Let us consider two incidents and one summary indictment.

In the early 1960s I was asked to participate in a scholarly panel at the University of Notre Dame. The session was to be strictly academic—professional papers and commentaries. The chairman of my presentation was an older man whose work had influenced me profoundly, a man for whom I had an enormous respect, and a man I considered my friend. His introduction was ten minutes of pretended comedy. No one laughed, however.

The text for his heavy-handed humor was the clerical-culture put-down that I "wrote too much" and "never had an unpublished thought." The chairman's critique of my work was not internal. He had no substantive or methodological objections to it. His argument was rather, *a priori*, someone who writes as much as Andy does can't possibly be good at it. His closing lines were: "Leave something for the rest of us to worry about, Andy. You don't have to write about everything yourself."

This was before I wrote columns, long before I wrote novels, yet the two themes were set and would recur for the rest of my life: Greeley writes too much and he has never had an unpublished thought. The themes would, however, expand.

In the late seventies, my colleague Teresa Sullivan (now of the University of Texas) was eating supper with five young Jesuit scholars. (Not including, as Terry is quick to remind me, her distinguished student Fran Gillespie, S.J.) My name came up in the conversation and the five Jesuits decided they had better explain to the young woman who and what I was. Terry, who has marvelous skills as a deadpan actress, listened to the five-point indictment:

1. He was not a good sociologist.
2. He was in the priesthood mostly to earn lots of money.
3. He was impossible to work with.
4. He never had an unpublished thought.

5. He despised ordinary priestly work.

Terry, as she admitted later, feeling a little guilt because she had led them on (but not much), let them finish and then replied that:

1. She worked with Greeley and thought him an excellent social scientist.

2. He was generous with his money.

3. She didn't find him impossible to work with at all and neither did the others on the staff at NORC.

4. He had lots of unpublished thoughts and ideas.

5. He liked ordinary priestly work and, in her experience of his performance as a parish priest in the traditional sense of the word, he was good at it.

One might have expected that the young Jebs would have acknowledged that her data were better than theirs. Such would be the case if there was not a myth much stronger than data. However, even though they had not met me and had not read my work and even though Terry had worked with me and knew my work, they attempted to persuade her she was wrong. Then she was put on the defensive and accused of being "one of Greeley's fans."

Money, professional incompetence, personality troubles, contempt for priestly work. It is possible, I think, to subsume the counterportrait under those headings, but to be fair to those who paint it, I will attempt a more extended indictment:

Andy is a writing machine, a gadfly, a man with some talent, but much more ability at production and self-promotion. He is the richest priest in America, the company sociologist of the Catholic church, the house intellectual of the Daley organization. He has serious psychosexual problems and authority hang-ups. Most of his writing is an attempt to work out those problems.

At times he has written good religious or sociological work, but when he turned to novels, he decided to write pornographic trash to make money. The novels are devoid of serious literary quality and theological content; they are prurient, puerile potboilers. They sell because of the novelty of a priest writing novels with sex in them and because they appeal to the kind of readers who buy books because there are naked women on the jackets chewing crucifixes.

Actually his sociology isn't all that good either. Much of his work is done by research assistants and colleagues who don't get credit for their work. His professional reputation is not strong among other sociologists. He uses his data to fight bishops because he is, as everyone knows, broken-hearted that he himself was not made a bishop. His scholarly research is inept and he uses his data to grind his own axes. He's nothing more than a workaholic gadfly, not a serious or important scholar. He doesn't say "Take a letter," he says "Take a book."

His sister is no better than he is. To hire her for your department is to ask for trouble.

He is thin-skinned, vindictive, and has a long and nasty memory. He is impossible to work with and cannot cooperate with other priests, despite his money and success. He has no feeling for what it is like to do real parish work.

His novels cannot be parables, because a parable isn't self-aggrandizing. His novels are self-aggrandizing because he attempts to prove that a priest can "know about sex."

He uses and exploits women in his steamy books. He is an ecclesiastical Harold Robbins.

His first novel was a success because it was a scarcely disguised *roman à clef* about Cardinal Cody. It was also a badly disguised autobiography, an unflattering self-portrait.

Moreover he's a paranoid. Anyone who would make a list of the above accusations is certainly paranoid. Anyone who would claim that a distinguished profeminist theologian tried to get his sister fired from her job (with the unrecognized sister listening) has to be paranoid.

A respected Catholic editor in Pennsylvania knows that he is paranoid because he had to suffer through Andy's paranoia when he was a student of Andy's in summer school.

He can't take criticism and reacts personally to any unfavorable comment on his work.

(Lady Wisdom: What they're saying, boyo, is that they don't like you altogether!)

Have all these things been said? Not really?
Really.

I have left out the names as I have in other chapters of this book, because I do not want to use the memoir as an occasion to get even, but every word has been said on the public record.

The reader now has two portraits to choose from.

CHAPTER
8
You Write Too Much

May it be said,
When I am dead,
His sins were scarlet,
His books were read!

—Belloc

I'd been at Christ the King for a year and a half when a woman named Henriette Mackin, urged on by Father Tom Hosty, who had written for her (and as curate at St. Angela anointed my father during his fatal stroke), appeared at the door of the CK rectory to ask me if I would write regularly for her catechetical magazine *Hightime*. Shortly thereafter, the editor of *Today*, another Catholic high school magazine, asked me to do an occasional article for him. I've never thought of it before, but the two short stories I wrote for Ms. Mackin were the first of my fictional efforts. Even then, I guess, I wanted to tell stories.

The stories for *Today* and *Hightime* were done under an assumed name, "Lawrence Moran," because it was taken for granted that priests did not write and I was still eager to please my pastor. I viewed both sets of articles as transient phenomena, certainly not the sort of thing I would do routinely.

Reflecting on the enthusiasm of Ms. Mackin and her readers for my two short stories, I wonder why I did not settle down somewhere for a course in creative writing. I suppose the answer is that I was too busy with the parish and I knew the pastor would never sit still for my taking any kind of course, much less one in writing. Or perhaps the thought never occurred to me that I could and should write stories. At that time the constraints of the clerical culture seemed so strong I could not imagine surviving as a priest if I wrote fiction or even a lot of nonfiction.

In 1958 at a summer study week that I had organized for kids in the parish at St. Procopius Abbey I was constrained to make a presentation of my own because one of the other speakers hadn't arrived. So I rehashed, without mentioning the name, the material in my St. Praxides memos. Donald Thorman, God be good to him, then the editor of the *Ave Maria*, was present at the lectures, and he asked me after I was finished if I would write it up as an article for his magazine. I did, once more under the nom de plume Lawrence Moran (middle and confirmation names), and he promptly published it. Then George Higgins asked me to make a presentation on the St. Praxides material at the Catholic Social Action Conference, which was in Chicago that year. Some of the social action types were highly offended. Was not the purpose of social action to serve the poor, the Negro (as they were called in those days), and the working class? I didn't much argue with them, but remarked that their approach ruled out perhaps three-quarters of the Catholic population and the enormous resources available of time and money and personnel and energy in that portion of the Catholic population which could be mobilized to deal with the social action problems. Dan Cantwell, a member of the Hillenbrand group and one of the leading social action figures in Chicago, was especially unhappy with me. "Take it up with George," I said. "He asked me to talk on the subject, I talked on it."

Ralph Gorman, editor of *Sign* magazine, was present at the conference and asked me if I might rewrite my presentation as four articles for them. I did and this time, a little more reckless than before, used my own name. I know the pastor read the articles but he never said a word to me about them and I never said a word to him.

Why the nom de plume? Why the fear of clerical culture? And why was the clerical culture so adamantly opposed to a priest writing magazine articles and stories?

The inevitable question would be "How do you find time to do your parish work with that writing crap?"

"I don't sit in front of the television set drinking beer all night long," I would snap back, my shanty Irish mouth getting me into trouble once again. An appropriate clerical culture response would have been, "Well, gosh, Father, I worry about the same problem a lot myself. So I normally do my writing on my day off or on vacation. That way I'm not interfering with my primary responsibilities."

To which the reply would have been, "You ought to be playing golf with your classmates at those times."

I'm kidding?

No way.

Sometime between the visit of Ms. Mackin and the appearance of my articles in *Sign* I must have gone through a psychological transformation. Perhaps the response to my articles convinced me I was on to something meaningful in my reflections about the emergence of well-educated upper-middle-class Catholicism on the city's fringes. What I had to say was worth saying and I would say it, and I would say it, henceforth, under my own name. Although the use of my own name was only a tiny break with clerical culture, the fissure created by my signed articles in Father Gorman's magazine would, with the passage of time, slowly widen so that now it is as broad as the Grand Canyon.

I wrote then mostly to clarify my own thoughts. The St. Praxides memo, despite my pastor's fear, was never intended to be published. I had written it to understand better the circumstances in which I found myself. The same thing is true, I think, of every book since then. It has been, first of all, an exercise in clarification for me. Even, I might say especially, the novels are an exercise in search of understanding. They are primarily stories I tell for myself so that I may understand the era through which I have lived and the impact it has had on my life. If I have written a lot of books, the reason is that I have many, many ideas I need to clarify and many stories I need to tell for myself to create the symbols and templates which interpret my life and shape the reality of that life as it continues.

Philip Scharper, God be good to him, then the senior editor at Sheed & Ward, read the *Sign* articles and wrote asking me to do a book on the same subject. I consulted with some of the priests in the Sunday Night Group and they all said, not without reason, that I was too young to write a book. What did a twenty-seven-year-old priest—going on twenty-eight—know about the world that would justify his writing a book?

The answer, I guess, was nothing. So I wrote Scharper back and politely declined, as did a number of my contemporaries from the seminary who were also scribbling things down on paper when they were asked to write articles or books.

I thought about it for a few months, pondered the problems facing the Church, decided that someone had to put in print the things I felt about the ongoing transformation. Since nobody else seemed to be ready to do it, then I'd better do it myself. (Something like the same line of reasoning was the final step before I began to write novels.) When I had finished the book, Jack Egan talked to his friend Monsignor Ed Burke, the chancellor, who in turn persuaded Cardinal Stritch to give me permission to write. Burke even agreed to an introduction written (by Jake Kilgallon) over his name to indicate Chancery Office approval of my work. Thus appeared *The Church in the Suburbs*. I was anything but a trained social scientist then but I was already reading widely in social science literature.

I gave the pastor a copy of the book with Ed Burke's introduction. He made no comment on it. I suspect that like most of the people in the parish he felt he knew what was in the book and wouldn't like it. I'm sure if he had read it he would have changed his mind, because *The Church in the Suburbs* was an utterly harmless book.

Harmless but, if I do say so myself, accurate. It was a book by a young and enthusiastic man who still lacked sensitivity and nuance and an appreciation for complexity, but he knew what was happening in the

American Church at a time when, if others were aware of the enormous social and cultural change in the Catholic population since the Depression, they weren't setting down what they knew on paper.

With *The Church in the Suburbs* a writer was born, though even to this day, twenty-seven years later, he has a hard time imagining himself as a writer.

Why was permission from the cardinal needed before I published the book? Permission was something quite different from ecclesiastical censorship, a necessary prerequisite before you even would seek out the *nihil obstat* for your work (you needed permission if you were to write articles regularly but they did not require the *nihil obstat* and the *imprimatur* of the bishop). The requirement for permission was part of the old canon law (it has been discarded in the new canon law, though the *imprimatur* is still needed for theology and canon law books—which I never write). I'm not altogether sure that Cardinal Stritch had any idea what he was unleashing when he said "Sure" to Ed Burke and then added what was heresy in those days, even coming from a cardinal: "We need more priests who write."

My fellow priests in the Sunday Night Group were saying exactly the same thing. In a switch from a few months before they enthusiastically supported the book (Leo Mahon had approved of the idea from day one).

Looking back on my first years of writing, I realize the canon law requirement which made self-expression of priests dependent on a bishop's permission was a violation of the fundamental right of a human person which a bishop can neither bestow nor take away. However, it is still useful to cite the permission given and never retracted. It is also useful to add that each of my bishops was placed under enormous pressure to "silence" me.

Shortly after his arrival in Chicago, Cardinal Meyer invited me to visit him at the Chancery Office (discreetly sending word that the purpose of his invitation was positive, not negative). He told me he had read what I had written, enjoyed it, thought it was excellent, and urged me to continue, assuring me I had his complete and total support.

He left it to me to decide what things he should see before they appeared—"either," as he put it, "because someone might raise trouble about them, or because it is something an archbishop can learn from." He quickly added that there were an awful lot of things archbishops had to learn.

175

As one might well imagine, I left the decrepit old gray Chancery Office building that day riding the clouds. This was not an approval the Sunday Night Group had pried out of a lazy (or perhaps very shrewd) cardinal and a cooperative chancellor, this was given by the archbishop himself on his own initiative because he liked my work.

I later found out that when he was preparing to leave Milwaukee, a delegation of older priests called upon him and urged him to "silence" me, expressing grave reservations about whether it was a good thing for a young priest to write—for *any* priest to write. A witness to the conversation told me Meyer's characteristic response: "I won't do that. It wouldn't be fair. I like what he writes. He should keep on writing." As Clete O'Donnell, bishop of Madison, remarked to me after Meyer was dead, "He was a genius, he was honest, and he was a saint. Besides that he wasn't spectacular." We shall not see his like again.

I was most vulnerable in the years between 1958 and 1965, a hesitant young priest who had begun to write and had already stirred up the animosity of clerical culture but had not yet achieved the base and the reputation and the influence and the independence required to stand up to oppressive authority. If Meyer had not supported and encouraged, defended and respected me, I would have been squashed by John Cody on arrival.

Many priests, I think, will feel that Albert Meyer has a lot for which to answer.

Albert Gregory Meyer was an outstanding man: brilliant, devout, stubborn when he needed to be, generous, flexible and, in the security of his office, charming. He stands head and shoulders above all the other archbishops who have presided over the Archdiocese of Chicago. His death at sixty was a personal tragedy for me, a terrible tragedy for the Church in the United States and in the world. For, despite his piety and his loyalty to the Church, Albert Meyer was a fighter. He loved to do battle with the apostolic delegate and with the authorities in Rome. He was one of the great leaders of the Vatican Council before he died, just after the third of the four sessions was over. If he had lived, he would have retired only a few years ago and the shape of the American Church would be very, very different.

Meyer intended, when the Council was over and my postdoctoral education at Chicago was finished, to move me into his household and have me teach him sociology at the supper table.

176

"Fair" was one of Cardinal Meyer's favorite words. The Roman Curia wasn't fair, the Secretariat of the Council wasn't fair in the way it tried to manipulate the votes, the apostolic delegate was not fair, and his fellow priests who wanted to silence me were not fair. Albert Meyer had a rigorous and stubborn sense of justice, a standard from which he would never depart.

His successor, John Cody, alas, did not know what fairness meant.

After Archbishop Cody had been in Chicago for a couple of months, I decided I ought to report to him and describe my work. I brought along the galleys of the first of our Catholic school studies—*The Education of Catholic Americans*—and sat in one of the uncomfortable chairs in a plush, pseudo-nineteenth-century parlor in the cardinal's house. By then everyone in the diocese knew the cardinal would actually see you only after you had waited for an hour and a half, and then he would charge into the room at full speed, attacking you. The secret was to stand up to him, and then he would back off.

He certainly attacked me. His first words were, "They all say you write too much. Do you have permission to write? What do you do with the royalties? Do you still hear confessions on Saturday?" (He didn't, by the way.) "How much money do they pay you at that center? What do you do about censorship of your books? You don't think I'm going to permit you to continue this, do you?"

My hands sweating and my stomach churning, I gave it back as best I could. The cardinal then, as predicted, settled down and began to tell his tall tales. He invited me to stay for supper and turned on his considerable charm. I was not fooled, because Cody already had in the Archdiocese a reputation for dishonesty and trickery. I was happy to escape, finally, from his house. If I had been a drinking man, I would have gone and swallowed six straight shots of scotch to cleanse the dirty taste out of my mouth.

Oh yes, I brought the galleys for *The Education of Catholic Americans* back to my car. Patently, the cardinal was not interested in them.

Cardinal Stritch gave me permission to write for reasons of well-intentioned indifference, Cardinal Meyer defended me from those who wanted me silenced, and Cardinal Cody, in effect, had defined me as an unperson for the rest of his years in Chicago, because the same kind of priests who wanted Meyer to suppress me had also got to him.

However, Cody never tried to silence me. My conflict with him was never a personal one. On the contrary, I flourished during the Cody years even though I was, without realizing it, slipping further and further into the fringes of the diocese. It was a strange quirk of the cardinal's personality that he did not suspend priests or try to silence them, especially when he knew there was a chance they would defy him. He understood instinctively that if you exercise power and that exercise is repudiated, you lose some of your own power; therefore, he conserved his reservoir of power for those cases where he was sure he could constrain obedience and consent. My permission to write, my assignment to academic work, and even my permission to live wherever I wanted went untouched during the Cody days. However, the encouragement and sympathy I had received at just the providential time from Albert Cardinal Meyer vanished, I suppose forever, from my own Archdiocese.

Why do you write so much? Wouldn't it be better if you settled down and just did one or two great books, instead of so many potboilers?

It's a terrible mistake to let the perfect get in the way of the good. If you wait to publish until you have written a great book, you will never publish anything. Great books happen by chance, not by design. The wise writer writes the best he can and leaves it to posterity to decide about greatness. I write what I can, when I can and how I can. Not with quantity as a goal but, as I've said before, to clarify my own thinking and to make available to others, for whatever use it may be to them, these clarifications. I will know that quantity is affecting quality when people stop reading the books and when some fair-minded and honest critic finds notable deficiencies in my work that can be attributed to "writing too much."

Moreover, while I've written many different kinds of books, catechisms, devotional books, books of meditation, popular religion books, I have also produced a fair number of serious works which, if they are not great books, are regarded as the definitive works in the field.

The books my colleagues and I at NORC have done on Catholic education have become the reference manuals for everyone interested in the subject. My book on the papal election of 1978 seems to be in the library of every major newspaper in the world. My *American Catholic: A Social Portrait* is the standard reference volume on the changes in the Catholic population in the last twenty-five years. I know of no other works in the field that are so frequently used as my books *Ethnicity of the United States* and *The American Irish*. My volume on the sociology of the paranormal is the only work in the field, and the work that McCready and I have done on ethnicity and alcoholism has also become standard on that subject. My theories in the sociology of religion (contained in *Religion: A Secular Theory, The Religious Imagination,* and *Religious Indicators 1940–1980*) have been hailed by my professional colleagues as a notable breakthrough in the sociology of religion, and my monograph *The Mary Myth* is, as far as I know, the first book to suggest that Mary's functional role in Catholicism is to reflect the womanliness of God.

I doubt that any of these books would have been improved if they were the only things I had ever written or that even one or two of them might have been improved if I had not written the others. On such sociological and religious work I will take my stand and only listen seriously to the quantity complaint when it comes from those who have read the above-mentioned books and find fault with their quality. It is embarrassing to have to cite these works, but I am doing my best to be honest in this volume, however awkward my honesty may sometimes be.

How do you write so much? That query is sometimes friendly, sometimes unfriendly, but it also merits an answer.

Celibacy and hard work.

And maybe a little talent, too.

As I said earlier in this personal exercise of self-clarification, I am a frantically efficient worker and I surround myself with all the modern technologies that facilitate work—word processors, phone modems, copying machines, dictating machines. Moreover, I have never experienced, in all my life, a writing block nor, even, much hesitation as to how to express what I want to say. I suspect that this is, in substantial part, a genetic matter, for my sister and her children also write and write frequently and write smoothly (or, if you prefer, glibly).

The "compiler," the synthesizer I mentioned before, takes over when I have found, stumbled on, discovered, teased out an idea or a theme for a book. As fast as an Intel 80386 it shifts through images, pictures, hunches, insights, ideas, rearranges them, outlines them, orders them, and provides me with the outline and much of the substance of a book within a few hours. After that it is merely a matter of listening and copying down what this wild, weird, frantically active, ingenious, determined, implacable dimension of me has done.

Both in fiction and nonfiction, once I have the basic insight, the plot line, the "hook" around which to arrange a story (popular religion, sci-

179

entific sociology, or fiction), I can see—in an instant—the beginning and the end of the book and the progress between, and I know what lacunae will be in the book that need to be researched. The actual exercise of word-processing or dictating the volume consists basically of a flexible integrity to that first basic insight.

In fiction, once I have created my characters and figured out what's going to happen to them, I merely sit back and watch them and listen to them and then copy down what they say and do on my word processor or in my dictator. Generally, in analyzing social science data, when I have finally figured out what the data are saying, I simply listen to them and get it down on paper. Often, especially when writing fiction, I am seized by a powerful compulsion to get the material down on paper quickly, partly, I suppose, because I'm afraid of losing it (though that's never really happened), but mostly because the storyline and the characters take possession of me, haunt my dreams, fill up my waking hours, and interfere with everything else I do—they become a burden which must be removed from my back and put on paper before I am free to relax again. After that there comes leisurely revision, greatly facilitated by the word processor. (I used to write, by the way, with a Radio Shack Model 12 with 12-megabyte "Winchester" hard disk. Then my friend Norman Nie bawled me out severely for my depression guilts: "Given the time you spend in front of a screen, not to use the top of the line and the state of the art shows that you have no respect for yourself." Norman is usually wrong when he disagrees with me, but on this occasion he was right. So the final draft of the present book is done with MS/ Word on a Compaq 286 with an IOMEGA Bernoulli Box holding two 10-megabyte cartridges—in addition to the 20-megabyte hard disk in the Compaq—and a Hewlett-Packard Laser Jet Plus Printer. I use Norman's SPSSPC on an IOMEGA cartridge for data analysis, Microsoft Chart for graphics, Keyworks for macro construction, and Turbo Lightning for spelling and thesaurus reference. In case anyone wants to know!)

I know from experience that this description of how I work infuriates many people. You ought to work harder at your writing, they say in the tones of the nun who was mad at me because I didn't suffer like Merton, or pretend to work harder. It shouldn't be that easy.

What can I tell you?

It's not that easy. Writing is hard, exhausting work. At the end of a week of solid writing on a novel (sometimes fourteen and fifteen hours a day) I am a basket case. Books, like babies, are easy to conceive and hard to deliver. A lot of grueling effort goes into my writing, if not much anguish.

The grace is not that I have this weird compiler working frantically away where my brain meets my soul. Everyone does. My special gift is that those thin boundaries of my personality give me more ready access to that dimension of my personality than most others have. Such quick access to the creative process (which does not excuse me from endless revision, by the way: my novels are revised at least ten times before publication, three times before they even go to the editors) has pluses and minuses, it's an asset and a liability, a blessing and a curse.

Sometimes I feel a little guilty, not because of mean-spirited fellow priests but because of generous storyteller colleagues, like Harry Petrakis (the great Chicago Greek-American writer), who applaud my success when in fact the quality and the terrible effort of their output should also have earned them success. That I don't suffer when I write and Harry does seems to me unfair.

"In my father's kingdom there are many mansions, if it were not so I would not have told you."

As I look over a list of my publications, the ones that seem to me to be the most significant are *The Hesitant Pilgrim* (1966), a post-Conciliar plea that the American Church make the most of the opportunities that the two changes—from slum to suburb, from reformation to ecumenical age—have created; *Religion and Career* (1963), my doctoral dissertation, which established definitively that Catholicism was no longer an obstacle to intellectual excellence or to academic career choice; *Life for a Wanderer* (1969); *The Friendship Game* (1970); *The Jesus Myth* (1971), a popular description of the work of scripture scholars on the core of Jesus's message as contained in the parables; *Unsecular Man* (1972), a refutation of the secularization theory of religion; *The New Agenda* and *Sexual Intimacy* (1973), which were post-birth-control-encyclical books that attempt to develop a positive aesthetic of sex, a contribution which seemed to be much more momentous than negative prohibitions; *Ethnicity of the United States* (1974); *The Sociology of the Paranormal* (1975); *Catholic Schools in a Declining Church* (with William McCready and Kathleen McCourd) and *The Communal Catholic* (that kind of Catholic who identifies with the Church but feels no constraint to keep all its rules) (1976); *The American Catholic* (1977); *The Mary Myth* (1977); *Neighborhood* (1977); *Re-*

181

ligion: A Secular Theory; The Religious Imagination; The Making of the Popes; Bottomline Catechism; Nora Maeve and Seby (1976), a children's story; *Women I Have Met* (poems). I also think that my forthcoming book, *Religious Indicators 1940–1980*, will settle definitively a lot of questions in the sociology of religion.

Before the novels, then, those books are the ones on which I would wish to take my stand as a sociologist, a social commentator and a religious thinker.

And, especially, a priest.

None of these books sold well. The Catholic marketplace is diminishing and is, moreover, controlled almost completely by book reviews in *America, Commonweal* and *The National Catholic Reporter,* which have been routinely nasty for the last quarter century. Since it produced a symposium attacking *Religion and Career, Commonweal* has a perfect record of never saying a nice thing about one of my books. Its onetime editor was only too happy to give anonymous quotes—and nasty—about me and my work to the *New York Times.*

I suspect, however, that even good reviews in those journals would not have notably increased sales. Seminarians read less than they used to, priests never read much, and nuns, who were great readers, now spend some of their surplus income on other things, thank God for the increase of their freedom.

(Lady Wisdom: You're welcome.)

I turned to fiction because, in part, I thought I might discover a much larger audience there. Obviously a writer should be satisfied if even two people read his books, but the favorable reaction, from people whose judgment I trust, to my nonfiction led me to believe that the same ideas expressed in fictional garb might be meaningful to many Catholics who had never heard of the Catholic marketplace and who were utterly unaware of the books being sold there.

There had to be a larger and more diffuse market of potential Catholic readers. The proportion of Catholics going to college has doubled in the last quarter century, but, somehow or the other, the sale of books in the Catholic marketplace has declined, in part, one suspects, because you can go through sixteen years of Catholic education and not know there *is* a marketplace and be unaware of such keepers of the gates to the marketplace as *America, Commonweal* and *The National Catholic Reporter.* I will confess, however, that I am astonished

182

by the size of the marketplace in which my novels are gobbled up.

Through all the years of my writing and through such fine editors as the late Philip Scharper, John Delaney, John Cox and Patrick O'Connor, my strongest support in my writing came routinely from the Thomas More Association and its genial and perspicacious president, Daniel J. Herr, something of a reject by the Catholic establishment, too. Mr. Herr and I have a lot of common interests and convictions, and he has suggested more good ideas for books to me than everyone else put together. Moreover, Dan Herr has been a fine reality check on my writing and is one of that committee of people who now read everything I write even before it goes to the publisher (save when he, through the Thomas More Press, is the publisher). A spunky, witty, ingenious man, Dan has made an enormous contribution to the American Church together with his colleagues at Thomas More, a contribution which is frequently unacknowledged because, like me, he fits into no ideological categories. I've learned in recent years that it's relatively easy to have foul-weather friends and difficult to keep fair-weather ones; apparent success turns more people away from you than does apparent failure. One of the highest compliments I can pay to Daniel J. Herr is to say that he is definitely a fair-weather friend and does not resent the success of my novels. Rather, he celebrates them, something that few of my other friends are willing to do.

Mr. Herr and I have similar vices—like loyalty to friends.

Moreover, he has coped with the crises at Thomas More caused by the turbulence of the last two decades of Catholicism with both grace and acumen—and never a hint of self-pity.

He has been a far better friend than many of the priests I thought of as friends and mentors.

For sixteen years I wrote a column in the Catholic press, and for nine of those years I also wrote three columns a week for the secular press (at the instigation of the late Jim Andrews, about whom more later when I talk about *The Making of the Popes*). The Catholic column was hugely successful and, for many, many years, was the most popular column in the Catholic press, both in the number of papers that picked it up and in the number of letters, positive and negative, that were received.

I abandoned the column writing in January of 1983. Archbishop Pio Laghi, the apostolic delegate, had sent secret letters to bishops, warning them of their responsibility about my column (it wasn't mentioned by name, but it was clear whom he had in mind) because I was causing grave scandal among the faithful. Ecclesiastical leaders need the stereotype of the easily scandalized faithful to justify their abuses of power. In fact, empirical evidence demonstrates that the overwhelming majority of the faithful are not scandalized, save by bad sermons, incompetent leadership and, now, financial corruption in the Vatican. When 90 percent of the Catholics in America reject the birth-control teaching, the image of an easily scandalized "simple" laity has become a fiction divorced from reality but essential to morale of ecclesiastical leadership.

It seemed to me that bishops and Catholic editors were looking for excuses to cancel the column after the delegate's secret letter. Since, clearly, the column would eventually be killed, I thought it better for me to end it when it was still the most popular in the country. After the column disappeared I received many letters from people who were saddened by its disappearance. Many of its fans have come up to me after lectures to tell me how much they enjoyed the column and how much they missed it.

Routinely I answer them by saying their complaints are too late and to the wrong person. They should have screamed blue bloody murder to their bishops and their editors when the delegate's campaign to destroy the column was publicly revealed.

June Rosner once commented, "You're a completely different man depending on what you're writing. Unless someone told me, I wouldn't believe that the sociologist and the columnist and the novelist were the same person."

They are not the same person, was my reply, or rather they don't have the same persona. As one moves across thin boundaries, one modifies the face one presents to the world. Why not? They are different crafts and different art forms and my style adjusts to each of these forms.

The most negative reactions I ever received on my columns and the most cancellations by editors came when I would write my annual column on preaching. I would point out that the empirical evidence demonstrated preaching to be the most influential thing priests do and yet that priests are rated poorly by their congregations on the way they do it. I was accused of discouraging priests and of being too harshly critical of their efforts. My response was that I was being far less critical than the people in their congregations and that at any gathering of Catholics a mere mention of homilies assures that complaints on the quality of priestly preaching will be the only subject of conversation for the rest of the night. Speak the truth about everything else, Greels, but not about preaching!

(In the winter of 1986 Frank Devine, the genial editor of the *Chicago Sun-Times*, charmed me into resuming the column. A somewhat younger priest demanded, "Does it give you a good feeling, Greels, to know that Joe wakes up with dread every Sunday morning wondering how you're going to embarrass him this week?"

Who, me?)

In this chapter on writing, I have been as candid as I could be. Marginal, porous, "odd" personality that I was to begin with, my involvement in various kinds of writing has, despite an occasional strong archbishop like Albert Meyer, absolutely destined me to be a square peg. Even many of the Sunday Night Group priests who suggested I go to the university because they thought a writer should have technical competence were none too happy when I began to exercise that technical competence in criticizing some of their pet projects, first in private, then in public.

As I will describe in detail in a later chapter, it was a lot easier to be a priest who wrote in Chicago in the days of Cardinal Stritch, Ed Burke and Albert Gregory Meyer than it is in Chicago of the present. I could do weekend parish work in those days, but in the last two administrations, I cannot. Joseph Bernardin is one of the best bishops in the American Church since the Vatican Council. John Cody was one of the worst. But if you're a square peg that doesn't make any difference.

Why does not the cardinal, who is a nice man and does not personally object to what I write and who would even like to be friends again if it were not for the complainers, treat me the same way Cardinal Cody did?

The answer, I think, is that I have become a massive inkblot for both the left and the right in the American Church. To have offended ideologues of both hues has often seemed to me no mean accomplishment. To stir up incoherent anger in both *Commonweal* and *The Wanderer* is a major achievement. To offend both the Liberation Theologians and the Charismatics takes considerable skills. I know of no one else in the American Catholic Church who has done it so thoroughly—and so effortlessly.

(Lady Wisdom: Sure, you're a terrible man altogether! Half the time your being the target of everyone hurts you, and the other half the time you love it! Even though I made you that way, more or less, don't be after expecting me to get you out of it!)

Portrait of the Artist:
Tertium Quid

Let me make a strong criticism of my own work.

It is arguable that survey sociology fails to capture the nuances of the religious imagination as effectively as I think it has. One might contend that I fail to understand the motivation or to show much sympathy for my fellow priests who were/are less confident in their vocations than I was/am. It could be that the birth-control teaching is more of a problem for the Catholic laity than my data suggest. It is possible I rely too heavily on mathematical sociology. It may be true that it is inappropriate for a priest to write quite as explicitly about sex as I do. (Michele, to her mother: *Well*, thank goodness there isn't any explicit sex in Father Greeley's novels.) Or perhaps my approach to the sacramentality of eroticism does not take sufficiently into account the sensitivities of older laity. Maybe I should ease up on the bishops. After all, they're human too, aren't they? (Don't push me on that one.) Could not one suggest that sex is more important in the life of my characters than it is in the life of ordinary men and women? And is it not true that the sections of my novels which deal with eroticism simply don't ring true? Are not the men in my novels consistently weaker and less appealing than my women? Doesn't *The Cardinal Sins* change genres in the last hundred pages? Don't I spend too much time on the theme of the womanliness of God? Am I not guilty of posing as an expert in too many fields, thus weakening my credibility? Don't I invite trouble by grinding out so many novels so fast? Are not the Ryan clan, for all their charm, too improbable to be true? Was not the narrative in the early stories too linear and the style too flat, utterly devoid of metaphor or atmosphere? Did not the breathless pace of the story limit the possibility of nuance in character development?

Is there not perhaps too much mysticism in my stories? Or too much violence? And don't my women, who admittedly save themselves instead of being saved by men, absorb rather too much pushing around?

I would disagree or agree partly or distinguish in response to those criticisms, but they are all intelligent comments with which it is possible to have responsible dialogue. A few of them have actually been written or spoken by others. Most I have heard only from myself. Yet it seems to me criticisms of that variety are proper, fair and reasonable and deserve to be taken seriously. Such commentary on my work is as rare as the hen's proverbial teeth.

I often think I could do a more professional critique of both my sociology and my storytelling than do any of my clerical-culture assailants.

I know I can do a better critique of my spiritual weaknesses and failings than they can, though perhaps not one nearly so satisfying to their emotional needs.

I make no claim to immunity from criticism, disagreement or attack. Fault can be found with both the techniques of my sociological analysis and the methods and themes of my storytelling. Critics can disagree with me on matters of taste or opinion or judgment or even theological content. Such reactions may be fair or unfair, arguable or unarguable. My protest here is that virtually no one within the boundaries of the clerical culture— or those outside it who absorb its clichés—seems either willing or able to engage in such criticism. There is an absence among Church people of patience and method and precision in responding to my work. That would take too much time. I must be destroyed as soon as possible.

Let me respond briefly to the charges I presented in the chapter before the last one (you really didn't think I'd let them escape without comment, did you?).

What is the content of the statement that someone "never had an unpublished thought"? It's obviously a rhetorical exaggeration. Stripped of its poetry, it says someone writes too much. Both charges then are the same. But what is "too much"? What does it mean? What would not be "too much"? Who defines "too much"?

"Too much" is too vague to have a clearly assigned meaning. It must mean something like "a lot on a lot of subjects." "Greeley has a tremendous output on a lot of subjects" does not seem an unfair summary of the charge. But so summarized, what do I do that is objectionable? Since content or quality is never analyzed in this charge, the objection must be to the sheer fact of a lot of writing on a lot of subjects.

Why is that wrong?

Maybe because he makes us feel we are inferior to him because we are not writing as much as he is. He is a reflection on us. Leave some things for *us* to write about, Andy.

Or maybe it is not fair in the competition for the scarce rewards of praise and income that the clerical culture makes available. The priest who "writes too much" is seen as possessing an unfair advantage. Is there not a risk that we will be cursed as the unproductive fig tree in St. Mark's Gospel?

Suffice it to say that such a reaction to a writer reveals small minds.

As to Terry Sullivan's five young Jesuits, what did you think, wise and gentle reader, when you heard about them? Did her story tell you more about me or about them? Cannot the question legitimately be raised about collective neurosis in such men? They don't know me personally, they are not familiar with my work; where do they get their information? Out of their own personalities. Their refusal to yield to the facts advanced by one who has had excellent opportunity to study the subject matter indicates a prejudice based on deep personality needs. The mechanism at work would be called by a psychiatrist collective projection. The subject has been reduced to an inkblot into which others can project their own fears, frustrations and self-hatred.

You got a better explanation for Professor Sullivan's experience?

Quixots as an inkblot. Stick with that theme.

Jim Coleman, just the other day on the UA campus: Andy, you're an inkblot.

Me: Tell me about it.

Do I like being an inkblot? Of course not. Am I going to practice literary contraception, change my personality and character, wander back onto the reservation so I can stop being an inkblot?

You gotta be kidding.

Now what about the multi-item indictment?

Let me be Irish and answer a question with a question: How does one respond to such charges? How do you prove you're not paranoid or money-hungry or sexually hung-up? Or an incompetent sociologist? Or an inept novelist? Or vindictive? Or difficult to work with? Or frustrated because you always wanted to be a bishop (and put words on paper anyway)?

You can trot out people like Terry who say no, those things aren't true, but is anyone committed to the indictment more likely to believe her than the five young Jesuits?

You can point out your citation index in sociology. But who knows what that is?

You can point to the theological themes in your novels, the favorable reviews, the research on your readers, but does anyone think that such weapons as facts refute a myth?

The difficulty is that those who bring the indictment are never required to prove it. I am required to disprove it, and no evidence of mine will be accepted. Guilty till proven innocent and you can't prove yourself innocent.

And if you're smart you won't try.

Note that none of the items in the indictment pertain to the substance

190

of my work or the methods with which I work. They are all unverifiable attacks on the person of the worker. None address themselves to the contents of my writing. They are all undocumented and undocumentable assaults on the writer's character. They are gratuitous and irrelevant.

Envy is both sickness and sin—sickness because it is rooted in self-contempt and sin because it is one of the cardinal sins, that is, a bent of the personality which is the source of many actual sins. Does the sickness mitigate the malice of the sins which flow from envy? According to the principle I laid down in the beginning of this book, I will neither deprive anyone of moral responsibility nor make judgments about his or her personal conscience. In general it seems to me that self-contempt mitigates the malice of sin. On the other hand, many envious people are like Salieri in *Amadeus*: they know quite well what they are doing, but feel justified in doing it, nonetheless. Remember Salieri threw his crucifix into the fire because God had dared bestow on Mozart talent which Salieri, the self-confessed patron saint of mediocrity, thought belonged by right to him.

Oh yes, about the Catholic editor from Pennsylvania who suffered my paranoia when he was my student in summer school. I have never met the man; he was never a student of mine. As a matter of principle, I have always refused to violate the summer by teaching summer school. So maybe I'm not paranoid after all. Maybe, like the creature in that wonderful poster, I'd be all right if all those paranoids out there would leave me alone.

Why, I often wonder, do people need to be envious? What is the payoff in it?

I suppose many of us need to be envious because other people's success seems to be success denied us; other people's talents, talents which should have been ours; other people's acclaim, acclaim of which we have been cheated; other people's work an intolerable judgment on our own work.

So kill him (as Salieri killed Mozart or thought he did or wished he did).

Sick? Hell yes.

But as common as leaves in autumn. And much less frequently denounced.

The man who is multiply successful and multiply rewarded is a special target for envy, particularly when he is part of the clerical culture. Bad enough that he takes away one success from others; what right has he to take away many? The animosity toward Hans Küng, in my experience of it, is caused by resentment that he is not only an influential theologian, but a successful writer, a popular lecturer, an international celebrity, a guru/folk hero to many, and, not unimportantly, a handsome Teutonic blond.

Can you prove even to yourself that you are not writing sleaze? How do you know that you are not suffering from frustrated ambition? Why are you certain you are not writing novels merely so you can laugh all the way to the bank? How is it possible to be confident you are not difficult to work with? Is it not possible that people read your books out of prurient curiosity and miss the religious themes you say are in them? How can you be sure your basic motivation is not self-publicization? Is it not possible that you are deliberately writing trash to exploit women?

Has any of this ever occurred to me? Indeed yes. You cannot be under sustained attack for years and not often wonder whether, however weird and improbable the things being said about you may sound and however angry you may feel about what seem blatant lies, the enemies may be speaking a grain of truth. The questions are especially troublesome when someone you have thought of as a friend, perhaps for most of your life, either joins the mythmakers or is revealed as allied with them for a long time.

However, there are three reasons why I resist the judgment that the mythmakers may be right.

First of all, some of the components of the myth are so obviously devoid of serious content that their envious origins are patent: never had an unpublished thought, richest priest in America, writes "too much," frustrated bishop.

Second, there are many who do not accept the myth either in its entirety or its components—two skilled feature writers in the *New York Times* (Ed McDowell, Mark Harris), astonishingly a long feature article by Michael Farrell in *The National Catholic Reporter*, a profile by Kevin Klose in the *Washington Post*, a story by Dodie Gust in the *Arizona Star*, a profile on "The MacNeil-Lehrer Report," several scholarly studies of my writing (Charles Fanning and Ingrid Shafer, for example), many secular book review writers (three favorable reviews in a row in the *New York Times Book Review*) including the majority of the reviews outside the Catholic press of *Ascent into Hell*, *Lord of the Dance* (over 80 percent of the reviews of the latter), and *Virgin and Martyr*, between a quarter and a third of the priests in the country, and millions of lay people to judge by both my mail and the research on readers of the novels, some loyal friends like Terry Sullivan who both in private and public give the lie to the myth.

I also reject the myth because of the enormity of its arrogance—the presumption of the mythmakers, most of whom have neither met me nor seriously examined my work, that they know my most inner motives, my most intimate hopes, my deepest vision better than I do. I have a pretty good idea of who I am and what I am about. I know my motives as well as most. I know the nature of my work and its weaknesses as well as its strengths, I know my own faults and spiritual weaknesses with dismaying clarity. This volume is primarily an articulation of my own spiritual development and self-awareness. When my critics inside and outside clerical culture address themselves to the real weakness of my work and the real problems of my soul, I will listen to them.

Professor Ingrid Shafer's study of the reactions of clergy to my novels confirms for me that there is a myth based on prejudice (in the strict sense of that word) about me and my work among the clergy, a prejudice which makes me an "inkblot" that reveals more about those who create the myth than it does about me.

A third of the priests in Professor Shafer's sample of Chicagoans had not read any of my novels. Nonetheless, this third of my fellow diocesans have strong feelings on the subject: 27 percent of them asserted the books were inspired by the love of money and notoriety; 18 percent found them devoid of theological content (even though they hadn't read them); 42 percent thought they were sleazy exploitations of the mass market; 42 percent would discourage their congregation from reading my stories; 64 percent thought the books would cause a loss of respect for the Church; 37 percent (without reading the books, mind you) thought they were slanderous and distorted; and 50 percent denied their essential accuracy. More than a third would not reject the proposition that I should be silenced.

These are not opinions—you can have opinions only about what you know. They are prejudices: judgments made before the fact. Would reading the books change their minds? That is unlikely. Men who have made up their minds so firmly before the fact are unlikely to change their minds afterwards.

What do the priests who have read at least four of my novels—and hence are better qualified than others to have an opinion—think on these matters? Fourteen percent think that the books could cause a loss of respect for the Church. On every other question, *all* of them reject the charges which the nonreaders so vigorously endorse.

And why are you such a made-to-order inkblot, fella?

When a priest who has spent a quarter century in scholarly analysis and trenchant commentary on American Catholicism in transition and has become famous and better paid than most of his fellow priests turns to "stories of God," comedies of grace in which the sacramentality of human sexuality is a major theme, and sells twelve million copies of his books in four years, he becomes one of your all-time favorite, made-to-order inkblots, especially if he has a "strange," "odd," "unusual" personality that makes him look vulnerable.

How do I feel when I experience an assault of *invidia clericalis*?

First of all, I feel revulsion, as if someone has vomited on me in a public place. Then I am embarrassed to be identified even as an adversary with someone who has so little self-esteem as to make such a display of himself/herself in public. Only after these initial reactions do I begin to feel some pain and anger, mostly at those who claim to be my friends and remain silent while I am being assaulted.

One reaction I do *not* have is a feeling of persecution, much less martyrdom. John Krump visits me each summer and "interviews" me for a couple of days, an exhausting and fruitful spiritual exercise. Last summer he asked why I did not take consolation from the fact that I was "configured" with Jesus, who was also attacked falsely and betrayed by friends. While I did not want to deny the value of such a spirituality, I was forced to reply to John that to apply it to myself would have seemed blasphemy. How can you think of yourself as a martyr if you sell three million books a year?

I still have a hard time drawing a line between trusting my fellow humans too much and trusting them not enough. At this stage in my life, however, I do not think it is bitter to be suspicious initially of anyone wearing a Roman collar.

Lately I have begun to experience a new reaction to the myth, a fitting ending to a couple of chapters about "writing too much."

And maybe the first sign of a mature response to the myth.

I'm flattered.

It is no small achievement to have become the most monumental inkblot in the contemporary American Catholic Church. Only someone whose work is far more influential than I thought mine was can possibly have generated so much controversy. Will my work survive, to return to an earlier question? If the durability of a work is to be measured by the amount of hatred it has produced in its own generation—not a bad measure—then, yeah, buster, my work will survive.

Oscar Wilde remarked that caricature is the compliment mediocrity pays to genius. I don't make it into the genius category. I'm talented and I work hard. So caricature, in the priesthood, is the compliment mediocrity pays to talent.

I accept the compliment.

It has been necessary to comment on the "Greeley Myth," rather bluntly outlined to Terry Sullivan by the young Jesuits, because the myth is part of the environment of my life and of my story. To those who know me only through the myth, I have no other response but to say that you should read what I have written, not what those from the clerical culture have written about me.

Now, reader, we have three portraits. Take your pick and read on. You haven't seen anything yet.

The Company Sociologist of the Catholic Church

GOOD HUMOR MAN

White truck turns the corner at four fifteen
Dime in hand we kids tumble down the street
Depression time, but his bell announces spring
Promises the sidewalk feel of summer heat.
Then one year vain wait on budding lawn
A better job? Another corner turned
Smile, bell white suit, sweaty dime—all now gone
Prosperity . . . our childish friendship spurned.
Good Humor trucks have never lost their spell
Entranced once more I dash among the cars
Back on the block with friends I knew so well
I munch my gooey ice cream bars
In every bite of chocolate savoring
The taste of a warm spring day at four fifteen.

The angel who was given charge of supervising in the name of Lady Wisdom the working out of the story of my life did me an enormous favor by nudging me out of the comfortable Catholic cocoon of Christ the King and into the more demanding, more hostile environment of the University of Chicago. I thought I was driving my battered black VW to Hyde Park each morning to learn sociology. I was also, without realizing it, receiving preliminary training for the Catholic world created by the Second Vatican Council, a world in which the comfortable cocoon disappeared for all of us almost overnight.

As a way station on my search for Paradise Lost, the university has never been particularly attractive. The Grail certainly isn't there. And Lady Wisdom turned up only occasionally despite all the divinity schools on or near the premises (maybe she avoided the place even because of the divinity schools!). Unappealing, never the object of a romance like CK, the university has been merely essential.

One Saturday morning in the summer of 1961, as I was finishing my first full year at the university, I stopped by NORC to see if the first run for my doctoral dissertation had come up from the machine room. I was eager to see the extent of Catholic deficiency in graduate school attendance in the 1961 graduates we were studying.

Everyone knew that Catholics were less likely to go on to graduate school. My doctoral challenge was to learn why.

I found a cross-tab (we had machines in those days that cross-tabbed data cards but did not percentage the tabulations). Catholics from the June 1961 class were more likely to attend graduate schools the following autumn than their Protestant classmates. Across the top of the printout, Davis had written, "It looks like Southern Methodist loses this year to Notre Dame!"

It was my first delightful experience of discovering that what everyone knows to be true is not necessarily true. An empiricist by disposition, I was now to become an empiricist by professional skill, an empiricist scholar in the service of the Church.

I had my first "unexpected finding," the first of a series over the last quarter century (the latest being that your picture of God as a mother and a lover affects how you vote in a presidential election) that, along with other forces, would both drive me to the margins of the Church and greatly deepen my Catholic loyalties and religious convictions.

I would be dismissed by a Catholic lay reviewer later as "the company

198

sociologist of the Catholic Church." It was a put-down which would be used still later with devastating effect by my enemies in the University of Chicago administration. It was not in fact true. At the time it was written the Church had never paid a penny for any of my research. It would only fund one project, the disastrous 1970 priest project. I was not the hired hack the reviewer implied.

It would have been closer to the truth to say I *thought* that I was being trained to be the company sociologist of the Church and ended up as the sociologist of American Catholicism (objective genitive, as we used to say in Latin class).

In my early days as a student and faculty member at the University of Chicago and as a full-time parish priest, I was often asked by people from the neighborhood whether the university was causing me any problems of faith. The faculty was a little more discreet. When I received my doctorate, Peter Rossi (finally working up the nerve to call me Andy) asked me in the privacy of his office after the exam whether I had any religious problems during the twenty months that I had worked for the degree.

My response to both my parishioners and to Pete Rossi was the same. My faith was only deepened by my university experience. The faculty, whatever their personal religious convictions were (and some of them were vaguely theistic and religious), did not engage in assaults on religion in the classroom. Moreover, I was now in my early thirties with a pretty clear idea of who I was and what I believed. Unlike a graduate student fresh out of college, I was not an appropriate subject for deracination. My roots were too deeply sunk for them to be yanked up by the academic socialization in graduate school. Moreover, I commuted back and forth from Christ the King to the university, from Beverly to Hyde Park, every day, so I never was part of the graduate school environment in which some people found their religious and moral convictions under assault.

How could one be intelligent and a graduate student and then quickly a staff member at the university and remain an active, practicing Catholic priest?

My answer was that it was easy. I had not come to the sociology department looking either for a faith in which to believe or an academic career. I was merely seeking certain professional skills which I hoped to use in the service of the church.

The priests in the Sunday Night Group, most notably Jack Egan and Bill Quinn, had three years previously, when Cardinal Stritch was still alive, begun campaigning to have me assigned to graduate work. They argued, especially under the influence of George Higgins, that I needed the discipline and the methodology of professional sociological education if I was going to be a commentator, an interpreter and a resource for the diocese and the Church. My own reaction was ambivalent: on the one hand I thought sociology would be an interesting and useful subject; on the other hand I hesitated to leave parish work and Christ the King. In the winter of 1960, at my annual stay at the retreat house in Mundelein, a priest who had been one of the heroes of my seminary years suggested I approach Cardinal Meyer directly. After all, had he not summoned me for a conversation when he had only been in the diocese for a couple of months? Obviously, he respected my work, and, just as obviously, he was a scholar. Should I not make up my own mind whether I wanted graduate school and then, having done so, not rely on go-betweens?

A reasonable enough position, but I finally decided to approach the cardinal on the subject for convoluted reasons.

During the early months of 1960, John McAvoy, one of the finest priests I'd ever known, was dying at Christ the King rectory of Hodgkin's disease. The pastor behaved most peculiarly through this interlude, his conflicts with McAvoy, whom he treated like a newly ordained priest, entangled with McAvoy's declining health. The pastor was firmly convinced that if McAvoy kept regular hours and did not spend much of his time dealing with the problems of people from his previous parishes and didn't receive phone calls from such people at all hours of the night, he would not be sick. The malignancy was partly the result of McAvoy's failure to be the kind of curate the pastor wanted. When the people in the parish took up a collection to pay for Jake McAvoy's hospital bills, the pastor appropriated the money and put it in the parish account, telling Jake he didn't trust him with the money because he knew he would give it away to his friends from the other parishes. "Send me the hospital bills and I'll take care of them," the pastor said in an extraordinary burst of paternalism which astonishes me even today.

McAvoy had more than just lay friends in other parishes. Many of the influential priests who had known him at the cathedral, including Monsignor James Hardiman (now one of the closest things to a saint we Chicago priests possess), who had been Cardinal Stritch's secretary, were

200

furious at the way the pastor had treated Jake, and they more or less moved into the rectory and took over the final moments of his brave life and the days of the wake and funeral, leaving the pastor to sulk unhappily in the background. In the meantime, the parish went on, and, as the pastor said bravely, "we're just going to have to double up to take care of the work Jake can't do." What that meant was that I was to do Jake's work and my own because no one would expect the pastor to take on any extra responsibilities. With two curates in those days, Christ the King might have been overstaffed, but with one curate and one nonworking pastor, it was decidedly understaffed. I felt health and sanity slipping from my grasp. The pastor stubbornly refused to remind the Chancery Office at the time of diocesan appointments in June that he was now under-staffed. "The cardinal knows we've lost a priest," he said confidently. "He will take care of us."

The cardinal respected and understood us even if Jake's friends did not. Right?

The cardinal, new in the diocese, and burdened with enormous administrative responsibilities and with intense preparations for the up-coming Vatican Council, had no idea about the staffing of any particular parish. We didn't get the new curate when the assignments were made. I was faced with a summer and a fall and a winter of doing all the work in the parish because the pastor was still sulking at the way he had been shunted aside when Jake died. I did not relish the thought of being the scapegoat for his hurt feelings. If he didn't remind the cardinal that we needed another priest, *I* would. That decision was the first fully mature choice I had made since I went to Mundelein thirteen years before.

I called the cardinal's secretary and asked for an appointment. I told him that I wanted to bring in galleys of my new book, *Strangers in the House*. The appointment was set for mid-July. So I drove in from one of the last class vacations at Lake Geneva (it was the summer I learned to water-ski).

The cardinal was relaxed and friendly, much easier to talk to than my pastor. He liked me, or to be more precise, he found me amusing.

"Is there anything I can do for you, Father Greeley?" he asked mildly after he had glanced at the manuscript of *Strangers in the House* and promised to read it soon.

"There has been some discussion, Your Eminence, of my attending graduate school. The argument is that I need the professionalism of scholarly training if I am to continue this sort of writing."

"That's an excellent idea." He glanced up alertly from his notepad. "I wish I had enough men to send you away to school. . . . Tell me, could you stay in Chicago, attend Loyola perhaps?"

He was not a man to waste time.

"Or the University of Chicago."

"That's closer to Christ the King, isn't it?" He made a small note.

"Yes," I gulped. For reasons of geography a feud of many decades with the university was swept away and a lifetime was decided.

"You think you could continue at Christ the King and pursue graduate work in, say, sociology?"

It was like having one's cake and eating it too. "Well," I said tentatively, "as you remember, Father McAvoy died and he hasn't been replaced."

"I guess I didn't remember that," the cardinal said, thus disproving my pastor's notion of the cardinal's omniscience. "I'm not sure whether I have anyone to replace him with." He tapped the desk again.

"There's always Father Hotchkin," I said. Jack, who was in the first class of Chicago priests of which two had been sent to Rome, was overlooked in the assignments. It had apparently been an unshakable law that there was only one North American College priest to be assigned. He'd spent the summer on the family farm in Tinley Park, wondering whether he was a permanent nonperson.

The cardinal made another cryptic note on his pad, with the little smile he always used when we talked, a smile which seemed to say, "We understand one another, don't we, Father Greeley?"

"You believe in doing your homework, don't you, Father?"

It was settled in ten minutes.

Apparently the cardinal promptly told Ed Burke that I was going to graduate school. Burke, never one to keep a secret for long, began to tell others. When I returned to the parish after my vacation, the pastor was incensed.

"Why didn't you tell me you were going to graduate school?" he thundered.

"I don't know that I am."

"Ed Burke is telling people the cardinal is sending you to graduate school."

"The cardinal didn't tell me that." He had not indicated any decision at the end of our conversation. I didn't know him well enough yet to understand his administrative style.

"Ed Burke says it, so it must be true." He turned away in disgust. "They tell me," he added as though it were an afterthought, "that they're sending a newly ordained Roman. Some fella named Hotchkin."

"No kidding."

"Got him, Jake," I murmured in a prayer of gratitude to McAvoy, who had desperately wanted me to go to graduate school and whose good spirit had, I was convinced, hovered over the whole enterprise.

That he was getting a second curate he did not expect was no consolation to the pastor. Losing one curate to a part-time graduate school assignment was a blow to his prestige, a blow against which his Wednesday-night bridge club of clerical cronies would urge him to protest for the next four years.

I applied to both Loyola and the University of Chicago. Loyola accepted me six months later. Phil Hauser, then the chairman of the University of Chicago, after a call from Jack Egan, accepted me on the spot. Almost before I knew it I was plunged into the world of the big-time academy, a world of, as it seemed to me, total confusion.

I didn't understand what anyone was saying, students or faculty. They seemed to speak a foreign language. My first class, at eight-thirty in the morning, was an introductory social psychology class taught by Jim Davis and Elihu Katz, two bright, witty, and attractive assistant professors. They were not particularly scary. But the students, many of them undergrads, asked questions whose content escaped me completely. You must be pretty dumb, I told myself, to be outclassed by undergraduates.

That class was followed by another course in which the professor was treated with infinite respect by everyone, though it seemed to me that he was around the bend completely. (It turned out later that he was.)

Then a stat class from Harrison White, who called me Mr. Greeley (the proper UC title for everyone in the classroom) in class and Father Greeley outside. "It must be a few years since you studied math," he remarked helpfully.

"Half a lifetime," I responded. "My last course was when I was sixteen."

"You'll do okay," he insisted.

I was not so sure, but I loved every second of the intellectual challenge. In the afternoon it was back to the different and more familiar challenge of Christ the King. I still loved that too.

The turning point came at midquarter. Davis and Katz required in our open-book exam that we analyze Shakespeare's *Romeo and Juliet* in terms of the social psychology we had learned in the course. I focused on Friar Laurence's role as a dissonance producer.

"Wonderful." Jim grinned as he gave me back my paper. "You must have produced a fair amount of dissonance in your life?"

"Participant observation," I murmured, noting with tremendous relief the A on the top of the paper, the most decisive grade I'd ever received. I assumed the young professors were both easy graders and most of us had received an A.

Then Elihu put the grade distribution on the board. Of the eighty-six of us in the course, six had received an A.

With the confidence that came from that grade, I sailed through graduate school. The only grade I received, besides a P in pass/fail courses, was an A. Even in statistics.

Occasionally when I see Davis or White I argue that I deserved the A from Jim and Elihu (now the director of Israeli state radio) but Harrison's A was a pure gift.

"We were afraid you'd put a curse on us," Jim insists.

After class that day he offered me a job at NORC. I told him I already had a job.

White, now calling me Andy outside of class, began to push hard for me to cut through the ritual and finish my degree work, especially since (foolishly) I thought the cardinal would give me only a year of graduate school. (I could have spent ten for all he cared, as long as I acquired the necessary skills.)

"Take the prelims in March and finish your M.A. by June," White insisted. (Twenty-five years later White and I are together again at Arizona where he became Department Head in 1986.)

Under his and Everett Hughes's direction I began an M.A. which I think even today exhausts the literature on the sociology of the country club. My subject was the peaceful self-segregation of Catholics and Protestants in an affluent quasi-suburban community like Beverly. My ultimate data were to be found in the country club's starting sheets. In the delicately balanced country club membership (half Protestant, half Catholic) both groups overchose as golf partners members of their own religious community by a rate of 11 to 7. Golf was not the great equalizer. Even with the ecumenical age upon us, Protestants and Catholics in Beverly lived behind benign and invisible walls, not fighting with one another and not noticing one another either.

On Sunday afternoons there would be a Catholic softball game on one corner of the public school playground and a "public" softball game on the other. Overlapping outfielders would carefully stay out of each other's way. Otherwise each game was invisible to the other.

Many years later John Larkin, my water-skiing precinct captain, asked if I minded if "Lance and Heidi" joined us on a ski venture at Pine Lake. Course not. A skier is a skier. Besides, Heidi was already a legend at Grand Beach, her name almost a common noun among little kids, a synonym for "lifeguard." She is not exactly like O'Connor the Cat, the fictional lifeguard in my stories. Yet it would not be an exaggeration to say of her as Blackie says of the Cat that she maintains order and safety with the same efficiency as that practiced by Ivan the Terrible (and considerably more charm).

Not long thereafter I was invited to dinner at the Hornaday house at the other end of the beach—"down by the mayor's" (in Grand Beach there is only one mayor, even if he has been dead for ten years). Their parents were quite properly curious about the strange priest from down the beach who was water-skiing with their kids. I assumed the Hornadays were Catholic because everybody in Grand Beach was Catholic but, nonetheless, the name being clearly non-Celtic, I made inquiries, just to be certain (a good empiricist always scouts the environment beforehand). Michele: "Of *course*, Father Greeley, they're Catholics. Heidi comes to Mass all the time."

For once in her life (probably the only time so far) Michele was *wrong*, like totally. Further investigation revealed that the Hornadays were Methodists. I brought a bottle of wine to the supper, nevertheless, and assured the whole family that if I'd known their kids were Protestant, I would never have taken them water-skiing. Bob Hornaday laughed and said that twenty years ago such a comment might be far more serious than today. Then he told me that both he and his wife had grown up in Beverly when I was a teenage priest and were utterly unaware of my existence, knowing Christ the King only as a modern church, most of whose kids went to Catholic schools and "kept to themselves." On the other side of the great divide, there was no more understanding than there was on our side.

Well, I drafted Heidi to do the diagram for my first mystery story,

Happy Are the Meek, and more recently for *God Game*, and they still water-ski with me, occasionally bringing friends along whom they promptly identify as Catholics, just so I will know what the environment is like!

Bob Hornaday insists that his kids refuse to believe that white Protestants are a majority in the United States!

In the human condition there is occasionally a little improvement. As Tom Fallers, one of the great saints of the University of Chicago community, once remarked, "Some things are so intimately important to us that we either laugh at them or fight over them. It is better to laugh."

By the end of the spring of 1961, I had passed the prelims, obtained my master's, and looked forward to two more years of graduate work. Again, Harrison White intervened. "That's ridiculous," he said. "Take five classes a quarter and go over to NORC and see if Davis has any work for you from which you can draw your Ph.D."

So I went over to NORC and asked Jim if he needed somebody to analyze something in the sociology of religion. "Funny you should mention that," he said, in his little cubbyhole in an old two-flat converted into a research center. "We're doing this study of career plans of college students and we need somebody to analyze the influence of religion. We'll find you a chair and a desk somewhere and go to work. Should we pay you?"

"Certainly not!" I insisted.

Later Pete Rossi, the director of NORC, would explain that he had to pay me in order to write overhead charges off against my salary. "We have to pay you so we won't lose money," Pete said with a crazy grin. "You don't understand that, but don't worry about it."

So my fall from grace began.

I checked around with various Catholics in education and asked what they thought would be a good focus for my Ph.D. research. We would have thirty thousand June 1961 college graduates with all kinds of information about their education and their career plans. Bill McManus, who was superintendent of Catholic schools in the Archdiocese at the time (and then and now a loyal ally), said, "Find out, for the love of God, why our kids don't go to graduate school."

There was a substantial literature, much of it commissioned by the Catholic Commission on Intellectual and Cultural Affairs, recording the anti-intellectualism of Catholics and noting their absence from the higher

206

reaches of the academy. Monsignor John Tracy Ellis, Professor Thomas O'Day, Professor John Donovan and a host of others had written extensively on the subject, and Gerhard Lenski, in a book that had just appeared and created considerable stir called *The Religious Factor*, had repeated this finding (though it seemed to me his research was weak because it was confined to Detroit and because he did not distinguish among ethnic groups and did not take into account the immigrant status of many Catholics). Nonetheless, I drew up a proposal of some eighteen hypotheses to explain why young Catholics were not choosing academic careers, the principal thesis being that the explanation could be found in immigration and ethnicity, that among third- and fourth-generation Americans, there would be little or no difference in graduate school attendance and the choice of academic careers.

Then came Jim Davis's Southern Methodist/Notre Dame game.

Despite what everyone knew, Catholics in 1961 were *more* likely to go to graduate school and more likely to choose academic careers than white Protestants. All the hypotheses of my dissertation collapsed, but now I was in the remarkably strategic position of having to explain why the conventional wisdom about Catholics and intellectualism was so powerful. Eventually I was able to point out that the Catholic population had gone through an enormous social change since the end of the Second World War and that graduate school attendance was not the result of any new intellectualism among Catholics, just as graduate school non-attendance was not the result of anti-intellectualism before. It had simply required a couple of generations in America and some affluence before graduate school became a possibility, but now Catholics had the money and the experience in America and they were going to graduate school and on to academic careers in large numbers.

The second year at Chicago, the autumn of 1961 and the spring of 1962, were devoted to writing my dissertation and to finishing the course work. Jim Davis said to me, "I don't want a long dissertation, I only want about a hundred pages plus tables."

Two weeks later, God forgive me for it, I appeared in his office with 101 pages of text and the tables. Jim looked at the stack of paper in astonishment. "What's that?" he exclaimed.

"One hundred and one pages plus tables." I must have been grinning wickedly. "You don't have to read the one hundred and first page if you don't want to."

Davis picked up the stack of papers. "You're the first one who ever believed me. I don't know what to make of you. When do you figure you're going to graduate?"

"In June," I said, now exuding confidence.

"Three years—that's pretty quick," Davis agreed.

"Two years," I responded.

"A record for the course." Jim slid the dissertation into his briefcase. "I hope they don't send any more priests like you, not right away."

Now I am less than enchanted with my record. Even by my own standards, I raced too rapidly through graduate school. My style of work leads me to turn in term papers three weeks into the quarter and do dissertations before courses are completed (I once walked out of a ninety-question history exam in my second year at Quigley after nine minutes—ten questions a minute, as the teacher remarked). There is nothing wrong with this approach, so long as you learn what you're about in the process. But my pace was foolishly hectic. I did not have the latitude to think and reflect and to play with methods and ideas. Even then, however, I concluded that sociology should be concerned not with elaborating *a priori* (and frequently Middle European) theories but rather with formalizing at a more general level the understanding of "how things work" and "how to get things done" which we call "street smarts" and which is to be found especially in cops, precinct captains, and good parish priests.

Only a few sociologists agree with me. For an allegedly empirical discipline sociology has strongly resisted learning from those who have learned empirically how society works. My friend Jim Coleman is a notable and brilliant exception.

Rossi wanted me to stay on at NORC for a postdoctoral. The cardinal was busy at the Council and thought it an "excellent idea." My pastor, whose approval was not needed, ungraciously said he supposed it was all right. (I volunteered to return to Saturday-afternoon confessions, to ease the blow to his prestige. He accepted.) The department, I would learn later, was willing to appoint me as a lecturer but not as an assistant professor. "I could no more support his appointment," one of them told Pete, "than I could the appointment of a card-carrying Communist. The Church will dictate the results of his research."

One's real training in scholarship begins after the doctorate. At NORC I learned slowly and carefully the tricks of my trade, the folk wisdom of research design, theoretical orientation, sample creation, methods and styles of analysis. One did not begin a project without a mental and usually an actual design of the key tables which would solve the intellectual question which underpinned the project. While my later debates with other priests about social research focused on the question of sampling (they arguing that probability samples were not required and my contending that without random samples, one does not have social science), in fact the disputes were mostly over design. I learned at NORC that you have to be testing verifiable or falsifiable hypotheses before you begin to collect data. My priestly adversaries could never quite comprehend this point. They asked scattershot questions and made up their designs for analysis *post factum*. Even with good samples, such methods won't work. We have computer programs for analysis, they would reply.

A computer is no substitute for sociological intelligence or imagination, I would insist. It can only answer the questions you ask it.

The issue has never been resolved. The other side assumes that my training at NORC is a luxury at best and not a necessity. I assume there is a right way and a wrong way to do social research. The sociological profession thinks so too, but not being part of the profession, my Catholic critics can easily dismiss it.

Everyone can be his own surgeon, engineer, architect, and lawyer too. Right?

Even today, the little bit of "Catholic" social research which is going on dismisses concern about sample selection and study design as "Greeley sociology." Actually it is sociology as it is practiced *everywhere*, sociology as you have to understand it to get through graduate school.

During the last year, however, there has been some shift. While poorly executed research is still material for PR hype from a certain Catholic university, two crucial appointments suggest that the ethos has changed and that professional competence is once more valued. Fran Gillespie, a Jesuit student of Terry Sullivan, has been appointed director of the Center for Applied Research in the Apostolate (CARA), and Jim Mahoney has been made the director of research in the diocese of Paterson, New Jersey. Both are able and competent and will not be intimidated by the NORC colossus (which we only seem from a distance, a great distance) and hence will be able to cooperate with us instead of having to put us down.

• • •

I learned three things from the University of Chicago which have been essential to me in the course of my life and my priesthood since then— in addition to the technical skills I acquired.

First of all, I learned there was a place in the world where talent was not held against you. Unlike the Church, the academy respected and encouraged intellectual ability. (So long as you didn't do a lot of other things too.)

Second, I learned that I was as good at sociology as any graduate student in the course and as good as some of the people who taught me. I could make it in the big world beyond the Church. The university was a testing time for me, an interlude in my life in which I could define pretty clearly what the limits of my abilities were, what I could and what I could not do well. I understood, then, that while I had no particular desire to be an academic, I could be a good one.

Third, I learned that my religious convictions could only be reinforced by exposure to the secular world. While many priests viewed the secular first as an enormous threat and then as an enormous attraction (many priests and nuns who came after me would discard their distinctive dress in order that they could be like "everyone else"), I discovered that the secular world was fascinated by a priest and was no particular threat to his religion or his morality so long as he knew who he was and where he stood. In the process, I discovered that I knew both these things.

I matured greatly as a priest and a human being in my years at the university from 1960 to my departure from Christ the King in 1964. I even began to learn a little bit more about sensitivity, the tender self. In CK, the married women were older than I was and the teenagers younger. Moreover, the relations with a priest were highly stylized, since the pastor kept us away from the adults and since I was wary of my emotional attraction towards the teenage girls. And also wary of the pastor's suspicions about those emotions. (When someone asked me later whether I was surprised that Tom Merton would fall in love with a student nurse, I replied that I was not surprised. If I had been locked up in a monastery for years and was cared for in the hospital by a kind and intelligent young woman, I could see the same thing happening easily. Any priest who cannot imagine that is without hormones.) In the university the convoluted structures of CK parish life did not exist. I discovered that I could relate to women easily and that, astonishingly, they seemed to like me.

210

I'm still kind of astonished about that.

It was one of the great graces of my life to be challenged outside the traditional clerical environment before that environment was swept away by the tornados of change that howled through American Catholicism during the late 1960s after the Council was over (a time of euphoria and confusion which I tried to chronicle fictionally in my book *Virgin and Martyr*). I was ready for change because I had already experienced it. I had perspective on the collapse of the house of immigrant Catholicism because I had been outside of it for half a decade before it fell. For me the changes of the sixties were slower, more gradual, and more supported by personal intellectual development and expansion.

Dear God in heaven, how fortunate I was!

In the late sixties I watched with a mixture of dismay and fascination what was happening to my fellow priests and to religious women. I was troubled by their sufferings and anxious to help in any way I could, but it was not my experience. My personal crisis, more gracious and benign and enjoyable, had begun in September of 1960, and was completed when Cardinal Meyer, on his deathbed, released me from parish work in the spring of 1965. My religious crisis—the word overstates the reality—was a crisis of growth, a benign and rewarding phase of my life.

I was a priest, a Catholic, a skilled researcher (not yet ready to use the word "scholar") in service of the Church. I would later expand that notion to define "service of the Church" much more broadly, since the institution didn't need or didn't want my technical skills.

Even in the middle sixties, I was beginning to comprehend, with inexcusable slowness, that my hard-earned and treasured professional skills might not be all that welcome to the Church to which I was offering them. While professional competence was being celebrated as a highly desirable goal in all the Catholic journals, the exercise of professional competence on a dearly held myth would be thoroughly unacceptable.

Naif that I was, I had presumed that my finding about Catholics going to graduate school and choosing academic careers would be the cause of considerable enthusiasm in the Catholic community. Exactly the opposite was the case. *Commonweal* ran a symposium attacking my findings. One professor called me a naive empiricist; one of the *Commonweal* editors suggested I was an "optimist" and wanted to be a bishop; still others attacked the sample design of our project. James Trent wrote a whole book to prove that Catholics were still anti-intellectual, the basic thesis of which was that NORC's sampling techniques were deficient. All his book revealed, however, was that he didn't understand multi-stage sampling. A subsequent replication of my project by Michael Schiltz, with a completely different sample, produced exactly the same findings. Lenski's response in a footnote to the paperback of *The Religious Factor* was to suggest that these young Catholics would shortly drop out of graduate school because they didn't have the psychological strength or the free and spontaneous intellects to survive.

The battle raged on for many, many years. Finally, however, in the late 1970s, two Canadian scholars reviewing the literature concluded that the NORC findings were basically correct—that there were no more obstacles to intellectualism in the American Catholic population than there were among Protestants. However, they added that the Catholic Church as an institution had not caught up with the Catholic population in its respect for serious intellectual pursuits. With neither finding could I possibly disagree.

The evidence for my conclusions in *Religion and Career* was unassailable. Those who assailed it, often on the grounds that I was refuting Monsignor John Tracy Ellis's historical work, simply had too much emotional investment in the myth of the anti-intellectualism of the Catholic population (on whom they could look down snobbishly) to concede the possibility that professional research could refute their myth. Therefore, my research had to be unprofessional and I had to have secret motives such as "optimism" or ambition to be a bishop. They paid no attention to my statement that I was not refuting Monsignor Ellis but describing an entirely different era. The data in his report did not go beyond 1950. Sometime between 1950 and 1961, I argued, American Catholicism had undergone a tremendous transformation.

The Greeley Myth was born.

Commonweal never forgave me. For *Commonweal* feeds on the self-pitying snobbery of a would-be Catholic intelligentsia that revels in its rejection by the leadership of the Church and by the ordinary "dumb" laity. The journal's principal function is to reinforce the feeling of intellectual superiority over the rest of the laity and the Church leadership. (Your typical "*Commonweal* Catholic" is smarter than your typical bishop, which does not mean that s/he would make a better bishop.) My research suggested that their self-image of a despised elite was in danger. Moreover here I was, a virtually unknown young priest already on the staff of a great university and presuming to disagree with one of their folk heroes, John Tracy Ellis.

With the years I came to realize that the *Commonweal* crowd were intellectual crooks and elitist poseurs. In the early sixties I was shocked that a journal which I had read eagerly every week and for which I had a deep respect would clobber my motivation and my character because of my factual findings.

The fact that Catholics are no longer the least-educated component of the white population (the ratio of Catholic college attendance to white Protestant college attendance is now 1.4:1—Catholics are almost half again as likely to attend college as white Protestants) and are entering academic careers is now part of the conventional wisdom. It proceeded from what everybody knew couldn't be true to what everybody knows as self-evident, with precious little gratitude to my colleagues and myself for our discovering the phenomenon and insisting on it for twenty years. The secular academic world, I learned, would accept as true something that was demonstrably true from the empirical evidence, but the world of Catholic "liberal intellectuals" would instantly reject sociological evidence that ran counter to their mythology.

It was not a fight that I would walk away from. For the liberals and the *Commonweal* crowd were not liberals but rigid ideologues. Later I would also discover the university could be rigidly ideological too. The Church has no monopoly on not living up to its principles.

Much of the talk of professionalism in the early and middle sixties turned out to be phony. Everyone in the Church wanted the "objective truth" from me, but against someone else. No one wanted his own assumptions challenged. The bishops did not want to know that the birth-control encyclical had been rejected by four-fifths of the clergy and the laity and that the crisis in the Church was the result of that decision and not the Council. Priests did not want to know that the laity gave them poor ratings on their sermons. *Commonweal* did not want to hear about the emergence of a new generation of Catholic intellectuals. Religious educators did not want to hear that the CCD programs were an abject failure. Amateur clerical researchers did not want to hear that their work was amateurism.

I would have no problem if I only told a little less unvarnished truth.

I was in those days totally insensitive to this dimension of the clerical code of behavior. That insensitivity led to the slow deterioration of my

213

relationship with Jack Egan, to whom, as this book has already made clear, I owed many and great debts. My criticism of the work of others, Jack kept telling me, was hurting the feelings of "nice guys" and earning me a reputation for being difficult.

All I was doing, I would reply, was telling the truth. You sent me to graduate school for professional training—do you want me to deny professional standards?

He argued that I should encourage others instead of criticizing them and hurting their feelings. They were "good men" and fellow priests.

Their work is sloppy, I would answer. Poor design, worthless samples, inept analysis. Any scholar would make the same judgment.

You're not a scholar, you're a fellow priest.

So the "nice guys" would come see me or call me on the phone, following Egan's advice that we should "get to know one another." I felt helpless in such situations. I was supposed to say that, well, I suppose your work has *some* validity; samples did not always have to be random. That's how one priest should react to another, humbly and sympathetically and "nicely."

I was not rude to any of them. Nor contemptuous, nor arrogant. I would chat pleasantly, listen sympathetically, nod politely, reinforce their occasional insight. Still, when push came to shove, I felt I had no choice but to speak the truth: you might find some use for the results of your research, but if the samples are not probability samples, you cannot in the name of social science generalize to the population.

You might as well listen to voices in the night or hold your finger up in the wind and sniff the breezes. Or read entrails or go to a cocktail party, or seek out a witch.

Actually I never *said* any of the things in the last paragraph. I merely thought them. However, they were true.

They could not complain that I was not personally nice to them or that I "hurt their feelings" during the conversation. I can play passive/aggressive nice guy stylishly if I have to.

However, they left or hung up knowing what I thought: their research did not measure up to any of the standards I had to honor.

So they went away convinced that not only was I not a nice guy, I was "difficult to work with" as well. Only Phil Murnion of New York gritted his teeth and said, in effect, "You're right."

Similarly, priest graduate students bluntly refused to enter into apprentice relationships with me. We were equals in the priesthood, were we not? Therefore we must be research equals. By definition I had no skill or craft or insight from which they could learn. Okay. But you only learn a craft—and social research *is* a craft—by apprenticing yourself to someone else. I was an apprentice to Rossi and Davis. I am even now an apprentice to Michael Hout, who is a quarter century younger than I, as I try to learn log linear model fitting. There's no disgrace, no loss of dignity, no servility in such a relationship. But priests, for the most part, will not establish it with other priests.

Sadly Egan began to agree that I was "difficult to work with." Subsequently he said it on the record to the *Wall Street Journal*. He wanted me to be a professional in every relationship except with my fellow priests. To them I was supposed to be the good guy who encouraged unprofessional amateurism.

Sorry, Jack, there are no exemptions, no clerical discounts.

A few years ago Cardinal John Dearden told a mutual friend that he felt bad about what happened to me. "Cody wouldn't let us use Andy at the hierarchical level. And X [a social action guru/administrator] is too threatened by his intelligence and skill. Hence Andy is lost to the institutional Church, maybe forever."

X, be it noted, is short on both social science competence and understanding of traditional Catholic social theory and long on ideological fervor—pacifism and watered-down Marxism. I once asked Joe Bernardin when I thought we were friends why he put up with someone whose competence he had admitted to me was minimal. "We can contain him," was his reply. I didn't realize that I, too, was being contained.

Dearden was not about to do anything but lament this phenomenon (maybe he felt he *couldn't* do anything). He was honest about the causes of it. Unlike Egan he did not try to kid himself or anyone else.

In the middle sixties I thought that advice on social policy (not decision-making—any administrator or bishop who lets his experts make decisions is criminally insane) in the Church in the years ahead would be offered by professionally trained pragmatists like me. But the Church would change under the impact of post-Conciliar trauma and anti-Vietnam demonstrations. The future would not be in the hands of skilled pragmatists but in the hands of romantic, ideological amateurs—who were nice guys.

To be fair to Egan, we came at the problems of the Church in the

215

sixties and the seventies from different perspectives. He was committed to working with priests (and nuns), and that meant working within the constraints of clerical culture. In his early days as a priest it was precisely his skills at manipulating (in the good sense of the word) clerical culture which enabled him to obtain acceptance for movements like Cana and CFM that would never have succeeded if Hillenbrand had been pushing them.

I was committed to professional standards of social research. Neither of us realized at first that these commitments were opposed. He might have argued eventually that reform of the Church and social justice could not wait for the scholars, that there was no time for professional research, and that he had to work with priests of goodwill who resented my high-falutin training if he wanted to accomplish anything as a national social action/urban ministry/peace and justice leader.

I could have accepted such a position, although I would have warned (accurately as it turned out) that ill-conceived and hastily executed projects often do more harm than good.

My problem in our friendship arose because something in his personal chemistry made it necessary not only to tolerate the clerical culture myths about me but to believe them and eventually to become a mythmaker himself.

He told the *Wall Street Journal* that I had a long memory and thin skin, a curious charge, since he was at that very moment attacking me for past offenses and I had never on the record or off the record said a word of criticism of him. Yet I was thin skinned and he was not.

It would later be said that about the time he was saying grace at my silver jubilee banquet and I was saying that in a well-run church he would be a cardinal, Egan was also telling a writer that I was paranoid and megalomaniac and had given the writer the name of a psychologist who had "made a study of me" so that the writer could confirm the charge. Moreover, after my private files were removed from Rosary College, I am told, he kept large excerpts from them without bothering to ask my permission or even tell me. It even has been said that Egan urged the writer who removed my files to sue me when I described his retention of my property as theft.

But I'm thin skinned.

And paranoid.

As near as I can find out, the reason for his anger is that I criticized

216

in my column three projects in which he was involved, the Call to Action (which was a 1976 conference by the "peace and justice" staff of the national hierarchy), the National Federation of Priests Councils, and the Catholic Committee on Urban Ministry. (In only the last was Jack the visible leader.) I said of the first that the research on which its meeting was based was poor research, of the second that it was not interested in improving the quality of preaching, and of the third that it had abandoned the American Catholic style of coalition building for confrontational politics.

The Call to Action vanished without a trace. The NFPC is virtually invisible and has no impact anymore on priests. Egan himself eventually broke with the radicals in CICUM and left the organization.

For all that my judgments seemed to have been correct, they were not worth losing Jack's friendship. I simply did not believe he would expect me to pull my punches. How could a columnist with integrity do that?

But it would have been better to abandon the column—which was not all that meaningful to me—than to have made him so angry.

The debate ought to have been not whether my criticism of the research preparation for the various social action projects in which he was involved was based on my being thin skinned (how would anyone know for sure about my motives?) but whether it was valid. The smoke screen set up by the "thin skin" charge hid that question.

In the long run, neither the advent of John Patrick Cody nor the ressentiment of Father X nor the conflict with Egan made any difference. My dream of being a sociologist in service to the Church was doomed to frustration. It was not a propitious time in the Church for a professionally trained sociologist.

It would take me ten years to fully understand that. And fifteen years to understand that after 1968 the action was no longer with the institutional Church. After the birth-control encyclical and the appointment of the post-Conciliar geek/bishops, the institutional Church became mostly irrelevant. The ferment moved to the Catholic community, to the writers, the artists, the musicians, the poets, the mystics, the parish priests, the prophets, the saints, and the storytellers.

Looking back on the beginnings of those times, 1960 was a providential year to show up at the University of Chicago. John XXIII was sitting on the banks of the Tiber and John Kennedy was running for the presidency of the United States. To have a Catholic priest as a graduate student was

217

a progressive, enlightened thing to do. "Hell," said Peter Rossi expansively, "we're so enlightened around here that we have a Catholic priest and a card-carrying Communist on the staff at the same time." I asked Rossi later why many of those who had been so happy to have me as a graduate student became bitter enemies when the question of my joining the faculty arose. "That's easy," he replied. "In 1960 they thought you were going to convert. By 1964 they knew better."

It was an exciting time—the university by day and Christ the King by night. Those were, I think, the best years of my life. If Hotchkin and I had not finally been swept out of Christ the King in 1964, I would have been happy to stay forever. Come to think of it, "forever" might well have been for only a couple of years, because trying to balance two fulltime jobs might have finished me off for good.

I am not sure I am a scholar; the label sticks in my throat just as does the label "writer." I'm a priest. I do scholarly things and publish scholarly articles, but the life of a pure scholar is not for me. Most of the skills I acquired were absorbed at the National Opinion Research Center, an institution as much on the margins of the university as I was finding myself to be on the margins of the Church. The NORC base was providential after Cardinal Meyer died. In addition to providing me with a base, it trained me in the logic of empirical research and in the skills and methods of national survey analysis. It was superb training—perhaps the best anyone could get anywhere in the world.

NORC is an unusual place. In the twenty-four years I have been there, there has never been a single factional feud among the senior staff. When occasional ill feeling erupts between individuals, the whole staff rallies around to dampen it down. This is not a matter of virtue on our parts, I think; it is rather a functional necessity. We have no subsidy; we live by our wits. We need each other's help. No individual can possibly have all the skills required to carry off large-scale survey research. We cooperate because we have to. Furthermore, we deal our students in early as partners in the research enterprise because we need their insight and their skills to carry it off. During the Cambodia/Kent State demonstrations at the University of Chicago, I walked into a room full of graduate students. "When are you guys going to close this place down?" I inquired, knowing full well that they wouldn't, because while the faculty would get salaries and students would get grades, the research assistants wouldn't get anything. They were all surprised by my challenge. One young woman

218

commented, "Why should we close it down? This is a nice place." Another said, "We passed the word to SDS to leave NORC alone. They better had, or they'll be in trouble with us."

Before the educational reform movement of the late 1960s petered out in shrill radicalism, I was committed in the attempt to combine liberal and developmental approaches to higher education. It always seemed to me that NORC, based on a colleagueship and apprenticeship relationship, without subsidy, with contract deadlines to meet, with no time to be wasted on endless committee meetings and departmental politics, was much more like what a real university should be than most actually are. Small wonder, then, that we are on the margins of the University of Chicago.

My early efforts at NORC were in the area of the sociology of education because, as Rossi pointed out, "that's where the funds are." Our first grant was from Carnegie to study the effects of Catholic schools. Pete insisted we pay a visit to St. Patrick's and light a candle before each of our visits to their headquarters. "If we don't do it," he argued with a Florentine shrug, "and they turn us down, we'll never forgive ourselves."

The parochial school study that he and I did in 1963 (which Bill McCready, Kathy McCourt, Shirley Saldanha and I redid in 1974 and which Bill, Terry Sullivan, Joan Fee and I redid yet again, partially, in 1979) was the first national sample study of American Catholics. The reaction to it made it crystal-clear to me that the skills I had acquired were not going to be of much use to the Church. The defenders of Catholic schools attacked the study on the grounds that it proved Catholic schools were not successful; the opponents of Catholic schools attacked the study on the grounds that it was a whitewash. Some people managed to attack it on both grounds. Professionally, *The Education of Catholic Americans* was a success. The hardback edition sold out, as did the paperback edition eventually. It was favorably reviewed in most professional journals and attacked in most Catholic papers. It still gets footnoted. As Pat Moynihan maintains, it was the first in a long series of studies that produced similar findings about the effectiveness of education. (More about the substance of our findings in a later chapter.)

I became a sociologist to serve the Church, but it became apparent that I had acquired the skills mostly in vain. However, I had not given up hope. The decision by Cardinal Dearden in the late 1960s to do a study of the priesthood after the Vatican Council buoyed my hopes. At

219

last there was a chance to become a scholarly technician for the Church, as had been my original goal. It was not to be, but that puts us ahead of our story. In the meantime, however, more fundamental sociological interests began to emerge.

(Lady Wisdom: Well, it's about time you got to me!)

Sociology and Myth: The Beginnings of Story

PARABLE

Lying in ambush
Truth, exploding rifle fire

Blasts me to the ground.

To understand how a parish priest became a novelist as part of being a parish priest, you have to realize what twenty years of reflection on the sociological approach to religion did to my thought processes, my perspectives, my imagination, my prayer life. I was trained in the seminary to reflect on religion from the top down—from dogma and theology down to practical programs—and learned in Christ the King to work with religion from the bottom up—from human problems and needs to religious responses. Sociology taught me to reflect on religion from yet a third perspective—from the empirical experience of the sacred to the articulations, imaginative and propositional, by which we try to share our experiences with others and to represent them to ourselves.

I began to comprehend, slowly at first, from my study of religion and of ethnicity that religion was storytelling before it was much else and that ethnicity was, in the United States, the locale for most religious storytelling.

Sociology forced me eventually to become a storyteller.

It didn't take me long to discover that what passed for the sociology of religion was mostly the blindest kind of empiricism, which NORC had left behind ten years before. Books like *Religion and Anti-Semitism* by Charles Y. Glock and Rodney Stark were being hailed as great works in the field. They would not have won approval at NORC as a doctoral dissertation. Sociology of religion was not only a stepchild of the sociological discipline, it was an inept one. Yet Clifford Geertz's notion of religion as a "culture system," which I had learned first from him personally when he taught in the anthropology department of the University of Chicago and later in his writings, especially *Islam Observed*, opened a whole new perspective in the social science approach to religion. Furthermore, Geertz's clear, elegant prose finally enabled me to understand Weber, Durkheim, Parsons, and the other greats of the sociological tradition. Reading other theorists like Peter Berger and Thomas Luckmann set me thinking along different lines about both religion and its sociology. From the Geertzian perspective I moved in two different directions. With Bill McCready I attempted to develop operational measures of a person's ultimate values. If religion is a person's ultimate worldview—his answer to the most basic questions a human can ask about life and death—then we should be able to find out what that worldview is and how it influences the rest of his behavior. This is far more useful sociologically than to know what he thinks about doctrinal propositions or what denomination he is affiliated with, or how often he goes to church.

Second, if one agrees with Geertz, as I do, that religion is a set of symbols that purport to give a unique explanation of reality, then the best way to approach the study of any religion is to find out what its symbols are and what they purport to say. This insight enabled me to move ahead toward what I had vaguely begun in the early years of Christ the King: an attempt to synthesize theology and the social sciences into a new style of religious reflection, a new method of theological thought.

My thinking about symbols was heavily influenced by three writers, Mircea Eliade (whom I had read even before graduate school and from whom I had taken a reading course at the university), Michael Polyani, the philosopher of science, and William James, the greatest of American thinkers, whom Santayana properly described as "an Irishman among the Brahmins."

From Eliade I learned that there were certain fundamental structures of religious experience and expression which seemed almost universal, even though they manifested themselves in dramatically different forms. (I still don't know what the philosophical explanation for this is—innate categories like Chomsky's deep structures of grammar? I kind of doubt it.) I saw that much of what is the Catholic imaginative tradition is in fact a baptism and conversion of good paganism. Catholic theology has always justified this both in the name of the sacramentality of creation and in the name of the nature and world religions, each in their own way anticipating and preparing the way for the coming of Jesus.

While reading Eliade's *Patterns of Comparative Religion* I had my first insight that Mary's functional role in Catholicism was to reflect the womanliness of God, a development from, not the same thing as, the female deities of the nature religions. (Even Yahweh had a consort in Hebrew folk religion—the "Shekenah" or the "Spirit" of Yahweh.) What had troubled an earlier generation of graduate students because they didn't know enough sophisticated Catholic theology (through no fault of theirs) became an asset to me. History of religions was not a threat to one who believes in the sacramentality of the created world.

It would take me another decade, however, to realize that the Madonna was the touchstone of the Catholic heritage—that Catholicism was its most radical, most refreshing, most salvific precisely when it said that

God's love is like the love of a young mother for her firstborn son.

(Lady Wisdom: You were finally beginning to find out who I really am. 'Twas about time!)

Chesterton had prepared me for this insight, especially in his book on St. Francis. Eliade pushed me strongly in that direction.

I did not take literally Mircea's notion that religious rites relate our daily lives to the ultimate realities which exist *in illo tempore*, in the uncreated Really Real. I understood him to be saying that's the way the ancients viewed religion, but I did not think he meant we actually live in Plato's cave. Only when he inscribed to me a copy of his *Forbidden Forest* "To Andrew Greeley who is also trapped in the labyrinth" did I understand that he meant the image (and the novel) to be taken literally.

As Chesterton said when he read Eliot's "not with a bang but a whimper," "I'll be damned if I ever felt that way."

Unlike Mircea, however, I'm an Aristotelian, or more precisely a transcendental Thomist à la Bernard Lonergan and David Tracy, with a strong dash of Whiteheadian process philosophy and Jamesian empiricism/pragmatism thrown in. In such a philosophical perspective one does not feel caught in a labyrinth.

No way.

From Polyani I learned that human knowledge did not follow the paradigm of the "scientific method," a confirmation of the way I observed myself and other sociologists working. We followed instinct, hunches, intuitions, much like a detective solving a mystery story. All our "method" did was provide us techniques for experiments which would prove what we already knew to be true—perhaps refining our intuitions in the process. The so-called conflict between scientific and religious knowledge evaporated in the light of Polyani's understanding. Subsequently, reading about the work of theoretical physicists (like the remarkable Stephen Hawking) I realized that on the frontiers of science men worked with symbols, myths, models and stories, much as did the searchers for religious truth.

Then James taught me that *all* quest for truth was an exercise in model fitting, a conclusion to which the cognitive psychologists were coming in the early seventies—and in the process rediscovering the genius of James. We fit our explanatory schemes (models, narratives, symbols, culture system, whatever we choose to call them) to the reality we experience and then modify the explanations to make them better fit reality. Knowledge is an empirical, pragmatic exploration through mystery. James's criteria—luminosity, congruence, and fruitfulness—were merely an empirical description of how the human mind worked.

And James was decisive on one point: science need not accept the truth of knowledge obtained in religious experience. But neither can science claim a monopoly on the ways of knowing.

I had, then, by 1970 the raw materials for my paradigm of religion—experience, symbol (image), story, and community—which would in later years shape my sociology (and become my principal contribution to the field) and give the impetus to my storytelling. The success of my stories would doubtless satisfy greatly the empirical, pragmatic William James. That success fitted perfectly the model of religion I had constructed.

My book *The Jesus Myth*, published in 1971, was my first tentative attempt to use my sociology of religion for a presentation, now not of religious facts, but of religious truth. From Eliade I had learned years before that a "myth" was not a legend or a make-believe tale, but a story which purported to tell us about the Really Real, about what the world truly meant. In my struggle to update my knowledge of the scriptures, I discovered that the best of the New Testament scholars were convinced that the mind and the religious experience of Jesus were most accessible to us in the parables. Jesus's life was the story of what God was like. The parables were stories which Jesus told to share with his followers his own experience of the Father.

Jesus was the sacrament of God and the parables were the best clues we had to the nature of the God Jesus came to disclose to us.

Who was the God revealed in the parables? He was the father of the prodigal son who welcomed back a ne'er-do-well and dishonest son, the crazy farmer who paid loafers a day's wage when they had worked only half an hour at the most, the judge who dismissed a case against an adulterous woman who had not even expressed guilt—a God of exuberant love who had been so captivated by His creatures that His behavior by human standards seemed mad.

What kind of a God is it who falls passionately in love with his creatures, especially creatures who seem so inherently unlovable as we are?

A God who is almost too good to be true.

The Good News seems too good to be true.

And in its Catholic manifestation the Good News is made even Better

225

because this God discloses Himself to us not only through Jesus but through all His creatures, especially those who are the most passionately in love with us.

I was dazzled by this image, convinced (then and now) that it was utterly Catholic and completely orthodox, and puzzled as to why there was so little of it in our teaching and preaching.

The Jesus Myth was a turning point in my development, just as later *The Mary Myth* would be. I was beginning to see that stories were not merely useful to religion, not even merely essential to it, but the core of religion itself. As Jack Shea would say later, religion is primarily "stories of God."

In my own personal religious life I began to appreciate that my faith was one of mystery, wonder, and above all surprise. As Robert Funk put it in his book on parables, "in the kingdom mercy is always a surprise." And Jack Shea in his book about heaven and hell would say it even more powerfully: the best way to prepare for death is to develop a capacity for surprise.

Note, however, how inevitably I was drifting away from the mainstream of American Catholic life. One of the nice-guy prophets whom Egan was defending against me (even though he was a student of mine) had left behind his professional training (analyzing political science data, at which he was rather good) to preach revolutionary relevance to clergy and laity, including a moralistic attack on priests who play golf! Romantic moralistic relevance was in, professionalism was out.

I had given up golf, with a sigh of relief, in 1960 when I enrolled in graduate school. No merit to me, however. I took up water-skiing.

Models and stories were out, concern was in. NORC was irrelevant, the Center for Concern was relevant. I was out, and the Berrigans were in.

The craziness of the late sixties was simply not my dish. Gradually that craziness has died, everywhere but in the Catholic Church. The kind of men who worry about priests playing golf are still calling the shots, as is evidenced by the slipshod, amateurish pastoral on the economy of 1984 which was devoid both of economic sophistication and comprehension of the Catholic social tradition.

However, when the Berrigans were burning draft records and going to jail, I was muttering about such unread and patently irrelevant, not to say unknown, characters as Mircea Eliade, Clifford Geertz, William

226

James, Michael Polyani, and later Paul Ricoeur and Alfred North White-head. What did they know of revolutions?

"You don't read all that junk, do you?" a priest asked me. What does that have to do with helping the poor or saving souls?

At the same time, I had become aware that ethnicity was a variable American sociologists had ignored for twenty years. Since it was assumed by the liberal media (contrary to the existing data, including the Gallup polls) that the hard-hat, chauvinist racist, blue-collar Catholic ethnics were the most likely to support the war, Catholic activists had become ashamed of their own people. To defend the Catholic ethnics then and the Catholic middle class (which is mostly ethnic) today is to be totally out.

It was only at the university and at NORC in the middle 1960s that I became explicitly conscious of ethnicity as a variable in social research. You grow up in Chicago, you attend a multi-ethnic seminary, you work in a Chicago neighborhood, and you take ethnicity for granted—as obvious as the Illinois Central, the Sears Tower or Michigan Avenue. The various ethnic groups have different styles and ways of doing things, different family structures. If you don't notice that, you're blind. Then when you arrive at the social sciences you discover they don't even ask questions about ethnicity in the survey questionnaires anymore. Pat Moynihan and Nathan Glazer write a book about ethnicity that sells over half a million copies and they *still* don't ask questions about ethnicity in national surveys. Something is clearly wrong.

Mary Jule claims that I discovered my Irish heritage in 1965.

Why ethnic questions were excluded and why the study of ethnicity was considered a dubious enterprise are questions beyond the scope of this book. Rossi and I pushed this through the middle 1960s, and finally in the early 1970s, the Ford Foundation took the lead in funding research and action in the ethnic area. Our Center for the Study of American Pluralism was established within NORC. Ethnicity is now just about the hottest area of research for graduate students in a number of fields. A lot of people are trying to discover their own identities.

In the study of ethnicity, three men have been particularly influential in the shaping of my thinking, Peter Rossi, Arthur Mann and Pat Moynihan.

First of all and of most decisive importance, Rossi, who from the very beginning of my insistence that the ethnic factor ought to be taken seriously even though most sociologists (again being very unempirical) had ruled it passé, said, in effect, "I don't like agreeing with a priest even when he's right, but you're right."

Arthur Mann, professor of history at the University of Chicago, has made it clear to me that ethnic diversity and pluralism has been part of the American way from the beginning. It was the ethnic and religious pluralism that generated its political pluralism. The 10th and 51st Federalist Papers of James Madison established America's pluralistic coalition politics not by inventing them but by articulating what was already going on. Such coalition politics are an affront to the political amateurs who periodically try to remake our system along neat, elegant, issue-oriented lines. I knew intuitively that these people were wrong from having grown up in the precincts of Chicago.

The writing of James Wilson, Martin Meyerson, and, in his earlier manifestations, Edward Banfield confirmed my intuition. But Mann's ideas and insights, as well as Gordon Wood's book *Creation of the American Republic*, convinced me that ethnicity (which we define as nationality, regional, linguistic, racial, and religious diversity) has been decisive for the social structure of this country from the beginning. To study ethnicity is to come to grips with the genius of American pluralism and to understand not only the various subgroups within the society but the protocols and procedures—largely implicit and even unconscious—by which this variegated, heterogeneous republic of ours manages to prevent itself from being torn apart. In so doing we also study what is happening to the Catholic ethnic groups in what I used to think of as the final stages of the acculturation process.

Ethnic diversity is not going away, although its operation in American society is becoming more complex and more subtle and hence more difficult to conceptualize and intellectualize. Social science is no more tolerant of people who go down strange back alleys than is the Church, but a handful of us who began research in ethnicity can be reasonably content that the next generation of scholars cannot possibly work in universities situated in the heart of great cities like New York, Boston and Chicago and think that ethnic diversity has vanished from American society.

Our research on ethnic diversity established eventually that ethnic subcultures were not disappearing, that ethnics were not disproportion-

228

ately blue-collar, and that they were not political or social or racial conservatives. The Irish, God help us all, were the most successful and the most liberal gentile ethnic group in America and still, God help them all, irredeemably Irish.

The third powerful influence on my ethnic thinking is perhaps the most unforgettable man I know. In 1962 Pete dragged me off at the ASA meetings in Washington to a Trotskyite reunion in a room in the Shoreham Hotel. The whole crowd that went to Townshend Harris High School, CCNY, and then Columbia after the war were assembled there— Bell, Glazer, Lipset, etc. There was one face that clearly didn't belong. The face looked at my collar and said, "What are you doing here?" I replied, "I might ask the same of you." The then Assistant Secretary and later Ambassador and still later Senator Daniel Patrick Moynihan and I knew we had each encountered one of our own kind.

Pat is not the stage Irishman he sometimes permits the imagemakers to portray him as. He is a sensitive, thoughtful, generous, haunted man with immense integrity (in this respect much like my father). The "Irish comedian" is a useful label to stick on if you cannot cope (the word used here advisedly) with his original, disturbing, penetrating and complex mind. If you are put off by his Irish wit and flair and elegance with language—which a lot of envious and inferior people seem to be—you will not appreciate a man whom historians of the future will no doubt conclude to be one of the two or three most amazing Americans of the era.

I never read an essay of Pat's that didn't have a strong intellectual influence on me. When the ethnicity business was uncertain and even risky, he was a tremendous intellectual and personal help.

In 1986 in a Washington restaurant, Pat held up his copy of *Angels of September* and demanded, "Do you know what you're doing with these books, Andy?"

"What?"

"You're bringing millions back to the Church! I meet them every time I get on an airplane."

"Well, maybe thousands?"

"Millions!"

An exaggeration, but a welcome relief after having to defend myself against the complaints of those who had not read my novels but were shocked because I wrote them.

I went to the university for two years and have been there at NORC for twenty-five years. My basic intellectual and religious interests have not changed, but the experience at NORC has deepened them, broadened them, developed them, given them, I hope, more rigor and discipline, more method and substance.

I became NORC's priest, with a letter from the cardinal assigning me there ("Does that make me a monsignor?" Rossi sniffed). I told an astonished Leslie Kish (one of the country's great statisticians) when he asked me at a professional meeting what I did at NORC that I was Rossi's confessor.

For a long moment there was a nervous silence.

Then came the laughter.

In later years many people at NORC would tell me that my presence there had changed their image of the Church and the priesthood. Which is one of the things priest workers are supposed to do (the wage scale at NORC is a bit higher than in the Paris factories). I was a Catholic presence in the world of the secular academy. The theory of the sacrament of Christian presence had become unfashionable by then too.

Which didn't make it any less true.

Looking back on the years, I regret that seemingly endless personal and organizational crises frequently made me anything but an effective witness to the religious worldview that grew deeper and richer because of what I was learning. Another way of saying the same thing is that I was probably at my best at NORC and my best as a priest when my leprechaun strain was most in evidence. Greels was no fun to be with on the pilgrimage when he was not playing leprechaun. In retrospect, I fear that for months and perhaps years at a time, the leprechaun was nowhere to be seen. One more opportunity blown.

The sociology I have described was often done with a heavy heart. Someone like me with intense institutional and community loyalties must suffer when his institutions and his communities don't want him. Perhaps I was naive to expect they would. And perhaps I should not have been disturbed: I had a career, influence, income, excitement. What else did I need? Perhaps I worried too much about rejection by the Church and the priesthood.

All such comments are valid—and easily offered by those who have never been rejected by their communities. Given who and what I was, however, rejection would hurt. It still does.

It is also, however, a grace.

I have finally come to understand that someone with my "odd" blend of personality and character traits will never be acceptable to an institution. My loyalty will always be rejected by any community of which I am a part—it is too passionate, too enthusiastic, too blunt, too determined, too wildly comic (with an intolerably Irish flair). It does not follow—and this is the key insight—that one should therefore abandon loyalties and commitments. It merely follows that one continues one's commitment from the margins and that one remains loyal even if one's loyalty is not returned.

Why leave? Stay and bother them.

The kind of person I am will survive—healthy and happy and still a priest—only on the fringes. But it is from among us on the fringes that there will come the men and women who will direct the Church into the next era. Leaders like Cardinal Bernardin and Monsignor Egan who permit themselves to be held in thrall by the frightened, the sick, the mediocre, the envious are trapped in the obscure swamps of the past.

Will my work help shape the future? How can I answer that. Only time will tell. I would be willing to bet, however, that both storytelling as evangelism and the novel and the screenplay as a valid part of church ministry will be approved wisdom in the next century.

Rejection equals freedom—only now, finally, do I begin to comprehend that. Without the freedom that comes from being a man on the margin, a perpetual pilgrim, the Grail will not be found, Paradise will not be recaptured. The stories will not be told.

My sociological training at the university, then, was the beginning of rejection and the beginning of freedom.

Meanwhile, to circle back a bit, the Church was bubbling fiercely in the crucible of the late sixties, a crucible created by the Second Vatican Council and the birth-control encyclical *Humanae Vitae*. It was becoming, as Blackie Ryan says in *Virgin and Martyr*, a supernova, an exploding star. For better or worse—mostly I think better—the Catholic Church in the United States would never be the same.

PART TWO

From Square Peg to Storyteller

From Council to Encyclical

MARY'S DAY IN HARVEST

The blue mantle hangs useless from the wall
Thick dust and darkness dim the summer skies
Air dry and stale presses down heavy on us all
Empty her house and so too all our lives.
Heaven's queen, Brigid, Astarte, gentle Nut
Now long gone, they used to wear the night.
Gone too bewitching teenage peasant
Who in Galilee set the world aright
Worthless the mantle and brown your garden,
Dei Mater Alma, to whom all once sang
Forsake us not, weary we come to you
Long gone Madonna, please come back again
To these rotten roses send your cooling rain
Wash us into life, laetare allelu

"Let me see that pass you have," Ernie Primeau, bishop of Manchester and once my French teacher in Quigley Seminary, said, just as the two of us pushed our way into St. Peter's for a Monday-morning meeting of the third session of the Vatican Council, surrounded on all sides by men, in varying degrees of senility and youthfulness, clad in colorful crimson and purple. I handed him my pass, which had been doctored by John Quinn, a Chicago priest who was one of the *periti* at the council. Ernie glanced at it disdainfully. "Quinn is getting clumsier every day. You'd better stick close to me, like you're on my staff or something. That way the Vatican gendarmes won't throw you out. Don't even *show* them that pass."

So I snuck into my first experience of the Second Vatican Council with a forged pass, escorted by a former teacher and now close friend. I got away with it, but not everybody did that day. From the observer balcony Dick Dempsey (who was also in Rome on a CCD tour) and I saw two other people from the Villanova House (where Ernie and George Higgins and John Quinn and Gregory Baum and Hans Küng and a whole host of influentials of the Council were living). They were dragged by Vatican gendarmes before the desk of Pericle Felici, the secretary of the Council, a charming reactionary. Archbishop Krol of Philadelphia, one of the assistant secretaries, lurked behind Felici, scarcely able to contain a grin. The gendarmes presented the doctored passes and Felici hit the ceiling, ranting and raving about the dishonesty of Americans who snuck into the Council. Krol moved forward to intervene, then backed away when he saw what Felici was doing. Across the face of the pass he wrote *"Falsi non ammitentur"*—fakers are not admitted—and then gave the passes back to the two priests, who were summarily escorted from the aula of St. Peter by the angry gendarmes. I later found out that Krol had murmured in English over Felici's head to the two Americans, "Quinn is getting clumsier every day."

The two priests returned shamefacedly and presented John Quinn with their invalid passes that night. Quinn produced his liquid ink eraser, blotted out Felici's condemnation, and rewrote the passes so that, as good as new, they could be used the next day.

That's how the Vatican works!

It was forbidden to bring cameras into the aula of the Council, but that stopped practically no one, because a cassock was a wonderful cover-up. One simply attached the strap around one's belt and walked blithely

236

by the guards. Despite the no-picture rule, cameras were flashing almost every minute from the various visitors' balconies.

The first day I was there Cardinal Meyer gave a brilliant "intervention" on the subject of the sacred scripture, which was, after all, the area of his professional competence. He received a huge ovation, and that night at the supper table with John Hotchkin (who was now in Rome pursuing his degree and living at the Chicago House on Via Sardinia) he said proudly, "That one I wrote myself. It received more applause than the talks written by Frank McCool or Barnabas Ahern."

(Later, after Meyer's death, Ahern in his lectures would quote at great length a brilliant Meyer intervention on the "cosmic Christ," i.e., Christ saving not only humans but the whole cosmos. It was pure Teilhardism, and Barnabas, quite properly, never bothered to note that he had written the intervention for Cardinal Meyer.)

"By the way, Jack," Meyer asked Hotchkin, "when did Andy get in town? It was yesterday, wasn't it?"

"I think so," Jack replied. "It looked like him next to me on the airplane, anyway."

"I thought so," Meyer mused. "It only took him twenty-four hours to get into the Council. Not bad."

Hotchkin agreed it was fast work. "I suppose it's another one of John Quinn's forged passes," Meyer said with a sigh.

Hotchkin could hardly wait to report his intelligence to us at Villanova that night. (I thought I had ducked around the corner before the cardinal saw me.) Later on I would see the cardinal, both at the Chicago House and on the Council floor.

The sessions themselves were dull, the interventions ranging from brilliance to folly; the real action of the Council, as in any deliberate assembly, was in the committees. It was there the theologians and the bishops, who were their allies, fought and won the battle against the Roman Curia. Pope John apparently summoned the Council so that the bishops of the Council would be a counterweight to the Curia, of whom he strongly disapproved. Through its four sessions, the Council was a fierce struggle between theologians and some of the residential bishops and the Curia. The theologians won, though not quite as brilliantly as they had expected after the first session. The evenings at Villanova House were swept by alternating waves of euphoria and pessimism. Every victory over the tricky Curial reactionaries was a sign the Church was changing and every setback in which the Curia people manipulated the Pope was a sign that the Church was not changing and that we were back to playing the same old game.

My own feeling, as my weeks in Rome wore on, was that the bishops had no idea *what* they were doing: they did not realize what the implications of their overwhelming majority of votes for a scientific study of scriptures, English liturgy, collegiality of Popes and bishops might do to their dioceses when they came home. Between sessions many of the American bishops came home to reassure their faithful (the bishops imagining a nervous and anxious faithful worried about the headlines they read in the newspapers). A bishop might have voted for every single document in the Council and still felt that the Church was not changing and that he could honestly tell his people that it was not.

The European theologians—Küng, Rahner, a much younger Ratzinger (who now conveniently forgets his contribution to the Council), Schillebeeckx, Congar—who had worked in the universities of Europe since the war and then thought through many new philosophical and theological interpretations of the Catholic tradition—were the real powers in the Council, because bishops knowing little theology would appoint theological *periti* to advise them and would pick the best theologians from the seminaries and universities in their area. Moreover, bishops, while they might be intensely loyal to the Vatican in principle, also came to the Council with a lot of grudges against individual Curial bureaucrats who harassed them. The bishops of the world, then, egged on by the theologians, delivered the Curia a number of sound drubbings.

The theologians were influential because they had worked through, in the World War II and post–World War II experience, many of the theological themes on which the Council was focusing. Thus, when a bishop, knowing rather little theology, found himself going to Rome for the Council, he hunted around for the best theologian he knew and brought him along so that he would not run out of ideas. Even Meyer, who was a scholar in his own right, had a whole stable of advisers and ghost writers. Those were exciting, exciting nights at the Villanova House, the most exciting nights, I think, in my whole life. I was not a *peritus*; no bishop was leaning on me for advice. I was, rather, a journalist there to observe and a sociologist there to evaluate, and most of all a tourist there to gape.

We often thought, amid much hilarity as the "creature" disappeared in prodigious amounts (Quinn had somehow found two ice makers, the only two in Rome, one for Villanova and one for Cardinal Meyer), that we were changing the Church definitively, that after the Council it would be almost unrecognizable. If John XXIII had lived, I think that would have been true, but Paul VI fancied himself a skilled diplomat and tried to mediate between the Curia and the bishops, with disastrous results. The Council, instead of being a 100 percent transformation of the garrison Church of the Counter-Reformation into the open Church of the ecumenical age, was perhaps a 60 percent transformation. The ambivalences, the ambiguities, the conflicts between the Curia and the theologians were structured into the Council documents—virtually guaranteeing there would be enormous conflict in the years ahead.

I made three good friends in those weeks: Hans Küng, the great Swiss theologian; John Wright, then an auxiliary bishop in Boston; and John Courtney Murray, the American Jesuit expert on Church-state relationships (whom I'd met once before during a retreat at the seminary)—three men who could not possibly be more different, but still three men who had an enormous impact on the Council: Küng, with his ideas on ecumenism, and Wright and Murray, on the religious liberty declaration and on the statement on Jews (both of which were of enormous importance to American bishops). In later years when I would visit Rome working on the Papal election book, I would always stop by Signor Cardinale's apartment—just up the stairs from Cardinal Baggio's apartment on the Piazza Città Leonina. Wright and I shared a love for Newman and Chesterton, for the Irish heritage and for Catholic literature. On virtually everything else we disagreed. As John put it one night, waving a wineglass at me, "Andrew, I disagree with everything you stand for. And I shall defend to the death my right to continue to disagree with you!"

John Courtney Murray was disinvited to the first session of the Council because the Curial bureaucrats thought his notions of religious liberty were so dangerous. He was present at the last three sessions, however, as the personal *peritus* of Cardinal Spellman—of all people—and was one of the concelebrants in the Mass that ended the Council. Murray was one of the heroes of my life who never did turn out to have feet of clay. His treatment by the young Jesuits in the late sixties, when the Jesuit order abandoned reason and civility in favor of radical romanticism, was shameless. And Garry Wills's description of Murray as the "theologian of the cold war" is characteristic of Wills's rather peculiar approach to the truth. As Hans Küng said in one of his books, Murray died far too soon.

Küng and I became friends at the breakfast table. We'd both made the decision that the Council sessions were mostly a drag and hence slept late and ate breakfast after the bishops and the *periti* had left. Küng was a great man even then. No one had much heard of me. I have always been cautious about bothering celebrities, but when one seems friendly, I quickly respond. Envy of the great and successful is finally counter-productive. Why envy them when you can *learn* from them?

Küng has taken a tremendous beating in the years since the Council. Yet, I must say that of all the Council theologians I know, he is one of the most conservative and also one of the most loyal. The doctrines he is alleged to hold which occasioned the Roman decision that he was no longer a Catholic theologian are doctrines he does *not* hold. Küng was condemned for positions he has resolutely stated are not his. He is a victim of the envy of the German cardinals who blend both academic and clerical envy into one monumentally evil amalgam. The German cardinals won their battle with Küng about the same way that Hitler won the Second World War. While I am not the theologian Küng is, I've learned a lot from watching him suffer persecution. Far more innocent than I, Hans really doesn't understand how much of the attack on him is based on sheer envy. Moreover, he does not seem to realize that when you reply to envious attackers, you play their game. Far better to ignore them and continue your own work.

Nonetheless, the attack on Küng by the Roman Curia and by some Catholics (like Michael Novak and Harvey Egan, who ought to know better) is a disgrace, a classic example of the Church trying to destroy its most gifted people. Küng continues to write, continues to teach, continues to be a world figure. But the Romans have taken away the joy, the flair, the playfulness which were characteristic of the younger Küng I knew at the Council in 1964.

Küng's major failing is not that he holds unorthodox doctrine but that he writes best-selling books. That is a sin his fellow theologians cannot abide. I think it was perfectly proper for him to refuse to go to Rome to face charges unless he was guaranteed elementary civil liberties—opportunity to cross-examine his accusers, counsel of his own choice, a report of the charges against him *before* the trial. I also think, however, that when Rome decreed he was no longer a Catholic theologian, Küng might have been better off simply to suggest they go jump in the Tiber River. I also think, by the way, and told him repeatedly, that he should have left the infallibility issue alone. His response has always been that it is linked to the birth-control encyclical, even though no claim was ever made that the encyclical was infallible (Pope Paul VI is reported to have crossed out the phrase "with infallible authority" which the drafter of the encyclical on birth control had inserted in it).

I stayed three weeks in Rome and was fascinated, exhilarated, depressed, and exhausted, like everyone else there. I then fled to the Near East—to Israel, Jordan, Palestine, Syria, Lebanon, Egypt. I did a lot of thinking in Luxor and Beirut and Jerusalem and Cairo and Tel Aviv during that trip.

Every time I looked at a body of water, be it the Nile or the Mediterranean in Beirut, or the Tiber or the Arno, I thought of Lake Michigan and the Chicago to which I would return and wondered what my role upon that return would be. It was on some of those quiet evenings staring at the water I made up my mind I could either do full-time parish work or full-time sociology, but not both.

I considered the data from our 1963 study and what they revealed to me about the American Catholic population. There were clear hints of rebellion. Less than half admitted that the Church had the right to teach them on social doctrine, sexual morality and similar subjects. While a majority were willing to accept its bans on artificial contraception and divorce, the majorities were only slight and almost half the American Catholic population were already dissenting from its teaching on birth control.

Moreover, an ever-increasing number of priests were making the same decision that I was making (after reading John Noonan's wonderful book *Contraception*), that if the lay people in good faith thought they could legitimately practice birth control, we were not going to refuse them absolution. From phone calls to the rectory at St. Thomas's after I'd left Christ the King (phone calls from Christ the King people, however) I realized that American Catholics, particularly American Irish Catholics, were shifting their birth-control practice. After all, had not Pope John set up a commission on the subject? And had not Pope Paul expanded

241

that commission? Why wait four or five more years, when clearly the Church was going to change? Did I think it would be all right for them to practice birth control for a while?

I would usually respond by saying that the Church's official position still forbids birth control but that husbands and wives must make, finally, their own moral decisions with the official teaching in mind. There wasn't much doubt what decisions they would make.

The Vatican Council, it seemed to me in those reflective weeks as I wandered the Mediterranean, was not only a group of specific documents on the modern world or on the nature of the Church or on sacred scripture or on religious freedom or on the Jews. More significant, the Vatican Council had legitimized change in the Church.

Most of us had grown up believing that it was impossible for the Church to change. Once, however, it became possible to turn the altars around and to say Mass partly, then totally in English, and once there was no longer an obligation to eat fish on Friday, then American Catholics, lay and clerical alike, began to believe that anything could change, including the birth-control rules and clerical celibacy. A trickle of priests began to leave the priesthood to marry, heralding a later tidal wave, and an ever-increasing number of the laity decided that they were blameless in anticipating what they thought was certain to be a change in the birth-control teaching. Hadn't everything else changed? Wasn't it then about time for a change that would benefit the laity?

I'm afraid a lot of us thought birth control could and would be changed. After all, in the nineteenth century the Holy Office had repeatedly cautioned confessors in France against asking married couples about their birth-control practices. So, too, had John Vianney, the saintly curé of Ars, when he gave lectures to confessors. Moreover, had not Leo XIII written an encyclical on marriage at the height of the birth-control problem in nineteenth-century France without once mentioning contraception when France was solving its population explosion in the nineteenth century by a mixture of *coitus interruptus* and abortion? Moreover, was it not true that because of the demographic revolution (decline of infant mortality rates), where seven pregnancies were needed to produce two children who would live to adulthood, now seven pregnancies would produce seven teenagers, as my sister was in the process of dramatically discovering?

Obviously, the Church had placed different emphases on marital sex in its history. Surely, there was room for change.

But, characteristically, Paul VI would not let his brother bishops debate this at the Council. The issue was taken off the agenda and turned over to the special commission on birth control. The Pope thought he understood better how change could be accomplished in the Church than his brother bishops did. His principal aim seems to have been to make the transition after the Council as smooth as possible. Unfortunately, as it turned out, he misread the signs of the times and thought change had to be slowed down. *It was too late.* Pope John had opened the window and the whirlwind was sweeping through. An attempt to dam and contain it was bound to lead to the explosion of every window in the house.

Despite all the thrills and excitements, the alarms and excursions, the ups and the downs, the agony and the ecstasy of Vatican II, it was essentially a theologians' Council, a battle between the theologians and the Roman Curia with the bishops, not altogether realizing what they were doing, allying themselves with the theologians. None of the human sciences were significantly represented. There was no one there, for example, to talk about the importance of marital sex for the human species. Nor was there anyone to say that this constitution on the sacred liturgy was a dreadfully aprioristic document which betrayed no understanding at all of the actual religious experience of the laity. Nor could anyone with expertise in international politics and social science challenge the document of the Church in the "modern world," a document which praised the "modern world" just at the point that those who had celebrated the "modern world" had lost their confidence in it. Thus, Vatican II, it seemed to me even then, was an aprioristic council, working in a vacuum with little awareness of what the religious problems and possibilities, the religious doubts and opportunities were among the ordinary people of God. The people of God were not consulted, neither through representatives nor through social research that could report on our experience of being Catholic Christians in the modern world.

I will not say that at that time I anticipated the troubles that would assail the Church in the wake of Vatican II. However, the handwriting was on the wall. At the end of the third session, just after I had arrived back in Chicago and on the last day when votes were to be taken on the religious liberty statement and the statement on Jews, Cardinal Tisserant rose at the beginning of the session and announced that these matters would be postponed and considered at the next session. There were shouts of horror and dismay from the assembled bishops. Cardinal Meyer, one of the presidents of the Council, slammed his fist on the presidential desk in a rare outburst of anger, and whispered moments later into Clete O'Donnell's ear, "They're not fair, they're not fair."

Quickly a petition was written and signed by hundreds of bishops, with Clete doing much of the legwork, pleading with Pope Paul not to postpone consideration of these two critical considerations. There were strong words in the petition. The bishops begged for a vote, "insistently, more insistently, most insistently." The Pope did not budge, however, and the third session was over with no votes taken on these two "American" documents. However, the outburst of Meyer and the quick collection of a petition had the desired impact on Pope Paul. At the next session, the documents were voted with virtual unanimity.

To this day it is not clear whether Tisserant acted on his own or at the Pope's instruction. Members of the Curia were quite capable of making their own decisions, enforcing them in the name of the Pope and then and only then informing the Pope. Alfredo Ottoviani, the conservative head of the Holy Office, who had resisted much of the change at the Council, grabbed his friend John Quinn and said, "Tell them I had nothing to do with that."

There were lots of headlines in newspapers about the Council being a failure, but Meyer, when he came home to be greeted by cheering crowds at O'Hare and even more enthusiastic crowds at Resurrection Parish Hall, later in December when he met with all the priests in the diocese, seemed confident victory was within his grasp on those two American issues. There was victory the next year, but Meyer was dead and John Cody had come to Chicago (he made no interventions as archbishop of Chicago during the fourth session of the Council, leading his sometime patron, Archbishop Joseph E. Ritter of St. Louis, to remark, "I really believe that man thinks he's going to be Pope someday").

One of the reasons for my decision to seek release from full-time parish work was my conviction that social research would be absolutely essential if the hierarchy was not to mistake the temper of the clergy and the laity. Hardly had they come home from the Council when the bishops were busy trying to reassure everyone that *nothing* had changed. In fact, *everything* had changed. Not because of any specific documents of the Council but because the principle of change in the Church had been revivified.

I did not return to Christ the King after the end of my first trip out of the country. As the Church was changing, so had my life changed. I was forced to choose between full-time parish work and scholarship, not because I wanted to, but because the choice had been imposed on me the previous spring.

"You've been changed." Walter Imbiorski's voice on the phone sounded like Jeremiah's predicting the fall of Jerusalem. "St. Thomas the Apostle."

"What about the work?" I gasped.

"No mention of it," he murmured. "Looks like Meyer couldn't protect you from your pastor."

Walter was the director of the Cana Conference and one of the most original and creative members of the Sunday Night Group, a loyal friend whatever the costs. Later Cardinal Cody would deny him Christian burial.

It was June of 1964. We were finishing the analysis in the first Catholic school study, struggling with NORC's erratic computer system. Without warning and out of the blue, my appointment to NORC seemed to have been repealed.

"Hotchkin too. He's going to Rome. Looks like your pastor cleaned house."

I called CK, congratulated Jack on his appointment to study ecumenical theology, and asked him to open my letter. Sure enough, no mention of my work at NORC.

"We had an election, only no one told us," Jack said glumly, "so we didn't get to vote."

It was a black moment in my life. What had I done wrong? Why had an assignment so graciously given been so abruptly withdrawn?

If I was to be pulled back from sociology, fair enough; but why in midstream and why when the cardinal had enthusiastically approved the project?

The monsignor assured everybody in the parish that he had nothing to do with the transfers. He did have nothing to do with Hotchkin's transfer, but he was responsible for mine. In fact, he was embarrassed by the two of us leaving together, since it made it look as if he had somehow conspired to get rid of us (as his Wednesday-night clerical bridge cronies had urged him to get rid of me) or that we had finally worked up enough nerve to walk out on him. The farewell party at Christ the King was one of the bleakest moments of my life. There is traditionally supposed to be music and singing, talks by various people in the parish with whom the priests have worked, a farewell statement from the pastor, and a farewell statement from the priests who are leaving. All of this had been carefully scheduled, but the pastor, who was supposed to be the master of ceremonies, never began the program. So people drifted away after it became clear nothing was going to happen, and at the end of the evening there was Hotchkin and myself, a bunch of teenagers, and the pastor, still sulking because the transfer of two curates made him look bad.

I reported to the pastor at St. Thomas's, a friend of mine from my seminary days in St. Ursula and also the one who, four years before, had urged me to see Cardinal Meyer directly about graduate training in the social sciences. However, it is one thing to urge someone *else's* curate to seek training in social research and quite another to tolerate a staff member of the University of Chicago replacing a full-time curate. His response to me was blunt: "You're an associate pastor here; you have no time to do anything at the university."

Once more I was a head of cattle, adding to the pastor's prestige. St. Thomas's parish at the time was in dire straits. The Catholic white population was moving out, to be replaced by blacks and by university faculty members. The pastor argued that for the morale of the parish he had to have four curates. Any diminution, he argued, would lead to panic among the remaining "cap and sweater" Catholics in the neighborhood. There were practically none left, but he didn't seem to notice that.

Dazedly I went back to Christ the King to pack. I should try to finish *The Education of Catholic Americans* as the senior survey director of the project, but the pastor at St. Thomas was not about to let me do that. I stewed for twenty-four dismal hours, then, pushed by some of my late-teenage and early young adult friends, most notably Grace Anne Carroll, two years out of Barat and running a big volunteer tutoring program, I decided to call the Chancery Office.

GAC: Don't be silly. Why would they send you to the university parish unless they wanted you to stay at the university?

Me: They didn't put it in the letter.

GAC: Maybe they forgot.

The reader will perceive who is acting maturely in this dialogue and who isn't.

When I called, Frank Byrne (the chancellor) and Clete O'Donnell were both out. I left word for them to call back. I was going to ask for an interview with the cardinal to straighten out my status. Clete O'Donnell, however, returned my call later in the day. He said he and Frank and the cardinal had been talking when my phone message came in and that the cardinal remarked, "Andy couldn't possibly have any doubts that we want him to continue to work at NORC, could he?"

"And I told him," said Clete, "there's nothing in the letter that says that."

"Well, I want him to continue there on the same basis as at Christ the King. Call him back and reassure him."

So Clete did.

"You'd better talk to your friend the pastor," I said. "He doesn't see it that way."

"I thought he was a friend of yours," Clete murmured.

"You can't be somebody's pastor and a friend at the same time," I said bitterly.

"I guess you're right," said Clete. "All right, I'll have a word with him. You are assigned to St. Thomas's, but only so it does not interfere with your major responsibilities at the National Opinion Research Center."

My new pastor, a generation younger than my former one, reacted with no more graciousness than had the older man. He made it plain to me he didn't like it and that he was going to expect me to carry "my share of the load" regardless of what the cardinal wanted.

Even today, twenty-one years later as I write about those terrible thirty-six hours, I feel the same emotions of helplessness, shock, and rage tear at me. Sure the cardinal should have realized what would happen, but fair and generous man he was, he could not comprehend how much meanness and unfairness had been institutionalized into the pastor/curate relationship.

I sweated through a lonely and confused summer, missing Christ the King as I missed my first love, and hopping out of bed almost every night for hospital calls because part of the deal that had been cut (*a priori* by the new pastor) was that I would be on call for hospitals three nights a week. Two or three calls a night exhausted me and I was looking forward eagerly to my first trip to Europe in the autumn, a trip about which the pastor was not especially enthusiastic but which he had to approve because he had just taken one himself.

On the European trip, particularly after those three crucial weeks at the Second Vatican Council, I was forced to address the problem of how much parish work I could mix with sociology or vice versa. When I got back from Europe I wrote the cardinal, saying in effect that I was willing to do one or the other but that I couldn't do both and I would leave the decision to him. I wasn't trying to escape parish work. I liked it; I hoped always to do some of it, but I needed to be released formally and officially from full-time parish work if I was to do sociology.

I mailed the letter around the first of December and learned shortly thereafter that the cardinal was in the hospital, sick. He died of brain cancer in March. Nonetheless, one of the last things he did from his sickbed before surgery was instruct Clete O'Donnell to see to it that I was assigned officially and formally to full-time scholarship, research and writing. While the cardinal was in the coma preceding his death, O'Donnell called me, invited me to come down to see him at the Chancery and told me the decision had been made: I was now free to devote all my attention to sociology and to do such parish work as I chose to do in my free time. He also said I could be free to choose wherever I wanted to live, in an apartment or a rectory; while he thought I might be happier in a rectory, that was not part of the obligation.

I searched all over for places in which to live and found out that pastors did not want me. They might lose one of their regular curates in a trade-off for me, and I would not, in fact, even be a half-time priest. Finally Gerry Scanlon, the pastor of St. Dorothy's, an upper-middle-class black parish a mile and a half away from the university, told me he was honored that I should think of living in the rectory with him; the best he had was a small room in the basement, but I was welcome to it and to all the freedom I needed to do my work.

I was off the reservation now, on my own, though I would not realize until the later sixties, when it dawned on us in Chicago what kind of man John Cody was, that I had escaped in the nick of time and that I likely would be off the reservation for the rest of my life.

I realize that in these last couple of pages I have sounded angry. I won't deny it, I am angry, but not at the men involved. Both my first pastors were good men—in one case, a wonderful curate, and in the other case, a wonderful seminary professor. The priest who was a curate at St. Angela when I was growing up and who later became my pastor at St. Thomas had told me, on a snowy February evening fifteen years before, that priests go through changes as they grow older. A pleasant, mellow, cheerful curate can become a sour, embittered pastor, and then, as time goes on and his health begins to fail, he can return to his earlier mellowness.

248

It struck me as being a very wise observation. I'll confess I was horrified to see it so perfectly fitting the man who had offered the explanation.

I came to NORC, then, in the spring of 1961 to write a dissertation. I stayed on through a two-year post-doc from 1962 to 1964. Gradually and subtly, without actually realizing what was happening, I was becoming a professional social researcher, something I would not have previously believed possible. My canonical status was moving me to the fringes of the institutional church at the same time my professional standards and intellectual concerns were pushing me to the margins of the priesthood.

Even after Cardinal Cody came to Chicago and I became a nonperson in the Archdiocese, I thought I could combine my many different roles the same way I had combined parish work at CK and research at the University of Chicago. It was still a physical possibility, but by the end of the 1960s it had become a cultural and structural improbability—as it would have, I think, even without Cardinal Cody.

By now I also had my own little parish or religious community (the "underground" parishes were flourishing in that time, but we never considered ourselves an underground parish), made up of the young people whom I'd known at Christ the King and who now were away in school or beginning their jobs or living in apartments outside the parish. This, I told myself, would constitute my parish work—the kind of small group experimental parish which, it seemed to me, would be absolutely essential in the post-immigrant, post-Reformation age of the Church. We would come together not in a tightly organized commune but rather as a free community meeting every week or two to celebrate the Eucharist and to discuss the meaning of faith in our lives. Perhaps we would also share social action projects and some recreational activities. It was a good idea and I would stick with it for a long, long time, another decade of my life, before I came to realize that while small group parishes might be the wave of the future, it is most difficult to protect them from the neurotic transference of unresolved family conflicts. (I will have more to say about "The Group"—maybe the worst of the many failures in my life as a priest—later on.)

My analysis of the Catholic school data continued.

There were a number of issues about Catholic schools that were being powerfully debated in the early 1960s. Mary Perkins Ryan summarized them in a book called *Are Catholic Schools the Answer?* Mrs. Ryan contended they weren't. Catholic schools, she argued, should be phased out and replaced by Confraternity of Christian Doctrine (CCD) courses, which would be able to reach a lot more people and free up a lot more money for the service of the poor and the oppressed.

Mrs. Ryan's book was innocent of systematic data. My position was that I should keep an open mind. I was not heavily committed to Catholic schools. My instinct said it was better to have them than not, but I was prepared to be refuted by the data.

The principal questions were:

1. Is there any religious payoff from Catholic schools, or is the apparent greater devotion of Catholic school graduates merely a function of the greater devotion of the kind of parents who send their kids there?

2. Are Catholic schools academically inferior? How do those who went to Catholic schools do in later life?

3. Are Catholic schools divisive? Do Catholic schools produce young men and young women who have little interaction with people outside the Church boundaries and also men and women who are socially and politically conservative and unconcerned about the poor and the oppressed?

The findings of the research were clear-cut and not particularly complicated:

1. Catholic schools *did* have an effect over and beyond the parental effect, and moreover it was precisely among those young people who came from already devout families. When parents and schools were cooperating the effect was striking.

2. Catholic school students were more likely to go on to college, even taking into account parental educational and economic background, and were also more likely to select academic careers and to attend graduate schools.

3. While three-quarters of the Catholics who attended Catholic schools said their three best friends were Catholic, exactly the same thing was true of three-quarters of the Catholics who attended public schools and true of three-quarters of the Protestants (claiming their three best friends were Protestants) who lived in the same part of the country as did our Catholic respondents. My finding in the master's paper about religious self-segregation was sustained in a national sample. While Catholic schools did not break down the segregation, they certainly did not increase it. Moreover, particularly for those who went to Catholic colleges after Catholic grammar school and high school, there were high scores on the scales

rejecting racism and anti-Semitism, a finding that led me to suggest to the American Jewish Committee that they should vigorously support funding for Catholic education because it led to a diminishing of anti-Semitism.

I made no particular effort at the time to distribute press releases explaining our findings, for it seemed to me then, stupidly I admit, that the sociologist does the research and journalists report its results. It was a disastrous mistake. Within a week there were stories all over the country distorting the project beyond recognition.

Some of the Catholic educators had opposed it from the beginning. One of the staff members of the National Catholic Educational Association demanded he take control of the project and that all questionnaires be cleared with him. I told him, in effect, to stuff it. Pete Rossi, more cool-headed in this than I, had a national advisory staff set up, which could make all kinds of recommendations and legitimize the project without actually controlling the questionnaire. Obviously, many Catholic educators were afraid I would find Catholic schools had failed. Many of the Confraternity of Christian Doctrine (CCD) enthusiasts and the Catholic liberals were afraid I would find Catholic schools had succeeded. Neither group seemed capable of comprehending what objective social research was—or that the scholar, whatever his predispositions, deals honestly with his data.

The first distortion was on the front page of the second section of the *New York Times* and occupied two columns. The author had gone through the report and systematically removed everything that could possibly be a credit to the Catholic schools (often ripping sentences and phrases totally out of context). Monsignor George A. Kelly, secretary of education in the New York Archdiocese, told me that "Spelly" was furious at me for criticizing Catholic schools. He advised I send Spellman a copy of the report with a letter saying that the *New York Times* had completely distorted it. I did send such a letter and received a friendly reply. I also protested vigorously to the *New York Times*. John Cogley, who was the religion writer then, wrote me a letter apologizing in his name and that of Clifton Daniel, the managing editor, for the article, saying they were both on vacation when it happened; however, the *Times* never did officially retract the article. I would later become friendly with the staff of the *Times*, but I never did raise the question of that particular article, figuring that bygones, after a while, should be bygones. In retrospect,

251

however, it was the worst distortion of objectivity I ever read in that most distinguished newspaper.

Exactly the opposite happened in the Catholic press. Robert Hoyt, the editor of *The National Catholic Reporter*, attacked *The Education of Catholic Americans* on the grounds that it was biased *against* the Confraternity of Christian Doctrine. Most of the findings he denounced were not in the book. When I challenged him on this he said, well, he had only glanced at the report but he knew he had a pretty good idea of what it said without having to read it because he knew my opinions on the subject.

Commonweal did virtually the same thing but went further than Hoyt, accusing me of deliberately distorting the picture to make the Catholic schools look good, and questioned my intellectual honesty and integrity. Neither *Commonweal* nor *The National Catholic Reporter* retracted their distortions any more than did the *Times*.

For many years it has been widely believed that *The Education of Catholic Americans* showed that Catholic schools had failed, whereas many Catholic liberals believe it was a biased report written to make Catholic schools look good. In neither case was there any awareness that a social scientist might simply be objectively reporting the data. As I have said repeatedly, I have no biases for or against Catholic schools. I've never been on the faculty of one. I have been treated shabbily by the Catholic school system. If I was to follow my own biases I would attack them. However, on the basis of the data, if I were ever in charge of a parish I would build a Catholic school—if my lay people wanted one. And most lay people want schools; it is the clergy and the hierarchy who no longer want to be bothered with the responsibility of administering Catholic schools.

Subsequent research on the Catholic schools in the sixties and the seventies and even the eighties has merely sustained the findings of *The Education of Catholic Americans*. *Catholic Schools in a Declining Church*, published in 1974, among other things established that Catholic schools were more important in times of transition than they were in times of stability, and also that Catholic schools, in fact, generated their own income because of the higher collection contributions made by parents. Moreover, in 1979, in our study of young Catholic adults for the Knights of Columbus, the finding was replicated again, even more powerfully. The life-cycle phenomenon of young people drifting away

252

from the Church in their twenties would tend to reverse itself as they approached thirty and then grew older, but the return was much more vigorous for those young people who had attended Catholic schools (and on all of these data we hold all possible background variables constant: parental education, income, religious devotion, etc., etc.).

Finally, in the work James Coleman and I did in the eighties, we have proved that, academically, Catholic schools are far more successful than public schools and especially with black and Hispanic minority students. The reason for the success, we found, was that the Catholic schools insist much more rigorously on homework and advanced course work, not having been *au courant* enough to drop the stiff academic requirements in the late 1960s and the early 1970s in the name of racial justice (the diminishing of standards in public schools on the grounds that one had to lower standards for the benefit of minority students was made almost entirely without any consultation with black parents).

The Catholic education issues have been solved; we now have clear, positive and definitive answers to all the questions one might have raised about them twenty-five years ago. The research my colleagues and I have done on the subject has gained general acceptance in the secular academic world.

Despite these findings, the clergy and their hierarchy close down old schools and do not build new ones. When I tell them this is folly—that they are giving up the best community building resource they have available without finding an adequate replacement—they look at me, nod their heads, but do not comprehend because they don't *want* to comprehend.

There are, to quote Rossi, many, many ironies in the fire. Catholic educators were afraid twenty-five years ago that NORC would find that Catholic schools were not the answer and that our research would be an enormous embarrassment to them. Now they find that Catholic schools *are* the answer and they are equally embarrassed because they do not want to offend the Confraternity of Christian Doctrine movement.

Even more ironic is that while bishops issue pastoral letters on poverty and pat themselves on the back for having exercised the "preferential option for the poor"—to use the latest meaningless ecclesiastical cant—they are busy closing down the one demonstratively effective ministry of the Church in the United States to the poor: the inner-city Catholic schools.

As I try to recapture my mood sitting in my windowless basement alcove at St. Dorothy's during 1966 and 1967, I recall myself more confused than angry. It seemed as if I were trapped in a mixture of Franz Kafka's Castle and Lewis Carroll's Wonderland, a peculiar place in which those who had not read a report could confidently claim that they knew more about it than the man who wrote it.

At that time, I didn't understand about the Greeley Myth, although it was already spreading. Some of the objections to *Education* were based on my alleged salary at NORC, the cost of the project (bargain-basement by the standards of large-scale research, but none of the objectors bothered to find out about the costs of comparable projects), and the suspicion that most of the Carnegie grant went into my own pocket. (In fact, I received no salary from the project.)

There was, however, a more fundamental problem, in the context of which even the Greeley Myth made some kind of sick sense. The Catholic Church was enduring its most volatile era certainly since the French Revolution, probably since the Reformation, and possibly since James said to Peter, "You take the suburbs and I'll do the city."

At the same time American society was in chaos. John Kennedy was dead, Lyndon Johnson was escalating the Vietnam War (Greels as political pundit: "Lyndon Johnson is too smart a politician to repeat Harry Truman's mistake. He'll have us out of Vietnam before the 1966 Congressional elections"), race riots were erupting in the streets. Young people were turning against their parents and their country. The Berrigans and their friends were burning draft records. Such professional prophets as Margaret Mead were hailing the beginning of a new age of human history. The Beatles were emerging from the slums of Liverpool.

'Twas the dawning of the Age of Aquarius.

My age, given my birthday, if I wanted it.

I didn't.

It was an age of romantic, self-pitying, anti-intellectual, self-defeating (it elected Nixon, didn't it?) nonsense.

In the Church it was the Age of New Certainties.

If those who did not live through the years before the late sixties are to understand what happened to the Church in those days, they must realize that the intellectual equipment of priests, nuns and many college-educated Catholics included a core of tidy, self-confident religious certainties. Creed, code, and cult—what you believed, how you acted, what you did religiously—were all neatly and cleanly specified. You might not know all the rules, but your parish priest did or the Catholic *Encyclopedia* could provide the answers. Catholicism had the answers to everything—polished, succinct, understandable answers.

Pope John's tornado demolished these intellectual structures. Once meat on Friday was possible, I argued even in those days, the whole ball of wax melted. Add a commission to investigate a possible change on birth control and you created a heady environment in which not only could anything change, but it was firmly expected (by the clergy and religious and many laity) that *everything* would change.

To make matters worse, the institutional leadership was losing control of reform during those madly euphoric post-Conciliar years. In what history will doubtless judge as one of the world-record misreadings of the signs of the times, both Pope Paul and the bishops who had voted in the Council reforms thought it was necessary to slow down the pace of change, lest the laity and the clergy be shocked and scandalized.

The Pope's classic self-revelatory comment about the bishops' inability to cope was "They don't understand." He pictured himself as the smooth, sophisticated diplomat who would preside over the changes with prudence, tact and discretion. The bishops pictured themselves as the protectors of the anxious laity. Alas, these self-images spoke more eloquently of the emotional needs of the hierarchy than they did about the reality of Catholic life in America. As I tried repeatedly to tell the leaders, the laity and the lower clergy were not shocked but delighted by the changes. Trouble would come only when they began to believe the hierarchy was trying to reverse what it had done at the council.

By 1966-1967 this belief was spreading. Gene Kennedy and I met with Archbishop Dearden in the Conrad Hilton Hotel in Chicago to plead with him to assume leadership not merely of the bishops but of the American Church. Unless the laity and the clergy, we insisted, sensed that there was a firm, confident and intelligently liberal hand on the tiller, the post-Conciliar euphoria would turn into destructive confusion and perhaps collapse into chaos.

Accurate prophecy, as it turned out. However, Dearden did not seem to hear us. Rather he talked about the problems he faced organizing a national hierarchy. He did promise us, however, a study of the priesthood. It was an excellent idea, on paper, and did not seem then what it and further studies would later prove to be: a strategy for buying time.

A study, nonetheless, was not what was needed if the leadership was to keep control of reform. However, a leadership which by now included such worthies as Carberry, Krol, Cody, and Medeiros was going to lose control of reform anyway.

I've often thought of that meeting with Dearden as a symbolic turning point, one that revealed the hierarchy was turning in on its own concerns and permitting the post-Conciliar energies to run wild.

I am now convinced it may take a century for the storms that were released to run their course and a new style of Catholic institution to emerge in which the leadership on the one hand and the people and the lower clergy on the other are once more in dialogue. The die was cast by January of 1968. The birth-control encyclical in the summer of 1968 would make the failure of the post-Conciliar era inevitable.

The Council, in most respects, was an enormous success. The most dramatic changes in the history of Christianity were implemented with only minor strain among the ordinary faithful—and often with enthusiastic approval. The American Church, disorganized and chaotic but vigorously pluralistic, survived and survived well. In 1963, 12 percent of those who were born Catholics were no longer Catholics. In the early 1970s, in the wake of the Council and the birth-control encyclical, the proportion of fallen-aways increased to 15 percent, where it has remained ever since. Church attendance has declined; so have vocations. The morale of the clergy and the religious have been at rock-bottom for the last fifteen years. But, as far as one can tell by observing the laity, the profound change of the Vatican Council has taken place, despite the Pope and the bishops, with little noticeable ill effect on the dedication of the laity in the United States.

The Roman Curia has retained its power; the theologians have been discredited; the bishops are confused and the laity are as enthusiastic as ever. However, young adults growing up in the post-Conciliar years, in the late sixties and early seventies, seemed to have a much more authentic and generous religious sensibility than did their predecessors (perhaps because their mothers were women who had to make a decision on birth control themselves and did so, finally, because they trusted God's forgiving love).

Since the bishops would not lead and scholars could not lead, everyone became a leader, every charlatan and lunatic with quick and easy answers who could find a platform at a summer institute and promise to diminish the uncertainty and confusion if only his magic solutions were followed.

256

Then leave the following summer to marry an Adoring Neurotic Nun. (There were lots of nonneurotic nuns but they weren't at summer institutes looking for husbands.)

Clerical culture came apart at the seams. The certainties vanished, but not the need for certainties. Therefore, and this is crucial to the understanding of what happened when the hierarchy lost control of reform, in the midst of the anarchy and the ambiguities of the late sixties, there was a desperate search for new certainties to prop up the emotional and religious lives of the clergy and religious.

Some of us could tolerate the ambiguities and the promise of even more to come. Others of us might even revel in the mess. But most of us wanted new certainties right away.

The result was new certainties. Every year. New theories to replace fish on Friday and the Sorrowful Mother novena, new authoritative sources to replace St. Thomas. European theologians were astonished when they came to America to discover that they had been transmuted from scholar to folk hero. They did not understand there was a desperate psychological need for a folk hero who spoke Truth.

The Neurotic Nuns quoted Rahner the way they used to quote St. Thomas and Our Lady of Fatima—with quotes that reflected the good Austrian scholar about as accurately as their quotes reflected Greeley/Rossi.

In pell-mell renewal chapters, the religious orders of women, with the best intentions in the world, "reformed" themselves out of existence, usually on the basis of a theological foundation provided by a handful of women who had picked up M.A.s in theology from summer school at Marquette. Priests and nuns dated and mated at the summer institutes. Weekly idiocies were reported in *The National Catholic Reporter*.

There was not an enthusiastic idiocy of the whole history of Christianity which has not been repeated, several times possibly, since 1966. All in search of a certainty to diminish the strain and the tension and the ambiguity. But there was no peace. The answer, whether it be Marxist revolution or tongue-speaking fundamentalism, was never certain enough. There was always a new answer coming down the pike next year.

In the midst of this fervid, frantic, fantastic environment, a guy got up and said, "Well, our data tend to show that you're all wrong and that..."

Can you imagine?

257

Who needed a sociologist with his, to quote George Higgins, goddam data that supported Catholic schools? Most especially a sociologist who was a smart-ass with a lot of money?

Could I have done anything about it if I understood what was happening then as well as I do now?

I don't think so. As Ed McKenna, who would later write an opera based on my first novel, *The Magic Cup*, would put it, "priests are fine, it's the clergy who are the problem." By which he meant that the terrible culture of the clerical caste system corrupted the natural generosity and loyalty of priests, unless they resisted it mightily. If I had known that then and accepted it, I would not have tried so hard or cared so much. Beyond that there was nothing else for me to do, save to hunker down and wait for the centuries.

Start writing stories earlier?

Maybe, but I didn't have the paradigm yet, the intellectual context which would free me to write them and the courage born of despair to take the risk. That would take another half decade.

There was nothing left in Chicago. The Sunday Night Group had long since collapsed. The cardinal had picked off the senior members one by one, saddling them with pastoral and administrative responsibilities which preempted their time and in many cases ruined their health. Leo Mahon was in Panama at the Chicago mission, to which Meyer had decided to send half of each ordination class for training at the same time he decided to release me from parish work. The Association of Chicago Priests, formed to contain the cardinal, lacked nerve and loyalty to one another. Chancery Office staffers were telling us the cardinal was a psychopathic liar who was stealing Church property—that long ago—although they continued to serve him faithfully to the bitter end.

I was in my basement alcove and on my own.

258

Grand Beach

Wild rainbow wit, lady dear, made the world
(Though we in loss of nerve often turn it gray)
Flowers red, foam white, lake green, sunset gold
Thunderbolts of color on your harvest day
And Matthew red, Mollie blond, Norae brown
Toothless grins, rotten kids, fun and funny faces
Mad comic God and a few Irish still around
Multicolored mischief, wild and merry chases
Too much for us, lady, you know the thought
He made them; from then on 'twas Mary's show
Like us, always watching kids, you've been caught
So praising you, God as Mother, we all know
That you look down with laughter from above
And God sees each of us with a Mother's love

"Well now, Father," said the cardinal, at his most charming, "men like you and me get our names in the newspaper a lot and attract a lot of attention." He eased the drink around in his hand carefully. "We get used to people who talk about us and say things that aren't true."

This was my second (and final) visit with Cardinal Cody. I had received a letter from him telling me he wished to continue the discussion of my work we'd begun over a year before. I had presented myself at the cardinal's house dutifully, waited the usual required hour and a half, and then was ushered into his presence. Oozing transparent charm, he invited me up to his room, offered me a drink (I said Coca-Cola), mixed one for himself (nature unknown), and began this seemingly friendly conversation.

"Now, I hear from some people," he went on, "that you bought yourself a great big house over in Michigan and that you're running retreats there. I'm wondering if that's true, Father. And if you have permission from the bishop over there to be giving retreats."

So *that* was it. He had no intention of talking to me about my work. He wanted to find out about my house in Grand Beach. I had heard some of the old-timers at Grand Beach were complaining to the cardinal and he, characteristically, was taking them seriously.

"It's not a retreat house, Your Eminence," I said, "just a summer house. Sometimes some friends of mine stay there for a weekend and we have discussions, but it's not a retreat house. I don't run retreats."

"Well now, Father, have you told the bishop up there about this house of yours?"

"As a matter of fact, Your Eminence, Bishop Zaleski knows about it, because I'm working with him on the priest study and he gave me the faculties of the diocese."

"Now how many retreats a year do you have there?" the cardinal went on.

"I don't have *any* retreats there, Your Eminence. It's a summer home for myself, my sister and her family and, sometimes, for friends. That's all it is. Whoever told you otherwise wasn't telling you the truth."

They had told him that it was a retreat house for blacks, and that I was using the house as a front to infiltrate blacks into Grand Beach.

"Well now, Father, you don't want it to get the reputation of being a rebel's roost, do you?"

"I'm no rebel, Your Eminence, and it's not a roost. It's just a summer home, like other priests have. There are several other priests who own houses in Grand Beach, and I'm sure no one has complained to you about them."

"Now, Father, do you think it appropriate that a priest own a house like that up there on the shore of Lake Michigan?"

I decided it was time to play my ace. "About as appropriate, Your Eminence, as it was for you to own that house up in the hills when you were bishop in Kansas City."

Bingo! Jackpot! Direct hit! Complete change of course in midstream. "You know about that house, do you? Well, it's always nice to have a place in the country in the summer, where you can invite your friends and your family and your fellow priests and have a wonderful time."

"I would hope you would consider yourself invited, Your Eminence, to come up to Grand Beach anytime you want."

"I'll certainly keep the invitation in mind, Father."

I had bought the house in the late summer of 1965. It cost approximately twenty-eight thousand dollars, ten thousand down. If I was to live in a one-room windowless basement because there wasn't any other place for me in the diocese, it seemed not unreasonable to have a house in the country where I could go and see some sunshine and blue sky, particularly in the summer. I suppose, to tell the truth, that the one room in the basement was an excuse for the summer house I'd always wanted, ever since Twin Lakes. So, my sister and Grace Carroll and I explored the shore from New Buffalo back to Beverly Shores—New Buffalo being the outer limit of how far I was ready to drive from my University of Chicago office—and found the perfect house. Ray Carroll, Grace's father, came up, glanced at the lawn, mumbled to himself, "Double lot." Then said to me, "How much do they want?"

"Twenty-eight thousand."

"Buy it."

So the house was bought. It was intended for many things, most notably, I suppose, a place for me to find some peace and quiet for my work, but also a place where the community which had gradually emerged from the young people I knew at Christ the King could occasionally meet for discussions and liturgy.

To put it mildly, I was not welcome in Grand Beach. I had paid relatively little attention to its social environment, because I did not figure I would be part of whatever social life there might be in the resort community. However, many of the Grand Beach people were from the

Christ the King/St. Barnabas area. They were convinced I was some kind of dangerous radical—even worse, a racial integrationist. They assumed I couldn't possibly have enough money to buy the house and therefore I had to be fronting for some interracial organization that wanted to move blacks into the neighborhood and destroy their summer community. While I was certainly committed to racial integration, I also was fully aware of the complex problems of integrated neighborhoods and had never in Christ the King taken a radical position on the subject. However, anyone who even *mentioned* race once in a sermon was considered radical. Moreover, many of the Grand Beachers had never met me, because of the pastor's policy of standing between me and the adults, and they were convinced that I was a rabble-rousing, dangerous radical. It was but a step from there for them to see busloads of blacks parking behind the house and pouring into it for interracial retreats. A letter of complaint went to the cardinal.

The myths about what went on in my house continued to expand. Not only were there interracial retreats, there were wild drinking parties and nude bathing on the beach. Presumably letters describing those bacchanals went to the cardinal too, but having been stung once in the conversation with me, he chose to leave me alone on the subject (though he would repeatedly tell other bishops about the palatial mansion I had on the shores of Lake Michigan). Needless to say, none of the rumors were true, but that didn't make much difference to the people who were circulating them.

It didn't take me long to find out who wrote the letter to the cardinal. He was a prominent Chicago civic and political leader with enormous clout in the Cook County organization (the mayor, who lived at the other end of the beach, had no part in the letter). Later when I became a more acceptable and then an honored person at Grand Beach, this fellow went out of his way to pretend to be friendly. I hope God gives me all kinds of points for never having said to him, "Now, Mr. So-and-so, are you *still* writing letters to the cardinal?"

(Lady Wisdom: Is it points you want now?)

Grand Beach became a refuge for me in the late sixties and the early seventies. It was there I heard of Bobby Kennedy's death and immediately said Mass for him. At Grand Beach I watched on television the rioting in Chicago after Martin Luther King's assassination. Similarly, I watched

262

the Conrad Hilton riots in which the Democratic Party destroyed itself in 1968 (never really to recover fully), the moon landing, and the first television announcements of the encyclical letter *Humanae Vitae*. Theoretically and ecclesiastically I was out of phase in the late sixties and early seventies, opposing the war but also opposing the antiwar movement, opposing the failure of the leadership of the Church to respond to the birth-control crisis but also opposing those who were leaving the priesthood and even the Church in discouragement and disillusionment over that encyclical.

The late sixties and the early seventies were a bad time for our republic. Many of the young people who matured in that era will forever bear the mark of self-pity and paranoia—those who shape the spirit and the ethos of a generation and those who occupy the key places in our society now who matured at that time. It often seemed to me the university faculty members betrayed these young people. Because of their good liberal guilt over the Vietnam War, they adored the younger generation that was opposing the war without ever forcing them to think through their political and social positions. It should have been possible to oppose the war with good sense and nuance. However, when the professorate abandoned its traditional obligation to challenge the enthusiastic but unrefined thinking of its students, then that generation matured without ever having had its self-pity, its paranoia, its sweeping, unfounded generalizations examined.

The Democratic Party reformed itself in 1972 and boasted that it had the most racially and sexually balanced convention in its history (later it would also add that even gays were properly represented). But affirmative action and quota representation at the convention produced first George McGovern, then Jimmy Carter, then Walter Mondale, three of the worst losers the Democratic Party has known since the pre–Civil War days of James Buchanan. Carter did win one election, but only barely—and that running against a President who had pardoned Richard Nixon, and in the wake of the Watergate scandal. The labor and big-city bosses were thrown out of the party in the 1972 convention, and the big-city ethnics were ignored. Somehow or the other, the liberals and the reformers who had seized control of the party were not able to count. The *New York Times* Op Ed page carried articles by Tom Wicker and Anthony Lewis announcing that the legions of the young would sweep George McGovern to victory. Well, the legions of the young didn't vote, and to the extent they did, they voted more for Nixon. (And now the legions of the younger vote for Ronald Reagan, as do the Yuppies, who are the sixties generation older but not wiser.)

James Carroll, a sometime Paulist priest, in his *Prince of Peace*, admits casually that the demonstrations at the Conrad Hilton in 1968 gave the election victory to Richard Nixon. Nonetheless, the book, a hymn of praise for the peace movement, never seriously raises the question of what is to be said of a movement whose tactics hand victory to its worst opponent. Carroll excuses his hero of adultery on the grounds that the adulterous relationship was *merely* a priest and a nun in love and all such love was, by definition, innocent and sinless. Carroll's book, written fifteen years after the fact, perfectly summarizes the ethos of the late sixties: a priest and a nun cannot sin if they make love to one another, and the movement is still a heroic and admirable one, even if it gives victory to its enemies.

In the Church, priests and nuns were now leaving by the hundreds and thousands, sometimes quietly and discreetly because they were tired and discouraged in their ministry and because they wanted the peace and the comfort of family life, but sometimes too they left, as did the controversial James Kavanaugh, with the confident proclamation that *they* were the wave of the future... that *they* were the ones that were being true to Christianity... that those of us who stayed in the priesthood somehow or other really weren't fully human and might, by remaining in the priesthood, confirm the Church in its old-fashioned, reactionary ways. "The best are leaving," they proclaimed melodramatically. They were the best and they were leaving. Those of us who remained probably didn't have strong sexual drives anyway.

Kavanaugh wrote an anonymous article in *The Saturday Evening Post* entitled "I'm a modern Catholic priest and I want to marry." And when he married he wrote an article describing the joys of being a married priest—complete with pictures of his wife in a bikini. Then when the marriage broke up, there was an article declaring, "I am a divorced priest." Each of these announcements was orchestrated in such a way that Kavanaugh was made to appear a progressive hero—a representative of the inevitable progress of history. There were many more like him who also, perhaps to assuage whatever guilt they might have had about leaving the priesthood, tried to present themselves as progressives and heroes and radical protesters.

Such priests were not typical. Most of those who resigned from the active ministry to marry did so quietly, though even many of those did not seem to consider the powerful impact their resignation would have on their parishioners. However, the much-publicized resignations of men like, for example, the theologian Charles Davis made headlines. Those of us who remained suddenly found ourselves on the defensive. It was a sign of weakness, it seemed, to keep your promises, to honor your commitments, to stand by your vows. Why weren't we leaving too? Were we homosexuals? Were we undersexed? Were we cowards?

In retrospect, most of those who left were men who were frustrated or unhappy or burnt-out or bitter. Only a small minority actually would have been willing to continue in the work they were doing as married priests (about 20 percent, according to our research). I felt abandoned when somebody I knew well left the priesthood. I certainly would not make any judgment on their decision. As I said to one close friend when he called to tell me tearfully that he was resigning, "If it's what you think you should do, then it's the right thing to do." Nonetheless, it made me feel the people standing on either side of me on the barricades were dropping off one by one.

In the years before the mass exodus in the late sixties, there was practically no discussion among priests about their unhappiness, their loneliness or their desire to marry. Thus, priests like me who were quite content in the ministry assumed, mistakenly it turned out, that everybody else was equally content. We were surprised and shattered to find out how many of our confreres were unhappy and would abandon their priestly commitment the moment it became possible to do so.

To the credit of the American Catholic laity, they were sympathetic to such men, much more so than I would have expected. Moreover, most families kept a stiff upper lip and supported their priest son when he left the active ministry and when he married, though occasionally they could be heard to murmur that, if it wasn't for "the woman," they were sure their son would still be a priest. In some cases I suspect this analysis was all too true.

In Chicago the numbers leaving were somewhat higher, and, moreover, some of the most active leaders in the presbytery were also departing, fractured by their endless combats with the cardinal. Some of them—the men closest to the cardinal, his vicar for religious and his secretary, for example—left the priesthood saying privately that they could no longer work for a man they found to be such a monster.

Unfortunately, they didn't say it publicly, and the cardinal continued to destroy the lives of other priests and nuns in the Archdiocese.

It was only much later when I would write *Ascent into Hell* and try to get inside the mind and personality of someone leaving the priesthood that I was able to become more sympathetic to the resigned priest. I now believe that perhaps a limited service vocation is appropriate for many men and for many women in the twentieth century. (When the issue of ordaining women was first raised in the early 1960s, it seemed to me that there were no reasons other than cultural ones for denying women access to the priesthood. It still seems to me there are no good reasons for excluding them. Hence, I'm in that modest minority of American Catholics who favor both ecclesiastical celibacy and the ordination of women.)

Some of those who resigned, particularly in the years between 1968 and 1975, did so because, as one priest admitted, "I don't want to be the last to leave." A kind of panic set in as one looked around and saw many of one's friends departing. If one did not leave oneself, and quickly, the supply of available women might diminish. Better to abandon the priesthood too early than too late.

"They're going to change the celibacy rule anyhow," I heard often. "Why should I wait four or five years until the change? By then maybe I'd be too old to marry."

I didn't think they were going to change the celibacy rule and I thought the prediction that they would was monumentally naive. Moreover, in truth, I also believed that some of those who were leaving were abandoning their commitments and promises all too hastily. At that time it was easier to resign from the priesthood and obtain a dispensation than it was to obtain an annulment of a marriage. The difficulties in obtaining a dispensation fluctuated, as did Paul VI's conscience. Sometimes the Pope thought the salvation of the souls of the men who wanted to resign depended on quick and easy dispensations, but at other times he was afraid that he might be too lenient with those who wanted to renege on their commitments and, consequently, tightened up the rules. When John Paul II became Pope, he virtually ceased granting such dispensations, but by that time it didn't make much difference. Many priests had decided that if they wanted to resign and marry it was their business, a matter between themselves and God, and ecclesiastical authorities had no right to intervene.

266

Paul VI's vacillation about matters such as birth control and celibacy did an enormous amount of harm to the credibility of ecclesiastical authority. If you put the birth-control issue in doubt by assembling a commission, then men and women feel that, well, there's going to be a change eventually anyhow, and why should we wait. And if you permit men to leave the priesthood and marry, then all of those who are weary or unhappy or discouraged will be inclined to leave. Then if you change the rules on dispensations and if you try to tighten up the regulations on birth control after being lenient for several years or seeming to be lenient, you lose all credibility as a teacher and a leader, and people cease to pay attention to you.

Wave after wave of fashions and fads swept the Church in the years after the Council as men and women strove somehow to recapture the certainties that had existed before 1965. Such quick, almost instantaneous "renewal" gimmicks as sensitivity training or the Cursillo or "marriage encounter" or the Charismatic Movement were hailed enthusiastically as the answer to all our problems and imposed on the laity whether they wanted such "quick fixes" or not—not infrequently doing serious psychological harm.

I remember a group of priests stopping by one night at Grand Beach to extol sensitivity-training workshops they'd attended. A week at Bethel, Maine, had made them experts on the dynamics of the human personality, capable of presiding over sensitivity-training sessions in which some people could have their self-confidence and personality integration shattered when the group turned viciously upon them. I attempted to explain that, hey, I am a trained social scientist, I know about group dynamics. I've read the literature. I am well aware that practically no measurable long-term effect has been produced by sensitivity training and that in some cases, for people who are not well stitched together, it can be a traumatic, a potentially psychosis-producing experience.

I might just as well have saved my breath. Sensitivity training was the new law and the prophets—the solution to all the Church's problems. John Hotchkin, who was visiting me that weekend, kept murmuring something about the need for "insensitivity" training. Priests and nuns, he impishly argued, ought to be taught to say no, firmly and strongly, in the face of nonsense. The visiting clerics didn't listen to him, either.

In the late sixties and early seventies I lectured often. I had become a "personality," and that's what the Catholic lecture circuit wanted in those days. The audiences were not all that much interested in what you had to say, but they were interested in what you "were like." To be able to boast that one had heard Rahner or Küng or Schillebeeckx or the most recently faddish American guru was what counted. It wasn't necessary that you absorb what they said. After my lectures the questions were almost always efforts to fit me into a category, a party line, a movement. Frequently there was anger in the audience when I simply refused categorization. As time went on, those invitations diminished while lecture invitations to secular institutions increased. Curiously enough, in the eighties I find myself once more invited often to talk in Catholic colleges after having been banned there in the years immediately beforehand. You can be so far "out" that you are "in."

And now the students come. Such are the advantages of storytelling.

It has always seemed to me that weekend institutes, study weeks, summer pastoral institutes and other weekend workshops are mostly entertainment and have little connection with serious scholarship or learning. I have refused to participate in them because I do not believe any subject worth learning about can be mastered in a couple of lectures or even in a week or two of classes. The summer workshops, pastoral institutes, etc., etc., etc., have done incalculable harm to the Church because they have continued the half-education of priests and nuns. In the old days we were half-educated in the liberal learning tradition and now we're half-educated in the new theology, the new scripture studies, the new peace and justice movements.

The ecclesiastical institution desperately needed and still needs well-educated men and women if it is to survive the present turbulence. I see no evidence, either in the seminary training or in the in-service training of the workshops and institutes, that the men and women in charge understand what good education is.

During those years I was going through my own theological and scriptural updating, learning my theology first from John Hotchkin and then from John Shea and David Tracy and my scripture studies by devouring all the books I could by our Catholic and Protestant scripture scholars. Even that, in the summer-institute era, was dissident behavior.

In the midst of the upheavals of 1968 the black priest who had become pastor of St. Dorothy's, after Jerry Scanlon stepped down to make way for him, came to my room one night and advised me that it might be wise for me to leave the rectory for a while because it was altogether possible it was about to be blown up by a black radical movement. I didn't particularly mind dying a martyr's death, but I wasn't going to die one for a cause that wasn't mine. So I moved out and shortly thereafter was transferred to St. Ambrose, which was at the north end of the University of Chicago community, a parish which needed my presence even less than St. Dorothy's. It was a place to stay, a canonical residence, but even less home than St. Dorothy's. Grand Beach had become home. It was the place where I thought, the place where I worked, the place where I relaxed. Sanctuary. Only looking back on the situation do I realize now that the time between 1968 and 1974, between, let us say, the birth-control encyclical and the resignation of Nixon, was the era when my "outside" status in the Church became fixed, and Grand Beach inevitably became my base as an outsider.

White cabin cruisers moving in stately procession down the shore, swarms of freckle-faced Irish kids, waves pounding the beach, water-skiers weaving and darting through the speedboat wakes, great dunes of ice in the wintertime, spring struggling to be born in early May, the fondue hat trick (cheese, beef and chocolate fondue in one meal!) on summer evenings, the blanket of stars late at night, the sun coming up through the trees, the village come alive on a Notre Dame football weekend, Lou Briody with the world's largest glass of sherry, little Nora and the cuckoo clock, big Nora searching for Liam, supper at the Brennans' on Friday night, with sausage hors d'oeuvres and Kelly Anne on the phone, swimming in the Connellys' pool, Mass on Saturday afternoon at my house (short sermon, no collection, according to the teenagers), routing Michele and Bob out of bed for the eight-thirty water-skiing obligation, their skills on the skis humiliating me, John Larkin ringing my doorbell at eight-fifteen, Jeanine wheeling Tommy Brennan—grace personified—to the beach, Terry Goggin and I trading stories about the old neighborhood, the fearsome beat of DIAMOND! (more recently renamed FRED!) cutting the night air, a new lifeguard chair for Heidi when "Max Gleason" refused to buy one after the vandals (from Long Beach, of course!) stole the old chair, the ballooning, multicolored spinnakers of the Tri State regatta on Labor Day Sunday (which one is Norman Nie?).

Enough story material for a couple of lifetimes.

Grand Beach is *not* an escape from Chicago. It *is* a part of Chicago, geographically and socially if not politically. I may have been rejected by Chicago (university and Church and later media), but I did not reject

Chicago (the city and its people—who would later read my stories by the hundreds of thousands). Chicago is and always will be *my* place— one of the world's most beautiful cities, even if it is not so perceived by many of the carpetbaggers who administer its large institutions and the copperheads of the local press who sell out to the superiority complex of the New York media experts (never more cravenly than in the summer of 1968).

The grandiose curve of the lake-front parks, the elegance of the Magnificent Mile, especially at Christmastime, the ingenuity of such wondrous interior streets as Dearborn, La Salle, Canal, Orleans, Halsted, Western and Wacker Drive (celebrated in my *Patience of a Saint* and *Blessed Are the Peacemakers*), the multicolored charm of the ethnic neighborhoods, the precise neatness of the bungalow belt, the glow of a winter sun on the frozen lake, the moon ducking behind Sears Tower, the reflection of the Merchandise Mart on the green ice of 333 Wacker Drive, the blurred ribbon of headlights on the Kennedy at rush hour, the caress of the morning sun on the loop, the Cubs, the Bears' Number 9 picking apart another NFL team's pass defense. The Fridge.

Not a perfect city, God knows. But something more than the hog butcher to the world—a title we gave up long ago anyway. My city at birth and my city as long as I live. Grand Beach and Tucson are places I go, from which I can come back to Chicago.

How can you justify your summer home? It is a question that comes up in almost every interview with a priest or a Catholic journalist.

The best answer is to say I don't have to. The use I make of the material resources available to me is my business and no one else's. Cooler heads, however, counsel me to assay a more detailed answer. Okay, but I doubt it will make much difference to those who complain.

I can work under almost any circumstances in the short run—airport waiting rooms, trains, buses, even standing in line waiting for a customs check or driving a car—but I have discovered the hard way that over the long haul my temperament and personality are such that physically drab and dreary (or dirty) surroundings slowly and subtly depress me. The house at Grand Beach was intended as a place for thought, reflection, work and recreation and an alternative to the basement with its glowering water pipes threading their way through the room.

I'm sorry if that offends people, but not so much that I will change my mind and sell the house. I learned in the seminary and I believe now

270

that we must each make our own decision as to how we allocate the material resources available to us. As long as we are generous with others, the precise use of our goods is a matter between us and God (and such spiritual advisers and reality checks as are available to us). So I am convinced that Grand Beach is an enormous help to my work and quite possibly essential. It's my decision, and I will live with it and not be afraid to face God with it. Yet that is not enough for the mythmakers. Although many priests have summer homes, that I have one is intolerable to them. The amount of hard work I do is irrelevant; what counts is how I relax, renew and recreate; and they consider themselves totally qualified to make judgments on that.

Many priests cannot afford a summer home, Father, they tell me with passive-aggressive piety. True enough, but if we are all to be held to what all priests can afford, we would have to live in huts and not drive cars. The point is that I can afford one and I have made a decision that it is appropriate for me in the context of my ministries, my responsibilities, and my physical and mental health.

And no one else's damn business.

I won't cut that line either.

Now your house in Tucson...

Shove it, friend. I teach a semester a year in Tucson. You want me to live in a tent?

Grand Beach became more and more my "place," the spot where I was most at home. Whether it is Twin Lakes reincarnate or not, as my sister suggests, it *is* a place that I think has a pervasive influence on my work. Anyone who is interested in the atmosphere in which a writer works must, I think, know about Grand Beach if he is to know about me, particularly in the summertime when I bury myself in books (neglecting neither my sailing nor water-skiing).

Now Grand Beach has been transformed into one of the loci of the Clan Ryan and an integral part of my stories, though I should hasten to add that neither the Ryans nor their compound are literal descriptions of Grand Beach. (Such institutions as our aforementioned indigenous rock group FRED! are, however, true to life.)

My friend Father Richard Dempsey commented after reading a somewhat earlier draft of this story that he missed in it the happiness he thought characterized my life when he visited me, usually at Grand Beach, on his leaves from the navy (he had been "volunteered" by Cardinal Cody).

I was taken aback. Rereading these chapters, they strike me as pretty grim. The times were grim. My life seemed grim as I had looked back on it. Yet the "Ace" found me happy. How explain the discrepancies?

Father Dempsey brings his own effervescence with him. Only someone with paralyzed facial muscles does not laugh when he arrives on the scene. As he once said of John Krump (or was it vice versa?), "That man's crazier than most people think he is!"

Yet I cannot explain his recollection merely as the result of the impact of his personality on me. I *was* happy through those troubled years. I continued to be happy through the even more troubled ones that lay ahead. In trying to record accurately in this story the confusion in my life between, let us say, 1965 and 1980, and the path I walked from square peg to storyteller, I have focused, perhaps necessarily, on the square-peg-making experiences. Such experiences, as may be evident to the reader, were not pleasant; but as Ace accurately observed, they did not destroy my fundamental happiness. I skirted close—too close and too often—to bitterness but never succumbed so completely as to become a cynic, thanks be to God and my genetic endowment.

(Lady Wisdom: You're welcome.)

Happiness, as my colleague Norman Bradburn established in his research, is a hydraulic affair, a favorable balance of payments of rewards over punishments, of reinforcements over sanctions, of good over bad, of payoffs over frustrations. I had to endure a crazy cardinal, a craven hierarchy, a bigoted university, and an envious presbytery. So?

So—and I never thought of it this way until the Ace challenged my earlier draft—what? So would I let those forces and energies destroy my fundamental happiness in my life option as a priest?

Maybe it is permeable boundaries or a tenacious core or some weird amalgam of the two; but the question did not even arise. Surely my faith *did* grow in those years. Surely I was protected under the shadow of the wings of God's grace. But the basic options of my life were not shaken. The issues over which I was doing battle did not touch the center of my goals and commitments.

I was not peaceful in those years, not nearly as peaceful as I am now. There was much about the anger and the hatred and the inkblotting I did not understand. Yet finally I was able to respond in the depths of my soul enough of the time to the rejection with the answer "That's their problem more than it is mine."

So what are the payoffs?

The most meaningful reward comes from being a priest. That's what I chose to do with my life, and I like doing it, even if the ways in which I do it are hardly what I had expected. As Bill Higgins, one of the St. Angela crowd reappeared, remarked, I have had an interesting priesthood.

Never dull, anyway. Whatever my life has been, it has not been *boring*!

In no special order, there are many components to my happiness as a priest:

I have the satisfaction of knowing that some of the things that I do in my ministry I do well. My friend Father Jim Mahoney, an able sociologist as well as a fine priest (and just possibly a model for Blackie Ryan in my novels), remarked recently that there is a connection between low clerical self-esteem and low job satisfaction—the latter lower for associate pastors than for unskilled workers. Self-esteem and job satisfaction, he argued, come from a sense that there is something you can do well.

I write well and I do sociology well, better than most, better if push comes to shove than most of those who were my foes at the university. Moreover, these are skills I exercise in the service of the Church even if the institution would just as soon dispense with such service.

The work of research and writing have an inherent pleasure of their own. Data analysis with Norman Nie's interactive SPSS is much like writing poetry, an activity which calls on the characteristics we associate with the right side of the brain, almost an altered state of consciousness. There is joy in formulating a problem, proposing hypotheses, testing them against the data, and then describing the results. It is not enough joy to sustain life, but it is better than not having it.

Though not enough, I think, to keep me happy.

I have been sustained through the years by loyal and dedicated friends, lay, clerical, and occasionally (as in the case of Cletus O'Donnell) hierarchal. More than most priests? I don't know. More than most people. Pat and Liz Moynihan, Joan and Tony Boyle in London, Jordan and Eleanore Bonfonte in Paris, Kevin and Sheila Star in San Francisco, David and Eva Riesman and Robert Coles at Harvard, Abe Rosenthal at the *New York Times*, Elizabeth and Chris Wallace, Joe and Yvonne Blotner from Ann Arbor, Norman and Carroll Nie, David and Joan Greenstone, Ken and Ann Prewitt, Leo Goodman, Jim and Zdzislawa Coleman, Ned and Peggy Rosenheim, Erika and Paul Fromm—all from the University of Chicago; a host of Arizona friends to be named later;

June and Marvin Rosner, Pastora Cafferty, Grace Barry, Rich and Maggie Daley (when they became neighbors at Grand Beach and invited me in for tea, I hesitantly invited them back for Mass and supper. "I don't want to embarrass you," I said. "Feel free to say no." Rich's laughter is always contagious. "I'm in so much trouble with Mayor Jane, I'd be the one to embarrass *you*"). My new friends from River Forest, acquired in the early eighties, the Brennans, the Gargiulos, and the Goggins. Priests like Nelson Callahan, John Cussick, Jack Wall, John Hotchkin, Pat Browne, John Coleman, Bill Clark, John Horan and the late Al Menarik, in addition to those I've named already. It would be hard not to be happy with such friends. If they are a trade-off for being a square peg in the Church and the university, it's a trade I'll make any day. Pure grace.

Grand Beach was a special grace because there I learned to practice and enjoy the virtue of hospitality. We solved all the problems of the world many times over at dinner parties and discussions there. Often the next morning we were not quite clear about the answers, but there was much fun and laughter and good conversation and good talk. Despite some lurking ghosts, Grand Beach is a graced place.

My cooking is, well, eclectic. At first it was things like the fondue hat trick. More recently it involves my bicentennial fruit salad, broiled whitefish, and Black Crow (chocolate ice cream with chocolate sauce laced with bourbon) followed by Bailey's Irish Cream out of devotion to the export trade of the Republic of Ireland.

Lot of chocolate, huh?

Well, I gave up sex, you don't expect me to give up chocolate too, do you?

Dinners like that require a lot of skiing and swimming to work off.

Grand Beach was also the site of some of the best (and some of the worst) moments in the history of my ill-fated small group church. The March Sunday when Nancy Gallagher (that was) read her "Yellow Yahweh" poem was a time of joy most of us will never know again—too much joy, I guess, because it was downhill for the group ever after.

Then there are the nieces and the nephews, seven attractive kids who grew up too soon but who are more fun every year.

Finally, underpinning or overarching all is my faith in a God of love and forgiveness (not the God of rules so popular these days in the Vatican) whose love I celebrate in my stories. However much the various rejections might have hurt—and some still do—there was no rejection in that quarter. With each passing year, the firmness of my faith grew deeper.

I regret only that, given these blessings, I have not always been as radiantly happy as I might have been. On the other hand, lest I violate Rita Brown's injunction not to be so hard on myself, the Ace did remember me as happy. So maybe I radiated more than I'm willing to credit myself.

Color me a square peg between 1965 and 1980, and a puzzled, sometimes angry one, occasionally a square peg who feels (not always without reason) betrayed. But don't color me sad.

Grand Beach had then become my Place, that corner of the world which, as Horace says, above all others *ridet mihi*.

A place to think, to write, to pray, to talk, to celebrate, to relax, to dream, and to begin to tell stories.

A place to dream, perhaps, of other windmills with which to joust.

CHAPTER
14
God Wouldn't Stay Dead

APPARITION

On the screen of black and white
A technicolor face
Liquid spinning movement
Within a frozen frame
Quadraphonic laughter
After a single-channel day
In a right-angled world
Your tridimensional shape
For my tundra mood
Your tropic hug
Despite my hopeless life
Your loving kiss

You can conceptualize what happened in the Catholic elites during the late sixties and early seventies if you consider a model of American Catholicism in the years before the Council as a central core of propositional rules around which were arrayed some doctrinal statements which one had to accept as a test of Catholic orthodoxy and some ethical regulations (in great part negative rules about sex) which one had to honor as proof that one was a "practicing Catholic."

Catholics did not, for example, eat meat on Friday.

And that was that.

In the years after the Council the propositions were swept away. Three new vectors from that vanished central core—radiation from a supernova—emerged. Two of them were in the direction of new sets of rules, more ethical and practical than doctrinal. One of these two went toward religious emotionalism of the charismatic and fundamentalist variety; in this vector the ethical rules were repeated, but now as obligations to undergo the approved experiences and emotions.

You may eat meat on Friday, but you also had to be baptized in the Holy Spirit.

The second vector involved rules for political and social commitment, as rigid as the sexual regulations but aimed at a different object. Both were attempts to replace the old certainties with new ones, either emotional and experiential or political and social. Both vectors also propounded simple answers to simple questions, because the quest for certainty cannot abide complexity.

You may eat meat on Friday, but you must also exercise the "preferential option for the poor" (which did not, be it noted, prevent you from paying your lay employees poverty wages) and support the Sandinistas and all other forces of "liberation."

These two vectors despaired of the Catholic tradition as outmoded and irrelevant, one searching for certainty in Protestant Fundamentalism and the other in (often Marxist) social relevance.

A third vector did not abandon the propositions as much as it bracketed them, while it explored what lay beneath them (in the images and experiences of the Catholic people) and behind them (in the overarching stories of the Catholic heritage).

What, this perspective asked, was the underlying religious symbolism which produced meatless Fridays and what did it reveal about the specifically Catholic religious experience and story?

To the social activists this vector was irrelevant because it did not immediately address itself to social and political concerns. To the Charismatics it was too abstract, rational and academic. Those of us who went in the direction of that third vector were concerned about the experiences, images and stories of the Catholic people past and present. We emphasized the importance of experience, but only that experience which resonated with the tradition. (If you rejected Mary the Mother of Jesus, you missed the point of the tradition completely.) We emphasized the importance of social commitment, but only that rooted in the unique Catholic social perspective, social commitment as a consequence of religious vision which one has not abandoned, instead of as a substitute for a vision on which one has given up because no "modern man" can believe it anymore.

We were talking about history and psychology and sociology and literary criticism and symbols while priests were impregnating nuns—in deplorably large numbers—and preaching revolution.

How irrelevant can you get?

Michele: Course I'm Catholic. That's the most important thing in my life. So I don't go to bed with my boyfriends.

Me: Because of what you learned in school?

Michele: Course not. Because of my Catholic values.

Me: Why are you Catholic?

Michele: 'Cause I'm Catholic, that's why.

Our vector, our paradigm, would insist that her position is not a tautology, but a profound religious insight. The challenge for the clerical elites is not to demolish that insight (as a lot of half-educated and half-assed clergy have tried to do in the last fifteen years—mostly in vain) but to enable Michele and the millions like her to explicate for themselves (and eventually their children) the stories and the reasons behind her insight.

Necessarily our paradigm was too complex, too elaborate and too intricate for it to have much appeal to those who wanted immediate new certainties to replace those lost. Moreover, we insisted on knowledge and skill and discipline and method, realities which were anathema to the other two vectors.

Two theological movements had an enormous impact in clerical culture at that time—the "death of God" movement and Liberation Theology. The former in its explicit, *Time*-cover-story form quickly

279

disappeared, but in its broader form it survives and flourishes. Its central argument, unchallenged by many priests and Catholic intellectuals, is that "supernatural" religion is "irrelevant" in the modern world and that therefore churches and denominations must turn to social and political action.

The "secular" and "death of God" theologians announced during the middle sixties that "modern man" was now capable of living a happy and fulfilling life without any need for religion.

This "modern man" inhabited Harvey Cox's secular city, found himself described in the beginning of most of Langdon Gilkey's books, and received honorable mention from almost all theologians of the era, including, for a time, even David Tracy.

I wanted to know who Secular Man was and where he lived, outside the halls of the divinity schools. I argued that while the theologians were proclaiming the death of God, religious sects and cults, practices from astrology to divination, and rituals from witchcraft to faith healing were happening right around the corner, on the secular university campuses. God may have been dead, I contended in my book *Unsecular Man*, but the gods were alive and well.

God was not dead and "modern man" was himself a myth. Protestant church attendance in America has not changed in forty-five years, and Catholic church attendance changed only once. As long as life needed meaning—and it does for most of us some of the time and for some of us most of the time—there would be religion. It was time for sociology to abandon the falsified hypothesis of "secularization" (the slow and inevitable decline of religion as a critical aspect of life) and study objectively how religion works in the so-called modern world.

Yet the secularization theory continued and continues to dominate education at the best universities, which turn out government officials who say, "Oh, no, religion doesn't matter any more in Iran. The shah has the support of the ordinary people for modernization."

Right.

Eliade has summed up the case against the "secularists" recently in a practically perfect paragraph (a case which all the data support):

"Meaningless[ness] seems to me the most antihuman thing there is. To be human is to seek for meaning, for value—to invent it, project it, reinvent it. So the triumph of the meaningless ... is a revolt against humanity. It is a desiccation, a sterilization—and a great bore! Naturally

280

I see that is sometimes a cry of distress uttered by certain artists in protest against the meaninglessness of modern existence. But repeating that message *ad infinitum* and thereby merely compounding the meaninglessness—*that* I don't see the point of."

My reading wandered far and wide, as it still does, probably because my character inclines me to intellectual playfulness—theoretical physics, cognitive psychology, literary theory, art history, anthropology, hermeneutical philosophy, the American thinkers like William James, Peirce, and Whitehead, the great novelists like Proust and Joyce, Faulkner and James, Lawrence, and Greene—all became grist to my mill of religious reflection.

And unconscious preparation for my own telling of stories of God.

At the same time I became conscious that there were a number of people in the country who were trying in various disciplines and fields to reinterpret the meaning of being American and Catholic. They were doing so neither defensively nor apologetically but rather because they believed that in the American Catholic experience there are insights and techniques that should be useful to the whole of society. The neighborhood, the trade union, the urban political organization, the parochial school system, as Ralph Whitehead pointed out to me repeatedly, all contain useful material not only for a self-understanding of American Catholics, but also for building a better city and a better world in which to live. In addition to Ralph, the people who were in one way or another working in this area and shaping my thoughts were the late Geno Baroni, Paul Asciola, Charles Fanning, Ellen Skerrit, Dominic Pasyga, Pastora San Juan Cafferty, Charles Shanabruch and my NORC colleague William McCready. This attempt to develop what Whitehead called "a Catholic ethic" or "a Catholic theory of society" was light-years away from trying to adduce practical solutions from Papal encyclicals. It is also light-years away from the current dominant fashion in Catholic social activism, influenced as it has been by the Berrigan mystique.

For most contemporary current Catholic peace and justice activists, ministry means guilt, hatred of America, and the repetition of the most fashionable current liberal or radical clichés. The notion that there might be anything in the neighborhood or the urban political machine that could contribute to the solution of serious social problems seems to these people uproariously funny.

It is clear if one reads the 1984 pastoral on the economy that Church leadership is not interested in its own historical social ethic. The tradition my friends and I represent has been grandly dismissed as beneath notice.

At precisely the time when brilliant sociologists like Jim Coleman are rediscovering the neighborhood.

So while we have lost to the ideologues at the Center for Concern (honest, folks, there is such a place) and the U.S. Catholic Conference, we're the wave of the future.

At the same time I was focusing on the religion of experience, symbol and story (without developing the paradigm just yet) and the social ethic of the neighborhood, the fashion in clerical circles was turning toward Liberation Theology, going in the opposite direction. Liberation Theology is in fact neither—not theology but political and social ideology disguised as religion—and it can be called Liberation only in the special sense that Marxist dictatorship means liberation. The supporters of Liberation Theology demand acceptance in the name of the poor, implying, it would seem, that Marxism and Marxism alone can solve their problems.

A simple look at the world (take Poland or Cuba, for example) would correct that notion, but the Liberation Theology people are too enthused about their mission to look at the world. Their "theology" is devoid of serious economic or social analysis. When one comes to the places in their books where one might expect them to demonstrate some under-standing of economic and social processes one finds either quotes from Marx or diatribes against the United States.

Just as opposition to the Vatican Council can only be intellectually satisfying to those Catholic traditionalists who have no sense of the history of the tradition, so Liberation Theology can be satisfying only to those enthusiasts who have no sense of the complexity of the world.

If all solutions are simple, Liberation Theology may make sense. But when one charges its supporters with enthusiastic oversimplification, they reply, "Our cause is the cause of the poor."

Unfortunately, they have no election credentials certifying that the poor have made them their representatives.

Such self-anointed messianism is offensive from anyone; when it comes from North American missionaries trying to stir up revolution in other countries despite the expressed wishes of the people, they become im-perialists indistinguishable from the multinational conglomerates they denounce, although the multinationals provide employment and in-

282

come for the poor countries and the missionaries provide nothing at all.

As the college student says to Cathy on the bus to Rio Secco in *Virgin and Martyr,* "Why don't you leave us alone? Why don't you take both your religion and your politics and go home?"

Liberation Theology is bad theology and worse social reform, but I don't believe those who teach it should be condemned by the Church. In fact, although it makes much noise in the seminaries of South America, it has had little impact on the life of the people. While the theologians have been preaching Marxist revolution, the actual historical trend in South America in recent years has been in the direction of social democracy.

Small wonder we were a minority and smaller wonder we were infuriating when we were also as loudmouthed and smart-assed as I was.

We had only two things going for us: we were right and we were the future. Both of which assertions will also qualify as simultaneously loudmouthed and smart-assed.

How do I know we were (and are) right?

Easy.

Anyone who thinks a tradition which is fifteen hundred years old (at the least) and has resonated to human needs for that length of time becomes irrelevant overnight and not worthy of reexamination is a fool.

And I subjected my model to an empirical test. I wrote novels based on hypotheses derived from the model. In a verification (model-fitting) process which would have delighted William James, they were tremendous successes, precisely because they were what my theory claimed should appeal to people—stories of God, comedies of grace, parables of divine love.

The years from 1960 to 1965 were a period in my life of excitement, hope and growth in professional skills and personal confidence and religious faith. From 1965 to 1970 I ran into the meatgrinder of the post-Conciliar failures and the rise of angry romanticism after the institutional Church lost control of the reform energies. The years from 1971 to 1980 were a period of discouragement, disenchantment and disillusion, a time of sinking into a rut, spiritual, emotional, moral. I kept trying and I kept failing. Often I would sit for a few moments in the parking lot at NORC after I had turned off the ignition, working up the energy to continue. Even my more ingenious schemes, like a study of the Papal elections, turned into disasters. My family was persecuted by priests. My work was dismissed briskly as irrelevant because I was a paranoid with whom it was impossible to work. Many of those who I thought were friends turned out not to be and never to have been friends.

Healing and renewal would wait for the end of the decade when I joined the faculty of the University of Arizona, developed my paradigm for a sociological model of religion, and began to write poetry and fiction.

I do not wish to exaggerate the theme of 1970s as rut. There were exciting times—a journey to Australia for the preliminaries of the Eucharistic Congress, a trip around the world lecturing on ethnicity for the State Department (arranged by Pat Moynihan), a study which vindicated the Vatican Council from the charge that it had caused the crisis in the Church, the development of the Pluralism Center (loyally supported by Mac Bundy, Mike Sviridoff and Basil Whiting of the Ford Foundation), continued growth in religious understanding as I responded to the "death of God" and "secular" theologians, persistence in many if not all friendships and the finding of new friends (including two men who had great influence on my thinking and imagining about religion, David Tracy and John Shea), the excitement of research in Rome on Papal elections, and the slow hammering out of my paradigm of religion as I worked on the Mary Myth and rediscovered Mary, now as a sacrament of God's tenderness.

Was I looking for a tender and womanly God because so much of my experience in life during that decade involved rejection and hatred?

There was one experience, however, that was pure grace—Jack Wall's First Mass. Jack had hung around with his contemporaries at CK, attended our summer discussion groups in the parish, and participated in some of the study weeks we sponsored for young adults. His class was ordained in 1967, but he postponed ordination for another year. Thus in the spring of 1968 I found myself in Queen of Martyrs Church listening to the sermon (I don't think it had become a homily yet) being preached by a big, broad-shouldered black Irishman who was a classmate of Wall's. (Jack Wall is now pastor of the oldest parish in Chicago, Old St. Patrick's. My friend Mary O'Hara sang her first Chicago concert there, my niece Julie was married there, and the Durkins have found refuge there, after the pastor made life unbearable in their home parish—and I gather for lots of other people too.)

The talk was dazzling, maybe the finest sermon I had ever heard till that moment. "Thank God our time is now, the enterprise is exploration into God." Christopher Fry. *Sleep of Prisoners*. Did seminarians and young priests still read Fry?

After that there was a continuation of the poem, which I didn't remember from Fry's play. I went home and checked it out. Sure enough, Jack Shea had written his own poem as a continuation of Fry's.

What the hell!

Me: (to Bill McCready who was in the seminary with that class) Who's the big fella who preached at Wall's Mass on Sunday?

Bill: You noticed him, too? That's Shags. He's a genius.

Me: It would seem so.

Bill: Mystic, poet, pool shark, basketball player, storyteller.

Me: Do *they* know about him?

Bill: Not really.

Shags is a towering genius, the most gifted human I've ever met. There are two ways you can react to such a person. One, which I have considered idiotic, is to resent him. The other is to make common cause with him. The latter is always the indicated procedure, especially when he is from the same West Side neighborhood you're from.

Shea's story theology is from the next generation. It will be a quarter century before the Church catches up. His poetry will last even longer, especially the story poems in the last three chapters of *Stories of Faith*, and most especially the last of them, in which Jesus is described as "The Storyteller of God," a poem which moves me to tears every time I read it:

> Now
> There was only the morning
> And the dancing man of the broken tomb
> The story says
> he dances still
> That is why
> down to this day
> we lean over the beds of our babies
> and in the seconds before sleep
> tell the story of the undying dancing man
> So the dream of Jesus will carry them to dawn.

Shags is a lot less likely to tilt with windmills than I am, mostly because he has much less confidence in institutions than I do (the result in part at any rate of being ordained in 1967 instead of 1954). His work is usually ignored, sometimes patronized in the Catholic media, but still widely read if not so widely understood.

As Jim Mahoney put it once in a marvelous Irish bull, "If Jack Shea were dead, he'd roll over in his grave at what they're doing to story theology."

One discusses theology with Shags under most favorable circumstances after a movie. In fact, we have a custom of seeing a double and sometimes a triple feature every season of the year.

I don't take notes, but I'm tempted.

My debt to him in *The Mary Myth* and *Religion: A Secular Theory* is obvious. If it had not been for his books and our conversations, I would have never developed my experience/symbol/story/community paradigm for religion.

Nor would I have ever written novels.

One of which is dedicated to him in gratitude for giving me a head start.

He is also the kind of West Side Irishman who defines friendship the same way I do.

I don't think the American Church values him enough. Certainly the Archdiocese of Chicago does not, but then we're not into talent just now. On the other hand, Shags is elusive; he avoids meetings, institutions, organizations, academics and administrators as though they were carriers of the bubonic plague. I must confess that this 1960s orientation of his is becoming more appealing. In theory I believe that the action had passed out of the hands of the institutional leadership by 1970. But there's enough of the Sunday Night Group's influence clinging to me not to accept that as totally in my gut as I do in my head. Jack begins with that assumption.

I was a priest when it still didn't have to be that way. He was ordained when it was almost inevitable.

The most notable thing about lost causes is that they are lost.

From those years there developed another theologian who, along with Shags and John Hotchkin and David Tracy, would have great influence on me.

One of the results of the changes in the Church was that my sister Mary Jule, at the ripe old age of thirty-one, decided in 1965 (after hearing Küng's famous McCormick Place lecture on honesty in the Church and with the encouragement of Walt Imbiorski) that she wanted to be a theologian. If the laity was to turn to theology, she asked, in anticipation of the feminist movement by five years, why not lay women?

She and her husband, Jack Durkin, were the chair couple of the Cana Conference the year of the encyclical, and this experience reinforced her decision, even if it did mean nine years of a class a quarter at the distinctly uncooperative University of Chicago Divinity School. She already had six children, and Liz, the youngest, made her appearance during Mary Jule's graduate training.

She took a lot of grief from women in her neighborhood for her decision and not a little later on from priests who ought to have known better. When applying for a job at the now happily defunct Jesuit School of Theology in Chicago, she was asked how she could possibly teach there and not neglect her children—this at a school whose president had bragged only a week before that women were receiving the training required for ordination to the priesthood. Women yes, mothers no!

Mary Jule offered to bring the kids and the husband along so the good Jesuits could judge whether they seemed neglected. That really wasn't the point, however. Their next question was whether the internal affairs of the school would be subject matter for my column.

You see why I say happily defunct.

Later when she and I toured promoting our book *How to Save the Catholic Church* there were hints of possible neglect of children. I would invariably assert that Liz—Elizabeth Maura Brigid Durkin—was obviously a neglected child: president of the student council, valedictorian, Merit Scholarship winner (with the most scorching Irish blue eyes I have ever seen) and recipient of a standing ovation from her high school classmates on graduation day. Yeah, neglected. Bastards.

As her oldest sister, Laura, whispered to me, "Well, Uncle!, three generations, seven kids, and we finally got our act together."

The Durkin kids (to whom I am Uncle!, always with an exclamation point) are rangy, resourceful, witty, articulate young men (two) and women (five). I do not believe in generalizing from one case to a universal rule. But in this one case, their mother's graduate work was obviously an asset in their maturation process.

The Divinity School, as much imbedded in absurd rituals as a pre-Conciliar Catholic rubricist, was not so much hostile as insensitive—and intolerably chauvinist.

When she began her program, certain requirements in philosophical theology were not part of the game. By the time she came up for her prelims, they had been incorporated into the ritual. Even though they knew she did not have the courses and had told her it didn't matter, her examiners spent most of her oral on those subjects—a very distinguished process theologian pushing her relentlessly on matter he knew beforehand was beyond her background.

At the end, an even more distinguished (world-class) Protestant theologian who considered himself a militant feminist consoled her with the thought, "This really shouldn't mean much to you. After all, you have your wonderful Irish Catholic family, haven't you?"

She received the doctorate anyhow, but only after much suffering.

And promptly discovered she was unemployable. One would have anticipated that a wife and mother with theological training would have been a welcome addition to any faculty. However, the Catholic schools in the Chicago area were busy adding Protestants and Jews and atheists and blacks. They had no room for a mother, even if she was an alumna. And especially if she was my sister.

At first neither of us could believe it. Then word drifted back to us that the faculties were uneasy about Cardinal Cody. Perhaps he would take punitive action against them if they hired my sister; Cody was certainly capable of punitive action—he repeatedly crossed her name off the list of speakers at Archdiocesan functions—but he left the Catholic colleges alone.

She taught part-time (full course load, but the salary of a part-time teacher) and did administrative work for a Catholic university. When a "full-time" position came open, she was turned down, according to a member of the theology department who was also the religious superior, the Drink having been taken, because "she is as bad as her brother and we don't want either of them around here."

In three instances we had sufficient evidence to go to court against the schools but decided it would be a waste of time.

The worst incident occurred at the Catholic Theology Meeting at Milwaukee the year Mary Jule accepted a visiting appointment at the University of Dayton (which meant commuting back and forth three days

288

a week in winter weather). A famous Catholic theologian, a man who had insisted repeatedly that the rights of women are the most important issue in the Church, jumped all over her department chairman for hiring her while Mary Jule stood by listening. Later in the conference David Tracy made him apologize, but it was obviously insincere. He was only sorry he had been caught.

There has never been in any of this persecution a shred of argument about competence. Her publications and credentials were in order. The issue was always something over which she had no control—her sibling.

I realized I was not imagining the envy behind the Greeley Myth (the priest who denounced Mary Jule to her department chairman had been turned down a few weeks before by the Universal Press Syndicate, with which he wanted a contract to distribute his column). Yet even today I continue to be astonished that priests, supposedly committed to the Gospel of Jesus, will deliberately and self-consciously try to punish a man through his family.

One of the happiest outcomes of the success of my novels is that I have been able to hire Mary Jule as a theologian, equip her with the resources she needs for her work and collaborate with her in that work. It's a way of having the last laugh.

During the late sixties many of the members of my small group church would suggest, not always with kindness, that I was a Don Quixote personality. Perhaps the model fit. I have certainly made it my own in this story, though perhaps giving it a more benign meaning than they intended. For a decade and a half I jousted with a lot of windmills. As I write this chapter I am tilting with the bishops again on their shabby pastoral on the American economy, a document devoid of wisdom on both economics and the traditional Catholic social theory.

Maybe that is quixotic behavior. Why was it necessary for me to take on so many windmills? I told myself I had the freedom and the platform from which to speak the truth and that if I remained silent, no one else would, for example, speak out on what everyone knew was happening in the Archdiocese of Chicago or on the impact of the birth-control encyclical.

But *who* appointed me knight errant of the American Church? No one, obviously. If the bishops wanted to hush up the findings on the change of priestly attitudes on birth control, why was it my mission to make certain the research was *not* hushed up? What difference did it make? Or if more recently they want to write patent nonsense about the American economy, why should I give a hoot? What difference does it make?

The argument I used repeatedly to myself was: "If you don't do it, it won't be done."

Was it bravery to take on the Maryknoll Marxists who were trying to bring revolution to countries whose people wanted no American imperialism of the left or the right? Or to challenge the Berrigan worshipers whose demonstrations helped prolong the war (some of them to this day admitted casually that sure their demonstrations helped to reelect Nixon, so what?) or to try to force sociologists to consider religion and ethnicity as major predictor variables once again?

What was the point in it all? *Cui bono,* as they say in the mother tongue. Why bother? Did I think I could withstand the wave of history which was sweeping away the intellectual and cultural foundations of the American clergy? Did I think I might stop the zaniness which was inevitable after the bishops lost control of the reform movement in the late sixties? Did I think I could single-handedly create scholarly standards for the American Church? Did I think I had a chance of turning Church leadership around on sex? Did I believe sociologists would begin to take religion seriously despite the fact that many of them were refugees from unpleasant religious environments in their childhood?

What can I tell you?

If we are only to attempt those projects which look as though they have a reasonable chance to succeed, then we will do almost nothing at all. By trying anyway, did I reveal delusions of grandeur? Should I have simply settled down and enjoyed life as one of my friends said when she broke with me over my first novel without having read it?

Was I a prophet, as Joe Bernardin said publicly in Dayton, or an embarrassment, as his spokesman in Chicago said off the record when I gave a million and a quarter dollars to the University of Chicago for a chair in Catholic Studies? Maybe both?

I doubt that. One or the other dominates. Which one?

I don't know the answer. The reader will have to make up her/his own mind. Finally, it comes down to the ideals, doesn't it? The tragedy of Quixote is that he lived for ideals which were both foolish and obsolescent and that therefore he fought worthless battles.

Are the things I fought for worth the effort? Are my ideals of honor and integrity and honesty and loyalty and friendship admirable or ridiculous?

(Lady Wisdom: Come on now, begorra, you do too know the answers to those questions.)

If I am a Don Quixote, then it is Don Quixote the novelist. It was precisely the argument which got me into most of the other hot water that led me to try to write theological novels, stories of God, comedies of grace: someone ought to do it; if you don't, no one else will.

Is that an ideal on which to base a life?

Perhaps. The reader again will have to judge.

CHAPTER 15

More Windmills

Low clouds—racing
maniac waves
Beneath a broken night
Lightning seared
Thunder blasted—
Briefly part

Calmly watching
With acetylene eye
A single star

As the sixties turned into the seventies and I was fighting intellectually with the "secularists" and the beginnings of "Liberation Theology" I was also jousting with the Church on our study of the Catholic priesthood and with the University of Chicago on whether I was a good enough sociologist to become a first-class citizen in the university community.

In the priest study I managed, without half trying, to offend everyone simply by reporting the truth as objectively and dispassionately as I could and then fighting fiercely when Cardinal Krol tried to discredit it.

In the autumn of 1970 I was sitting with some of my staff from the NORC Study of the American Priesthood at the hotel near O'Hare International Airport. The historical and liturgical and theological and psychological studies had reported their preliminary findings. The bishop's committee listened with interest—and some sleepiness, for it was late in the afternoon and most of the bishops had traveled a long way. The committee was made up of Cardinal Krol, Archbishop Carberry, Bishop Primeau, Bishop Zaleski and Bishop Bernardin as secretary of the hierarchy. First of all, I told them the good news, relatively good. Most American priests are happy in their work, priests are as emotionally mature and as capable of intimacy as comparable married laymen. Perhaps as many as 15 percent of the priesthood would eventually resign but the others would remain. Eighty percent of the clergy favored optional celibacy; 80 percent favored a married clergy. Only a minority still said their office every day. Those who had left the priesthood thus far or were thinking of leaving were doing so because they wanted to marry, but their desire to marry was in its turn the result of unhappiness in their work. Only a minority of those who had resigned, approximately 20 percent, would want to go back to doing the work they had done before they left the priesthood—parish work and teaching. Another 20 percent would come back if they could be Sunday priests but do other work during the week, and 60 percent of those who had left had no desire to return to the active ministry.

Some of this was controversial, but not terribly so. The bishops around the table relaxed visibly. Sociology was not that dangerous after all. There were problems, but the problems were specific, and could be dealt with, either by practical programs or by well-chosen words.

Then I gave them the bad news.

First of all, priests were no longer interested in recruiting new aspirants,

294

in great part because they had lost confidence in their own priestly identity.

Moreover, there had been a dramatic swing away from support for the official birth control teaching since the publication of the birth control encyclical. More than 80 percent of the clergy said they would not enforce it in the confessional and a slightly lower number said they did not believe that the teaching was valid.

Instead of falling in line under the Pope's rule, the American presbytery had revolted, quietly and secretly, but emphatically. The Pope and the bishops no longer enjoyed any credibility on matters of sexual morality. It was as though the entire room had been wiped out by a laser gun— absolute and total silence. Archbishop John Carberry left the room at once so as not to hear any more scandalous doctrine. Ernie Primeau leaned over to me and whispered in my ear, "Even I didn't expect it to be *that* bad."

I have been told often it would have been much better if I had not confronted the bishops with the truth. Prudence and discretion would indicate I should have held it back. How *else* did I expect them to react?

I am convinced it would have been horrendously dishonest not to tell the bishops the truth. They had not objected to the birth-control questions in the questionnaire because they assumed, gratuitously it seemed to me, that the clergy had gone along with the encyclical. Cardinal Krol was far more concerned about the question of whether the priests said the breviary—were we not, after all, asking them whether they were committing sins?

Priests were not saying the breviary but even worse, they were rejecting Papal teaching on birth control. For the hierarchy, now that the late great Archbishop Paul Hallinan was dead and the committee had lost its most dynamic, progressive leader, the question was how to establish as much distance as they could between themselves and the NORC survey.

If that were the only bizarre episode, I would have little to complain about, but from beginning to end, the NORC priesthood study was trouble. By the time it was over, I had learned two lessons—never trust priests, and never trust bishops. Unfortunately for me, one of the bishops I had learned to distrust during the priesthood study later cultivated my friendship, and I began to trust him again. Then he became archbishop of Chicago and I realized I had swung on a curve ball twice. One more strike and I would be out.

The idea of a multidisciplinary study of the priesthood had been Archbishop Dearden's. With characteristic political skill, he persuaded the national hierarchy that a committee should be set up to oversee such a study and that his seminary friend Cardinal Krol, the vice-president of the bishops, should be its chairman. Thus it was a study suggested by the progressive John Dearden but to be supervised by the conservative John Krol—the conservative who, even though he was only vice-president, was made a cardinal before Dearden of Detroit was made a cardinal— the first of many signs from the Curia that the Americans were not to be forgiven for what they did at the Council. Then the vice-chairman of the committee was Dearden's seminary contemporary Archbishop Paul Hallinan of Atlanta, one of the great liberal leaders at the Council. It was his job to make sure Krol did not turn the study into too conservative an operation. Bishops Primeau and Zaleski were added to fill out the committee, and Bernardin was there in his role of general secretary (and protégé of Hallinan).

The trouble with the study from the outset was that everyone wanted to make it a political study, i.e., the bishops wanted the study to establish what they knew in their hearts was true, namely that priests were basically satisfied and that there was no reason seriously to consider changing the celibacy rule. On the other hand, many of the priest activists in the country wanted exactly the opposite: they wanted the study to prove that a change in the celibacy rule was essential.

I explained repeatedly to all questioners that the study could neither prove nor disprove the value of the celibacy rule—it could merely report what its implications were in the modern world. Scholars were not policymakers. Researchers could find the facts but they could not make the policies. No one on either side of the controversy seemed prepared to believe me. Why else did you do a study if it didn't force you to make a decision one way or the other? The distinction between facts and decisions seems to have escaped everyone, yet it is an elementary distinction in scholarly research. The scholar does not know the values or the directions or the principles under which the policymakers work. He reports his findings, then leaves the policy decisions to whoever is sponsoring the study. He may have his own inclinations about what decisions are appropriate, but these go beyond the data he has collected, analyzed and interpreted. Then and now this distinction seems totally invalid to Catholic clergy and hierarchy.

The first problem we encountered when the project was launched was the announcement of its cost. The Catholic press reacted in outrage when it heard the NORC study was going to cost three hundred thousand dollars. The howling was led by a monsignor in the *Pittsburgh Catholic* who somehow or other seemed to think I owned NORC and all the money was going to come to me. He led the pack of critics who did not believe in social research and bitterly resented the fact that I was ripping off the hierarchy.

Actually three hundred thousand dollars was a modest price for the kind of research being done. In fact, we were producing three studies for the price of one—one of priests, one of bishops and one of resigned priests. Moreover, despite the Pittsburgh monsignor, I didn't receive any salary for the project. At that time, I was recovering from the first phase of my long battle with the University of Chicago and I was a full professor at Chicago Circle, which was paying my salary for two years.

The second problem was the National Federation of Priest Councils, presided over by a Chicago priest with some political skill but limited intelligence. He wrote to me, much as the National Catholic Education staff member had written at the time of the Catholic School Study, demanding that all our data be turned over to scholars he would appoint to analyze them from the priests' perspective. "You," he told me, "are doing a study for the bishops. We also must have somebody doing a study for the priests." I wrote back to him and suggested somebody was writing crank letters and signing his name to them and added that NORC was doing a study in the interest of truth and not in the interest of the policy proclivities of either priests or bishops. Moreover, while NORC data were available two years after the ending of a project for any scholar who wished to work with it, I could not legally turn over data to anybody prior to that time and he had no right to demand it of me.

So the National Federation of Priest Councils launched its own project as a rival to ours and, as was strongly implied, a corrective to keep me honest.

Yet another problem was internal to the study staff. Foolishly I hired priests to work on the project, figuring they would understand the subject from the inside and we could save a lot of time and energy in orienting the staff.

This created a serious role conflict on the project staff, for we were all priests, I no more so than the others, and I with no priestly authority over them. I was the senior scholar, the only one who had done national survey research before, and the one responsible to NORC and to the client for the project's outcome. This "authority" of mine was bitterly resented by the others. I had no right to make any command decisions. All had to be reached collectively (it was 1969, when "participatory democracy" was fashionable).

One of the staff members was the most arrogant and supercilious student I have ever encountered at NORC. He came to the project thinking he knew everything about sociology, social research and the priesthood and had nothing to learn about the techniques of survey research. In the NORC environment, staff seminars are a context for criticizing ideas and methods in order that the younger scholar may learn to improve his technique of survey data collection and analysis. The criticisms of the staff seminar this particular priest dismissed with a contemptuous sneer. His theories were clear, and the simple cross-tabulations he had done to support them left no doubt of their validity. He didn't need to know about beta weights, multiple regression, correlation coefficients, path analyses, or anything of that sort. When I suggested there were weaknesses in his line of reasoning and that any professional sociologist would dismiss his findings out of hand he once again simply waved his hand contemptuously.

It soon became clear that the priests on the project were convinced I was an authoritarian interested in providing the bishops with a report that confirmed the existing celibacy discipline. It was their job, as they saw it, to keep me in line and issue the accurate and valid report recommending that the celibacy rule be abolished. I insisted repeatedly that we were not making recommendations, we were reporting facts. My staff no more understood this distinction than did the national hierarchy or the National Federation of Priest Councils. One priest simply stopped working. He collected his salary, appeared occasionally at the office, and produced nothing. Later I found he was spreading the word to everybody he could that I was a creature of the bishops, doing their bidding. I should have fired the whole lot of them and hired a group of agnostics to complete the project, but by then it had become so thoroughly politicized there would have been cries of outrage from the priest organizations around the country and from the liberal catholic press, like *The National Catholic Reporter*, so I endured my colleagues on the project, knowing that whatever they thought about the collegiality, I was nonetheless the senior study director in charge of the project and the report would contain what I wanted to put in it and not what they wanted—i.e., it would objectively analyze the data and not make *a priori* recommendations about the abolition of celibacy.

Although the priest who was the staff director was, and is, a competent sociologist, it became clear in the spring of the final year that he was going to leave the priesthood and marry an ex-nun. Unfortunately, he was and is a slow, cautious and methodical worker, the kind of man who produces good research but only after many years. In the NORC business, reports have to be done on time and cannot, of necessity, be as perfect as if they were being done by a sociologist without a deadline. Summer turned into autumn and there were still no data ready to analyze, even though data collection had stopped almost a year before. The staff director was slowly, carefully preparing the data to make sure they were all flawless before running a single table.

In the professional survey business, such caution is inappropriate. One could work years in preparing data for analysis and find an occasional mistake or two, but nothing that would notably change the findings. Again, I should have absolutely insisted he stop tinkering with the data and actually begin the analysis. However, his own emotional life was, at that time, quite turbulent, and finally, in September, he informed me he was going to be married in early December, three months before the report was due.

This would be the ultimate disaster to the project. It would have no credibility at all with the bishops if one of its senior authors had already left the priesthood. Norman Bradburn, the director of NORC, was in Europe, so Paul Sheatsley, the acting director, and I journeyed to Philadelphia to talk to Cardinal Krol about the situation. Krol was, to give him full credit, sympathetic and helpful. The compromise we reached was that the report, when it appeared in the following March, would be a report from NORC without any author's name on the cover but an introductory paragraph explaining who had done what on the project.

The man who was about to leave the priesthood accepted the compromise reluctantly. When Bradburn returned from Europe he was critical. We should have fired the young priest on the spot because his behavior was irresponsible and endangered the credibility of the report to the client who was paying for it. Norman was theoretically correct: we should have fired him on the spot, but, once more, the political concerns raging around the project made such a decision impossible.

The stall in data preparation continued through the autumn with my colleague assuring me that the tables would be ready for me to write the report when he left on his honeymoon. The day before his wedding, I went to his office to collect the data. Not a single table. "It can't be done," he said. "We are not going to be able to finish by March. We have to go to the bishops and ask for more time and more money."

"They won't give us more time or more money," I replied. "If we don't have a report by March fifteenth, they are going to accuse us of violating the contract."

"It can't be helped." He shrugged. "We are not going to be able to do it right in the time they've allowed us."

"NORC does things right in the time it is allowed," I said. "I'm taking charge from here on."

Badly shaken, I went back to my office, where the NORC editor was waiting for me to inform me that if I wanted the report by March 15, I had to get the final draft of the text into her hands by January 6. This was an unreasonable demand, but with Bradburn away in Europe, and her complete control of the typing and duplicating process at NORC, I had no choice but to go along. That meant I had three and a half weeks to do all the analysis for the project as well as write the report.

So while my colleague was on his honeymoon, I did just that, spending the whole thirty-five-thousand-dollar data-processing budget in approximately two weeks. The report was written and written on time (Christmas didn't happen that year), and despite comments from some priest-sociologists that I had done none of the work on the report but was claiming credit for it, no one ever found any technical weaknesses. Doing a major report in three weeks is an exercise I cannot recommend to anyone.

If there was one thing we learned in the study, it was that the national hierarchy ought not to directly fund research because of their fear that Rome would hold them responsible for their findings. Moreover, given the turbulence in the priesthood, it would not be a wise thing either to have priests working on projects whose director was another priest, their equal in the ministry, but their superior in research experience.

However, I had not heard the last of the report. Cardinal Krol had commissioned a three-person team of sociologists to evaluate it, which was perfectly within his rights. Several months later I learned from an article in the *New York Times* that this team had turned in a highly unfavorable evaluation and that the evaluation was going to be printed in the official U.S. Catholic Conference publication of the report. I called Joe Bernardin (he insisted that everybody associated with the project call him by his first name) and screamed blue bloody murder. Why hadn't I been given a chance to see the evaluation? Why was it going to appear as an appendix to our report without us being told, and without us being given an opportunity to respond to it in the same report? Nervously, Joe said there had been an oversight somewhere in his office. I said it was more than an oversight, it was betrayal, and I would not tolerate it.

A couple of days later he did send me the evaluation, a curious, nasty, supercilious document. The three evaluators could find nothing technically wrong with what we had done. Their principal theme was that had they done it, they would have proceeded differently, and relied much less on surveys and more on personal observation. Like many sociologists who do not use the survey techniques, they saw little value in national sample data collection and analysis. Their "know-nothing" contempt for survey research was to be found in almost every paragraph.

From the point of view of sociology, they didn't lay a finger on us, as Jim Davis, who had replaced Bradburn as the director of NORC, pointed out. However, from the point of view of the ordinary reader, it would seem their evaluation thoroughly discredited it. Cardinal Krol had been consummately clever.

The bishops were perfectly within their rights in commissioning and publishing an evaluation. But we were within ours in demanding an opportunity to respond to the evaluation in a book which was published over NORC authorship.

I phoned Archbishop Dearden and pleaded with him to intervene. He said that was a problem I should take up with Cardinal Krol. I didn't argue with Dearden. He knew I thought he was betraying the project, and I think, deep down inside, he realized himself that he was. The political realities of the power structure of the American Church at that time, he believed, gave him no choice.

I was asked to make a presentation to a committee set up to "implement" the reports, presided over by Archbishop Hannan of New Orleans. The hierarchy now had become deft at burying controversial materials in committees. There was no question of Philip Hannan's personal integrity. He took the various research documents seriously and did plan that they be implemented in the life of American priests. Unfortunately, with the passage of time, all that would happen would be another office set up in the U.S. Catholic Conference bureaucracy and our research documents read but forgotten. I prepared a presentation for Archbishop Hannan's committee, charging the bishops with spiritual, intellectual and moral bankruptcy, because of their attempts to discredit their own research project, and then, to make sure my remarks were not overlooked, I released the document before the meeting to *The National Catholic Reporter*. If Krol and Bernardin wanted a fight, they were going to get one.

Hannan was shocked, more by the treachery of the leadership than by my statement, and at the next administrative board meeting, moved that the offending evaluation be eliminated from the report. There was a bitter battle, but Hannan and his allies (strongly supported by two Chicago auxiliary bishops, Thomas Grady and William McManus) won the day and the evaluation was published separately—and read by no one. The idea of tearing it out of the report—and they had to go to the bindery to remove it physically from the document—was not mine. I would just as soon have the evaluation appear in the report with our response because I was sure I could devastate the criticism. However, Hannan thought— correctly, I suppose—that the controversy had gone far enough, and that any further controversy would have a negative effect on his committee's work.

The two and a half years of research and controversy on the priesthood study were, in fact, a waste of time. *Nothing* was accomplished. While we did provide the most extensive study of the priests, bishops and inactive or resigned priests ever attempted in the world, the findings satisfied no one because reality resolutely refused to fit anybody's preconceptions. The temper of the times in American Catholicism was such that dull, objective, nuanced, factual analysis was calculated to offend everyone. The book was distributed to the libraries, where it was occasionally read but, with the exception of the birth-control findings, systematically ig- nored. Social scholarship in the service of the Church, the reason I had become a sociologist, was out of fashion, and was likely to remain so for a long, long time.

The hierarchy and the Church, however, paid a heavy price for the bishops' fear of the results of our report. We warned them that there was a serious crisis brewing in the priesthood. They did not listen, not really. Their committee, while well intentioned, did not care to fully understand what the data suggested about that crisis. So the morale of the clergy fell apart and the lack of vocations—a clear result of failure of morale and loss of nerve in the clergy—has now become an acute problem.

Why the crisis in clerical identity? At the heart of the matter is the low job satisfaction of priests. This seems to be caused by our lack of a sense of adequate performance of tasks at which we were professionally trained. Moreover, our job performance is not adequately recognized by either our colleagues or by our people. We were trained in the seminary to believe that we should not be good at what we did because that would lead to pride. Being incompetent was not a problem because our status was a given, not the result of achievement. But now ascribed status has been swept away. We feel inferior because we have to earn respect, and we suspect that we can't do it—often a well-founded suspicion. Moreover, now that the laity are no longer an inferior caste and other people seem able to do as well as we can some tasks which were once our preserve— religious instruction or marriage counseling, for example—what is there left to give us dignity, importance and the right to respect?

The crisis is mostly self-imposed. The laity think priests are more crucial than ever, which is precisely why they demand high standards of professional performance from us. We hear the latter demand, but we do not hear the former assertion. We don't know how important we are— or could be.

No one can say that fair warning wasn't given a decade and a half ago.

While I was fighting the perhaps senseless war of the windmills on the priest study I was engaged in a running battle with the University of Chicago. It was not one I chose or wanted.

Some curious background to the battle:

In 1966 I had purchased in Germany a Mercedes 190, drove it through Europe, and then brought it home. The car (which turned out, incidentally, to be a lemon) cost twenty-five hundred dollars, only six hundred dollars more than my VW, which I had bought in 1959.

A man who would later become my implacable enemy in the sociology department was offended. "Priests shouldn't drive Mercedeses," he told everyone who would listen. I didn't take him seriously. It was, after all, none of his business what I drove. Moreover, since he was not a Catholic, why was he worried about the life-style of a priest?

I am assured, however, by those who know him that the Benz was the origin of his animosity against me.

Weird.

(For those who care: since then I have driven VWs, Plymouths, and most recently Chevies.)

Another implacable foe told his colleagues that I had been a student of his and had a second-rate mind. The latter may have been true, but the former was not. I encountered him later at a restaurant (myself in clericals) and congratulated him on a recent article.

Foe: Thank you very much, uh, Father...

Me: Greeley.

Foe: Oh yes, Father Greeley.

I've often wondered who the priest was with whom he had confused me.

Finally, the sociology department had decreed that my work on Catholic schools was not concerned with "important" matter and that my work on ethnicity was irrelevant, because ethnicity was not "important" either.

I'm not the only one against whom such tactics have been used and the Chicago department isn't the only one to play such games. But the cards were stacked from the beginning, and if Quixote had been smart he wouldn't have played the game.

In 1968 I had accepted an appointment in the education department at Chicago Circle (jointly with NORC, where I was directing both the priest study and the alumni study) with tenure. I left it after two years because it had become clear to me that NORC was the place where I belonged. Let it be emphasized for the record (since the newspaper accounts have usually been confused) that I *had* tenure and gave it up. My future battles at Chicago were not about tenure, but about anti-Catholic prejudice.

When Bradburn returned from Europe, he was appointed chairman of the new behavioral sciences department and assistant dean and informed me I was the obvious choice to replace him. I had not thought of myself particularly as the director of NORC, but when I was approached about that possibility, it seemed that it would be a useful learning experience for me. The same faculty influence that intrigued against my appointment in the education department also intrigued against my appointment at NORC. The trustees voted to delay and look for someone else to fill the position, the reason being that most of the understaff at NORC were blacks, and that blacks would be offended by my emphasis on white ethnic research. The trustees never bothered to talk to the blacks of the NORC staff, most of whose children were in Catholic schools, and virtually all of whom were friendly to me (when the priest on the USCC study resigned from the active ministry to be married, the word went around NORC with some contempt that "he's not a priest anymore").

Jim Davis came back from Hanover and assumed the reins at NORC after asking me whether I minded. Obviously I didn't mind and was just as happy to be freed from the administrative burden. However, for the second time now, I had been offered jobs at the University of Chicago and had them snatched away at the last minute for reasons which, then and now, looked to me like anti-Catholic prejudice.

The best summary of my ongoing battles with the University of Chicago at that time is that they were a mistake. I should never have become involved in them in the first place. The dice were loaded against victory from the outset, both because the other side made up the rules as it went along and had more influence in the administrative bureaucracy and because the people that were on my side were simply not the ruthless alley fighters, the veteran academic politicians, that my opponents were.

I was voted the rank of tenured full professor three times by different units of the university, and each time these recommendations were rejected at higher levels of the administration. The sociology department did not want me on the grounds, as they had said before, that my sociological work was trivial (what they meant was unusual and unorthodox). Favorable votes were then taken on various occasions by the education department, the school of social service administration, and the divisional social science program—in each instance the recommendation was rejected by higher officials, always because of politicking from a couple of people in the sociology department. In one instance, the then provost of the university intervened directly to persuade a faculty unit to reverse a tentative favorable vote it had previously made.

I remember vividly the winter night in 1972, between the two lake storms which almost destroyed my house at Grand Beach, when I wanted to call it a day. My friends insisted the battle must go on and that they would resign their administrative positions in protest against what we thought was the provost's trickery. I argued against them, they insisted, I was won over.

Who can say no to such dedicated allies?

The smart man, that's who. In retrospect they were doing what they thought I wanted.

Did I?

I don't think so. I was willing to end the nonsense. My better judgment said we would never win. Still, we continued the fight, and that's my fault more than theirs. One by one they faded away over the next several months. They had excellent explanations for what happened. Academics are good at analytic explanations as a substitute for action. Like the French in the song in *My Fair Lady*.

What were the reasons for this complicated academic politicking?

My sociological interests were on the margins of the profession. I could make a case that the sociology of religion was scarcely marginal to the mainline sociological tradition. However, *de facto* sociology of religion is scarcely a respectable subdiscipline. Moreover, as I have since learned, academic departments love intricate, convoluted and nasty tenure fights. It provides those scholars who have abandoned their own work with entertainment between lunch at the faculty club and a late-afternoon squash game. Some departments in particular rarely if ever promote anyone who is part of their own university community. While I was never an assistant or an associate professor (always a research associate at NORC), I was still part of the University of Chicago environment and its sociology department has, in the last quarter century, rarely promoted any-one from its staff of assistant professors. Turning down a younger scholar seems somehow to reassure the older generation of their own potency. The department at Chicago had a long record of hassling younger schol-ars, including one of the finest sociologists in the world, Otis Dudley Duncan. I was in good company.

Moreover, I managed to acquire a lot of public attention by doing things that weren't sociological, like writing columns and especially like writing articles. The typical academic has an ambivalent attitude toward an article in the *New York Times Magazine* (the reading of which is, according to David Tracy, the liturgy of The Word on Sunday mornings in the University of Chicago community). On the one hand, the scholar would dearly like the public recognition that comes from having one's name on such an article; on the other hand, he asks himself how any responsible and serious scholar can engage in such "popularization." As one of my friends at the University of Chicago remarked facetiously,

"Every article you do in the *New York Times* costs you two scholarly articles. You've ended up owing us scholarly articles!"

Finally there was the fact that I was a Catholic priest—not the only reason why I never quite made it to full faculty status but, as most people in that community will admit today, the decisive reason: "There were a lot of things going on, but if he wasn't a priest, he'd be a tenured faculty member, no doubt about that"—such seems to be the usual comment of named or unnamed faculty types talking to reporters who, in the eighties, were doing feature articles about my novels and my academic career before the novels.

As I mentioned earlier, Rossi, who intended to have me made an assistant professor in the sixties, was frustrated explicitly on religious grounds. Those who voted against the appointment then were still voting against it ten years later. Having rejected me themselves, the politicians in the sociology department had to campaign vigorously against appointments in other units of the university lest the charge of anti-Catholic bias be given some credibility.

Other academic appointments materialized and then vanished in the next couple of years, at Notre Dame, at Loyola, at the City University of New York and at Northwestern. In every instance, the initiative was taken by the other institution and somehow or other, the initiative later went up in smoke—at Notre Dame and at Loyola because the president of the university backed off in the face of pressure from his sociology department (the Notre Dame department has always argued that I simply wasn't good enough to be appointed there). The distinguished appointment at the City University of New York was ready to go when New York teetered on the verge of bankruptcy, and the Northwestern University appointment was again stopped at the higher level of university administration. Charles Moscis, the chairman of the sociology department at Northwestern and a close friend, told me it was sitting on the provost's desk awaiting approval when the provost received a phone call from a member of the faculty of the University of Chicago urging him to reject the appointment and offering as a reason the fact that I was a close political ally of Mayor Daley and the house intellectual of the Daley organization. This argument was decisive with the Northwestern provost, who was also a sociologist, and the appointment was turned down.

In fact, I was not a friend of the mayor's, I did not know him at the time, and I was *certainly* not the house intellectual of the Daley organization (the mayor didn't need house intellectuals). Charlie didn't tell me the name of the faculty member, though it wasn't hard to guess because there was only one sociologist who had such violent animus against Mayor Daley. The University of Chicago sociology department, or some of its members, was not content merely to block my appointment in other departments of the university; it was ready to intervene at any university of major stature to make sure I was not appointed professor of sociology.

In the Catholic community there was no support in this time of troubles. On the contrary, the fact that there was some not-too-subtle rejoicing at the university's refusal to "vote him tenure" was proof of what a lot of priests knew all along—I wasn't a good sociologist.

I only became a good sociologist when I turned to writing novels and people could say, "What a shame such a great sociologist should waste his time writing steamy novels."

I learned long after the fight was over that the men in the department I most respected—men like Stanley Lieberson and Leo Goodman and later Jim Coleman—were on my side. To be fair to Stanley and Leo, both of whom are now close friends, I have to admit that in my pessimism about my own abilities, I thought they would be voting with the opposition and was flattered and delighted to learn they thought my skills merited a professorship. As Stanley said to me when he was recruiting me for the University of Arizona, "Andy, they screwed you!"

Tell me about it, Stanley!

Why give a million and a quarter to a place that screwed you?

First of all, I cannot blame the university or the faculty for what a few administrators did. It is a great university and while there are (or were) strains of anti-Catholicism in it, those strains are not typical. One does not have to love some of the people involved to respect the quality of the institution.

More to the point, if one wants a chair of Catholic Studies at a distinguished university in the Chicago area, one starts there.

How good a sociologist am I?

In an earlier draft of this memoir, I sketched out a defense, still, I suppose, arguing with the Chicago sociology department. But such an effort would be ridiculous. If the reader really wants to know, he can check my publication record, my citation list (the number of times professional colleagues cite a scholar's work), the ranking of the sociology department at the University of Arizona, the comments of men like Jim Coleman in the feature articles which have been done about me.

That is a good enough record on which to stand, without any further arguments.

Ah, but why so many windmills?

Why indeed?

'Cause they were there?

The Vanishing Dune

So, what mighty lord made you mad this time?
Banshee winds, killer waves, psychotic surf
This storm no chance, you must have me in mind
The house shakes. Quit rocking my poor turf!
I take your noise personally, of course
For waves of this absurd and foolish size
You must cause, not low pressure, natural force
Such a storm I will not demythologize
I mean, tell me what have I done wrong?
Still the frenzy, calm yourself, postpone my fate
My verses inept maybe, but not too long
Let's clear this up. I promise I'll go straight
Okay, if you say so, I'll wait awhile...
Whatdaya mean, some angel lost my file?

I looked out at the sullen, restless lake and for the first time in my life understood the metaphysical concept of nonbeing. Where there had been terraced lawn, concrete steps, steel seawall, dilapidated boathouse, graceful trees, wide beach and soaring dune, there was now nothing at all, save rubble and the lake relentlessly eating away at the eroding cliff to which it had reduced my dune.

On that grim, nasty March day in 1972, the lake was only twenty feet from my house—and sixty feet straight down. Two winter storms, storms of the century within six weeks of one another, and the highest water level in recorded history were threatening all of Grand Beach.

I half expected to look up and see the glacier reappearing on the horizon, two miles high.

Lou Briody, across the street from me and one tier in from the lake, talked of his "lakefront property."

The threat to my home—repelled by massive concrete-and-wood walls and five hundred truckloads of sand—seemed typical of that year, the worst year in my life until then: mindless destruction which I was powerless to resist. I found myself rejected by my Church, my community, and my university for reasons I could not comprehend. I would struggle through much of the decade with the constant pain of uncomprehended rejection.

In 1972, when the University of Chicago kept me dangling in the wind most of the year, for the first time in my life I was not sleeping well—falling asleep and then waking up and remaining awake for much of the night. My physician, Marty Phee, said it was a sure sign of depression and asked me what I was depressed about. I told him and he observed, "Well, some forms of depression are neurotic and some are based on real causes. You have plenty of real causes to be depressed."

The collapse of my community at about the same time as these other 1972 problems was actually a far more serious blow than the battle at the university. The latter I could understand. The violent anger and the nastiness of the community collapse was much more difficult to understand.

We had started out as an informal discussion group and then after several months added a private Mass, all low-keyed and relaxed. Most of the members were young, unmarried or just married, filled with enthusiasm for the promise of their lives and loves. With astonishing speed the emotional intensity of the community increased. Religion, common

312

background (most of the young people were from Beverly), friendship and my (perhaps misguided) enthusiasm turned us into a community which became the most important reality, outside of our families, in each other's lives.

We would do great things together, support one another, be friends to one another in God's love for the rest of our lives.

We were also playing with fire.

So-called "underground" parishes were flourishing in those days, but their half-life was usually pretty short. Either they broke up in recrimination or became authoritarian groups, with the guru running everyone's lives. The sweetness of friendship reinforced by strong faith commitment was appealing, but the energies released in such situations were normally too intense for the members to handle.

We were aware of these phenomena and vowed we would not become a commune. We were just good friends who had Mass and discussion together and spent much of our social time with one another.

Intimacy held dangers none of us recognized. I swore I would not become a guru. Instead I became, unwillingly, at once inkblot and father figure.

My message was that we needed one another if we were to achieve our ambitions for our lives. There was verbal agreement with this proposition, but, looking back on it, there was also much fear that if you let others as intimately into your life as the dynamics of small group religion seemed to demand, they would also control your lives, they would close off the escape hatch from the risks that "Greels" was saying were necessary for happiness.

We were not making decisions for one another or anything remotely approaching that—partly because I wouldn't tolerate such behavior and partly because there was too much suspicion in the community to turn in that direction. The usual pattern was, rather, for someone to say, for example, I want to be a writer, please help me; then become bitterly angry when others asked, innocently enough, how the writing was progressing; and then finally get on the phone and say I was trying to force the person to write because of my own emotional needs.

I realize it sounds odd. It was.

It was also what happened.

The house at Grand Beach seemed to become haunted by ghosts of unspoken and perhaps inexpressible anger.

313

I guess there was not enough maturity or enough trust to cope with the powerful dynamics of a small group church. Moreover, the young people, the first-generation offspring of the Irish new rich, were sufficiently uncertain of their own personal worth to take the risks that deep religious commitment demands and, for many of the members, the risks that life demands. The pattern is not unusual. What *was* unusual was the duration of our efforts—on and off for almost fifteen years. Partly this was because of my refusal to give up and partly because the love aspect of our love/hate relationship was powerful. We had all invested in the illusion of religious community long after the reality had died. It was a wonderful hedge between a life of faith and a life just like everyone else's.

The odds were heavily against success in such a (perhaps naive) effort. Clearly we had become a surrogate family, and, equally clearly, all the unresolved parent/child and sibling rivalries of our collective past were projected onto the community.

Still, I couldn't quite understand, and still can't, how something that began as a mixture of religious faith and close friendship could end so painfully. Some of us tried again in the late seventies with the same result, this time the anger and the hatred being even more violent, perhaps because it was all too obvious time was running out for many of the members.

While small group communities may be the religious wave of the future (someone had to try it and no one was, so . . . Don Quixote saddled up Rosinante again and sallied forth), we must, as a species, develop skills at creating these communities so that they are immune to the unresolved sibling and generational conflicts that we carry from our youth.

Some of the survivors have argued that only through a common therapy experience can such conflicts be worked out in a small group church. This seems to me a dangerous cop-out. First of all, I don't have the time or the inclination to go through an experience in which others finally come to realize that I am not their father. On a more general level, when a religious group turns into a therapy group, its own processes rather than the religious vision become the principal concern. And a perennial concern that is never resolved. Why talk about God when we can talk about why you don't like me the way I think you should like me? Family therapy may work fine (sometimes) in the family, where the motivation—to save the family relationships—is strong. It will not work in a religious group, both because the motivation to struggle for success is much less poignant and powerful and because the collective neurosis exists precisely to avoid what the group is supposed to be for: the challenge of religious vision.

I suppose something like this demonic process has affected every religious order which has ever existed. The escape into canon law has always been an escape from the awful challenge of religion and intimacy combined.

So, we must as a race and as a Church find a way to short-circuit the transference dynamics when they rear their ugly head, usually at the end of the first really moving liturgical service, without at the same time exorcising all the real freedom and affection (as opposed to the imitations to be found in many Charismatic groups) that small group church can generate.

All I can tell you about such a goal is that it won't be easy to pursue.

The pain of the various community breakups was the worst suffering so far in my life, even worse than the agony that would come in the early 1980s when my most private files at Rosary College were violated.

One of the worst parts of the pain is that I have known many of these men and women since they were grammar school children, presided at their marriages, baptized their children, helped them through some of their early sexual dilemmas. Now I see them in the midyears of their lives, miserable, unhappy, frustrated. Often their marriages do not work well and their careers are severely constrained by fear if not outright failure. Their lives could have been so much happier. I suppose everyone from an older generation wishes he could preserve his/her young from painful mistakes. The wiser among us know it is impossible and that we must suffer through their mistakes even when they are disastrously destructive of happiness. We must leave them free even to destroy themselves. It's never easy.

It's especially difficult when you realize that most of the problems that are ruining their lives are rooted in a failure of religious vision and nerve. My group, given who they are and where they were from and when they were from it, was fundamentally afraid of risk-taking, pathologically afraid of it—even when there was a good chance the risk could transform their lives.

I'm sure I've made a lot of mistakes in my perhaps reckless and certainly stubborn attempt to build a small group ecclesiastical community, and I'm also certain that my own personality defects contributed their own fair share to its collapse. Moreover, I doubt that any of us will ever understand what finally went wrong. The human race is going to have to progress in wisdom before it learns the skills required to prevent small intimate friendship communities from turning into collective neuroses.

Through all of the harrowing psychological trauma a few of the friendships survived intact, and several more have been reconstituted, as far as I can see, on a healthy and relaxed basis. A couple of folks even want to try the community experiment again. I'd have to have holes in my head to run that risk a third time. Common sense says that what we tried, we tried twice and it didn't work, and if we try three times and it doesn't work, that is a strikeout. But when a community wants a priest, the priest should not refuse. On that one, time will tell. If there is another go-around, however, I won't make the mistake of assuming that reconciliation can take place without a clear understanding of what went wrong before.

Some of the relationships of those days, some of the most treasured of the relationships, are, I much fear, fractured for the rest of my life. Pain can and does eventually destroy love, and while reconciliation can never be completely excluded, fear of more pain imposes an almost physical caution that inhibits the risk-taking necessary for intimacy.

Tentatively, and with some self-doubt and hesitation, I accept the explanation for the disasters of our community offered by one of those friends who survived the explosion: "The message scared us so we set out to destroy the messenger."

Many years after the end of my small group church Jack Shea helped me to reflect theologically on the meaning of the experience (Shea is superbly skilled at facilitating theological reflection).

An English theologian, James Dunn, observes in a book about the early Church that St. Paul tried to create in Corinth a "charismatic community," what I would call a "small group church." His project failed, but the ideal of an intimate band of the followers of Jesus still persists. Says Dunn, "It may be, of course, that the Pauline vision is unworkable in practice, so deeply does the inner contraction within individual believers run that it prevents the sort of mutual interaction that Paul envisages as the functioning of charismatic community. But the alternatives suffer from even graver weaknesses and are exposed to more serious dangers, so that the Pauline vision retains its attractiveness."

Joutte Bassler, another theologian whose work Jack showed me, contends that the Johanine community—the other early Christian small group which we know well—theologized out of its own experience of being cast out of the synagogue. It therefore developed its own internal theology. But the Corinthian community did not and/or would not reflect on its own experience of grace, so that Paul imposed his own experience of grace on it and that imposition did not work. The problem, of course, is that the rigid, defensive community of John has little attraction for us while the open, outgoing community of Paul in Corinth, for all its weaknesses, is very attractive, just as Dunn says.

As I reflected in this fashion, it became clear to me that I had done the same thing that St. Paul did—made the same mistake, if you will. Since the community would not or could not articulate its own symbols and stories, I imposed my own on them. With the same kind of results as occurred in Corinth.

If there is a lesson to be learned it is that when a community refuses to tell its own story of its experience of grace, the story which will emerge from within the community will be demonic. One outsider compared the women of my group to a teenage "pajama party"—giddy, arrogant about their own worth, contemptuous of others. At first I thought this was unfair, then I thought that their demonic story was aimed at me, and finally I realized that it was rather aimed at their own tragic rejection of the grace experience which bound us together in the very early days— an experience of keeping alive our friendships formed while we grew up.

Dunn writes an appropriate epitaph for our attempt to replicate Corinth (without realizing that we were doing that):

"Perhaps the biggest challenge to twentieth-century Christianity is to take the Pauline exposition seriously, and to start not from what now is by way of tradition and institution, but instead to be open to the experience of God which first launched Christianity and to let that experience, properly safeguarded as Paul insisted, create new expressions of faith, worship and mission at both individual and corporate levels. One thing we may be sure of: the life of the Christian Church can go forward only when each generation is able creatively to reinterpret its gospel and common life out of its own experience of Spirit and word which first called Christianity into existence."

That's what we tried. We failed.

At least we tried.

317

At the time of the 1972 breakup I realized I had no longer any direct pastoral work to perform and that it was necessary to my priesthood that I engage in such work. Therefore I applied to the personnel board for a change of residence to a rectory where I could do weekend parish work (the pastor of the parish was enthusiastic about having me). It's worth noting that I had written the statute establishing the personnel board in the early days of the Association of Chicago Priests—before it began to contribute money to research on the priesthood that would refute mine because I was thought to have sold out to the bishops!

The personnel board hemmed and hawed—not quite able to fit me into its set of categories, and also relishing its newfound power over me. However, it finally approved the appointment. The cardinal resolutely refused to give his approval for it, however. "I'll see this man myself. If he wants to do parish work, then we can put him back in the parish full-time."

Observe what was happening: I was merely asking for an opportunity to do more work and the cardinal was using it as an occasion and an excuse to withdraw my appointment to academic and literary work that had been made by his predecessor. A member of the cardinal's staff, an auxiliary bishop, actually, phoned me and said that whatever I did, I should not go to the cardinal's office to see him about this change of residence. "He will order you *viva voce* to stop your sociology," the man said. "He's afraid to do it in writing because then it will make the news-papers. He wants to be able to give you an oral order and then to spread the word around among the bishops of the country that you're a diso-bedient priest. Stay away from him and he won't be able to give you such an order." So when Dan Ryan, the cardinal's secretary, phoned, I told him I had no desire to see the cardinal and would not see him until he approved my change of residence. Knowing that the words scared the living daylights out of the cardinal, I added, "It's a matter of academic freedom, Dan. The cardinal is persecuting me in order to inhibit my academic freedom."

I suspect it was the only time in his service of three cardinals that Dan Ryan heard a priest say "No, I don't want to see the cardinal." I must say he was smooth about it. "All right, Father," he said calmly. "I'll tell the cardinal that."

The cardinal later called St. Ambrose to demand to talk to me, and the pastor, John Cassidy, told him I wasn't in Chicago and that he didn't

318

know where I was. In fact, I was in Washington visiting the new apostolic delegate, Jean Jadot, who had expressed interest in my work and wanted to meet me. Upon returning I wrote the cardinal and told him where I had been and said that doubtless he would wish to disabuse the delegate of the idea that there was anything he could possibly learn from me. A curious situation, surely, when an apostolic delegate initiated a long friendship with a priest at the same time that the priest's archbishop was maneuvering to remove him from the work about which the delegate wanted to talk. And it all started merely because I wanted to add weekend parish activity to my responsibilities.

It was one of those opportunities for a response about which we all dream.

Since then I have been effectively barred from parish work in Chicago. Oh, anytime I want to give up my writing, I'm sure the personnel board would find a nice parish for me to preside over as pastor.

They really can't imagine that a priest would want anything else in life but a rich suburban parish. Or that they have any obligation to protect oddball personnel like me.

Would you come back to the reservation for Christ the King?

No. But I'd be tempted.

In any case I have filled up my life with other activities which also pertain, perhaps more importantly, to the preaching of the Gospel. Besides, now no pastor or no parish in the city would want me, save on direct orders from the cardinal. With reason, perhaps. The controversy would start the day I arrived.

Just as in CK thirty-two years ago.

Do I still miss CK?

Always.

After the troubles with Church and university, to make matters worse, I went on two long trips in 1972 and 1973—in '72 to give a lecture series before the Eucharistic Congress in Melbourne, Australia, and in '73 for an around-the-world lecture tour. My emotional state was certainly not helped by the profound weariness at the end of both these winter trips. More windmills.

In 1970 I was forty-two; when the decade ended I was fifty-two—the time of the crisis of the middle years. Did I have a crisis of the middle years?

What can I tell you?

Although they are closer than the previous decades of my life, the 1970s are the most difficult to write about because they are the most difficult for me to put into any pattern of meaning and even to remember accurately.

My emotional resonance with that period of my life is that it was one of acute pain. Yet when I look at the work I did, I find there is often a serenity of vision and a growing confidence in faith and vocation. My friends Chris and Elizabeth Wallace, with whom I had breakfast in Washington while I was preparing this part of the book, recalled the summer of 1976 at Grand Beach (Chris was working for Channel 2 then) as the best summer in their life. When Elizabeth—née Betty Jane—turned down a water-skiing opportunity, I raised an eyebrow. She said to Chris that night, "He's already guessed I'm pregnant." Sure I had. Why else would she refuse to ski, especially since she was better at it than Chris?

A man as discouraged as I remember myself at that time could hardly have presided over a shining summer for two young friends. (I would later baptize both Peter and Megan Wallace, a fact which delights Mike Wallace when I bump into him occasionally.)

My best "fix" on the seventies is that in addition to being a time of intellectual and religious development, both of which would lead me to turn to storytelling before the decade was over, it was a ten-year purgation which would be recognized only in retrospect.

I must strive for nuance in describing what I mean by the purgation. My "sufferings," if such they can be called, were not serious compared to what others of my generation have had to endure. No broken marriage, no vocation crisis, no terrible conflict within the family, no rebellious kids lost to the drug culture, no exhausting family worries, no embittering failure in career activities.

Quite the contrary, it could well be said that during the 1970s I became a well-known and influential priest, perhaps even something of a mini-celebrity. (Very mini.)

Such an observation suffices, I'm sure, for those who think there is only one kind of personality and one kind of purgation and that what I think was my purgation is more than a little weird.

I used to say I thought of myself as a failure in the priesthood; in fact, in the original draft of this book, I asserted that boldly in the first chapter. One of the payoffs for me in struggling through this appraisal and reappraisal of my life is to understand that such terminology is inappropriate and misleading, finally even to me.

I would have said—and did say in the first draft—hey, I don't get much in the way of kicks from writing books that a couple of million people read, or jetting around on promotion trips (in fact I hate those ordeals with a purple passion), or living in three different parts of the country (in three homes, owned mostly by the banks), or appearing on the "Today Show" or the cover of the *New York Times Magazine,* or in being recognized on Michigan Avenue or even in Fortnum and Mason's tearoom in London. I didn't become a priest because I wanted to do or experience those things. With the exception of the trials and tribulations of the promotion trips, most of these phenomena leave me indifferent. I'm glad I have achieved some professional skills at doing TV interviews during which I can talk about God's love, but there is no great personal emotional payoff. Heaven knows, I'm pleased that people read, enjoy and, despite the Catholic critics, understand my "comedies of grace." Yet they have always seemed, and still seem to a considerable extent, how shall I say it, a sideline.

I don't mean that I question their priestliness. On the contrary, they are surely the most effective priestly activity in which I have ever engaged. I mean rather that they don't really represent what I wanted to do as a priest or hoped to do—and that the cost of doing them is giving up forever what I wanted and hoped to do.

They are, however, pretty likely what God wants me to do, whatever the price to be paid in abandoned dreams. Purgation was learning that.

It's taken me a long time to understand it, to comprehend that one's own ambitions and God's plans are often not quite the same.

So for a long time—through most of the seventies—I said "failure." Now, more wisely, I say "grace."

(Lady Wisdom: The saints be praised! You finally figured it out. It took you long enough, God knows.)

As someone remarked recently, "You *should* give all that money to the University of Chicago, because if those bastards had made you part of the faculty you never would have written novels."

And, he might have added, never done my book on Mary and never developed my theories on the religious imagination.

I might also have been tempted by the Church. Archbishop Bernardin once said to me, when he knew he was going to be archbishop of Chicago, that he would not be able to make me part of his administrative structure but that he would see I became an honored and respected member of the Archdiocese. Even then I was perceptive enough to express doubt that he could overcome the animosity of my fellow priests. If he had tried to live up to his promise, I might have been coopted even a couple of years ago. A friend and a sociological adviser to a cardinal—with perhaps weekend parish work back in Beverly?

Would I have settled for that even in 1982?

To be able to do weekend parish work in my own diocese—say Mass, talk to people in the back of the church, make faces at the little kids, hang around with the teenagers, visit the sick, bury the dead, console the confused—as I do in Tucson may seem a trivial and minor ambition. It becomes temptation when I am willing to compromise with nervous ecclesiastical authority to be able to do it.

Would I have to give up some/most/nearly all of my personal freedom to write in Joseph Bernardin's Archdiocese for even such a small ambition?

Maybe.

The temptation then is not so much to do the right things for the wrong reason as to accept the right things at the wrong price.

It is now clear to me as anything can possibly be that God put me together to be a man with the creative freedom which—in the present era of the Church and the Academy—is granted only to square pegs. The purgation of the seventies, as I see it now, was God's way of saying, "Hey, dummy, I don't want you ever to be an insider, because if you become one, you'll sell out cheap and not do the things I want you to do."

These truths should have been self-evident to me in 1970. That they were not is proof of a false innocence that was inexcusable.

I think I have grasped the inevitability and the gracefulness of my square-peg vocation in the writing of these words; but I have yet to integrate such gracefulness sufficiently into my personality to be sure the temptation to escape it or the alternative temptation to sink into bitterness has been overcome on anything more than a temporary basis.

When I look over the facts and the publications of that ten-year period, I realized I enjoyed a remarkable outburst of creativity—developed a new religious paradigm, began to write poems and novels, made new friends, celebrated my silver jubilee in the priesthood (Cardinal Cody complained to the delegate because Clete O'Donnell showed up for it, making the bishop of Madison angrier than I've ever seen him), found a new home at the University of Arizona, did major research in many different areas, wrote the definitive sociological book on American Catholics (*The American Catholic: A Social Portrait*), launched a new enterprise in my Papal election research, and became the confidant of some of the Church's most influential leaders. I apparently did more than merely survive. Many of the projects did turn bitter, but they were exciting and enjoyable in their early phases.

As I consider 1975 and 1976 I see that one of my projects was on the cover of *Time*, that I began my research for *The Making of the Popes* and wrote thirteen books, several of which were influential—in addition to *The American Catholic* and *Catholic Schools in a Declining Church*, there appeared *The Mary Myth, Neighborhood, No Bigger Than Necessary, The Great Mysteries*, a new kind of catechism, and *The Ultimate Values of Americans.*

And I began my poems and my novels.

Despite my memory of pain, the decade might be more appropriately described as a roller coaster, highs and lows, jolts and thrills racing after one another with no discernible meaning or pattern. The highs were rewarding, but I no more understood them than I did the painful lows.

The good and the bad were going on at the same time. While I was trying to recover my violated records, Warner Books accepted *The Cardinal Sins* and my community erupted in savage resentment. While the book was riding the top of the best-seller list, my secret documents were being published in a sleazy Chicago weekly and some of my former friends were denouncing me without having read the book for embarrassing them by writing it. The roller coaster continued into the winter of 1982, and then with the publication of *Thy Brother's Wife*, the healing forces at work in the late seventies began to take their effect.

I do not say the worst is over; who can say that about life, especially when the Vatican is engaged in what may be its last witch hunt? (What consolation is it to know that you may be the last witch to be burned in the last Vatican witch hunt?) I do say I have come to understand what was happening and so am better prepared for what happens next. What more can you expect from a midlife crisis?

So I survived. Not elegantly or gracefully all the time, not like the leprechaun I would like to have been. But I didn't quit. My faith in God was hardly as strong or resilient as I would have liked during those years, but it survived. And, I think, grew.

I'm asked occasionally by interviewers how I picture God. My automatic and spontaneous response is, "She's a comedienne."

I usually don't add that She's Irish.

(Lady Wisdom: I'm any and all ethnic groups. If it makes you happy to picture me as Irish, sure 'tis fine with me.)

You can only picture God that way, I am often told in reply, because you haven't suffered. Well, I certainly haven't suffered much in comparison to others, but that has little to do with the validity of my insight; it only means that faith in a comic God may be (marginally) more easy for me.

How can you believe in any God, much less a comic God, after Auschwitz?

I understand, surely, the terrible assault on faith that the death camps are. But I have to respond that death wasn't invented there, nor mass murder. How believe in God after the potato famine? How believe in God after the death of Abel? How believe in God after the death of one innocent child? How believe in God despite the fact that each of us must die?

Those who reject God (by which they mean the goodness of the cosmos and the purposefulness of life) would picture themselves as braver, more realistic, more hardheaded, than we wish-fulfillment types who still accept God, especially a comic God.

But the decisive question is not hardheadedness or wishful thinking. The issue is truth. Obviously we wish that there would be a loving comic God who wipes away every tear. That wish does not necessarily prove that there is such a God, but it does not prove that there isn't one either. The question is not whether wishes are wishful. Surely they are. The question is whether they will be fulfilled or not.

And the agnostic does not solve his problem by arguing from the existence of evil that there is no loving comic God. For the agnostic must still face the problem of good and the problem of why there is anything at all.

To use the terminology of social science, my loving comic God is not a model which fits all the data, but She fits it better than any other model.

And the data that do not fit—evil and suffering, great and small?

The game isn't over. It's only the First of the Ninth, the Two-Minute Warning has just been sounded, we have yet to see the Last Act, the Final Scene.

In which God, I do believe, becomes the passionate lover who WINS!

On the subject of lovers, this part of the memoir is as good a place as any to refer again to the women in my life. As I said before, I have both loved and been in love many times in my life, though none of these loves ever became love affairs. I mentioned the intense but ephemeral affection for the girl who lived down the street when I was in first and second grade and the long-distance crush on one of my grammar school classmates (both of which experiences have found their way into my stories, but not as autobiographical episodes). There have been and continue to be (and please God, there will continue to be) relationships with women that are rewarding, compelling, disturbing, demanding and exciting. Some were, are and I hope will continue to be of sufficient intensity (in my own experience of them) to become mind-twisting preoccupations. But that none of them have thus far turned into "love affairs" doesn't mean that there does not exist or will not continue to exist the radical possibility of that happening.

With the passage of time all of us, married or celibate, become skillful at the art of loving or falling in love and at the same time honoring our realistic promises and commitments. It doesn't follow, however—however skillful we may be at this delicate balancing game which is part of the agony and the ecstasy of the human condition—that we ever become immune to the possibility of disastrous mistakes, frailties and weaknesses. Celibacy is not served, however, by denial or repression or pretense. It is rather served by honest recognition of the power of one's own emotions, enjoyment of the pleasures such emotions can create, and discretion and prudence at following the impulses of such emotions. The balancing act is difficult for celibates but probably no more so than it is for anyone else.

So have there been women in my life who on occasion will deprive me almost entirely of my power of rational thought? About whom I awake in the middle of the night with powerful hunger? Sure. And for that delightful delirium I am grateful. I am also grateful that thus far the delights have led to no shattered promises or commitments.

Suppose such delights should get out of hand—what then would happen?

325

With God's help, I would attempt to put the pieces of the commitment back together.

All abstract, you say?

Anything less abstract than that, at this stage of the proceedings, you are not going to get, however much it might increase the sales of the book.

It would be telling, now, wouldn't it?

(Lady Wisdom: Stop teasing the readers. We know you're not going to tell, mostly because you don't have all that much to tell, do you now?)

There also have been women (some of them the same women) who have forced me to face the implications of the Grail quest, the search for the womanly aspect of my self. The nurturing aspect of femaleness is a complex mixture of biology and culture too intricate to sort out. Women bear children and nurse them. They have breasts and men do not. They are equipped physiologically to provide tenderness in a way men are not. Interacting with history and culture, this biology has created a situation in which, on the average, women are more likely to be tender, nurturing, healing creatures than men. The proper goal of feminism, it seems to me, is not that women become more macho but that men become more tender—there is too much machismo in the world and not nearly enough tenderness.

Whatever the Grail quest for women might be, for men it is a quest to discover the tender God revealed in their own self, to discover their own tenderness and the divine tenderness as sacraments of one another.

Whatever we may teach women about the captivating power of God, they teach us about Her gentle, lifegiving, healing grace. Given a chance, they rip away our harsh pretense at masculine superiority and reveal us as the bowl of soft warm mush that we really are.

It's an ongoing struggle, a continuous improvised dance, in which the players can never be sure that yesterday's melodies and rhythms will work today.

And the dance goes on with the Lord of the Dance calling the tune.

One of the most surprising results of fiction writing has been the discovery of the anima of my personality in the woman characters, which, like God, I have created and with whom, like God, I have fallen in love. As I try to explain it in my novel *God Game*, just as we are sacraments of God and reveal what He is like, so the characters in a novel are sacraments of the storyteller (negative in his bad people, positive in his good people). I don't find at all unattractive my anima as revealed in my women characters—who in their turn are preconscious composites of the various women who have influenced my life.

Creating my women characters—Ellen Foley, Nora Cronin, Maria McLean, Noele Marie Brigid Farrell, Cathy Collins, Lisa Malone, Anne O'Brien, Mary Kate Murphy, Eileen Kane, Ranora, Ciara Kelly, Diana Marie Lyons, Cardinal Deirdre Fitzgerald—has forced me to face the nurturing aspect of my own personality and of my own experience with women and to try to integrate that dimension more fully in my life and in my religious faith.

A curious path to grace.

And, good God (a prayer), there are a lot of strong-willed Irish women in the above list, aren't there?

I can hear the cries of narcissist and sodomite (from the conservative Catholic press) in the background.

They have the wrong myths. Instead of Narcissus, the appropriate pagan myth would be Pygmalion. And instead of Sodom, the appropriate Yahwehistic story would be Hosea—a God who fell so passionately in love with His people that He would forgive their infidelity almost before they asked for forgiveness.

I survived the alternately painful and exhilarating roller coaster of my midlife crisis decade mostly by work. It seemed to me then that I had to go on, researching and writing about the subjects that had taken possession of my intellect and curiosity. With the freedom, often unwelcome, which came with my square-peg status, there came a recklessness that was almost absolute. No idea seemed too big to scare me off—study a Papal election, take on a cardinal, write novels. What was there to lose when you think you've lost almost everything that matters anyway?

Or as John Kotre would remark to the *Wall Street Journal*, going far beyond his data, it looked as if I kept expecting acceptance and then doing something which precluded it.

He might have more accurately and less vindictively said that I would have liked acceptance (and still would, I suppose—who wouldn't?) but was not willing to pay the price (and still won't). However, long before I turned to storytelling, I knew what was happening and had decided that if I had to choose, the freedom which came from rejection was better than acceptance.

I now understand the messages in what was being said about me in

327

those days by the "murmurantes" in the Church, in the university, in the priesthood and in my community. Fit into a category. Do what other priests do. Be a mainline sociologist. Don't challenge us so much. Don't write so much. Don't have so many interests. Don't be so outrageous.

And whatever you do, don't write novels too. Especially successful novels.

If you don't do all those offensive things, we'll accept you. Tentatively and provisionally because we don't really trust you. But we'll give you another chance.

Single-minded Don Quixote that I am, with full awareness of all my faults and all my mistakes, I won't buy those terms. I've never even been seriously tempted by them.

In the middle 1970s, my terms were both freedom and acceptance. They still are.

CHAPTER 17

"That Goddam Encyclical"

*Smog broods over the sacred hills of Rome
Dimming the city's pastel pink and white
Hiding the tarnished northland-losing Dome
From the early sun's purifying light.
In drab palaces high heels click down the stairs
Soon tiny cars will clog the ancient ways
And make parking lots of quaint old squares
With churches placarded by PCI displays
Passion unfulfilled but spent, they rise,
Old and new, from a couch of anxious lust
With a mate they adore and yet despise
Dreading to return at night though they must
And glum marriage broker, devoid of mirth
The Church wrings its hands, grimly waits for birth.*

An American bishop and I were sitting in the bar of the Seven Continents Restaurant at O'Hare Airport in the late summer of 1976. He called me to say he would fly out of Chicago after a meeting. Could I meet with him for an hour or so?

Why not?

Our book *Catholic Schools in a Declining Church* had been published earlier that year. The bishop had issued a curious statement which seemed to indicate surprise at the report, as though we had not briefed him on its findings, the most notable of which was that the birth-control encyclical and not the Council was the cause of the decline in Catholic religious practice.

He placed his glass on the table and began slowly, choosing his words carefully as he always does. "I had to say what I did." He paused again. "But I want you to know that I think you're right. Often I can't sleep at night because of what that goddam encyclical is doing in my diocese."

That incident is both dense and multilayered. It reveals much about the condition of the Catholic Church in the modern world. It also describes my own fringe position in the Church in the middle seventies.

The apostolic delegate and the general secretary of the NCCB were going out of their way to ask my advice, to listen to my opinions, to read my books. By opting for the fringes I had seemingly achieved the role of sociological expert for the ecclesiastical institution which I thought I had given up.

It was an illusion, a temptation, the result of deception as well as self-deception. But it was an illusion which tempted me during the middle and late 1970s.

The bishop's comment pointed at another phenomenon which was not an illusion—the necessarily Janus-faced position of American bishops who are caught between their priests and people on the one hand and the Vatican on the other.

The "Encyclical/Council" study, my most famous (or notorious) sociological work, came about by chance. So too did its most controversial finding.

In early 1973, while I was sorting through the mail, I noticed a request for a proposal from the National Institute of Education on alternative educational forms and particularly on education in time of change. It occurred to me there might just possibly be a chance of submitting a

330

proposal for a redo of our 1963 study of Catholic schools, asking the question of whether a private school system would have the same effects in times of rapid change as it did in times of stability. I went home that night, wrote the proposal in a couple of hours and sent it off to the National Institute for Mental Health. To my astonishment, it was funded in part. (Other projects, months in preparation, were routinely turned down—such is the rationality of federal social science funding.) The NIE people said they would fund the data collection and the Church would fund the analysis.

Well, obviously, the Church wouldn't do the funding, but my colleagues in the project and I could do the analytic work in our spare time, while we were working on other projects. Thus was born the study which ended in the controversial report *Catholic Schools in a Declining Church*.

The methodology of survey research analysis had changed notably in the ten years since *The Education of Catholic Americans* because more advanced computers made it possible to use correlation analysis, unthinkable in 1963. Thus, it was necessary to reanalyze the 1963 study in order that the 1974 study might be comparable. The basic educational finding was by no means trivial; in almost every category the correlation coefficients *increased* between 1963 and 1974. Catholic schools were more crucial to the Church in a time of change than in one of stability. Moreover, we were able to demonstrate that declining enrollment in Catholic schools was *not* a function of declining enthusiasm for them on the part of parents but, rather, the reluctance of Church authorities to build schools in the new suburban areas to which the Catholic population was shifting. Third, we were able to estimate the cost of Catholic schools and come up with a figure that was virtually the same as the one compiled by the National Catholic Education Association from collecting data from all their schools. Since we also knew the contribution of our respondents to the Church in the Sunday collection, we were able to demonstrate that the extra contributions of parents of Catholic school children more than made up for the subsidy provided the schools by Catholic parishes throughout the country. Finally, since those who had gone to Catholic school as young people were more likely to contribute to the support of their parish, a case could be made for the proposition that Catholic schools were actually a financial asset to the Church.

The real issue in the study was the reason for the "declining Church" part of the title. The conventional wisdom blamed the obviously declining

Catholic practice on the Vatican Council, a position recently repeated by the Lord High Inquisitor, Cardinal Josef Ratzinger. In the late 1960s and the early 1970s, three different groups of observers were arguing that the great mass of the "simple faithful" were shocked by the changes: conservative priests and bishops, reactionary journals like *The Wanderer* and *The National Catholic Register*, and the more liberal and radical journals like *The National Catholic Reporter* and *Commonweal*. The former two groups claimed to be protecting the poor, simple laity and argued that there was an obligation on the church to slow down the pace of change in order that said poor, simple laity might not be any more shocked than they already were. In the case of the Catholic liberals, there was a certain snobbishness—snobbery is the vice of Catholic liberals: we who are *Commonweal* or *National Catholic Reporter* readers understand the changes and approve them but the ordinary folks out in the pews— hard-hat, conservative, chauvinist hawks—do not understand the changes and are against them.

I thought these commentaries on the Vatican Council were wrong and subscribed to what I called then the "meat on Friday" theory—you make it all right for people to eat meat on Friday and they will feel less obligated to follow the other rules. The decline in church attendance and other observable forms of religious behavior, it seemed to me, was the result of a decline in respect for rules, but not the result of opposition to the Council.

There was no support for a Conciliar explanation of the decline in our data. Three-quarters of the Catholic laity approved of the Vatican Council changes—seven-eighths approved of the English liturgy. Moreover, three-quarters could accept the idea of a married clergy and half actually supported optional celibacy. A little less than half (at that time) supported the ordination of women. At all age levels, there was majority support for the Vatican Council changes—even 60 percent support among those who were over sixty years old.

Most of the laity, therefore, approved of a changing Church. Obviously those who didn't were much more likely to write letters to bishops. But the masses of simple faithful, digging in and resisting change in the Church, simply did not exist. Nonetheless, the "simple faithful" (85 percent of whom no longer accepted the Church's birth-control teaching) were too critical for the personality needs of both bishops and conservatives and liberals to be abandoned. The same simple faithful who would be shocked by a married clergy or by the ordination of women or by the English liturgy were also supposed to be shocked by my novels ten years later.

Moreover, support for the changes instituted by the Council correlated positively with religious devotion: those who approved of the changes were more rather than less devout—so much for my "meat on Friday" theory. I began to hunt for an alternative explanation. Could it be that what so many of us considered a post-*Conciliar* decline in Church attendance and religious devotion was in fact a post-*encyclical* decline?

Suddenly the pieces of the puzzle began to fall into place.

We were able to compare the birth-control attitudes of the Catholic population in 1963 with those in 1974 and demonstrate that while in 1963 about half of American Catholics accepted the birth-control teaching, ten years later this had declined to less than 15 percent. Moreover, acceptance of Papal authority in these matters had declined almost as precipitously. Finally, by a complex social change model we were able to demonstrate the decline in Catholic practice between 1963 and 1974— a decline of 20 percentage points in Sunday church attendance—was the result not of the Vatican Council but of the birth-control encyclical. All the changes in Catholic religious behavior—church attendance, support for vocations, Sunday contributions—could be accounted for in our social change model by the decline in the acceptance of Papal authority and of Papal birth-control teaching. The model indicated that the Council itself had been a huge success and that left to itself it would have led to an increase in Catholic religious practice (and it had, in fact, led to a considerable increase in the weekly reception of Holy Communion— now half the people who went to church every week received Communion, so that the proportion of Catholics who are weekly communicants had doubled in the ten years). However, the positive change brought about by the Council was canceled by the negative reaction to the birth-control encyclical.

We quickly found supporting data from other studies. Between the end of the Council and the issuing of the encyclical, the Gallup measure of Catholic church attendance ("Did you attend church last week?") fell only 1 percentage point. Between the encyclical and 1973 it fell 11 more points. Later we noted that between 1973 and 1985, the net decline has only been 3 more percentage points.

Moreover, in 1965, 28 percent of the Catholics and 50 percent of the

Protestants in the Gallup data said they thought the Church was losing influence in American society. In 1968, the year of the encyclical, the percentage increased 9 percentage points for Protestants and 34 percentage points for Catholics. By 1974, with the war winding down, the percent thinking the Church was losing influence had declined to 52 percent for Protestants but remained at 59 percent for Catholics. In ten years Catholic opinion about the waning Church influence had increased from 28 to 59 percent. Protestant change had been from 50 to 52 percent.

Something had happened to American Catholics during that decade which had not happened to American Protestants.

That goddam encyclical.

As one might well imagine, this led to a big contretemps, a contretemps which produced a cover article in *Time* magazine.

McCready and I also briefed Archbishop Jean Jadot and Thomas Kelly, the associate general secretary of the bishops (now the archbishop of Louisville). Both seemed interested in the research, impressed by its precision, and not surprised by its findings. I was confirmed in my feeling that, in a curious twist, the outsider was able to do what the insider had not been able to.

This curious development began in 1973 when Jadot was appointed apostolic delegate. I was informed by a friend in Europe that Jadot was a close ally of Archbishop Benelli, the chief of staff of Paul VI. Benelli had visited the United States the previous year and been shocked at how out of touch with the problems of the people were many of the American bishops and how ineffective was the apostolic delegate. He also, my European friend told me, concluded that Cardinal Cody was a "madman" and had to be replaced.

I wrote a column shortly after Jadot's arrival in which I repeated this conversation obliquely, leaving out the Cody reference.

At the next meeting of the bishops in Washington, Kelly, a young Dominican on Jadot's staff, strolled up to Tom Grady, once my English teacher and now an auxiliary (chosen by Meyer) in Chicago.

Kelly: The delegate was interested in Father Greeley's column.

Grady: What column?

Kelly: The one about the delegate.

Grady: We don't carry it in Chicago.

Kelly: (reaches in his pocket and removes clipping) Here.

Grady: Oh . . .

Kelly: The delegate would like to meet Father Greeley.

Grady: I can imagine.

When we did meet in the delegation, Jadot never mentioned the column but rather asked a steady stream of probing and sensitive questions about the American Church. We became friends that day and still are, even though I am sure he was part of the later deception.

The trust and confidence of Jadot and later Kelly made me feel I still had a contribution to make, however indirect and unofficial and off-the-record, to the institution. I was a nonperson in Chicago, but the Church leadership still recognized the importance of my work.

And I didn't understand my own capacity for being taken in by devious churchmen who were offering me what I had always wanted—not purple buttons on my cassock but respect for my work.

In retrospect, Jadot, Kelly and even Bernardin doubtless did respect the work. But as the seventies rolled on they had me on another agenda, one they did not disclose to me. They wanted to "contain" my criticisms of Cardinal Cody while they worked discreetly behind the scenes to engineer his removal.

You'll remember how successful their tactics to replace the cardinal were.

My colleagues and I in *Catholic Schools in a Declining Church* insisted repeatedly that we were not suggesting morality could be achieved by data collection. Repeatedly we also said we were not judging the theological wisdom of the birth-control encyclical, we were simply pointing out the sociological effects, which were threefold: (1) Catholics ignored it; (2) Catholics turned even more against the birth-control teaching; and (3) there was a notable decline in Catholic practice because of the encyclical. From various other surveys we were able to demonstrate that in the early 1960s Catholics turned from the practice of rhythm to the use of the birth-control pill, apparently confident the Church was going to change its teachings. When Paul VI overrode the majority on his birth-control commission and rejected a recommendation for change, he offended many otherwise devout laity. Some stopped going to church and others simply rejected the Church's right to teach on sexual morality and the credibility of its teachings.

When the birth-control encyclical was issued, the Pope and his advisers doubtless assumed Catholics would accept it and return to the traditional practice. Many Catholic liberals, on the other hand, assumed Catholics would leave the church or cease their religious practice. What in fact had happened was somewhere in between the two. Most Catholics rejected the birth-control encyclical, some stopped going to church, but the vast majority both rejected the encyclical and continued to go to church and receive the sacraments. Seventy-five percent of the weekly communicants rejected the birth-control teaching. A new era in Catholic life in the United States was dawning; an era of "do it yourself" or "selective" Catholicism, in which men and women would affiliate with the Church and engage in regular religious practice, but on their own terms and according to their own judgments, no longer listening to the Church as arbiter of sexual ethics.

A number of bishops and Catholic writers have blamed me for this change (most notably George A. Kelly), ignoring the fact that *Catholic Schools in a Declining Church* appeared in 1976—eight years after the birth-control encyclical. It's hard to see how a report explaining the Catholic reaction to the encyclical eight years afterwards could have *caused* that reaction. Logically, our critics were saying that Catholics didn't know that other Catholics were ignoring the encyclical until we reported that fact. Any priest hearing confessions in the parish, however, would know better. Birth control as a frequently confessed sin simply disappeared from the confessional in the years after the encyclical.

Paul VI had attempted to rally Catholics to the traditional teaching and to acceptance of his authority. In fact his attempt, however laudable and necessary, backfired. *Humanae Vitae* turned most American Catholics (and most Catholics around the world, if one is to judge by surveys done in other countries) against the birth-control teaching and against the credibility of the Church as an authority in matters sexual. There is no reason to believe on the basis of the evidence available that John Paul II's insistent reassertion of the teaching has had any effect. Occasionally a Catholic leader like Archbishop Bernard Law of Boston will announce that the Catholic faithful are grateful to John Paul for his insistent repetition of the traditional teaching. But Archbishop Law is making up such a judgment out of whole cloth (cardinal-red cloth, as it turned out). There is no empirical evidence whatsoever to support it.

Periodically I am accused of attacking the Church's doctrine on birth control. However, I have never publicly attacked it. The birth-control teaching of *Humanae Vitae* is the official teaching on the subject of the Catholic Church. Along with Archbishop Quinn of San Francisco, speaking at the synod of bishops on the family, I believe the teaching is subject to reexamination and change but, for the moment, it is the official teaching. I am not a moral theologian; I am not competent to make a public judgment on the teaching. I am a sociologist, capable of reporting the simple fact that whatever people ought to be doing, they do not in fact accept the teaching. Once more I find myself in the peculiar position where many Catholics are incapable of distinguishing between fact and value. The sociologist who reports the fact does not necessarily endorse it, he merely says it is true. For a sociologist to pretend Catholics do accept the teaching of the Pope when in fact they don't (which is apparently what some bishops and Catholic writers like Monsignor Kelly want) is to lie. And lie on empirical findings I will not.

The birth-control encyclical disturbed me as much in its style as in its conclusions. In the early paragraphs the Pope lists all the reasons for changing the teaching advanced by the majority of his commission. However, he does not respond to any of these reasons but simply dismisses them and reasserts the traditional doctrine because it is tradition, even though the majority of his own commission had provided reasons for him, if he wanted to justify a change without violating the tradition. The encyclical was, then, a naked exercise of authority and not a reasoned response to the theological arguments advanced against it. As soon as I realized that this was the sort of document it was, I felt reasonably confident it would not work. In the modern world, a well-educated Catholic population will not accept naked authority that feels no need or obligation to offer explanations for its decisions.

So, while one hears of the politics of the Curia after the birth-control commission made its report and went home, the argument against the change was neither one of moral theology nor one of sexual ethics. Rather, the argument was one of authority and power. The time was not ripe for a change in the doctrine, the Pope was told. The Catholic laity would not be able to understand the reasons for the change. Should there have been a change in birth-control teaching, grave scandal would have been caused among the faithful and they would have doubted all forms of Catholic authority. Therefore, the birth-control teaching must be preserved, not because of its internal rationality but as a matter of protecting the authority of the Vatican. To the extent that this argument was efficacious (and my Roman sources report it was the only argument that was decisive for the issuance of the encyclical), it turned out to be false. The laity, instead of respecting authority, came to have contempt for it. More-over, in something as intimate and poignant as marital sexuality, to make a decision based on political power is to do terrible violence to human beings. If the reason for the birth-control encyclical was not internal arguments over sexual ethics but external arguments over the power of the Vatican, then the encyclical will be harshly judged by history. Not only did it destroy the sexual credibility of Church authority, it also was a terrible injustice to the married lay people.

My own position on this is not greatly dissimilar from that of John Paul II, who in his encyclical on the family said that because of the charism of the sacrament of matrimony (the wisdom which comes from the experience of marriage), married lay people have a unique and in-dispensable contribution to make to the Church's understanding of the theology of marriage. He continued by adding that the "sense of the Church" in these matters cannot be obtained exclusively by social data collection, no matter how useful. A number of people think that that passage in *Familiaris Consortio* was aimed at me. If it was, then the Pope made the same mistake a lot of others have made about what I have written. I have never argued and do not believe that survey research is the only way of arriving at the sense of the faithful. The most I would claim for it is precisely what the Pope concedes to it, a useful and partial way of learning about the sense of the faithful. It is a curious experience to see yourself condemned (implicitly) in a Papal document in which the Pope in fact embraces a position which coincides exactly with your own. The problem with *Humanae Vitae*, as I see it, is that the experience of the married faithful did not make its unique and indispensable con-tribution to the formation of the encyclical.

Moreover, for all the talk in Papal documents about the human sci-ences, the contribution of the human sciences in matters of marital sex has been totally ignored. We know now from such disciplines as paleoan-thropology and comparative primatology that what is unique and special about human sexuality is not its procreative but its pair-bonding aspects. A specifically human sexuality had to evolve before *Homo Sapiens* could appear. It is relatively simple and easy to procreate a higher primate. The other species—orangutans, baboons, gorillas—do it much more neatly and efficiently than we do. The female is ready for sex only once a month and the male is attracted to her only at that time. As far as we can tell from observing them, none of the other higher primates are constantly

338

and obsessively preoccupied about sex as we humans are. To say that our sexuality is "animal" might be unfair to the animals. We are pervasively instead of episodically interested in sex, ready for it at almost any time, and attracted to members of the opposite sex precisely because these characteristics were selected in the evolutionary process to bind together the male and the female in a quasi pair bonding of the sort necessary to sustain their relationship so that the infant of the species, weak and defenseless for many years, might have two parents to protect him/her during the infancy and childhood years. We are not pair-bonded like birds, for example (the Gambel quail in Arizona being the classic case of full pair bonding) but only quasi-pair-bonded. Pair bonding is not so much programmed into our genes as it is a propensity reinforced by our powerful and pervasive sexuality.

Thus, for those interested in natural law, frequent and passionate sex between the male and the female of the human species is "natural" because it reinforces the quasi pair bonding, and to abstain from sex is to some extent "unnatural" because it weakens the quasi pair bonding. It would appear, therefore, that the Catholic attempt to minimize marital sexuality in the name of the natural law in fact betrays that law. The refusal of Church leaders and Church theologians to take seriously what the human sciences say about the nature of human nature is a violation of the tradition which in the great natural-law thinkers like Thomas Aquinas was always empirical, seeking to learn by investigation instead of deriving propositions on *a priori* grounds about the nature of human nature.

Serious natural-law investigation has long since been abandoned because the Church leadership is inclined whenever there's debate about the nature of human nature to foreclose such investigation with statements from what is alleged to be the "deposit of faith," in effect attributing to the traditional teachings and finally the teachings of Jesus the solutions to natural-law questions which did not exist in His time. A reexamination of the natural law of human sexuality, it seems to me, would provide, finally, a way out of the Church's impasse on marital sexuality. A way out which, as my sister and I have pointed out in our book *How to Save the Catholic Church*, is in perfect accord with the Catholic tradition. However, the Vatican has painted itself into such a corner on birth control that a consideration of the natural law of human sexuality is at the present time out of the question.

339

I suspect Catholic historians of the future will describe the Church's obsession with sex and particularly with an attempt to deny the pleasures of sex to married men and women as a chapter in our history comparable to the Inquisition and the Crusades. For reasons of political power and, I believe, fear of and dislike for women, Church leadership has interjected itself into the marriage bedroom (ignoring the wisdom of the nineteenth-century response to the bishops of France) and tried to prevent husbands and wives from having sexual intercourse.

In this foolish and ultimately self-defeating attempt, ecclesiastical authority has ignored the teaching of the human sciences about the nature of human sexuality, the demographic revolution which has diminished the number of pregnancies required to continue the species, and the testimony about the meaning of married sex from its own lay people. It has listened neither to natural law nor to the sense of the faithful—and the latter despite John Paul II's explicit statement that the Church *had* to listen to them. It has insisted that every marriage act must be open to procreation, even though both the human sciences and the experience of sex in marriage have said the opposite. It does so in the name of "natural law" and the "teaching of Jesus," although it provides no evidence to support either argument. It has by this disregard of its own premises caused suffering to millions of married couples and demolished its own credibility as an authoritative teacher.

None of this is to argue that the decision of Paul VI was wrong. It is merely to describe objectively what happened.

My guess is the debate will become moot before the end of the century as "natural" means of birth control become so easy, so effective and so popular that Catholics and others alike will use them. Then theologians of the future will reassess the present controversy.

That will be fine for the future. What about the sufferings and the anguish of devout Catholic husbands and wives today?

The local leadership will shake its head and murmur about that "goddam encyclical" and continue enthusiastically to endorse it.

The reviews in the Catholic journals of *Catholic Schools in a Declining Church* were, as I had come to expect, distinctly unfavorable, rejecting in principle the possibility that the birth-control encyclical could alone be responsible for the decline in Catholic practice. Three sociologists from the University of Notre Dame pointed out that a lot of other things were happening in the Church in the 1960s—the civil rights demonstrations, the peace movement, Father James Groppi, the 1968 Democratic Convention riots. Doubtless such things were happening, though it is absurd to think they made as much difference in the personal lives of ordinary Catholics as did a Papal decision on birth control. Moreover, the Notre Dame critics paid no attention to the mathematical models we had developed to measure social change between 1963 and 1974, apparently fearing to dirty their hands with such dreary things as statistics. The most typical Catholic review or editorial-page reaction was to express "disagreement with Greeley's opinion." Unfortunately for this frequently self-righteous stand I was not expressing opinion, I was describing a mathematical model. The distinction between fact and value or opinion was apparently beyond the comprehension of the Catholic journalists too. There was a long review article in *America* by a professor from Fordham who also simply did not understand the nature of our social change model and who completely misinterpreted it. He confused an explanation of the *change* in religious behavior (which is the analysis in which we engaged) with an explanation of the *total* variance of religious behavior—a mistake a first-year graduate student would avoid.

The hostile reviews, however, did not prevent the findings about the Council and the encyclical from being generally accepted in the Church. Too many laity knew what the encyclical had done to them and too many priests knew the laity were no longer bothering to confess birth control for there to be any doubt of the accuracy of our findings.

Later research done by Michael Hout and myself confirmed the findings of the Catholic school study and also demonstrated that in 1974 we had observed the end of the post–*Humanae Vitae* decline in Catholic practice. Church attendance stabilized in the middle 1970s at 50 percent almost every week and has not changed in the ensuing decade. Moreover, the generation born in the 1960s will be as likely to attend church in the middle years of life as was my own generation. Unlike other countries (most notably Germany), American Catholicism survived the *Humanae Vitae* crisis without a mortal wound.

Interestingly the crisis of church attendance correlated with the crisis of political affiliation for Catholics. The decline in churchgoing between 1968 and 1975 paralleled the decline in Democratic affiliation and *correlated* with it. The attendance of those who strongly identified with either political party diminished by only 4 percentage points while among those who were "pure" independents—leaning towards neither party—the decline was more than 30 percentage points.

Using a complex model-fitting technique called a Rasch model, Hout and I (mostly Mike) demonstrated that there was an underlying factor (a "latent variable") which we called "loyalty" that constrained Catholics to stay in their party and continue regular churchgoing after 1975. Both religion and political affiliation, we surmised, were too intimate a dimension of self-definition and social location to be readily yielded by American Catholics. The social structure of American society had protected the Church through its post-encyclical crisis.

Lucky us.

I must admit that on the whole, I thought these findings reassuring. If the hierarchy and the Papacy intended to enforce the birth-control encyclical as strictly as possible, the churches would be empty. Seventy-five percent of the weekly communicants would be banned. Obviously, the hierarchy had no intention of trying to enforce the encyclical that way, and just as obviously the Vatican did not expect them to. The old Mediterranean argument about sympathy for the weakness of human nature would justify their position, as offensive as it might be to the lay people who did not think sexual passion in their marriage was a weakness of human nature. The Church in the United States would survive *Humanae Vitae*. It would survive it because the hierarchy pretended it didn't know what was going on as a result of "that goddam encyclical" and because the clergy chose to take sides with the laity, and because the laity in their turn chose in substantial part to remain Catholic while still ignoring the Church's sexual ethic.

Usually, when I offer this explanation, somebody rises up to say that "they can't do that." Catholics are bound to obey the teachings of the Papacy on birth control. I would not for a moment deny that Catholics are bound to follow the teachings of the Papacy on birth control. All I am saying is that they don't, and if they did, what we would have is empty churches, something neither the Papacy nor the hierarchy really seem to want.

How do the lay people get away with it? In later research, after I had developed my theory of the religious imagination, I was able to demonstrate that the critical variable is *how people imagine God*. Those who reject the Church's sexual ethic and nonetheless have an image of God as kind, gentle and loving are the ones who are most likely to go to weekly Mass and Communion. The laity justify their continued reception of the sacraments despite the violation of the Papal birth-control teaching by an appeal from the Church to God. The Pope might not understand the importance of sex in their marriage, the laity are saying in effect, but the loving God does. The official Church has caught itself in a bind in which the laity think that God is on their side and not on the side of Papal teaching.

The major questions, then, about post-Conciliar American Catholicism had been answered: the Council was a huge success. Much of its success, however, was canceled out, even reversed, by the birth-control encyclical. A fair number of Catholics had stopped going to church because of that encyclical but the majority continued to be devout despite their rejection of the teaching. The era of "do-it-yourself Catholicism" had begun. Later research, in which we teased data out of NORC's annual General Social Survey, indicated that many of those who had drifted away from the Church because of *Humanae Vitae* would drift back into the Church in their late thirties and early forties. A life-cycle dimension to Catholic practice seemed to have arisen since the early sixties. Young people in their twenties would drift away, then drift back again in their early thirties. This return (which my sister and I describe in a book called *A Church to Come Home To*) was part of a larger reintegration into society that occurred at the time of marriage and immediately after marriage. Young people during their single years disengaged from all social institutions and then tended to return to them once they were married. The drift of young Catholics back to the Church and back to the Democratic Party seemed correlated. There was, for example, a .20 correlation between frequency of spouses' communion and the propensity of a newly married young Catholic to associate strongly with the Democratic Party!

After marriage, the return to the Church continued, simultaneous with the coming of children but apparently independent of children and more closely correlated with the simple fact of aging. The older one became, the more likely one was to take religion seriously, perhaps because after a certain age in life, one discovered that prayer and religious devotion seemed to "work."

We would try again, in the 1980s, to fund a study of the American Catholic population twenty years after the Vatican Council, but Church institutions had learned their lesson. Don't give money to social researchers, for while they may find much news that is good, the bad news is likely to cause considerable trouble with the Vatican. Better that the

343

Vatican be permitted to keep its head in the sand than to find out the truth from social research that the Church's organizations have funded—particularly when the research is directed by a priest who writes dirty novels!

CHAPTER
18
Yet More Windmills

FOR NORA MAEVE

What mirthful liturgy, feast of red and gold,
Mounts laughing incense from burning leaves
Makes joyful autumn don its vestments old
And wind hymn merrily in the waltzing trees?
Why do warm-hearted celebrants sing and dance
As their tired, snowdrift-dreading souls revive?
What festival causes such a happy trance?
Don't you know? Nora Maeve is five!
Though yet the spiteful blizzard winds will howl
As death's-head winter spews its bitter lies
And despair snarls a sharp-teethed frigid growl
We see God's sparkling love in her ocean eyes.
Barely, perhaps, till spring, life and love survive
Let us sing of hope: Nora Maeve is five.

AMBASSADOR PAT

The black mountain ranges
Turned white in winter snow
But fed by warm springs
Flow the racing streams
Tumbling down the mountainside
To laughter exploding waterfalls

My novels, it is complained, are about the Chicago Irish. Chicago, a *National Catholic Reporter* critic protests, is not the center of the world.

To which I reply that it is too. It is the center of my world and I'm writing about my world, since I don't know any other. My research on ethnicity during the 1970s was unintended preparation for fiction rooted in the culture of the Irish Catholic neighborhoods. I sought neither in sociology nor in fiction to celebrate the Chicago Irish so much as to understand them.

It is a terrible thing to be numbered among the Chicago Irish.

Until you consider the alternatives.

While the project reported in *Catholic Schools in a Declining Church* received considerable attention, it was not the principal activity of my colleagues and me at NORC during the seventies. We had formed a Center for the Study of American Pluralism to analyze religious and ethnic diversity in American society. The basic support for this project through the seventies came from a grant from the Ford Foundation, not from the research division, which never did like us, but from the national affairs office, presided over by Mitchell P. Sviridoff and Basil Whiting. McGeorge Bundy vigorously supported this research.

The day after my final battle with the University of Chicago, Bundy was on the phone (having heard about it from Pat Moynihan, who, in his turn, had heard about it from Pete Rossi) to assure me that no matter what the university did, the Ford Foundation would continue to support our work.

The Ford money was not for specific projects, though we squeezed several primary research projects out of it, but to build and hold together a staff of researchers who could design and raise funds for projects. NORC was and is an institution that lives by its wits, receiving no subsidies from the University of Chicago or from anywhere else. Grantsmanship is a difficult, unpredictable business. The funding institutions follow unpredictable cycles of fads and fashions. Moreover, good work does not necessarily guarantee grant renewal because the funding agency can argue that the work has been done so well that further research in that direction is no longer needed. Nonetheless, by dint of many trips to New York and Washington, McCready and I kept the program going for ten years. One of the reasons for my accepting an appointment at the University of Arizona was that I had had it with grantsmanship, and one of the marvelous things about novel writing is that now I can become a grantor instead of a grantee!

It was during this grant that I met one of the more impressive human beings it has been my pleasure to encounter.

Mike Sviridoff kept telling me that I ought to get to know a man named Mario Cuomo who had mediated a community dispute in Forest Hills. "He's going to be President someday," Mike insisted.

I have great respect for Mike's political instincts, but I doubted that one. "We're not ready for a president named Mario."

"Read *Forest Hills Diary*, his book about the mediation out there."

"Sure," I said, with no intention of reading it.

Finally, however, I figured I'd better do what Mike said.

It was an astonishing book, thoughtful, sensitive, profoundly religious.

"I gotta meet this guy," I said to Mike.

So a few weeks later in Jimmy Miller's home in Queens, I met Mario and his wife, Mathilda. I wrote a column suggesting that on the basis of *Forest Hills Diary* Mario Cuomo might be President someday.

I have no reason to question that prediction now. Not in the slightest.

What impresses me most about Governor Cuomo is that he stands so solidly on his own traditions—Queens Italian Catholic, New Deal Democrat, Thomistic legal philosophy. His wit and passion, his articulate rhetoric, his profound commitments are all rooted in a clear sense of his own faith and identity.

He is a neighborhood ethnic, an excellent qualification in my judgment to be President. It's time the country was ready for a President named Mario.

Some scholars, most notably Orlando Patterson, argued against ethnic research—ethnicity was not even a legitimate subject for social research because ethnic groups were "particularistic" and divisive. Patterson and his crowd, however, were playing the old game of thought control, attempting to police ideas and determine which ideas were appropriate to investigate and which were not. Having lived through an era when the Catholic Church tried the same thing, I was in no mood to accept such control in the academic world.

Much of our work on ethnicity was done on grants from the National Institute for Alcohol Abuse and Alcoholism, where it was not necessary to persuade people that ethnic subcultures did exist in American society and that there were different patterns of drinking behavior in such sub-cultures.

Briefly, we were able to establish that the Catholic ethnic groups were, on virtually all measures of political attitudes and behavior, more liberal than the national average. They were also more likely to support equal rights for women, more likely to oppose the Vietnam War and, in fact, were no longer predominantly blue-collar, the majority of them having crossed into the white-collar category in the time after the Second World War for the Eastern and Southern European immigrants and the time after the First World War for the Irish ethnic group. The Irish, in fact, were the most successful gentile ethnic group in America, an achievement which offended many Irish-Americans' need for self-pity!

A curious controversy developed around this finding. The black economist Thomas Sowell, analyzing Irish data from the United States census, argued that the Irish were the poorest ethnic group in America and the one least likely to have achieved success in this country. Somehow Sowell could not be persuaded that half the Irish in the United States census data were Irish Protestants, mostly rural and Southern, and that the data on Irish ethnics were worthless because the census could not ask a religious question. Sowell argued that he could not imagine a Protestant claiming Irish background. When told that a national sample survey showed that slightly more than half of those who claimed Irish ancestry also gave their religion as Protestant, Sowell dismissed the finding as *a priori* impossible and wondered whether we distributed questionnaires in shopping plazas for sampling methodology. Sowell has argued, quite correctly it seems to me, against black tokenism, claiming that blacks ought to be given a right to earn their way in the academic world, just as much as anyone else, and not be given academic appointments for reasons of racial background. Unfortunately, Sowell's sloppy methodology and arrogant polemic would be tolerated only by those who believe in tokenism.

We were also able to isolate specific ethnic subcultures, not totally different from the national culture, but with different propensities and tendencies and proclivities. In such matters as religion, family structure, politics, attitudes to aging, and alcohol use and abuse, there were different ethnic subcultures, subcultures which were handed on quite independently of any self-conscious ethnic identity. The various ethnic behavior patterns were learned early in childhood, mostly by imitation of one's parents, without any necessary ethnic self-consciousness. Jewish teenagers drank little, and Irish teenagers drank a lot, not because they were self-consciously Jewish or Irish, but because they were following cultural patterns learned early in life from their parents. If one made up a series of propositions about the Irish-Americans and the Italian-Americans based on the anthropological literature that arose from fieldwork in the home country, and then tested these propositions against the data collected in American surveys, approximately four-fifths of them would be correct, i.e., you could predict differences between Irish-Americans and Italian-Americans on the basis on literature from the old countries and be right four-fifths of the time.

Ethnic subcultures have remarkable durability, precisely because they are acquired unself-consciously early in life and consist most fundamentally of a network of expectation concerning one's most intimate role opposites—parents, spouse, children, aunts, uncles, cousins. (When Geraldine Ferraro said, "You know what Italian men are like!" she was not engaging in ethnic stereotyping, she was rather describing a statistically demonstrable correlation.)

Just as Catholic elites were upset by our findings on the lay acceptance of the Vatican Council changes, so were many secular elites upset by our findings about ethnic diversity. Somehow such diversity was wrong: we all ought to become like one another in the great melting pot, ought we not?

No one objected to Hispanic subcultures or black subcultures or even Jewish subcultures. It was the Irish and the Italian and the Polish subcultures that were objectionable. So I came to believe that anti-Catholic nativism—disguised, urbane, sophisticated, but profound—continued in American society, not merely and not even principally among the rural redneck population but among the cultural elites at the great universities and in the major national media outlets. I wrote a little book on it called *The Ugly Little Secret* which seems to me still to be accurate: the great unacknowledged bigotry in America is nativism. The attack on Congresswoman Ferraro during the presidential campaign seems a classic example. Reporters would admit off the record, though they'll never say it in print, that the principal reason for going after the Ferraro finances was their conviction that one could not be a well-to-do Italian real estate man in Queens and not have Mob connections. They were convinced Mr. Zaccaro was hesitant about releasing his financial data because they would reveal a connection with organized crime. It turned out that there were no such connections and Mr. Zaccaro's reluctance to make public his business dealings was what one would expect from an Italian male small businessman with a strong sense of privacy. Much of the antipathy toward Mrs. Ferraro which astonishingly appeared in the press during the campaign was based on the fact that she was attractive and successful and well-to-do and *Italian*!

Related to, but not necessarily to be identified with, our research on ethnic diversity was the ethnic activism pioneered in the sixties in part by the American Jewish Committee, under the leadership of Irving Levine and David Roth in Chicago, and in Washington by the late, great Monsignor Geno Baroni, one of the finest priests it has ever been my pleasure to know. Geno's instincts went in the same direction as our research. Both showed that while the ethnics had made it in America, they were still victims of both cultural and economic discrimination—cultural discrimination because they were looked down upon and their neighborhood communities were viewed as reactionary and racist, and economic discrimination because they were still excluded from positions of influence and power in the banks, the law firms and the universities.

The great state universities no longer discriminate against Catholics or against anyone whose name ends in a vowel, but the great private universities, Harvard, Yale, Princeton, Stanford and the University of Chicago, may well engage in affirmative action for blacks and Hispanics and women but have little if any representation from the Catholic ethnic groups. As one scholar remarked, "Is it our fault that your group just isn't good academically?"

It was interesting to me to see how the Catholic liberals, like Notre Dame's Monsignor John Egan, changed their opinion on Baroni when he switched from being a black activist to being an ethnic activist. Geno certainly didn't abandon his earlier support for racial justice, but he came to realize that in American society, justice for one group means justice for all, and that when Catholic leaders abandon their own kind because of concern for justice for other groups, they not only betray their own but they also break the rules of America's pluralistic political game. His vision of power alliances between whites and black ethnics did not materialize, save in a few isolated situations during the seventies. It was a brilliant idea, however, but there simply was not enough support from those who provided the funds for such projects for it to materialize. If the Italians and the Poles and the Irish, on the one hand, and the blacks, on the other, ever do manage to put together a grand alliance of the sort Geno envisioned, it could remake American urban society.

One of Geno's best stories (like Mario Cuomo's, his stories were all about his mother) has to do with an argument on ethnicity at the family dinner table on Thanksgiving between Geno and his brother. Mrs. Baroni finally intervened, "Shutta ya face, Geno. In this country, everybody is American. Now eata your spaghetti!"

Muddying the waters in this ethnic "revival" (it wasn't a revival because those of us who are Irish or Italian or Polish or Greek or whatever were well aware we were that all along—what was revived was the larger culture's awareness of us) was the highly idiosyncratic writing of Michael Novak. As in many other subject areas, most recently Catholic tradition and Democratic capitalism, Novak was never one to be held back by the absence of scholarship or research or data. He wrote about his own opinions and his own impressions as though they were statistically demonstrated facts. Unfortunately for the rest of us, Novak was a marvelous target for the Orlando Pattersons of the country. The ethnicity he claimed existed (and which, in fact, we could never find with our data) was precisely the narrow, rigid, racist, reactionary ethnic stereotype which the cultural elites liked to imagine. Small wonder that Novak became their favorite white ethnic: he confirmed all the prejudices they already had.

Our research on ethnics in the seventies was successful. We answered all the questions we set out to, and on the intellectual level won the argument. Moreover, a whole generation of younger scholars is continuing the work of studying the various ethnic communities in the United States, undeterred by the Orlando Pattersons and other thought-policing critics.

Ethnicity survives. Undoubtedly there is much ethnic intermarriage. It does not follow, as some scholars assume, that intermarriage eliminates ethnic diversity, both because children exercise the option to choose one ethnic group or the other and because sometimes it requires a parent of only one ethnic group to transmit the ethnic subcultural pattern.

(McCready is an excellent example of this. On affirmative action questionnaires he legitimately claims his Dakota Indian ancestry, while in the neighborhood in which he lives, he claims only to be Irish!)

Thus, one needs only one Jewish parent for the Jewish nondrinking subculture to be transmitted across generational lines and only one Irish parent for the Irish drinking subculture to be transmitted. The marginal increment in one's drinking behavior from a second Irish or a second Jewish parent is slight. What happens in Irish/Jewish intermarriage? We had only four cases in the study, but my suspicion is that in this area the Irish win!)

In the early eighties with my translation for part of the year to Tucson I became interested in Hispanic/American ethnic subcultures and together with Teresa Sullivan, Pastora Cafferty and Barry Chiswick embarked on a study of American immigration policy in which the four of us argued strongly against what seems to us to be the monumental injustice to Hispanic Americans in this so-called reform of the Simpson/Mazzoli bill, and of the President's select commission on immigration, presided over by Father Hesburgh. It seems to us ironic that Father Hesburgh can lecture the rest of American society on its obligations in justice to the third world and still accept the near-genocidal conditions under which the undocumented immigrants must live along the Texas, Arizona and California borders. Sometime Father Hesburgh ought to read Joe Wambaugh's book *Lines and Shadows*, and see the wonderful motion picture *El Norte*, and then examine his conscience carefully. The recommendations of the Dillingham Commission on immigration at the turn of the century (keep the Italians and the Poles out!) do not differ greatly from the recommendations of the Hesburgh Commission at the end of the century (keep the Hispanics out!). Father Hesburgh is the Congressman Dillingham of our time.

As long as there is a large labor market on one side of the border and a large labor supply on the other, no nation in the free world can prevent immigration. Moreover, despite the alarms raised against the swarms of undocumenteds crossing the border, in fact, no serious economic research has ever found any particular danger or even threat to American employment. The undocumenteds, for the most part, take jobs no American citizen would want. Most of their migration is cyclic. They come to the United States and work awhile and then return to their villages in northern Mexico; they are the conduits for a flow of American money into the third world of which Father Hesburgh ought to approve.

America has gone through periodic infections of nativism. The prevailing feeling about Hispanics at the present time is simply one more recurrence of that nativism and it is linked in its fundamental fear of the foreigner. I will take seriously the peace and justice activists at the U.S. Catholic Conference when their justice activism also includes the Cath-

352

olic ethnic groups which are still victims of discrimination, Hispanics at all levels in the society, and Italians and Poles and even Irish in certain critical elite positions in society.

During the seventies, my roller-coaster ride on some occasions notably affected my judgment. The recklessness which came from rejection could become foolish imprudence. It was hard to tell, especially when I was weary and discouraged—which was much of the time—when my defiance was appropriate (as in my conflict with the bishops over the priest study) and when it was mindless. It was also hard to tell when Don Quixote would have been better off not to pick up his lance.

In the ethnic business I let myself be entrapped in a battle with the American Jewish Committee that was ridiculous from start to finish. I am not proud of it. I hope those responsible in the AJC are not proud of it either.

I had become closely involved with the AJC in the late sixties, in the first flush of ecumenical enthusiasm. In fact, it became a joke that I was their house priest. I served on committees, went to meetings, made presentations, formed friendships, worked hard for them. I enjoyed these activities, especially because among their many other civilized traits, Jews serve not only coffee and tea but sweet rolls at midmorning snacks. (Protestants serve only coffee, if that. Catholics serve coffee and tea, but no sweet rolls. Except for Poles, who serve whiskey and brown bread and sometimes, bless them for it, sausages.)

Nonetheless, when one of their ecumenical rabbis invited me to make a presentation at the annual AJC meeting on Jewish anti-Catholicism, I demurred. No group is free of bigotry; tension between Catholics and Jews is too critical a problem to be ignored. But I had enough trouble without taking that subject on. Don Quixote resolutely refused to pick up his lance.

He said, "Do it for me as a personal favor."

That's a request which no neighborhood ethnic can resist. I picked up my lance, but only on the condition that he vet every word. First mistake.

There was some hostility at the meeting. Wasn't Catholic anti-Semitism worse than Jewish anti-Catholicism? Sure it was. Terrible historical evil. Yet in a pluralistic society everyone must fight all forms of prejudice. I think most of the audience was intrigued, troubled and thoughtful. The rabbi thanked me profusely.

A few days later I was on a platform at NYU with Abe Rosenthal, the new editor of the *New York Times*, then and now a close friend. (I was talking about the use of social science in court decisions. My position: better to rely on meteorology because it is more certain.) I gave Abe the paper, he read it, liked it, and asked if they might use it.

Sure, Don Quixote said. Why not?

Second mistake. I should have demanded a chance to see how it was edited for the Op Ed page (Abe later apologized for the slip-up, the only one who ever apologized in the whole incident).

I came home from Europe a few weeks later to see a mangled excerpt on the Op Ed page, nothing I wouldn't have agreed to, but without the necessary qualifications and nuances. And without any reference to the fact that the AJC had commissioned the full paper and vetted every word.

The roof fell in. A whole page of letters conjuring up all the anti-Semitism of the past and blaming me for it. The best of them said that some Jews may be anti-Catholic but that because of Catholic guilt from the past, we ought not even to mention it.

A dumb position.

The worst letters were from priests in ecumenical work.

I replied in kind. (Third mistake.) I also pointed out the AJC origins of the paper. Which no one seemed to notice.

Then I read later an attack on the article by the rabbi who had commissioned it. He neglected to mention his role in it.

I wrote a furious column denouncing the AJC for double dealing. (Fourth mistake.) A rabbi wrote me to say it served me right for trusting the first rabbi.

The *New York Times* picked up the column and an AJC response which, ignoring the fact that I had done it all as a favor for a friend, tried to tar me with the brush of anti-Semitism. Again.

A furious attack on our funding was made at the Ford Foundation by the WASPs in charge of their foreign operation who wanted our money. It was barely beaten back by Mike Sviridoff (who was Jewish).

Now I was really angry and sulked through the summer and into the fall. I wrote yet another column (fifth mistake) proposing a joint Jewish/ Catholic study of interreligious attitudes. Let the AJC put its money where its mouth was. (Not a bad idea, but hardly the time for it, what?)

Finally, about to return to Europe (for more research on the Papal election project), I began to think straight. I phoned Bert Gold, the head of the AJC, and proposed we meet at the United lounge at Kennedy and end the nonsense. We did it in fifteen minutes. Bert issued the statement calling off the fight and more or less admitting that (1) I had made the presentation originally at their request and (2) all interreligious bigotry was a problem.

(First nonmistake for Quixote on this one.)

When *Ugly Little Secret*, my book on anti-Catholicism, appeared the next year, it contained the full text of the talk and my version of the background. (A Quixote trick, but no more reckless than writing this memoir.) Fewer people probably read the book than read Gold's exoneration of me from the charge of anti-Semitism. And fewer read that than read the original charge of anti-Semitism.

The fires died down, although for the next couple of years, I would occasionally be asked about my "anti-Semitic outburst."

I make no case for the AJC rabbi's behavior, which was shameful. Nor would I argue that the move to take away our funding at Ford was anything but vicious. Finally, the response of many Jewish leaders was inappropriate. As I said to Gold, if you do not listen to the Catholics who are your friends, then you are going to have to listen to many who are not your friends later on. If my credentials were not good enough to protect me from this sort of reaction, whose would be?

I should have stayed out of it in the first place. It was not my fight. Then, when the battle was joined, I should have hopped the first plane to New York, driven right to Bert Gold's office and said, "Let's settle this now."

I may not be the son of a cop, but I'm enough of a West Side Irishman to know that.

Why didn't I?

Does it help to say I was tired? Worn out from jet lag and a rough semester of work? Battered, bitter, despondent. Not really good excuses. They are the only ones I have. There were lots of harassments at Grand Beach that summer (I don't remember now what they were) and the thought of another jet ride was more than I could bear.

Physical weariness I can deal with. The pain of rejection I can tolerate, more or less. The two together leave me spiritually and morally vulnerable. The anger the mythmakers see in me all the time is part of their neurosis. My real anger is rare—like with Phil Doran at Hi Club—but when it erupts in the midst of weariness reinforced by feelings of rejection, I'm in trouble. So is everyone else.

It didn't happen often in the seventies, but once was more than enough. And it happened substantially more than once.

Eventually, I managed to straighten out most of the damage as I did with Bert Gold, apologizing sometimes for the substance and sometimes for the method of my rage (the latter in the case of the AJC). I not only felt sorry. Worse, I felt like a fool. A dumb Quixote.

Perhaps I should stay out of airplanes. Yet at that time I was taking on both novel writing and a job in Arizona which would mean more rather than less air travel.

Anyway, I'm sorry for the blunders to which I succumbed in my moments of weariness and rejection.

Our third emphasis in the pluralism program during the seventies was the sociology of religion. Unfortunately, despite the tradition of sociological concern with religion, there were virtually no funds available in the last twenty years for the study of the sociology of religion because the intellectual and cultural elites in American society had ruled that religion was "irrelevant." The sociology of religion, of critical importance to the Holy Father Founders of sociology, Emile Durkheim and Max Weber, has become a backwater subdiscipline which bright students are advised to avoid.

These bright students became the teachers who presided over the classes of the State Department officials who were unprepared for the Ayatollah Khomeini. And the media wise-persons who were unprepared for Jonestown. And for the so-called "revival" of fundamentalism.

(Fundamentalism hasn't revived; like white ethnics, the fundamentalists have always been there. However, Reagan's first presidential victory sensitized the New York media elites to the existence of a large and powerful fundamentalist component in American society. Characteristically, when the media discover something everybody else knows about, they call it a revival, not a rediscovery.)

I proposed that one ought to attempt to study religion as an explanatory system, a culture system, a set of symbols explaining what life means. Martha Wallace of the Henry Luce Foundation supported this proposal, and the foundation made a major grant for the study of religion as a meaning system, the only grant of which I am aware for a national survey of religion in the 1970s.

McCready and I devised a technique of "vignettes," life situations to

356

which we would ask our respondents to attach meaning, combined with a series of agree/disagree items which also could be expected to give some hint as to what basic meaning a respondent attributed to life. The vignettes were, for example, the slow and painful death of a parent, the death of a child, a natural disaster, the news that one has only six months to live. The report from the study, of which Bill was the senior author, on the ultimate values of Americans did not, I fear, have too much impact on the sociologists of religion, who, in any case, were not interested in what we were doing. We did derive meaningful factors from our vignettes and from our agree/disagree items and were able to use them to explain behavior in ways that made sense. However, as interesting as these correlations were, they were not especially large. We were able to distinguish between several different religious styles—optimism, pessimism, resignation, and hope. Those who were committed to the last worldview— those who saw both good and evil in the world and good marginally stronger than evil—were the most likely to be politically and socially enlightened and to have the happiest family relationships. Moreover, the roots of their hope could be found in patterns of early family relationships when they were children.

In retrospect, however, we were too clever by half. The vignette questions asked people to assign propositional meaning to life situations, but Geertz had defined religion as a set of symbols, not a set of propositions. We should have gone directly for our respondents' symbol system and not tried to get at it indirectly through propositions. Such is the nature of empirical research: you keep making mistakes until finally you hit upon a method of exploration that works. Unfortunately, the technology of survey research is so expensive that two-hundred-thousand-dollar grants to profit from one's mistakes come along but rarely.

I was beginning to understand, however, that religion was image and story before it was proposition—poetry before it was theology, experience before it was catechism. I had already written two popular religion books, *The Jesus Myth* and *The Sinai Myth*, in which I tried to explore the symbols and the stories of the New and the Old Testament for what they were, symbols and stories, pretheological, prepropositional, prerational accounts of an encounter with the sacred. But it would take time, and the development of Tracy's and Shea's ideas on religious experience, symbol and story, as well as my own reflection on the symbolic experiences that arose out of my self-hypnosis experimentation, to realize that the study of the sociology of religion ought to be primarily the study of the religious imagination. And even then I would make many mistakes before I finally found, in 1984, a measure of the religious imagination which really worked.

There was one unexpected payoff from the Luce study, a payoff that led me to duplicate my venture with the study of Beverly Country Club. Just as I owned the patent on the sociology of the country club, McCready and I invented and monopolized (through no intention of our own) the sociology of the paranormal.

You can imagine how all the windmills with which I was tilting liked that!

I was interested in the prevalence of ecstatic religious experiences of the sort described by William James in his classic *The Varieties of Religious Experience* in American society. McCready suggested that in the survey, before we came to the question about ecstatic experiences ("Have you ever had the feeling that you're in the presence of an overwhelming spiritual power which lifts you out of yourself?"), we should also ask questions about ESP, *déjà vu*, clairvoyance and contact with the dead. Later, we also added a question on out-of-body experiences, at Nancy McCready's insistence.

The exact wording of our question was:

> How often have you had any of the following experiences:
> a) Thought you were somewhere you had been before, but knew that it was impossible.
> b) Felt as though you were in touch with someone when they were far away from you.
> c) Seen events that happened at a great distance as they were happening.
> d) Felt as though you were really in touch with someone who had died.
> e) Felt as though you were close to a powerful spiritual force that seemed to lift you out of yourself.

The responses were astonishing: three-fifths of the American people reported ESP experiences, three-fifths reported *déjà vu* experiences, 25 percent reported clairvoyance, 25 percent contact with the dead, 20 percent out of body experiences and 32 percent religious ecstasy.

We had become epidemiologists of the paranormal. The paranormal turned out to be normal and ecstasy turned out to be good for you. There was a high coefficient of association between a mental health scale routinely used in our surveys and frequent ecstatic experiences—the highest correlation ever recorded with that scale. Contrary to what the psychiatric profession believed (as stated in a book called *Ecstasy* published by the Group for the Advancement of Psychiatry) the ecstatic was not a quasi-schizophrenic, not someone escaping from mental problems, but, rather, the healthiest and the most "normal" of persons. While there did not exist such coefficients of association for the other paranormal experiences, there was no evidence that the people who had such experiences were unusual or had serious emotional problems or were in any other respect different from typical Americans.

We soon discovered that researchers in other countries, England, Switzerland and Iceland, for example (most notably Alistair Hardy and David Hay in England), were doing similar work. Using our questions, they replicated both the percentage of people reporting mystical experiences and the correlation with positive mental health. I also found that when one would discuss these kinds of findings at dinner parties, there would almost always be several people who would describe their own ecstatic experiences and admit it was the first time in their life they had mentioned them. As Clifford Geertz remarked wryly, "In many countries of the East, thirty-two percent would be considered a small proportion of mystics."

We published a little booklet called *The Sociology of the Paranormal* and wrote an article for the *New York Times Magazine* called "Are We a Nation of Mystics?" The result of the article was overwhelming—letters and phone calls poured in from all over the country—and so began a series of interviews with "modern mystics" for a book which, unfortunately, has yet to be published. We did everything we could to raise money for further research. Surely if the .40 coefficient of association between frequent mystical experiences and psychological well-being had been found for any other phenomenon, the National Institute for Mental Health would have fallen all over itself endeavoring to fund more research. But after years of rejections, when we finally did get a project approved and recommended for funding, the priority was not sufficiently high for the funds to actually appear. We gave up, realizing that while religious experience might be a strong predictor variable of human behavior, it was not one that it was legitimate to study.

Psychic experiences are commonplace in society, and hence are the kind of phenomena for which survey research funding agencies are ordinarily willing to pay out monies. Nonetheless, just as it is inappropriate for a Catholic priest-researcher to find that the laity rejects the Church's birth-control teaching, so it is inappropriate for a scientific sociologist to find out that ecstasy correlates with positive mental health and that a quarter of the American people have had contact with the dead.

As a social scientist, I have nothing to say about the "reality" of these experiences. I am, myself, the least mystical, the least psychic of persons. As a social scientist I am merely interested in the correlates of paranormal experience, their antecedents and consequences. What kind of people have these experiences and what impact do the experiences have on their lives? Moreover, I want to know the phenomenology of the experience. What is it like to make contact with the dead? Does one dream about the dead person? Does one sense the dead person's presence? Does one actually see the dead person in the room? (In informal anecdotal interviewing I have been astonished at how many ordinary sensible people have actually seen the dead person sitting in the room with them.) When a clairvoyant experience occurs, when one sees something happen in the distance, what is it like? Is it actual physical vision? Is it something that seems to be happening inside one's brain? Is it as though one is operating a video camera miles away from where one is? (Again, the anecdotal interviews suggest that the last may be the best description.)

None of the experiences we studied in the Luce project are abnormal in the sense of happening to maladjusted individuals or in the sense of being rare. They are also commonplace in some of my novels, leading a reviewer in the *New York Times* to complain that such extraordinary events should not be introduced lightly into fiction writing.

They are *not* extraordinary events—they are part of the warp and woof of everyday life. The scientific community may pretend they do not happen, but such pretense is pure dogmatism. I don't know what to make of either psychic or ecstatic experiences. I suspect, as does Blackie Ryan in some of my novels, that psychic capabilities are a "neo-Neanderthal vestige" and that mystical experiences are some kind of direct, intuitive and immediate contact with reality (whether one spells it with a small r or a capital R).

These questions are not my primary concern as a survey research sociologist. I can leave the answers to them to the practitioners of other disciplines. As a sociologist I am concerned with the phenomenology, the antecedents and the consequences of these experiences which are

360

frequent in our society and happen in fact to a majority of us. That the scientific establishment refuses to approve such research proves only that bigotry and bias are by no means limited to religious institutions.

Do I put such incidents in my stories to get back at the scientific establishment?

Is the Pope Catholic?

Why get involved in such bizarre research interests as ethnicity, religious experience and the sociology of the paranormal?

Dare I say again, "Because no one else was"?

CHAPTER
19

"The Blessed Mother and the Catholic Schools"

A BLESSING FOR MARY'S DAY IN HARVEST TIME

May your family never lack food to eat
May you feed the hungry before you dine
May your table be heaped high with tasty meat
At your feasts may you serve the best of wine

May our lady guard you from all God's foes
And may her loving care you never lack
If the front gates of heaven are firmly closed
May Mother Mary sneak you in the back

In the summer of 1975, my tranquillity at Grand Beach was disturbed by a phone call from the *New York Times Magazine*.

NYT: We noted with interest a recent statement of Pope Paul about feminism. We wonder if you could write us an article about Mary.

Me: Mary who?

NYT: (surprised) Why, Mary the Mother of Jesus. Who else?

Me: You really are the *New York Times*.

NYT: Of course. Are you interested?

Me: Well, she was Jewish, wasn't she?

NYT: (faint and uncertain laugh)

In the back of my head there echoed again one of Bill McCready's best dicta: All the Catholic Church has left is the Blessed Mother and the parochial schools.

Curiously enough, one of the great victories of the liberals at the Council was the elimination from the agenda of a draft document on Mary the Mother of Jesus. Mary was to be discussed as part of the document on the Church and not as a religious symbol distinct from the Church.

There were sound historical and theological reasons for this decision. Mary in her most ancient manifestations *is* a symbol of the Church— the symbol par excellence. Nor was there much reason to doubt that any Mariological decree coming out of the Council would be heavily laden with the baggage of the professional Mariologists and hence offensive to Protestants and meaningless to most Catholics. There was no reason to multiply titles or saccharine devotion.

So Mary the Mother of Jesus became an ecumenical embarrassment; the most momentous religious symbol in fifteen hundred years of Western history was tossed unceremoniously into the ashcan of irrelevant and out-of-date stories.

No one asked the laity what they thought about Mary, any more than anyone asked them what they thought about married sex.

She was rescued for me by my old friendly adversary Professor Harvey Cox, who, having come a long way from the Secular City, was now singing the praises of Our Lady of Guadalupe. If Harvey thought Mary was still relevant, maybe she was.

A few months before the *NYT*'s call I had begun an intensive study of the role of Mary in Catholic history and devotion, perhaps because I did not have enough windmills to joust with just then.

364

It was a major turning point for me both professionally and personally. Through preconscious processes I don't fully understand myself, theology and sociological theory merged and my future sociology as well as my storytelling—and my own prayer life—were heavily influenced, indeed shaped, by the work that went into my book *The Mary Myth*.

I would come to realize that in addition to failures of implementation, aggravated by the birth-control encyclical, there were two more fundamental flaws in the work of the Second Vatican Council:

1. The Council was concerned with institutional structure and doctrinal propositions (the role of the bishop, the nature of revelation, collegiality, etc.), and not with religion.

2. The Council was aprioristic rather than empirical; it reflected on the schema of administrators and scholars rather than on the experience of the faithful.

These phenomena result in substantial part from the failure of the Council (a failure for which no one is to be blamed, by the way) to consider religion.

Religion (to paraphrase Clifford Geertz and John Shea) is the set of answers a person has available to the fundamental questions of the meaning of life and love, answers which are normally encoded in pictures, images and stories (symbols) and purport uniquely to give purpose and meaning to human existence. A layman or laywoman may understand only vaguely the formularies of the Council of Chalcedon and have only little concern about the Christological debates of the present (not even knowing of the existence of Karl Rahner or Walter Kaspar or even Hans Küng, much less struggling through their books) and still understand clearly and powerfully that God's love has been revealed to us in Jesus and is stronger than death. Such a person may be, and usually is, perfectly willing to assent to the orthodox doctrinal formulations; it is not, however, the propositional formula but the "story of Jesus" which, in fact, provides meaning and purpose to this person's life.

The doctrinal formula is essential as a critique of the story, as a safeguard in its transmission and as an intellectual explanation required by a reflecting animal such as humankind. But in an individual life the story is normally more influential in providing meaning than the schematic and abstract formula.

The research evidence confirms the low to nonexistent correlation between religious devotion and both doctrinal propositions and institutional structure. My colleagues and I, in our study of young Catholics, found that there was little relationship between propositional orthodoxy and religious behavior but a powerful relationship between "stories" in the religious imagination and such behavior. Moreover, there is also no relationship between the leadership style of a bishop and the religious behavior of the people in his diocese.

Behind these two findings (and many similar) lie two unpalatable truths: religiously, bishops don't matter much, and neither do theologians.

Over the long haul, leadership and scholarship will have an impact on religion. But in the short run—which may take centuries—the stories are handed down by parents, spouses and parish priests, quite independently of what goes on in the halls of the Curias (diocesan or Roman) nd the academy.

The precise definition of the nature of revelation will not affect much either the Sunday homily (won't make it better and can't make it much worse, given the quality of preaching) or the individual reading of the Bible. Nor are the lives of Catholic lay persons, nor their loves, hopes, aspirations, fears and sorrows, likely to be affected in the slightest by a clarification of the institutional role of the bishop vis-à-vis the Pope.

If Vatican II had devoted itself only to doctrine and power (and sex), it might have been not so much traumatic as unnoticed. However, it also introduced changes, allegedly pastoral, which, while popular in themselves, severely damaged the existing religious paradigm, called into question some of the stories that were essential to its integration. In terms of their doctrinal importance, practices like fish on Friday may not have been critical, but in terms of what it meant symbolically to be Catholic, they were crucial.

Thus we found out that the following images were no longer to be part of our story system: mixed marriages are bad; Protestants are not to be trusted; we don't eat meat on Friday; priests must be called Father, sisters wear special clothes; the Mass does not change; men do not leave the priesthood; mortal sins must be confessed in full detail before receiving Communion; weekly confession is, if not necessary, almost a prerequisite for frequent Communion; no one criticizes the Pope; the most important thing in life is to save your soul; Catholics should have large families; Catholics can't divorce and remarry; sexual sins are the worst and are dreadfully easy to commit and always mortal; the man is the head of the home, the woman the heart; etc., etc.

366

Catholic novelists (Mary Gordon and John Powers, for example) have had a field day with nostalgia for these images and pictures. A majority of American Catholics do not lament their passing. Yet these stories were, mistakenly perhaps, vital to the religious symbol paradigm of many Catholics both elite and mass. Call them into question and the whole symbol system, which is not logical but imaginative, is in serious jeopardy.

Or to quote perhaps the most frequent comment of Catholics about the "new Church": We don't know the answers anymore. They do not want the rigid answers of the past, but they *do* want something by which to give meaning to their lives and their loves. They want a reconstituted symbol paradigm, a revivified story system, a "Second Naiveté."

They can't get it from the clergy because the clergy (and the other elites) don't have it. And they certainly can't get it from the *magisterium*, which is preoccupied with power and sex (and negative sex as a means of preserving power). You can survive as a do-it-yourself Catholic, clinging simultaneously to the remnants of your heritage (which you do not fully understand and cannot clearly explain but which are so dear to you that you do not propose to give them up) and to your own understanding of, for example, the importance of sex in your marriage. But such clinging is not the same thing as having a firm grasp on the stories of your tradition and a clear sense of how these stories illumine both the ambiguity and complexity of your life.

Let me illustrate by three examples.

The souls in purgatory were useful symbolically and narratively. We could offer our sufferings up for them, whether we were a little kid with a sore tooth or an adult with terminal cancer. What ever happened to the souls in purgatory? The doctrines still exist, but they are no longer part of our religious story system, oddly enough just as D. M. Thomas revives purgatory in the shattering Coda to *The White Hotel* (Greeley's second law: When Catholics forget something, others remember it). Okay, so we have had to give up the souls in purgatory, but there is no substitute story to give meaning and purpose to our suffering. What do you tell a little kid who is bravely enduring the dentist's drill?

I'm sorry, but that's a crucial question and I don't think the *magisterium* or the theologians or the religious educators have found a useful substitute for the Holy Souls.

Second, I remember the horror at a meeting of the editorial board of *Concilium* when René Laurentin told us that pilgrimages had increased since the Second Vatican Council. In a "secularized" world how could that be? How could such mythological superstition persist? Had not Bultmann demythologized religion for us? Yet the human hunger for sacred places continues unabated. Such places seem essential to our "story," and so many of us continue to pursue them regardless of the academic assumption that modern humans can dispense with the sacred.

Third, despite institutional neglect, the Mary story persists and continues to exercise great influence. The *magisterium* would turn her into a negative sex goddess. The theologians and the religious educators would try to forget her as an ecumenical liability. Yet the Mary story contributes to passion between lovers and appeals to Protestants as well as Catholics, once the largely irrelevant (religiously, however important they may be doctrinally) arguments over titles are set aside.

A few years ago, Catholic, Anglican and Free Church leaders led a pilgrimage in honor of the fiftieth anniversary of the revival of the shrine of Our Lady of Walsingham. This, gentle souls, is religion, and it was not imagined by the fathers of the Council and, I suspect, was deemed inconceivable by many of the theologians.

And one classic example of the opposite. The most directly pastoral effort of the Vatican Council was liturgical reform. Yet, as Father Patrick Collins acknowledged a few years ago in a painfully honest interview in *U.S. Catholic*, most liturgies are "lousy" precisely because they are attempts at imposing on the laity *a priori* master plans for what the people should get (thirty-second pauses, counted to the millisecond, for example) instead of the result of listening to what the laity *need*.

Surely the purpose of Christian worship is to amplify, reinforce and rearticulate the religious experiences of the faithful and link these experiences (as encoded in their religious stories) to the overarching experiences of the tradition (as encoded in the great stories of the tradition, Christmas, Easter, Jesus, Mary, etc.). But from the Conciliar document on the liturgy to the present, liturgists have been listening not to the experiences of the present but to the experiences of the past. They have tried to reconstitute worship on historical models with little or no concern for present needs, experiences and stories. Surely liturgical history has a contribution to make, but, as Father Collins admits, so does the religious experience of the present. Yet liturgists with their marvelously elaborate intellectual structures have been quite uninterested in the religious experiences of the Catholic people, save insofar as these experiences can be forced into preconceived molds of *a priori* scholarship and planning.

Of course, liturgy is "lousy"—but an excellent example of the weakness of the Vatican Council as a pastoral enterprise, a "symbol" of that weakness. The old religious story system was torn apart (though powerful, if unconnected and unarticulated, remnants survive and will continue to flourish. You don't give up images of the womanliness of God, for example, no matter how unfashionable they may be with theologians). There was perhaps no intention to destroy the integration of the symbolic paradigm. But anyone save an academic or a bishop would have anticipated that when you change what was unchangeable for fifteen hundred years, you are going to create a religious crisis. Attempts to cobble together a new system of religious symbols were halfhearted, unplanned and, most of all, insensitive to the actual religious needs and conditions of the Christian people.

It will be said that you reintegrate a symbol system only slowly. Sure, but you can make a beginning, and neither the Vatican Council nor the post-Conciliar efforts of the *magisterium* or the academic theological community have made that beginning.

The Vatican Council was not empirical enough. I do not mean here that it wasn't social-scientific enough. I mean rather that the Council was shaped by men, bishops and scholars, whose worldview and style were for the most part anti-empirical, who would not even have thought that a contribution might be made by the ordinary laity, by social scientists or by poets, prophets, storytellers and saints (and for whom the idea of a contribution by the womanly half of the race was beyond imagination).

When you have the answers, you see, you don't need to know the questions.

When you know what collegiality ought to mean and when you know what sex is all about, you don't need to listen to the agonized questions of the ordinary folk about how, for example, the pain and poignancy and pleasure of sex may be integrated into a life of meaning and purpose within the overarching Catholic stories. You certainly don't have to ponder the riches of the heritage to see how the stories might be retold and the answers reformulated to such questions.

My study of Mary took seriously the role of Mary in the lives of the Catholic people, especially as that role could be judged from art, literature and music. In principle the professional theologians would agree that such an exercise was a legitimate investigation of a theological "locus" or source. Unfortunately none have bothered to explore in any detail the Catholic tradition as it is passed on through image and story from parents to children, and from art to ordinary people. I had begun an exploration, both sociological and theological, of what I would come later to describe as the "Catholic sensibility." It was sociological, because the exploration would provide me with theoretical perspectives on the sociology of religion which I could test against empirical data. It was theological because it probed the imaginations of the people of God as a source of Catholic faith.

Without realizing it, I was also building the intellectual and religious perspective which would later compel me to write stories, almost all of which were notably influenced by my vision of the womanliness of God.

My first published story in *U.S. Catholic* was called "Ms. Carpenter." In it, Mary, a pert, charming, olive-skinned teenager, visits an archbishop to "ask a favor." It won the Catholic Press Association award as the best short story of 1978. If the judges who voted me that prize realized what they were starting, they might have had second thoughts.

Does religion exist first of all in the heads of theologians, bishops and priests and then, after it is taught, in the minds of the people? Or does it exist first of all in the experience of the people and then in the reflections of the elites?

In theological Catholicism of the last five hundred years there has been no doubt of the answer. The religious experience of the people is highly suspect. It must be purified, filtered, refined through the thought processes of theologians and Church leaders before it becomes acceptable as a manifestation of the presence of God. The essential mission of the Church is to impose right doctrine on its people, not to listen to the people for the voice and presence of God.

Religious stories are charming tales, perhaps, but they must be examined, abstracted, digested, schematized and codified by the skilled theologian before they can be considered safe paradigms of belief and behavior. The theologians and the clergy, you see, know the right answers. It is their job to teach them and the laity's job to listen. The laity have access to God through the propositions taught by the clergy and hierarchy. The theologians and the clergy have access to God because they reflect on propositional texts and listen to the bishops and the Pope. The bishops and the Pope have direct access to God by means unspecified.

The only religious experiences that matter are the experiences of the Pope and to a lesser extent those of the bishops.

Religion, finally, is an ecclesiastical matter. It goes on in the Church. It is not a secular matter; it does not exist in the world apart from the Church.

Such a model of religion has its uses. Essentially it is a description of how at this stage of the development of the Catholic heritage the community through its institutional authority examines belief and practice and determines whether they are congruent with the ancient heritage. Obviously, experience must be the subject of reflection. Obviously, too, experience and reflection must be challenged by the community as representative of the tradition. Theological and propositional religion becomes inadequate only when it is thought to be the only model of religion, when theologians and church leaders, often without regard to the history of the tradition or the experience of the faithful, claim for propositional theology a monopoly on religion.

No more pathetic manifestation of this claim can be found than in a recent book-length interview with my friend Father Edvard Schillebeeckx. When did he first become aware of religion? With obvious regret, the great theologian admits that it was around the Christmas crib with his family—a narrow, superstitious, shameful origin of his Catholic awareness. When you're dealing with the high problems of theology and political relevance, of Islam and Buddhism and Christianity, how can you possibly take seriously the charming but primitive little scene around the crib at Christmastime?

Right?

An American theologian, protesting solemnly against my claim that Christmas is the Catholic feast par excellence, admitted this was probably true in the minds of the faithful, but the faithful were wrong. They had to adapt their festivity to sound theology.

What can I tell you?

Christmas is the first hint in the lives of almost all Catholics that God loves us as a mommy loves a little baby. The link of love between mother and child, Christmas hints, is what God is like.

This is a revelation of extraordinary luminosity. It may not be true, but if it is true, it is good news. The Catholic heritage has always stood for the truth of the Christmas illumination. Theological explanations of how God and humanity are joined in Bethlehem are significant, but they are reflections on the Bethlehem experience itself, as it first happened, as it happens again for us every year at Christmas, as it can happen every time our hope is renewed by the sight of a young mother with her baby.

Life is stronger than death. The mother's love is stronger than hatred. God loves us as the mother loves the baby. Only more.

The theologian's temptation is to rush in with a theology of the virgin birth and the incarnation; the exegete's temptation is to rush in with an explanation that the story of Christmas is not necessarily accurate and precise history. The social activist's temptation is to rush in with a demand for food for hungry children.

Grinches.

Not because their work is unimportant or unnecessary, but because they try to impose it at the wrong time.

They wish to replace our experience of God's love as quickly as possible with concerns that are derivative of that experience—concerns we will ignore unless we are caught up all our lives in the power of that experience.

To put the matter differently, most of us begin to learn ecclesiastical religion only when we go to school. Until then we have learned secular— that is, daily-life—religion. Even after we become propositional Catholics we still are sustained by our secular religion even though it does not seem to articulate with the answers we have memorized.

The sociologist in me wanted to learn about the religion of daily life— the experiences of God's grace which we learn not so much from the Church as from the phenomena and relationships of our ordinary existence. I wanted to approach religion as best I could from the bottom up instead of from the top down. I suspected (and would later prove) that it is the religion of daily experience and not the religion of propositional theology which has the greater impact on our behavior.

Such an exploration was sociologically justified, an empirical study of how religious consciousness develops in the human personality. Its theological relevance to Catholicism is to be found in the firm Catholic conviction that God reveals Himself/Herself through the whole of creation as well as through the official teachings of the tradition. Everything is grace, as Karl Rahner has put it. For some things to be a "Sacrament" with a capital S all things must be a sacrament with a small s; for God to lurk in the official acts of the Church, S/He must also lurk in all the objects and events and persons of creation.

Okay, says I, let's see what we can learn about this sacramental-with-a-small-s action of God and determine whether it ought to have something more than the trivial place it now enjoys in official Catholic thinking.

Influenced by Eliade's work on the history of religions, I began with the obvious notion that Mary was a mother goddess, different from the others, better doubtless, but still similar. What Catholic theologians had tried to discount for years—the fact that Mary was replacing Diana and Venus and Astarte and Nut and that bunch—I took as an asset instead of a liability. The early Catholics had found something good and true and beautiful in the pagan goddess and had therefore baptized and converted her. Behind the picture and the story of the goddess, there must lurk an experience of grace, a hint of what God is like, that they found religiously valuable.

(Brigid was integrated into Mary, but in a special Irish way. She was transmuted from goddess to saint, with about the same responsibilities for spring, poetry, storytelling, and new life; but she was also considered by the Irish who had not quite given up their belief in reincarnation to be the Mother of Jesus reborn—hence quite literally the "Mary of the Gaels.")

The experience that leads to the woman goddesses is obviously that of sexual differentiation. The power and the pleasure, the mystery and the wonder, the compulsion and the delight of that experience had been interpreted by most human religions as a hint about the nature of God. Sex is sacrament. St. Paul said it and the Church made sexual union a Sacrament—and has been afraid of the implications ever since.

God, the ancients believed (again Eliade), was an androgyne. If the deity did not combine both male and female traits, then there were male and female consorts who shared divine power. The Catholic tradition played this theme in a minor key. Medieval mystics and theologians (most notably Anselm and Bernard, the latter urging us to drink milk from Christ's breasts) wrote of God as Mother as well as Father. Nicholas of Cusa wrote of the perfections of male and female being combined in God. Julianna of Norwich called God a mother in her mystical writings. Pope John Paul I spoke in one of his all too few audience talks of God as our loving mother.

In such a context I saw that Mary was a symbol of the sacramentality of sexual differentiation, of the fact that God is revealed and perceived in the experience of human sexual differentiation. Mary represented the womanliness of God's love.

She is a link between the womanliness of God and our experience of woman in our daily life; she focuses our experiences of woman (whether we be men or woman, differentially, one presumes in either case) as occasion of renewal of life and hope, and interprets them as revealing similar lifegiving, nurturing, healing tenderness in God. Mary is the story of a God who loves us with those strengths that we attribute to both men and women—and thus in the ideal frees us to develop those traits in each of our personalities which culture tends to attribute to the opposite sex.

All of this is on the level of symbol and story, not theological reflection. If one analyzes, as I tried to do in *The Mary Myth*, the art and the poetry of Mary, this sociological function of Mary in the Catholic tradition becomes obvious. She tells us Madonna love animates the cosmos.

If true, not bad. That's why the Mary Myth will never die in Catholicism, no matter how much the elites may neglect it. The story that God loves us with Madonna/virgo/spouse/pietà love is so attractive that even the possibility that it might reflect Reality is too radiant ever to be discarded.

The fourfold typology of our experience of woman and our experience of the womanliness of God I borrowed from the Jungian Erich Neumann, as a paradigm to organize the data, not as a datum from the collective unconscious. We experience women/they experience themselves, among other ways, as the origin and nurturance of life, as inspiration, as passion, and as caring tenderness. That's the way God is, only better. Choose another paradigm if you wish. But should Mary be a sacrament of God, so is every woman, and therefore the fear and hatred of women which has obsessed Catholicism since it emerged in the neo-Platonic world is blasphemy.

Three objections might be posed to this position, although the work I did in *The Mary Myth* was so completely ignored that only the first was ever actually posed.

1. The Mary story has been so corrupted by the life-denying, sex-denying, woman-denying, male-dominated Church that the symbol has lost all its power for modern women.

374

2. My paradigm ignores the theology of Mary.

3. It is not linked with Mary the historical mother of Jesus, a woman about whom (some would add) the present work of exegetes makes it clear we can know little anyway.

There are replies to all three objections.

1. Symbols are not logical or ideological propositions. They are dense, polyvalent, multilayered, polysemous, resilient. One draws from one's experience of a symbol on the basis of what one brings to it. Because churchmen and theologians may have put the Mary story to corrupt uses, it does not follow that others cannot draw other experiences from it. A symbol has a structure, a history, and an integrity of its own; one cannot, as the Modernists are alleged to have thought, draw whatever one wants from it. But my version of the story comes straight from the Catholic tradition, only in slightly different language.

2. I deny none of the theological propositions about Mary. I am merely describing the secular religious experience of woman as source of hope renewal that gives these propositions both their durability and their appeal.

3. We know a good deal about Mary because she is reflected to us in her son. Mary the mother of Jesus, my teenage Jewish imp, was a historical woman who was deeply involved in the work of her son. Hence our image of her, reflecting in part the God whom her son came to reveal, is solidly rooted in history.

(Jack Shea has written a long unpublished essay called "A Biography of Mary" which dissents from the exegetical conclusion that we can know little of the historical Mary. It illustrates Jack's theological method of seeking for the sources of religious truth, among other places, in the devotions and beliefs of the Catholic people. Again his theology and my sociology converge.)

Reading for and writing *The Mary Myth* changed my life. My intellective and affective dimensions had existed side by side all my life, with, as I now understand, thin boundaries between them. They had operated in close harmony in all my writing, but I had never devoted any self-conscious attendance to the "compiler" at work within me, much less looked to it explicitly as a source for materials, ideas, theories to test. Now, under the influence of the self-hypnosis with Erika and the works on the imagination of Tracy and Shea, I permitted my imaginative/affective dimension full partnership. This "rubicon" in my life was really a "crossing over" (in the words of the theologian John Donne) to another kind of existence, more self-knowledge, different perspectives, greater alienation from those on both the right and the left who condemned the imaginative/affective dimensions of human life on the grounds that they were not relevant—either to the authority of the *magisterium* or to the pursuit of social relevance.

In his *Models of Revelation*, Avery Dulles has recently summarized why symbols are so important:

> Symbols by their evocative power arouse the imagination and invite participation. As contrasted with literal discourse, symbol induces a kind of indwelling in the world of meaning to which it points. Symbols frequently make known a meaning too deep or too comprehensive for clear articulation; they arouse tacit awareness of things too vast, too subtle, or complex to be grasped in an explicit way; they bridge constraints that defy conceptual imagination . . . they exert a dynamic, transforming influence on the consciousness of those who apprehend them.

If one believes that, one almost has to be in the process of becoming a storyteller.

I was not flaking out, not abandoning intellect, not giving up the left side of the brain for the right. Quite the contrary, under the influence of what I had learned in reflecting on *The Mary Myth* I would elaborate new and more powerful propositional theories for the sociology of religion.

Then I discovered in the use of interactive SPSS (a software data analysis program developed by my colleague Norman Nie, as true a genius as I've ever known) that analysis with instant access to data was much like writing poetry—imagination and intellect combined. The human intellect, I learned empirically, is most effective when it is working in partnership with the imagination.

And vice versa.

The "compiler" works not as an independent agent but in service of the whole self.

A few years later I would do research on the religious imaginations of young Catholics and find evidence which sustained empirically the expectations I had derived from the socioreligious reflections in *The Mary Myth*. The Mary image was alive and powerful among younger Catholics, even stronger than the image of Jesus and God. (Strong, too, among younger Protestants, for whom her story if not her theology has great appeal. "You Catholics have no monopoly on the Mother of Jesus," one of my Protestant students told me briskly.) The strength of that image correlates with warm relationships with mother in childhood and warm relationships (for men) with a spouse in marriage. There is a significant relationship between the strength of the Mary image and sexual fulfillment in marriage, and no hint of a correlation between the Mary image and sexual repression.

Regardless of theology and ideology, Mary stands for life and love.

Not bad.

Michele: *Everybody* knows that, Father Greeley.

Me (wearily): Tell me about it.

Moreover, precisely *because* of the Mary image, Catholics are notably more likely than anyone else to accept the image of God as mother and father. Even though it has been a minor theme in the tradition, more than two-fifths of the Catholics in the country think of God as both mother and father. The experiences of the people enshrined a religious truth the theologians and official teachers had barely noticed.

Out of my religious and historical reflection there had come sociological hypotheses which could be tested and which having been sustained contributed to more theological reflection.

What can the Madonna's smile or the joy of sex, a Jesuit dean recently asked, contribute to the Church's service of the world, to nuclear disarmament, capital punishment, world hunger, race?

The implication is that the answer has to be "not much."

If, however, the Madonna's smile and sexual love give us a hint of what God is like, then the potential contribution is monumental. If God loves us with the tender passion of a mother and the fierce passion of a sexual lover—only more so—then those caught up in the message of such passionate love have a powerful contribution to make to the service of the world. They must love others even as they *are* loved.

If we cannot make this contribution—and it is finally the only unique religious insight sacramental Catholicism has: human passion reflects divine passion—then we have nothing special to offer and we will arrive at the site of social problems, as Bernard Lonergan once remarked, a little breathless and a little late.

The Mary Myth may be the most decisive book I have ever written. It pulled together the theology that Tracy and Shea and John Navone were doing with empirical sociology. It changed my life.

The best story of the womanliness of God in our time—and one which had a considerable impact on me—was Bob Fosse's film *All That Jazz*. Fosse/Gideon in a brush with death on the operating table experienced death not as ugly or evil or hateful, but as tender and loving and attractive, much like his wife and his mistress and his daughter. Can this be death? he asked. Can this be God?

He shared the experience with us in a story in which woman became a tentative image of God. Angelique, the angel of death, the angel of Yahweh, he asks us, can she be God? Can God be as lovely and tender as Jessica Lange?

We are given two choices at the end. In the ultimate scene, Gideon's body is zipped into a shroud to be taken off to the morgue. In the penultimate scene, Gideon walks down the long corridor described by those who have had resuscitation or near-death experiences toward the figure of light, also part of those experiences, which waits at the end.

Angelique, in filmy bridal robes, arms outstretched in waiting love.

Which is it, he asks us, the shroud and the slab in the icy morgue or the warm and delightful body of the beloved in a marriage bed?

That, gentle souls, is the only religious question that matters. Is life absurd or is life love?

Is the renewal of life and love in sexual passion finally a deception or is it a hint of an explanation?

Is God really as sexy as Jessica Lange?

She'd better be even more sexy.

As I was rediscovering the imaginative, the poetic, the experiential dimensions of Catholicism I was also rediscovering or perhaps discovering for the first time my own imaginative, poetic and experiential dimensions. My fellow priests were becoming more prosaic and secular (in their sense of the word). Don Quixote was characteristically turning to poetry and story. I was working on *The Mary Myth* when my self-hypnotic interludes with Erika began. During a return trip from Ireland that spring I began literally to hear verses in my head. The poem "Lady's Day in Harvest" quoted earlier was literally dictated by my preconscious before the Aer Lingus plane landed at Kennedy. It was, incidentally, the summer of 1975, the same time I was fighting my battle with the AJC. I was writing the Mary article for the *Times*, working on *The Mary Myth*, thinking up the idea for the Papal election study, writing poetry, worrying about the renewal of our Ford grant, finishing the *Catholic Schools in a Declining*

378

Church report, and fending off those who called me anti-Semitic—all at the same time.

Grand Beach was supposed to be for rest and relaxation. Not much that summer.

I also began to face the need to write stories. From Nathan Scott's book on the Michigan poet Theodore Roethke, I learned two things. First, analogy and metaphor can return God and the sacred to the world. Primitive people believed in spirits which animated everything. We now know that natural explanations suffice to explain material phenomena. Yet if all beings participate in Being (and Father Scott, an Anglican, was here being much the Thomist), then they all reveal Being. God is everywhere not in a pantheistic sense but in a sacramental, i.e., revelatory, sense. Second, stories are for meaning. The little kid's plea "Mommy tell me a story" is in fact a plea for meaning. "Mommy, please help me understand what it's all about, put all the pieces together. *Please.*"

I knew both these things from the work of Shea and Tracy, but in reading Scott's *The Wild Prayer of Longing* I understood that the longing was for stories which give meaning.

Everyone was writing about stories about God, it seemed to me. Ought not someone do what Greene and Waugh and Mauriac used to do, actually write stories about God?

Quixote reaches for his fountain pen. Well, typewriter.

My sociological theory, later developed in *Religion: A Secular Theory*, contends that religion emerges from the ordinary experiences of secular life which renew our hope, that these hope-renewal experiences (sometimes but not always ecstatic) are encoded in the images or symbols we inherit from our religious traditions, that they are told as stories which correlate with the stories of our tradition, and that they are shared with members of a storytelling community which share the same set of symbols and the same collection of overarching stories.

The emphasis on the narrative dimensions of religion can be found in many different disciplines, one of the most fascinating convergences of scholarship that I have ever witnessed—hermeneutics, exegesis, anthropology, literary criticism, cognitive psychology. All now tend to agree that a person's religion is that set of stories (narrative symbols) which s/he uses to provide directive interpretation for himself and others about the most fundamental meanings and goals of that person's life. Tell me your story and I will know who you are. Tell me the basic theme of your story and the experiences which constitute it and I'll know your religion.

As Kathryn Morton recently noted in the *New York Times Book Review*, "Narrative is the only art that exists in all human cultures. It is by narrative that we experience our lives. I would propose that . . . imaginative narrative . . . was decisive in the creation of our species and is still essential in the development of each human individual and necessary to the maintenance of his health and the pursuit of his purposes" (December 23, 1984).

I suspect that about half the fundamental Catholic religious sensibility is passed on from mother to children around the Christmas crib, the greatest religious storytelling "audiovisual" device human ingenuity has ever created. For most of human history, stories have been the only way of handing on religion. They may still be the most effective means of religious socialization. The best parts of the Gospels are the parables and also, the scholars tell us, the closest we can get to the religious experience of Jesus. Hans Küng has suggested that Jesus was perceived at first by the crowds as a wandering storyteller. The size of the crowds was a tribute not to the miracles but to the excellence of his stories. The most interesting parts of the Jewish scriptures are the stories—Moses, David, Joseph. Robert Alter has recently shown that they are not the rough-and-ready tales we might think, but highly refined exercises in the narrative art.

My respected prefect of discipline at the seminary had said fiction was a waste of time. I knew he was wrong, but it took me till the middle 1970s to realize how wrong.

Ms. Morton again: "More than just show us order in hypothetical existences, novelists give us demonstration classes in what is the ultimate work of us all, for by the days and the years we must create the narratives of our own lives. . . . so you say reading a novel is a way to kill time when the real world needs tending to. I tell you that the only world I know is the world as I know it and I am still learning how to comprehend that. These books are showing me ways of being I could never have managed alone. I am not killing time. I'm trying to make a life."

I didn't have Ms. Morton's words available through the fall and winter of 1975, but I was thinking the same thoughts. At the same time my own inner life was vibrating with the access provided by Erika's self-hypnosis. I hesitated. Perhaps writing stories would be a mistake. I could do nonfiction well. My catechism *The Great Mysteries* was a story approach to catechetics. Wasn't that enough? What if I devoted considerable

380

time and energy to fiction only to discover I couldn't do it? There was just so much time in life. Should I not stick to my last?

Chicken? Sure. But I was not afraid of self-revelation, much less of anger from my fellow clerics. I was afraid of wasting my time and failing.

Yet on the island of Martinique (with a bad cold and fierce winds) after a January lecture stint in the winter of 1976 to Barbados and Trinidad, I read John Fowles and began to think of a trilogy around the original Irish version of the legend of the Holy Grail—in which the searcher gets the magic cup and the magic princess. One story would be the original Grail legend set in the past, a second would be set in the present, and a third in the future. All the heroes would be named O'Neil, the name of the ancient Irish kings, and all the stories would be in the finest tradition of Celtic antiquity and Catholic sacramentality. They would be, unlike the legend as we know it, life-affirming, flesh-affirming comedies of grace.

So the next year I wrote novels and short stories with almost obsessive passion. The summer of 1976 at Grand Beach was devoted to fighting off attacks on *Catholic Schools in a Declining Church* and pounding away on novels and stories.

Of the three novels, *The Magic Cup* was published in 1979 by McGraw-Hill and *Death in April* was issued by the same company in 1980. *The Final Planet*, a science fiction story about an Irish space monastery presided over by one Deirdre Cardinal Fitzgerald, will be published in a drastically revised form by Warner and Tor in the spring of 1987.

The books disappeared. Only seventy-five hundred copies were printed. There was almost no advertising and few reviews. A Catholic editor of the *Chicago Sun-Times*, a contemporary at the seminary, was more interested in who was the real-life counterpart of Lynnie in *Death in April* (there wasn't one) than in either the story or its theological message. He had it figured: Since I had dedicated my book of poems (*Women I've Met*, some of which appear in this memoir) to "Erika," obviously I must have been in love with a girl named Erika when I was growing up.

As I complained in a letter to the editor (to which he did not deign to reply), no one was named Erika on the West Side of Chicago in the 1930s. Mary Lou, Betty Anne, sure. But not Erika.

Would he believe a professor emeritus at the University of Chicago's Committee on Human Development? A psychoanalytic hypnotist who was a refugee from Hitler's Germany?

By 1980, then, I had learned I could write novels, that I could get them published, that they would be received with as much hostility as anything else I had written, and that few would read them. My theory of the importance of religious stories might be valid enough (and it was by then being confirmed by the data from our study of young Catholics) but the world was not exactly hungering for stories of God that I might write.

All right. Quixote doesn't quit easily. No way.

CHAPTER 20

The Making of the Pope

Our great glacier melted lake turns most fair
When, troubled, it gropes for uncertain calm
Like a girl combing wet and twisted hair
Rain-swept and twisted by a manic storm
Hair-line traced, fragile vase more lovely made
Lightly marked by steel pointed sorrow's knife
Ready still for flowers too long delayed
To grace subtle lines in the bloom of life
For the half day lost children do not mourn
When the noon sky lifts after summer rain
But praise the blue with an afternoon of mirth—
Hope broken, shattered, stomped on, then reborn
First life lost, it was said, then found again—
See death as the vespers of rebirth

A warm Roman moon shone benignly over St. Peter's Square. An Italian military band played brisk tunes. The great door of the balcony of St. Peter's swung open, for the second time in six weeks. Pericle Felici strode out on the balcony. Those around me heaved a sigh of relief. If Felici was announcing the outcome of the election, he himself had not been elected.

"*Annuntiabo Vobis Gaudium, Gaudio Magno. Habemus Papam, Carolum. . . .*"

There was a gasp in the huge crowd that filled the moonlit piazza of St. Peter's. "*Carolum?* Who was that?"

"*Sancte Romanae Ecclesiae,*" Felici droned on. "Wojtyla!"

Felici didn't seem happy about it. Neither did the crowd. Who the hell was Wojtyla? Italian he certainly was not. Finally the Italian monopoly on the Papacy had been broken, and the Italian crowd didn't like it.

"*Padre, Padre!*" An Italian man grasped my sleeve. "*E Papa Negro?*"

"*Non.*" I couldn't help myself, I was laughing. "*E Papa Pollacho!*"

Later John Paul II would emerge on the balcony, speak in almost flawless Italian, and win the crowd over. The drama of the year of the three Popes was coming to an end.

But not the drama of the Papacy. In the spring of 1982, in a hotel in Pittsburgh, on a promotion tour for my second novel, *Thy Brother's Wife*, I had a call from my secretary. He told me the Pope had been shot. I flipped on the television set and watched with dismay for the rest of the afternoon. John McMeel, of the Universal Press and Andrews and McMeel Publishers, and I talked repeatedly on the phone. We both remembered the days in Rome in the summer of 1978, we both remembered our friend and his partner the late James Andrews, and we both wondered whether we had the courage to go to Rome again for another conclave. Fortunately, as it turned out, we didn't have to choose.

I'm sure now, however, that I would not attend another Papal election should one happen in my lifetime. It's great theater—among the most spectacular in the world. But it's a bad way to elect a Pope. Almost invariably the outcome of the conclaves is disappointing to the Church, precisely because it is a bad way to elect a Pope. I no longer believe the long-overdue institutional reform, which is desperately needed to free the riches of the Catholic tradition from the stranglehold of a decrepit and corrupt bureaucracy, will come from the Papacy. Like all institutions, it will eventually respond to pressures for reform but will not create its own pressures. Pope John XXIII, one of the great Popes in history, was an extraordinary man, but his election was a fluke. The cardinal electors are not likely to repeat such a mistake. So the institutional Church will drift on, ever more irrelevant to the lives of the Catholic faithful and to the riches of the Catholic heritage and tradition. Council, encyclical, conclave: these were the big events in my life and in the life of the Church from 1960 to 1980. The Council was a success, the encyclical was an organizational disaster and the conclaves of 1978 were ambiguous— fascinating, exciting, dramatic, but in their outcomes, finally, not what the Church needed.

That fact became clear to me the day after the shooting of the Pope. I had been dragged early in the morning to an NBC studio outside of Pittsburgh to share time on the "Today Show" with a manic Malachi Martin. Before Malachi began to babble, the "Today Show" made the usual round of clips of Catholic churches in which the faithful were allegedly swarming to light candles and offer Masses, so little did the media understand contemporary Catholicism, for the Pope's survival. Virtually all the churches were empty despite the enthusiastic prattling of the NBC correspondents.

The rector of Chicago's Holy Name Cathedral (not like his fictional counterpart in my novels, Blackie Ryan) made a fool of himself prating piously about widespread Catholic grief despite the background of an almost empty cathedral which seemed to suggest little grief. The morning after an attempt at a Papal assassination, there were no more people in Holy Name Cathedral—or in any other church that NBC had shown— than there would have been on an ordinary weekday. Catholics around the United States were undoubtedly upset by the attack on the Pope, possibly even somewhat more upset than they would be later by the attack on President Reagan, but not so much so as to dash off to church to pray for him. The Papacy was important to the media, and important to the clergy and hierarchy, but not so high on the agenda of the laity.

The crowds had cheered him when he had come to America, though the crowds were a tiny fraction of the Catholic population—a phenom- enon the media never seemed to appreciate—but even the people in the crowds continued practicing birth control despite the Pope's warnings against it. Whether they had been in the crowds or not, Catholics un- doubtedly whispered a prayer or two the day after the assassination attempt, for his recovery. But the bitter truth was that while the Papacy, for American Catholics, was a symbol around which we would cheer, it was no longer a particularly relevant institution in our lives. We had a globe-traveling Pope with a charismatic public presence and he no longer made all that much difference.

The idea for a book on the Papal election came to me on a summer afternoon in Grand Beach in August of 1975. I had been sitting on the beach reading a political science account of previous American elections prepared by the brilliantly gifted survey research team at the University of Michigan. I reflected that if one combined the survey research of the Michigan team and the fascinating election journalism of Theodore White in his *Making of the President* books, one had a brilliant history of Presidential elections for the last two decades. It was a shame, wasn't it, I thought to myself, that there was no similar study of Papal elections. Conclaves did not come with mathematical regularity and they were far more difficult to cover, for neither candidates nor electors gave interviews, but that would make them more interesting, wouldn't it?

Why wasn't somebody doing for the Papacy what Theodore White did for the presidency?

As at many other times in my life, including when I began to write novels, the next thought was "If you don't do it, no one else will."

Okay, Quixots, grab the lance and saddle up the nag.

I climbed the stairs, phoned Jim Andrews, and proposed the idea: a book on the making of the Popes, election coverage to be distributed to American newspapers and pre-Papal election features and speculations. Many trips to Rome, lots of expenses, but great excitement.

And we would be in the piazza when the new Pope was elected!

I suppose that was the bottom line. I remembered Winston Burdette on television the day John XXIII was elected. I remembered someone in the rectory remarking that it was a pity to elect such an old man to such a demanding job. I remembered the vigorous voice of Angelo Giuseppe Roncalli when he imparted his blessing to the City of the New World. The next time that happened, I wanted to be there.

The memory plays odd tricks on you. Jim Miller, my streetwise New York Irish friend to whom I owe many debts of gratitude, had suggested the idea for such a book a couple of years before and I had forgotten the suggestion.

And in one of my self-hypnotic experiments with Erika earlier in the year I had found myself in Rome cheering at the end of a conclave.

"That is strange, Andrew," she said. "Coming over here I said to myself, where shall we send him today? I thought, yes, Ireland and then Rome for a Papal election. You were at both before I even mentioned them to you."

My one experience of ESP. A make-believe conclave. I wanted to be at a real one.

I was, twice, in a few months, and I do not want to do it again.

It would mean a lot of traveling, visiting Rome a couple of times a year until an election occurred, and I hated to travel. Nonetheless the excitement and the appeal of the story and the sociological fascination with the oldest election process in the world were irresistible.

I will not repeat the whole story of *The Making of the Popes* here. If anyone is interested, the book is still available in libraries, I'm sure. One of the first persons whom I called, however, was Archbishop Joseph Bernardin of Cincinnati, the president of the American Hierarchy. While our relations had been chilly since the priest study, it nonetheless seemed to me that I should both inform him of the project and see if he would be willing to cooperate to the extent of setting up for me interviews with various people in Rome. I made an appointment to visit him in Cincinnati and laid out the project. With scarcely a moment's hesitation, he leaned forward and said: "Don't content yourself with merely reporting the election afterwards. Write about it beforehand. Try to clarify the issues. This will be a decisive conclave, and public discussion of the issues and the candidates may well influence the outcome."

He was the first one to suggest that the outcome of a conclave might be influenced by journalistic/sociological articles written before the conclave. It would, I suppose, have occurred to me anyhow but, nevertheless, I heard it from him for the first time. The articles I wrote before the election, especially my long article in the *New York Times Magazine* on the issues of the candidates, were read by Archbishop Bernardin before publication and in some cases modified according to his suggestions.

The conversation about the Papal election was the beginning of a renewed and, it seemed to me, close friendship between me and Archbishop Bernardin, a friendship he publicly proclaimed with notable praise at the University of Dayton in 1976. Looking back at our conversation in Cincinnati, I speculate that he and Archbishop Jadot and possibly Archbishop Benelli were already worried about my public criticism of

Cardinal Cody's closing inner-city schools in Chicago. They were also worried about how much I knew concerning the situation in Chicago (I wasn't the only one who knew the story, but I was the only one with easy access to the media).

I will not ever forget the Dayton meeting. Mary Jule and I were standing at the other end of the lobby when Archbishop Bernardin entered the meeting center. His eyes swiveled around the room until he spotted us. Then he promptly ignored everyone else, cut across the room, and joined in a long and intense conversation. He sat with us at supper, gave a little talk about my birthday (which was that day and which had been celebrated with a birthday cake) and said it was a shame I had to leave Chicago to be honored. Then he introduced my presentation in the auditorium with elaborate praise as a friend, a scholar and a prophet.

"If I were in your position, I would not have done that," I said afterwards.

He shrugged. "It was time someone did it."

If Benelli was worried that I might blow his plan to quietly replace Cardinal Cody (a plan which, as we will see, failed even *with* my silence) all he had to do was to call me himself or have Bernardin or Jadot call me and in the traditional parlance of the Chicago Irish say, "Hey, do us a favor. Cool it on Cody for a year or two."

That would have done it. But that is not how the Romans work, it is a tactic that is not nearly devious or cynical enough. Instead the order was given, "Cultivate his friendship, praise him, flatter him, help him with his research, provide him all sorts of information to which he does not expect to be privy, and keep him quiet about Cardinal Cody."

There are many things wrong with the way the leader of the Catholic Church is selected. First of all, the present form of Papal election violates the tradition of the first thousand years of Catholic history, which demanded—under pain of grievous sin, as Pope St. Leo I put it—that Church leadership be selected by the clergy and the people of the diocese. If the Pope is now *de facto* the bishop of the world, then he should be chosen in some fashion by the clergy and people of the world ("He who presides over all should be chosen by all" was St. Leo's flat dictum on the subject). The cardinal electors are supposed to represent the clergy of the city of Rome because they all have titular churches in or around Rome. In fact, however, the representation is purely symbolic, and one can be quite certain that's not what St. Leo had in mind. Moreover, no one represents the laity of the world; no one these days even thinks that's necessary. One needs to say it repeatedly: for the first thousand years of Catholic history the tradition would have said that such a way of selecting the bishop of Rome was immoral. If one wants to be a Catholic traditionalist, one has no choice but to say that the present form of Papal election is immoral.

Second, custom and to some extent law dictate that there is to be no discussion of the Papal election while the Pope is still alive. Thus, at the Synod of Bishops immediately before the 1978 conclaves when many of the candidates were there in Rome, when it was clear that Paul VI's health was failing, and when the Church's institutional problems were patent for all to see, there was virtually no explicit and little implicit discussion of either candidates for the Papacy or the issues that would have to be faced in a Papal election. The Roman Curia was busy politicking behind the scenes, but the Curia was now a divided and faction-ridden collectivity (more divided and more factioned than usual, that is).

It no longer had the votes necessary to swing an election in the direction its principal factions wanted. As one cardinal elector remarked to me, "How do we know who the candidates are? Or what their qualifications are? Or what the issues are? We read about them, perhaps, in the international edition of *Time* magazine. How else would we know?"

Finally many electors go into the conclave with virtually no clear notions about either qualifications or issues. They're following bad, really heretical, theology in waiting for the Holy Spirit to inspire them, unaware that others are not so waiting and are engaging in the perfectly normal and honest and utterly human activity of politics. Many of the reelectors (between thirty and forty in the elections of 1978) are utterly uninformed and go with the wind, eager only to have supported the winner before the last ballot. It's embarrassing to have to say it, but such was the case with almost all the American cardinals in the 1978 conclave.

During the pre-conclave restlessness I phoned Bernardin from Rome and told him how sadly disorganized the preparations were. I pleaded with him to pressure his friend Cardinal Dearden to assume some kind of leadership. I'll try, he said with a shrug in his voice. But it won't do much good. That's not his style.

The strategy, then, of many of the electors is to sort of wait around and see what happens, thus leaving, as they would put it, everything in the hands of the Holy Spirit. One might just as well spin a roulette wheel with the names of all the cardinals on it to select the Pope, because that would leave things even more directly to the Holy Spirit. The peculiar notion that the most influential religious leader in the world should be elected with the most minimal of human activity and intelligence is damnably near to heresy. It absolves the cardinal electors of all responsibility to consider the issues facing the Church, the qualifications of the candidates and the implications of their choice. For anyone else to behave recklessly in a situation of great delicacy and responsibility would be called tempting God. I can find no particular reason to dispense many of the cardinal electors from that charge.

Under such circumstances there is a pernicious tendency to concentrate on electability—as one Cardinal remarked to me, to follow "the mathematics of the Holy Spirit." The question becomes not who is best qualified or who will best serve the interests of the Church in the present time or who is most likely to be responsive to the needs of the Christian people; the question becomes, rather, who can we most quickly elect and get the hell out of these cramped, hot (in August), uncomfortable conclave quarters with the whole world waiting eagerly outside.

Albino Luciani was elected simply because he was the only Italian candidate who could have obtained the necessary seventy-six votes. It is highly unlikely that any more than a handful of the non-Italian cardinals had ever met him and even less likely that they had read his books (or even knew he wrote books). Nor is it reasonable to suppose that they voted for him because they knew he was "soft" on birth control. Rather, they voted for Luciani because everybody was whispering in everybody else's ear as they went into the conclave that Luciani was the one. The real "great electors," in this case Western Europeans and Brazilians presided over by Leo Suenens of Brussels and the Italian Curialist faction (relatively moderate) presided over by Pericle Felici and the Italian residential bishops led by Giovanni Benelli, had all agreed beforehand that Luciani was electable and would make a good Pope. Whether or not they realized he had poor health—if he had poor health—was a matter of some debate. I do know as a fact, however, that after the conclave but before his death, some of the cardinal electors reported that his health was not good. Presumably, however, it must have been thought he would live long enough to put more men in the College of Cardinals and make it possible to find other compromise Italian candidates besides himself.

Luciani if he had lived would, I think, have been a wonderful Pope. He would have fit my sociological job description of the Pope as a "hopeful holy man who smiles."

John Paul II was also elected because of the "mathematics of the Holy Spirit." Few electors knew he had written books or read them. One of the leading figures in the conclave said he hadn't read the books. He was interested to learn that I had and asked me my impression. Few if any of the people who voted for the Polish Pope gave any thought to the political message it would send to the Soviet Union. "Afterward," said one of my informants, "oh yes, afterward we thought it was a good idea. But we were only interested inside in getting those seventy-six votes." Apparently no one wondered what it would be like to turn the administration of the Church over to a man who had spent most of his life in a country under foreign occupation.

The mathematics of the Holy Spirit is essentially an exercise in collective irresponsibility. And that collective irresponsibility is reinforced by the secrecy of the conclave. There is great drama in the white smoke/ black smoke question. (People inside the conclave had a hard time with white and black smoke in both the August and the October conclaves. By October, however, it dawned on some genius that you could announce the color of the smoke over the public address system and thus solve the problem.) Yet the tight secrecy of the conclave is a relatively recent event, introduced after the election of Pius X at the beginning of the twentieth century, because in that election the Austrian ambassador had entered the Vatican and exercised the emperor's ancient claimed right of "veto" against a cardinal who was unacceptable to Austria (and who probably wouldn't have been elected anyhow). So the strict secrecy and all the oaths and ceremonies around it are designed to keep out the Austrian emperor. You may have noticed there isn't an Austrian emperor anymore.

The secrecy means there is *no accountability*; no one is to be held responsible for what he has done inside the conclave. Such absence of accountability merely reinforces the collective irresponsibility of the present process. Even in the nineteenth century when the election was in the Quirinali Palace in Rome the electors would walk out of one building where they'd had their morning breakfast, walk down a street chatting with the crowd and go into another building where the actual voting would take place. Such a system might not be appropriate for the present. Surely the media of the world would quickly know how the ballots were going. That, however, might not be a bad idea.

Whether it is true that in the election of Paul VI in 1963 Cardinal Spellman had a radio with which he signaled the result to the CIA resident in Rome is a debatable question. However, it is most likely that all the major intelligence services of the world routinely bug the conclaves and that it is virtually impossible for the Vatican's technical experts to keep the conclaves bug-free. Under such circumstances the pretense of secrecy is ridiculous.

How does one do research on the Papal election?

The question is not how one gets information, for information is as easy to come by as a cup of coffee or cappuccino on the Via della Conciliazione. The real challenge is to sort the good information from the bad. Thus, even the accomplished Vaticanologist Francis X. Murphy tried to persuade the world for several months that Luciani had been elected on the third ballot (causing considerable embarrassment for *Time* magazine's brilliant Rome bureau chief, Jordan Bonfonte, who had reported in *Time* a four-ballot election). Murphy eventually retracted his explanation in a passing phrase in a book review, scarcely responsible journalism.

My analysis, presented in *The Making of the Popes*, of the dynamics of the elections has never been seriously challenged. Although the cardinal electors are not supposed to say anything about what went on inside, most of them do, and none of the American cardinals, despite excellent reason for doing so, ever said, "Greeley doesn't know what he's talking about." Moreover, there is a convergence among the more serious and responsible books done since the year of the three Popes on the processes and dynamics leading to the election first of Luciani and then of Wojtyla.

A computer decision-making program developed by James S. Coleman and applied by Coleman and myself to data collected by Jim Andrews on the cardinal electors anticipated the outcomes of both elections. We assembled data on each of the electors on fifteen different variables and then, through an iteration in a decision-making program, selected out the various factions within the sacred college (seven different ones emerged) and then through further iterations combined these factions until the seventy-six necessary votes were achieved. We then asked which

392

of the candidates seemed to have the score that would be most typical of the electors. The first program was run only after I'd left for Rome and hence was not available at the time of the first election. Nonetheless, it chose Luciani. Then, when I flew home after the death of the September Pope to run the program again and ask it which candidate was most like Luciani, the computer came up with Wojtyla (an .02 difference from Luciani on a scale of plus or minus 1.00).

Actually, the decision-making program was helpful in figuring how the coalition of factions would take place inside the conclave. I was able to use it when I came back to Rome from Chicago to reassure a lot of frightened folks who believed what they were reading in the Italian newspapers, that support for Cardinal Siri, the archconservative of Genoa (who really didn't approve of the Vatican Council), had become overwhelming and even decisive. The Siri forces had cleverly manipulated the Italian press to give the impression that this time their man was a shoo-in. In fact, on the first ballot in the October conclave he received forty-one votes, fifteen more than he received in the first ballot in the previous conclave—thus fifteen electors had shifted their vote mostly because of the propaganda in the Italian newspapers. However, if one counted noses with our program, there was no way one could find seventy-six men inside the College of Cardinals who would vote for Siri, no matter what happened. It took me twenty-four hours of terror in Rome— "Our whole lives will have been wasted," one of my Vatican friends said, "if that man is elected"—to realize that I was an empiricist and a nose-counter and that despite jet lag and depression I should count the noses and realize Siri didn't have a chance.

I might conclude from the success of the computer program in predicting the outcome that the Sacred College is likely to end up with a candidate who more or less scores pretty close to the mean of its members on attitudes toward the current situation and the Church. Despite the speed, the lack of discussion, the absence of knowledge of the candidates and the irresponsibility of many of the electors, the system still seems to produce a Pope who runs pretty close to the average of those who vote for him.

I guess that's not bad, if you think the election of the Pope ought to come up with somebody who is right on the mean of the Sacred College on most critical issues. If it's an average Pope you want, then presumably it's an average Pope you're going to get. It is not clear to me, however, that that's what the Church wants or needs at the present time. Or at any time.

There were, nonetheless, moments of high drama: being dragged away from Bill McCready's birthday party on August 6 by CBS with the news that the Pope had died, having a late-afternoon Mass interrupted by a helicopter from CBS seeking my comment (the film of which was lost by the reporter), taking off early in the morning with Jim Andrews and John McMeel for the trip to Rome, the press conference at which we enunciated our "hopeful holy man who smiled" job description (ridiculed by many European journalists but never seriously challenged), Jordan Bonfonte's moment of terror when it turned out that the black smoke was white and that Luciani had been elected in a single day (Jordan had eight hours to do a cover story, a brilliant one, by the way), the horror and the anger of the solemn, sullen crowd at the Luciani wake, the irreverence at the Montini funeral, Luciani's incredibly winning smile on television the day of his inauguration (I watched the ceremony at Grand Beach just before the Chicago Bears game), the sheer physical exhaustion of crossing the Atlantic five times back and forth in the space of a few weeks and the terrible depression that came from that exhaustion, the euphoria of the night of John Paul II's election (many Italian middle-class families bringing out champagne to toast the end of Italy's era of domination of the Papacy—an era they believed was disastrous to the Italian Church), Jim Roache's splendid press briefings in the Vatican press office—so good that even the French reporters came to hear him—a final visit to Rome in December on a brilliant chilly Sunday morning, watching the Pope give the Sunday Angelus address with his white robe shining in the sunlight and thinking to myself what an easy target he'd be up there for somebody with a high-powered rifle—drama, excitement, thrills, memories aplenty. Those of us who were there, like Prince Hal's men on St. Crispin's Day, will never forget the experience and are bound together in the memories of those dramatic moments—men, for example, like Kevin Starr and Jordan Bonfonte will be lifelong friends precisely because we were there when it happened.

And yet, what did it all mean?

The reader will guess by now that I am convinced the Vatican is not only corrupt but, worse, incompetent. There are few evil men in the Vatican, but there are many who are not qualified to be doing

394

what they're doing and many others who are utterly devoid of moral principle and conviction. Lord Acton said that power corrupts and absolute power corrupts absolutely. With the Papacy in mind, as a sociologist I would refine the dictum: power without accountability corrupts and absolute power without any accountability corrupts absolutely. The big scandals of the Vatican in the last several years are the result of incompetence, total unaccountability and large, large sums of money. But they are, in a way, the tip of the iceberg, the base of which is many small incompetences, small irresponsibilities, small abuses of power and small unaccountabilities that permeate the Vatican bureaucracy.

Pope John tried to balance the bureaucracy by calling a council. Pope Pius XII tried to run the church independently of the bureaucracy with the help of Sister Pasquelina. Paul VI made Archbishop Benelli his hatchet man to keep the bureaucracy in line. John Paul II apparently is following the model of Pius XII, running his own office with relative independence of and relatively little attention to the rest of the Curia. None of these strategies will finally work. The incompetence, the irresponsibility, the unaccountability, the corruption, must be swept out of the Vatican from top to bottom, and the Vatican offices must be as publicly accountable and responsible as are any government offices in the free world. And the Papacy, too, must exist in the light of openness and publicity, which is the way all governmental structures in the free world operate. Or rather, more precisely, the Vatican must realize that it now has no choice and the Papacy must understand there is no alternative to openness and honesty. What is whispered in the chambers, as the Lord Jesus said, will be proclaimed from the housetops. It will either be proclaimed by honest, official sources or it will be pried loose anyway— *there are no secrets left.*

Whatever can be said of the past, the Vatican and the Papacy can no longer work in secrecy. The Pope must no longer be chosen in secrecy. We must go back to something like the old days when the cardinals (the priests of Rome) would go into St. Peter's to select the bishop of Rome, come out and present him to the people, and if the people booed, go back into their conclave and select another Pope. Perhaps that most direct form of democratic government is no longer feasible. But unless we approach something like that, we are going to continue to have disasters like the two-billion-dollar Banco Ambrosiano scandal and a declining credibility of the Papacy in almost every area, so that however powerful its symbolic value may be, it will no longer have any influence on how people live and act and believe.

In fact, I'm afraid that such is dangerously close to being an accurate description of the way things are now.

Was the September Pope murdered? David Yallop in his book about the death of John Paul I, *In God's Name*, raises that question powerfully. The only honest answer, as far as I'm concerned, is that I don't know. To be forced to give that answer is to reveal how badly the Vatican fouled up the death of the September Pope. I had supper the night before his death with my friend Roberto Tucci, the director of Vatican radio, and two couples who were traveling with me. It was a wonderful night at Sabatini's, across the street from Santa Maria in Trastevere, a soft, lovely September evening with the bright moon glowing above us. We joked about the Pope being "a hot property," that he should be "syndicated" around the world on TV (even though the Vatican radio at that time did not have TV capability). The next morning Ernie Primeau called to tell me that the Pope was dead. A few moments later Tucci phoned to say that when we were talking about the Pope as a hot property his own body was already growing cold.

It was an incredible experience, like the death of the President in 1963, the attack on Pearl Harbor, the death of Roosevelt—something you simply can't believe is happening and the exact circumstances when you first heard it you'll never forget.

Between Tucci's phone call and noontime the Vatican lied five times. It did not tell the truth about (1) who found the Pope's body, (2) what time the body was found, (3) what the Pope was doing when he died, (4) what time he died, and (5) what was the apparent cause of death.

Moreover, it presumably lied when it said there was no autopsy, because it seems a mini-autopsy was actually carried on in the *aula* of St. Peter's during the wake. These lies are not necessarily proof of murder. They can be the result of the self-serving Vatican argument that the laity would be shocked at any "indecency" (like an autopsy) in the Papacy. They also could be simply the result of the stupidity of Cardinal Villot, the camerlengo and secretary of state, in the face of a crisis (in dealing with the Vatican bureaucracy, never underestimate the stupidity factor). I remember saying to several reporters as we waited for the first viewing of the

Pope's body in one of the beautiful rooms of the Vatican palace, "They have fouled this up so badly that the conspiracy theories will never die. It's going to be like the Kennedy assassination only worse."

Revelations in years to come of the Calvi, Sindona, Banco Ambrosiano scandals—which made Vatican corruption headline news all over the world—gave apparent motivation for the murder of John Paul I. The combination of the corruption of the Vatican's finances and the lies of the Vatican's public relations staff on the day of the death of Luciani gives plausibility to the charge that he was murdered. This does not, in fact, mean that he *was* murdered. His family certainly did not think so. His family's willingness to accept the official explanation, like the Kennedy family's willingness to accept the Warren Commission report, strikes me as providing *prima facie* evidence of the general truth of the official story. ("Rich Daley couldn't get an indictment in Cook County with the evidence in that book," a cop remarked to me.) Nonetheless, the proper questions about the death of the September Pope have never been answered by the Vatican and I suppose they never will be. The Vatican, in other words, continues to lie "for the good of the Church."

I'm often asked in interviews what I think of John Paul II or even more specifically whether I agree with his conservative thrust. Unfailingly I reply that John Paul II is far too complex a man to be described in a single sentence and that I don't think the term "conservative" is a fair assessment of him. The present Pope is an Eastern European romantic intellectual phenomenologist, and each of those words is meaningful. He has never in his adult life, I think, had an unnuanced thought. Virtually everything he says is qualified several times. There is nothing, by the way, wrong with nuance and qualification, for the world is a complex and intricate place and can only be described intelligently by nuanced and qualified statements. Unfortunately, the world media, including the world Catholic media, are quite incapable of dealing with the complexity of Papal thought and expression, and, therefore, what he says is frequently misunderstood and even distorted totally out of context.

For example, in one of his audience talks when he said that a man who lusts after his wife is as guilty of adultery as if he sinned with another woman, the Pope was in fact saying that a man who objectifies his wife, turns her into a thing, is guilty of adultery, a statement with which the most radical feminist could not disagree—but one would only understand the context if one had read his previous audience talks, and the fifteen talks he had already given on the same passage from St. Matthew's Sermon on the Mount.

I think my sister is the only one in the world to have carefully studied the audience talks other than the Pope himself. She's certainly the only one to have published a book on the subject.

The audience talks, she believes, quite correctly it seems to me, are a revolution in Catholic sexual theory, a turn in the corner from the long road down which we have walked since St. Augustine's time. They are the most powerful, positive evaluation of human sexuality yet produced in the Catholic Church. Yet the Pope himself does not seem to realize their implications on the practical daily lives of his people and sees no inconsistency between his insistence on the importance of sexual passion for human love and the audience talks and stands on birth control which make it difficult, if not impossible, for those few who accept such stands to have much in the way of sexual passion in their lives. He apparently sees no inconsistency between the radical feminist theory of the audience talks (which insist on the total equality of men and women) and the refusal to ordain women (on the bad scriptural grounds that no women were in the upper room—how do we know?) and also the continuing discriminatory treatment of women in the Catholic Church.

The Pope also apparently perceives no inconsistency between his brilliant defense of human rights and human freedoms when he is lecturing the institutions outside the Church and the continuing abuse of human rights and human freedoms inside the Church. The day that Hans Küng was excluded from the ranks of Catholic theologians, the Pope also criticized those who would deny freedom of expression to those who dissent —apparently utterly innocent of the seeming inconsistency of these two statements.

In response to questions, I normally say that John Paul II is one of the most gifted men who have ever been Pope. Theoretically he is a liberal and a brilliant philosopher of the sort who meets yearly with such distinguished philosophers as Godamer, Ricoeur, and Kolakowski. On the other hand he is often a theological and administrative conservative who has little taste for the daily administrative burdens and struggles with the Curia. I believe this is a fair summary of a complicated man (who skis and swims and does other things that would have been unthinkable in previous Papacies), but it is not the impression many Catholics, and particularly Catholic women, have. They only read the headlines and the short summaries on television and in the newspapers, and they picture John Paul II as a reactionary who is trying to undo the work of the Vatican Council. I am afraid this is the image that is going to endure, in part because neither the Pope nor those around him seem terribly concerned about persuading the Catholics of the world of the nuances, the complexities, the intricacies of John Paul's thoughts and pronouncements.

In some ways he is a stern conservative—for example, his refusal to continue dispensing priests of their vows and his intractable attitude towards the freedom of nuns in the Church. The Küng case was less his fault than that of the German cardinals who got rid of Küng—a rival on both academic and clerical grounds, since most of the German cardinals are academic—with the same kind of skills with which the Wehrmacht won the Second World War. (Küng's bishop had prepared a compromise solution with which the Pope was prepared to live until the German cardinals stormed down to Rome and blew the compromise out of the water.)

I am told by those who have been closer to the situation more recently than I have that the Pope feels his attempts to restore some sort of order and discipline in the Church have been mostly successful and that now the principal problem is Liberation Theology.

In a way, I hope he and his staff actually believe that. Order and discipline have not been restored in the Church and will never be what they were in the old-fashioned Church of the Counter-Reformation. We are back to the pluralistic Church of the Middle Ages, whether we like it or not. Any further attempt on the part of the Papacy to impose order and discipline again is simply going to create more chaos. It would be far better for the Pope to believe this mistaken policy has succeeded than to forget about it. Liberation Theology, it seems to me, may merit condemnation because it is preached by Catholic theologians who seem ignorant of history and sociology. They seem to be the only ones in the world who do not appreciate that when Marxism comes to power it *always* creates greater tyranny than that which it replaces. I don't believe, however, that it's worthwhile condemning specific Liberation Theologians because, despite the newspaper publicity about them, they are really not influential in Latin America. The basic political trend in recent years is to social democracy, and the basic religious trend is toward folk religion. The Macumba and Condumble, mixtures of Catholicism and African paganism in Brazil, for example, are what really matters in that country. They are the religion of the millions; Liberation Theology is the religion of hundreds or thousands, at the most.

The present relationship between the Papacy and the Church is not a healthy one. The Pope is a marvelous public presence, a brilliant symbol, for whom people cheer enthusiastically even though they pay absolutely no attention to what he says. There is something hollow, I'm afraid, in brilliant public ceremonies of acclaim when what the dazzling symbol says is ignored. On the one hand, such a mixture shows that the ordinary Catholic is not about to leave the Church. On the other hand, it also shows that what the principal teacher of a Church says goes almost completely unheard.

In my pre-conclave sociological job description, I said that the most effective Pope would be a hopeful holy man who smiles—a pope like John XXIII. Papa Luciani was that man. Papa Wojtyla is a holy man who smiles but he doesn't seem to generate much hope. Those around him and those who have studied him say he is an abidingly pessimistic man who expects world disaster. It is precisely this dark dimension of his personality which, I think, makes him finally ineffective as a Pope. Statecraft is a skill like any other—some men are more gifted at it than others. Religious leadership, however, is an entirely different matter. It has nothing to do with administrative competence.

The challenge to the Papacy is not, as some Catholic conservatives would have us believe, of a Pope teaching "hard truths," i.e., truths the world does not want to believe. Nor surely does it consist of the Pope merely repeating negative sexual prohibitions. Nor does it consist in a Pope repeating all the modern clichés, as the Liberation Theologians would like to have him do and as the Conciliar document on the Church in the modern world certainly did. To be effective, the Pope is not required to preach either hard truths or fashionable truths but rather "good news." To be an effective follower of Jesus of Nazareth in the key position of the Catholic Church, the Pope must both comfort and challenge, and the comfort and challenge must be based on excitement over having heard incredibly good news. Paul VI, whatever his intellectual brilliance and his good intentions, finally failed as a Pope because to the people of the world he seemed to be a nervous, whining hand-wringer. Pope John Paul II seems to be failing because he appears to much of the world as

400

a man with powerful public presence who is speaking a message of gloom and doom. John XXIII was effective at popecraft because he preached a message of joy and hopefulness.

Just as Jesus did.

Much of this is a question of style and emphasis and personality and not a question either of doctrine or sociological analysis. You can believe the world is in for some pretty grim times and that you have to tell it some pretty grim truths and still be a man of joy and hopefulness. If you want to make people listen to your bad news, you'd better win them over first of all by the power of your good news. My experience in studying the two conclaves persuades me that it's unlikely that we can count, in the future, on men like that being selected Popes. Both Roncalli and Luciani were flukes in the system.

However, one must concede the fact that the system is sufficiently chaotic and irresponsible now that such happy flukes do happen occasionally. It is not all bad.

Neither is the Vatican bureaucracy, but my experience in studying the Papal elections persuaded me it is pretty bad. While many, if not most, of the men are good, the system is corrupt and perverse and ought to be truly reformed, and probably the only reform that would work is some kind of permanent abolition and the establishment of a different kind of governing structure for the central authority of the Church.

When the present nuncio sent out his letter hinting to the bishops that it was time to force my column out of the Catholic press, he said it was guilty of attacks on the "person of the Holy Father."

In fact, I was the only Catholic writer, beyond the tiny core of knee-jerk Pope worshipers, who was defending John Paul and the only one, besides my sister, who was consistently praising the audience talks. All I had ever said was that the laity were not listening anymore, an empirically demonstrable fact. We were back at the same old game. He who reports the truth is assumed to approve of it and to have caused it. The only acceptable stance for a Catholic writer is such total adoration for the Papacy that he suppresses unpalatable truths and insists that the Pope has no credibility problem when in fact he does.

Such an attitude is not only oppressive. Worse, it is stupid. The real enemies of the Papacy are not those who tell the truth about its current ambiguous situation. The real enemies are those who lie to the Pope (and perhaps to themselves) about the relationship between the Papacy and the world. Apparently the Vatican prefers the liars to the truth tellers. So much the worse for it.

Unlike some Catholic radicals, I do not rejoice in the breakdown of communication between the laity and the junior clergy on the one hand and the Papacy on the other. In addition to whatever may be said about it theologically, the Papacy is one of the greatest sociological inventions in human history. If we did not have one, we would be trying to establish it. The Pope is the most significant religious leader in the world—more important than all the others put together.

I do not say that the distance between the Pope's pronouncements and the life of the Catholic people is vast and growing broader every year, because it represents an opinion or a hope of mine. I say it because, sadly, it is true. I say it not out of a spirit of revolt but out of loyalty to the Papacy—because I believe that loyal human beings tell the truth.

As long as those who tell the hard truths are condemned, there is no hope anything will change or that the Holy See will begin to recapture the possibilities of those holy moments in the early sixties when John XXIII was Pope. The opportunities of that blessed time were lost by Paul VI, despite all his good intentions. They will not be recaptured by orders or condemnations or attempts to silence those who say the opportunities were blown sky-high—and that what is left of them continues to be blown.

The worst offenders are the bishops, men whose charism of office should make them the intermediaries, the messengers, the angels (in the sense of the Book of Revelation) between the local and the central Church. Many of them know the truth of the ineffectiveness of the present Papacy as a source of religious teaching. They are afraid to tell the Pope the truth for fear they will be treated the same way I was by the nuncio and be accused of disloyalty for telling the truth.

The difference between me and them is that they are bound in conscience by the solemn obligations of the office to be *accurate angels*. To violate this obligation is a grave failure of their most profound duty. It is also to cut the Pope off from the voice of the Spirit as the Spirit speaks among the people, and it's strict traditional Catholic doctrine, repeated by John Paul in his exhortation on marriage, that the Spirit speaks among the people.

No one is listening.

Even to listen is to run the risk of being judged disloyal. Only when the Papacy begins to listen again will it begin to recapture its lost credibility.

As I reflect on the experience of my Papal election study, I find that it reveals a personality trait that has dogged my whole life: I'm plagued by ingenuous ideas to which I do not have the ability to say a sufficiently vigorous "No."

What? Quixots say no?

I had more than enough to do in the late seventies with my column, my sociology, my catechetical writings, my lecturing and my responsibility to my small group community, which was trying to put itself back together. The idea of a study of the election appealed to me because of its ingenuity and novelty, its fun and challenge, its excitement and drama, and because it was something someone *ought* to do. Therefore I did it, even though I realized dimly that it would lead to exhaustion, depression and frustration. Ever since I wrote *The Church in the Suburbs*, original and ingenious ideas have had a fatal appeal to me and I never have developed the ability to reject them out of hand.

I am not saying that all my crazy schemes should be abandoned but merely that, in retrospect, I might have been better advised to have picked and chosen among the projects instead of doing them all with reckless disregard for the effort and energy demanded. My imagination, as I suppose my novels reveal, is restless, frantic and uninhibited, especially when I'm relaxed. In the days when Bill McCready and I were working closely together, he used to dread my return from vacations because he said vacation was a time when my imagination stirred up all kinds of new projects, which meant all kinds of new work for everybody involved. The idea to study the Papal elections and to write a book about them was a wonderful one, as almost everyone admitted. Looking back on it, I would have been better off, perhaps, if I had not followed up on the idea. Certainly my private files would never have been ransacked.

Maybe part of the appeal of this exciting idea was that some corner of my personality saw it as an antidote to the pain of rejection. The book was a moderate success, selling perhaps thirty-five thousand copies hardback in this country and several thousand more paperback in England, not nearly what Jim Andrews had expected. No American paperback house was interested in it. (In retrospect perhaps if Warner Books had published it, *The Making of the Popes* would have been a best-seller. This involves no negative judgment on Andrews and McMeel, only a positive judgment on Warner's ability to market and distribute books.) It would be seven more years before a string of monumental Vatican scandals would finally stir up enough interest in the internal workings of the Papacy to make a Vaticanology book a best-seller. Oddly enough, the first book to rise to the top of the *New York Times* best-seller list was David Yallop's account of the death of John Paul I, an account which unlike some of the other Vaticanology books treated *The Making of the Popes* with considerable respect.

I was disappointed in the book's modest success. The drama of the year of the three Popes made a great story. More people should know that story.

Perhaps it ought to be retold, this time in fictional guise.

Which has to be the craziest of the kinky ideas that I've ever had.

Quixots the storyteller of papal elections!

CHAPTER 21

The Unmaking of the Cardinal

Transparent curtains
Slip aside as I push through
Burdened soaking air

We were eating lunch in the President's Room in the First National Bank Plaza shortly after Ed Wall had come to Chicago as editor of *The New World* (which would soon be renamed inappropriately *The Chicago Catholic*). Ed had regaled me with the usual stories of the sometimes comic difficulties of trying to work with John Cardinal Cody. All of his bureaucratic staff told stories behind his back. (I use the word *all* advisedly.) "I don't like to say this about anyone," Ed sighed, "but it's the truth. He is the only truly evil man I have ever known. He is a complete monster."

Wall may deny the statement, as most people in the Church and in the mass media will deny in public what they have said in private about Cardinal Cody. Wall, alas, is one of the many victims of the Cody era. He came to Chicago to take over *The Chicago Catholic*, in his own version encouraged by his good friend Archbishop Bernardin and feeling as many who were "in the know" in those days that Cody would be shortly eased out as archbishop of Chicago. He'd stayed on to serve the cardinal faithfully and loyally while, at the same time, inviting to his house for supper such known opponents as Roache and Bernardin and myself. When the *Chicago Sun-Times* began its investigation of the cardinal, the pages of *The New World* under Wall's editorship exploded in hysterical defense. So closely had Wall become identified with Cody that it was necessary for Bernardin eventually to ease him out as editor. He had ridden with the hounds and was now hunted with the hares, a man who played the ecclesiastical power game with skill—and lost.

Before he was eased out of *The Chicago Catholic*, Wall had written an adulatory biography of the new archbishop. Now, reduced to issuing a "Florida newsletter," he says he may write "the truth" about Cardinal Bernardin. If that happens, which book should one believe?

When my diaries, which had been removed from my confidential files at Rosary College, were printed in an article in *Chicago Lawyer*, Wall sent copies of the article to every major Catholic newspaper editor in the world, so loyal was he above and beyond the call of duty to the cardinal he called a monster.

I suppose Wall's story is as good a symbol as any I know of the Cody years of Chicago: large numbers of men loyally serving a cardinal whom they would privately admit was bad or evil or monstrous or crooked or just plain crazy, then piously rising to his defense when someone dared to say in public the same things they said in private. If watching the process of the Papal election was disappointing, watching the Cody years in Chicago made me sick to my stomach.

Thinking about the acquiescence of the clergy and the hierarchy and the mass media in those years of madness *still* makes me sick to my stomach.

Are you not ashamed of what you did to Cardinal Cody? I'm frequently asked.

I really didn't do much to him. I only disagreed with and criticized him in public and said bluntly that he ought to be replaced, something many others, including his successor, were saying in private. No, I'm not ashamed of speaking the truth during the Cody years; rather I'm proud of it and I hope I will be remembered in the future as one of the few priests in the Archdiocese who *did* speak the truth.

It didn't take any particular courage for me, since the cardinal wasn't paying my salary and couldn't cut off my hospital insurance as he did to a few other dissident priests who dared raise their voices. Incidentally, when I made the charge that the cardinal routinely cut off the hospital insurance of those clergy of whom he did not approve, his then chancellor, now bishop of Arlington, Virginia, John Richard Keating, denied it ever happened. Keating knew better then, and he knows better now. To deny that is simply to speak a falsehood. But then on the subject of John Cody, lots of people spoke and continue to speak falsely.

Wall's description of Cody as thoroughly evil and a monster are popular descriptions of what went on in Chicago during those years. They are not the words I would choose. I would prefer much more clinical and neutral words. The cardinal suffered from what is clinically known as an antisocial character defect, a little-understood syndrome, not uncharacteristic of many who rise to high power, in which the person and possibly an overwhelming mother figure are the only "real" persons in the world. Everyone else is a pawn and a potential enemy to be manipulated and has no rights or dignity or even basic humanity. In the antisocial character's orientation one is utterly and completely blameless if one injures all the others in the world because they, for all practical purposes, do not exist as human beings—surely not as human beings with whom one would consider entering any relationships of trust, or mutuality, or loyalty or friendship ("I don't have any friends," the cardinal proudly told a

Chicago reporter). The antisocial character is bound by no moral code other than the protection of himself and perhaps the overwhelming mother figure.

This syndrome is well enough known to clinicians, and the cardinal's personality and behavior in those years fit it well. He was a deeply troubled and badly disturbed man. Virtually no one who worked with him, either in the Chicago Chancery or in the national hierarchy or even eventually in Rome, had any doubts of that. Neither did those who knew him in the Chicago media. They may not have known the clinical names but they certainly knew the symptoms. Early in his years, some of his closest staff members told him to his face he was a pathological liar, a charge which did not cause him to replace them or them to resign from his service.

That is the one charge against which, however, I must vigorously defend the late cardinal. The *Chicago Sun-Times*, in its blundering investigative reporting of the Cody years, broadly hinted that his relationship with his woman friend was sexual. Moreover, I am told, some of the *Sun-Times* staff who were involved in the investigation would snidely comment on the physical similarity between the cardinal and his friend's son. I suspect many people outside of Chicago, especially, and around the world, assume that the woman and the cardinal were lovers. This is nonsense. While the relationship was intense and, in its own way, intimate, the woman's psychological role in Cody's life was that of a powerful mother surrogate and not a sexual lover.

The priests, the bishops, the archbishops, the cardinals who refuse to speak the truth about what happened in Chicago during the Cody years will tell you privately that they remain silent for the "good of the Church." They do not seem to realize that the good of the Church is ill served when psychopaths, sociopaths, antisocial personalities, pederasts, crooks, alcoholics and incompetents are routinely appointed to the American dioceses and that even such an important diocese as Chicago is not immune to such a disastrous appointment during the most critical period of the last five hundred years of Catholic history. To continue to pretend the Cody appointment was not a disaster is dishonest. When men get caught up in lies "for the good of the Church" they eventually are no longer able to distinguish the truth. Far better no investigation than one that may satisfy a small group of restless, old-fashioned laity but that is patently, especially to those who know what really happened, a cover-up.

Quixote again?

Yeah, sure.

I shall leave it to the future historians to sort out the complicated financial and administrative and interpersonal tragedies of the Cody years. By and large, I was not affected by them. I had and have no personal vendetta with the cardinal. He did nothing to me; under his administration, I prospered. He left me alone. I went into public dissent for the first time when he abruptly closed several inner-city Catholic schools without any consultation. I was asked by some Catholic journalists how priests could remain silent as the cardinal phased out perhaps the most significant work and the most generous charity the American Catholic Church had ever done, the maintenance of alternative education for poor black and Hispanic children in the inner cities. I decided I was one priest who could speak out and if I did not do so I would violate my every deepest conviction. It is no easy thing for a priest to take on his bishop. I did not do it lightly but I certainly do not regret doing it, nor do I feel guilty about the results of my opposition.

I am not picturing myself as a stern crusader for honesty and integrity and against falsehood and corruption. That has never been one of my themes and it is not now. Honesty in the Church—a critical theme, heaven knows—is Küng's message, not mine. If I insist on the truth and on integrity in this chapter it is because in Chicago during those years the corruption was monumental and monstrous and the lie was and is vast and perverted. My protest was of the sort that if I didn't say something the stones would cry out.

Can't you leave the cardinal alone now that he's dead? Haven't you done enough to him already?

My intent is not to do anything to the cardinal. It never was. My intent was and is to tell the truth, not because it will have any immediate practical consequences, but so that it will be on the historical record. I have no fear how historians will judge my part in those years. I wonder how many of the others involved can be similarly confident.

The extent of my public opposition to the cardinal seems greater to many people in retrospect than it actually was in fact. I criticized his closing of the inner-city schools. I referred to him, quite accurately, as a "madcap tyrant." I later said he was destroying the structure of the Archdiocese and quoted a fellow priest (a wise and learned one) as saying it would take to the year 2000 to undo the harm of the Cody years. Such accusations are mild compared to the obsessive attacks on him which occurred every night in the city at almost every rectory dinner table. I refused to take part in such conversations because I believed they were psychologically unhealthy. To complain about the cardinal but not to do anything about him was immature and neurotic. My complaints, both in public and in private, were milder than the routine complaints of priests who had to put up with the diocesan administration every day, as I did not. If someone is destroying my Archdiocese, and everyone knows he's destroying it, and everyone else is silent for one reason or another, I will refuse to be silent because the norms of clerical culture forbid speaking the truth about a characterologically disturbed archbishop.

That's why I went into public opposition, that's the *only* reason I went into public opposition. The cardinal did not persecute me personally, he did not interfere with my career, he did not take from me anything I wanted. I had no personal resentments against him. I advocated his replacement for the same reasons that Archbishop Benelli had advocated them years before I spoke about him in public.

Was there a plot to "get" Cardinal Cody, as was charged by *Chicago Lawyer*?

"Plot to get" are smear words, implying something illicit and immoral. If the question is rephrased—were there plans to remove or attempts to investigate Cardinal Cody?—then the answer is that there were at least five of them. I was not directly involved in any of them, though, as I have said repeatedly, I would have been proud to have been so involved if the opportunity had been made available to me.

The first and most serious attempt to remove Cody began when Archbishop Benelli visited the United States, spent some time in Chicago and was horrified by what he took to be patent evidence of the cardinal's psychological problems. From that time on Benelli was determined to replace the cardinal, though, finally, some six years later his efforts would fail. The story of this Vatican "plot to get Cody" is generally known among those who are close to ecclesiastical matters in Rome or the United States. I outlined it in some detail in *The Making of the Popes*. Cardinal Cody denied it vigorously but he was, once again, simply not telling the truth. Ecclesiastical authorities will, one way or another, deny it again after the publication of this book. They are not telling the truth and they know they're not. Those involved in the attempts to replace the cardinal have not attempted to keep the "plot" secret. It is a commonplace of ecclesiastical conversation. Moreover, journalists who have studied the Chicago situation in the seventies also know it to be true in vague outline. Their failure to investigate it and to report it is but one more manifestation of the incredible journalistic irresponsibility in Chicago during the Cody years.

It must be emphasized that Benelli and his colleagues were working with the full knowledge and approval of Pope Paul VI, who, characteristically, okayed the "visitation" to Chicago by the investigative commission but wrung his hands and vacillated when presented with its report.

In broad outline, those who were appointed some time in the middle seventies to investigate Chicago, after the cardinal had deflected several attempts to "kick him upstairs" to meaningless Roman offices, were Cardinal Villot, the secretary of state, Archbishop Benelli, the undersecretary of state, Monsignor Caprio, a staff member of the secretary of state, Cardinal Baggio, the head of the Congregation of Bishops (who in a conversation with me in 1975 defended Cardinal Cody in such weak terms as to make it clear he was advocating replacement) and Archbishop Jadot, the apostolic delegate to the United States. Evidence was collected secretly from various Chicago priests who were familiar with the situation in Cody's administration.

As I reported in *The Making of the Popes*, the principal conclusions of the investigation were as follows:

1. *Racism.* The arbitrary and seemingly capricious closing of schools serving blacks in the inner city of Chicago (many of them non-Catholics) gave the Church an appearance of racism, to which Roman authorities are sensitive. In fact, the cardinal was hardly a racist but closed the schools because he did not believe the Church had any mission to educate non-Catholics (to provide an alternative to public schools for middle-class blacks). However, the Romans were correct in thinking that annual public conflict about closing of inner-city schools had given the appearance of racism to the Archdiocese of Chicago. An American black bishop from a diocese where Cody was archbishop (New Orleans) has publicly called Cody a "classic example of an unconscious racist."

2. *Financial maladministration.* Roman sources told me it was generally known in the Curia that after his term as treasurer of the American

411

bishops was over, but before he turned the money and books over to his successor, the cardinal had unwisely invested several million dollars in Penn Central commercial paper a few days before that railroad went bankrupt. I have documented this in a column which appeared in the *Chicago Tribune* in 1976. In addition there were allegations that sixty million dollars of parish funds were on deposit at the Chicago Chancery, and no accounting had been made either in the diocese or to Rome as to the investment of these funds. (It is a fact that no public audits of these funds had been released.) Finally, while closing inner-city schools because of the allegedly impoverished finances of the diocese, the cardinal had poured millions of dollars into a TV network which operated only in rectories and schools. Added to his rumored proclivity for lavish gifts to Curial bureaucrats, these facts and rumors made Roman authorities uneasy about the finances of what is generally thought to be the world's most affluent Archdiocese. "How come he doesn't have the money for schools, when Cardinal Cooke in New York does?" one Roman official asked me. It is possible that ecclesiastical authorities have more detailed information about the finances of the Archdiocese of Chicago—reported by present or former staff members troubled in conscience about what was going on. "For Baggio to be going after him," I was told, "he's got to have more information on Cody than you can imagine."

3. *Poor administration.* Many American bishops, including some who had been auxiliaries in Chicago, had complained to Rome about the arbitrary, highhanded, and frequently inefficient administration of the diocese. The cardinal concentrates all power in himself, Rome was told, delegates no decisions, and consults no one; hence major decisions and appointments get put off for months or even years. The Association of Chicago Priests has complained of most of these matters publicly and bitterly for several years. There had also been complaints to the Congregation for Catholic Education about the lack of a coherent seminary policy. "It's the worst disaster in the history of American Catholicism," one angry bishop told me, "and all we do is stand by silently and fume."

4. *Conflict with the clergy.* There is always some tension between priests and bishop, but Roman authorities know that most of the Chicago clergy, normally respectful, had lost all regard for the cardinal. He had been told in public at meetings of the Association of Chicago Priests that he lied to them habitually. This charge was made by three Chicago priests in a UPI story in the summer of 1978. The Romans had some confir-

412

mation of this charge in the cardinal's public statements that he had requested auxiliary bishops when in fact no such requests had been made. Protests at the apostolic delegation in Washington and in Rome came not from fringe clergy, but from the most respectable and responsible priests in the Archdiocese. Rome's inclination to take these protests seriously was reinforced by the fact that the cardinal often did not respond to letters from the various Roman congregations and in one case did not respond for several months to a handwritten personal letter from Pope Paul VI (he bragged to others about ignoring this letter, saying that "Baggio made the Pope write it"). A senior priest with excellent reputation and a responsible position had said publicly, "It will take a half century to undo the harm." Rome never sees things quite that apocalyptically, but there was more urgency than one normally encounters in the Vatican's anxiety about Chicago.

5. *Unpopularity with the laity.* While Vatican officials would not take seriously a public opinion poll sponsored and conducted by the *Chicago Tribune* which showed that the cardinal was no more popular with the laity of Chicago than Richard Nixon was with the American people the year before he resigned, they were upset by the steady flow of protest letters received both at the apostolic delegate's office and in Rome. "They're not nuts," I was told by one informant. "The letters are neatly typed on impressive stationery by influential laity. The stack is a couple of feet high."

6. *Extraordinary personal habits.* Rome was also upset about the rumors of the cardinal's behavior—tales of his involvement in complex political and military machinations, obsession with keeping track of every outside priest who came to Chicago, vindictiveness against those who disagreed, a passion for secrecy and mystery, allegations of spy networks in the diocese, reported refusal to make annual spiritual "retreats." While it did not have the resources to sort out fact from fiction in these rumors, Rome operated on the assumption that where there was so much smoke, there must be some fire.

As one Roman said to me, "Any bishop on whom they have all that material would have been a chaplain in an old people's home five years ago." But Rome was reluctant to move against a cardinal, no matter how bad the case and how great the potential scandal.

It was of this passage from *The Making of the Popes*, I am told, that Pope John Paul II said when he read it (the first day it was available in

Rome, if my source is to be believed), "It is all true, but he shouldn't have said it."

I would differ with the Pope. If it is true, it is sufficiently bad that it should have been said.

This evaluation of Cardinal Cody was not a secret in Rome in the months immediately before the death of Paul VI. You could pick it up from several cardinals at dinner or from many different Vatican bureaucrats in café conversation along the Via della Conciliazione. Nor was it any secret then that the only possible successor to Cody would be Bernardin, a man who was thought to have the skill and the tact to act as an administrator until Cody's official retirement or death and to pull together the tattered pieces of the Archdiocese. In the early summer of 1978, Baggio, on the way to a Latin American conference, was dispatched to Chicago with orders for Cody to resign. He was stopped at Fumicino Airport by a call from the nervously hand-wringing Pope, who said the whole plan was to be implemented only if Cardinal Cody accepted it. Disheartened, Baggio flew to Chicago in any case and tried to persuade the cardinal to accept it. He refused in a shouting match at the cardinal's mansion at the seminary in Mundelein.

A few weeks later, Paul VI was dead. A few weeks after that, late one afternoon John Paul I ordered Baggio to revive the program and to remove Cody from Chicago as quickly as possible. The next morning, John Paul I was dead. John Paul II vacillated. He wrote a letter to Cody informing him the plan was to be implemented, but the cardinal's pathetic plea postponed its implementation until after his visit to Chicago. Then, finally, on Ash Wednesday of 1980 the Pope demanded the cardinal's resignation in a tumultuous confrontation in Rome and backed off when the cardinal threatened a public fight. The Pope had not learned what any priest in Chicago could have told him, that Cardinal Cody's style was always to attack at the beginning and then quickly back off when someone stood up to him. A touch of Papal backbone at that time would have saved the Archdiocese of Chicago a lot of trouble.

There were three other investigations of which I am aware, one by the *Chicago Sun-Times*, one by the Gannett News Service, and one by the United States attorney for the Northern District of Illinois. Before discussing them, however, I should remark that during one of my visits to Rome I speculated in the diary I kept about the possibility of a journalistic investigation of the Archdiocese. I am not ashamed about such speculations or about the fact that Jim Andrews and I discussed it further in a subsequent meeting in Kansas City. Ecclesiastical corruption is as much a legitimate matter for journalistic investigation as is any other kind, especially because the Church by its tax-exempt status is indirectly subsidized by all the rest of American tax-paying individuals and institutions. The Church will only be accountable in the use of the funds it collects from the laity when it knows it can no longer hide anything it does with its funds. The absolute identification of personal whim with Church mission, which was characteristic of Cardinal Cody's finances, ought to be exposed, it seemed to me, so that such behavior would be impossible in the future.

In fact, that good has already come from the explosive end of the Cody Years: Church finances in the Archdiocese of Chicago will be publicly accountable for the imaginable future. If I made some small contribution to that outcome, I am proud of it.

I know relatively little about these three investigations, although Jim Andrews, a couple of years after our conversation in Kansas City in 1976, had suggested to Gannett that there was a good story in Chicago. I was interviewed by reporters from both the Gannett News Service and the *Sun-Times* but there was little I could tell them beyond what was already in *The Making of the Popes*. I had little information about the internal financial workings of the Archdiocese or about the cardinal's relationship with his friend, who had been on the diocesan payroll for many years. All I did know and I do know now is that tens of millions of dollars of Church money disappeared in an as yet unexplored and unexplained financial machination, involving, among other institutions, the diocese of Reno. That story has yet to be told and perhaps will never be told.

I know practically nothing of the investigation instituted by the U.S. attorney, though if such a distinguished Catholic layman as Thomas Sullivan instituted it, he must have had *prima facie* evidence of violations of the law. I am told on good authority, but I cannot confirm, that in part of its own probings into the finances of the Archdiocese, the *Chicago Sun-Times* came upon a Chicago Chancery Office employee whose conscience could no longer tolerate the uses to which the cardinal was putting church funds. (The employee, I gather, was lay. Previous clerical employees of the cardinal had grave difficulties in conscience with the "alienation" of Church property—its use for nonecclesiastical purposes—but somehow or other managed to live with their consciences.)

It has been reported to me that the *Sun-Times* brought this man and his information to the United States attorney, who then launched the investigation. Sullivan's successor, Dan Webb, in a classic exercise of political opportunism, stalled the investigation, perhaps under pressure from Washington, where a powerful attorney had been hired by the cardinal to lean on the Justice Department to quash the investigation (at a cost, I am told, of hundreds of thousands of dollars of attorney's fees). When the cardinal died, Webb dropped the investigation with a notable sigh of relief. Jim Hoge, the editor of the *Sun-Times*, had also aborted the publication of the results of his paper's investigation, under pressure from the attack of the Chicago Catholic newspaper and Ed Wall and also criticism from Catholics on his own staff.

At the time of the *Sun-Times* preliminary stories, many priests and laymen in the Archdiocese spoke out in defense of the cardinal, pleading his age and infirmity and the sanctity of the office. What right did newspapers have to investigate a cardinal? Hoge apparently took these objections seriously and thus blew an almost certain Pulitzer Prize for his paper. He should have either never authorized the investigation in the first place, or stuck to his guns once it was launched. But Jim Hoge, while he may look like Jason Robards Jr. playing Ben Bradlee, does not have Ben Bradlee's guts.

What, then, about my own private files, which when released to *Chicago Lawyer*, caused the Gannett newspapers to flee in panic and may have influenced Jim Hoge's decision to abandon his investigation?

There was, to begin with, nothing in my diaries which had any relationship to the three investigations going on in 1982. *Chicago Lawyer* manipulated the diaries to make it appear that I had engineered the plot against Cardinal Cody. It was a smoke screen, a reasonably successful one in that the full story of the Cody years has not been and may never be told. However, I doubt that the publication of my diaries—a scandal of a day or two in the Chicago papers which never made either *Time* or *Newsweek*—had much influence on anything.

Briefly, what happened was this. In February of 1981 a staff member of the Notre Dame alumni magazine wrote to me about doing an article about me for that magazine. I replied tentatively. However, when the writer visited me in Tucson, his naive charm overcame my objections and I agreed to an interview, which went on for several days. He asked me if it would be possible to "visit my archives" and I said yes. Later in the interview, he asked if he might look at the manuscripts of my books and I told him that it would be all right—they were at my archives in Rosary and he could inspect them.

It was the last I had heard of the subject until I learned in the following summer that the writer was talking to reporters about my "plot" to get Cody, a "plot" that he had uncovered by reading my diaries. I phoned Rosary College to learn whether someone had been at my personal papers and private and confidential correspondence. I was told abruptly by the nun in charge that someone had and that she had given permission for him to do so. I asked her why and she again abruptly replied because the writer had asked, and hung up on me. After consultation with my lawyer, I phoned and then wrote a letter to the writer requesting the return of my property, saying that the permission I gave him only covered the inspection of manuscripts, and not the removal of anything—much less inspection of files marked "Personal and Confidential" and the copying of these files. He replied on the phone and then by mail that he would not return my property and that the First Amendment guaranteed his right to retain my property.

Apparently he interpreted the word "visit" to mean take everything in sight, copy personal letters and private diaries and even physically remove cassette tapes.

The reader may imagine what it would be like to permit someone to visit your house and then discover that he assumed your hospitality meant that he could make copies of your private papers and physically remove from your home your personal cassette tapes.

I understood then and understand now that any retention of my papers after my letter to him correcting his assumption was tantamount to theft. Whatever good faith he may have had about his rights to copy and remove the materials (whatever vast stretch he gave to the word "visit") ceased with my specification of what was permitted him and what not.

If you are a writer, finders, keepers.

Losers, weepers.

Two points to be noted. He claimed the right to interpret "visit" to mean take everything. In the name of the First Amendment he denied me any right to specify what I meant by "visit" or to require the return of my papers. What had been mine was now his because he was engaged in newsgathering which involved obtaining files and documents.

Do I need to say that the First Amendment bestows no such right to

417

retain the property of others which you might come upon by mistake or chance? Or that the courts have never granted anyone the right as a writer to retain someone else's property?

His good faith I will not question. But his legal advice about his First Amendment rights was bad. Culpably bad.

Father Hesburgh, the president of Notre Dame, ordered the writer to return the papers (and the tapes he had also removed from the files) to me, and the writer told an aide of Father Hesburgh's he had done so.

Subsequently, despite his word to Father Hesburgh, according to published accounts, the writer attempted to peddle a hundred-page story without telling Father Hesburgh, to Chicago newspapers, which rejected it. One published account said he even demanded employment as part of the purchase price because Hesburgh would fire him if he found out what he had done. It was at that time apparently that copies were made of the documents, and the following year in the midst of the *Sun-Times* stories on the cardinal they were transmitted, according to rumors, by an associate of the cardinal to *Chicago Lawyer*.

Nor did the writer seem to comprehend (a failure which also marked the behavior of the publicity-hungry *Chicago Lawyer*) that it cannot be assumed that notes five and six years old are linked to a current investigation. The link has to be demonstrated, and none was or can be.

It was a distasteful experience. It still is. However, I am now persuaded that in the stress and strain of the interlude I attributed to it more importance than it actually merited. An editor of the Notre Dame magazine and Rosary College had violated my trust. So what else is new? It served me right for trusting either institution. Many in the Notre Dame community rejoiced at my embarrassment. What more should I have expected? The writer, as quoted by Father Hesburgh, summarized the case against me perfectly: "Greeley's a success so it's all right to bring him down."

It was a tempest in a teapot, a minor footnote to the tragicomedy of the Cody years. When the infection of an antisocial character defect gets into a large social system, all kinds of evil things are likely to happen. I was only one of the minor victims of the Cody years. I survived this foul violation, on balance, rather well, and despite the attempt of the Notre Dame writer, supported in substantial part by his own university community, I have not been brought down. I will not be. Not by the likes of them, anyway.

The cardinal is gone now and God rest him, but the harm he did to the Church in Chicago will continue for a long, long time—long after I'm dead, long after the end of this century. The ingenuity, resourcefulness, creativity, energy and imagination which had marked the Archdiocese of my youth had been destroyed—"killed by Cody," as a priest, discouraged by what he saw as the bland mediocrity of the present administration, remarked, "buried in cement by Bernardin." None of this needed to happen: Archbishop Cody's behavior in New Orleans and Kansas City before he came to Chicago was well known. Any kind of serious investigation of him by the Vatican would have revealed, long before his appointment to Chicago, that he did suffer from an antisocial character defect. Rome knew, only a few years after the appointment, it had made a tragic mistake, but the system is such that not only does it make such tragic mistakes and make them often, it is unable to undo them once they are made. The Cardinal's Office is a sacred one like the Papacy. One must lie, deceive, cheat, falsify to cover up such mistakes "for the good of the Church"—even though such mistakes eventually become public knowledge and even though they would, if anything could, destroy the Church.

My faith in that tradition and the God it represents is in no way dependent on the intelligence, the ability, the courage, the integrity, the honesty or even the sanity of the men who preside over it. I recognize, however, the absolute need for an institution to preserve the tradition. Further, I recognize that the institution is subject to all the weaknesses and frailties that beset any human institution (I've written novels about that subject!); moreover, I understand that the Church, like all human institutions, has its high and its low points, its apexes and its nadirs. Unfortunately at the present time it is pretty close to rock bottom. When a man who manifestly has a monumental antisocial character defect is appointed to one of the most momentous positions in the Church; when such a man is maintained in power long after the leadership realizes what a tragic blunder has been made; and when that man's successor sees as one of his principal obligations to cover up and to smooth over the tragedy that preceded him, then the Roman Catholic Church as an institution has reached the bottom of the barrel. It won't stay there. The future will be better and different, but I'm not likely to be around for the future. For the present, those who are on the margins are the blessed ones.

Arizona: "It Sure Beats Elba"

Skilled ballerina spinning on the spray
She slices through the wake with disdainful ease
A mature woman, elegant at play
Aloof, discreet in her capacity to please
Then the tizzy teenage trickster topples from her skis
Cartwheels through the air
A carnival comic choreography
A somersaulting epiphany of grace
Devised by God to guarantee the race
Who gifted them with smiles to incandesce the day
Sculptured summer sunbursts to celebrate in space
And with technicolor splash our humdrum gray
A designer impeccable in taste
Such sacraments crafted to delight us on our way

Stanley Lieberson phoned me the week after Easter in 1978 at the motel in Phoenix where I was spending a few days recovering from too much travel and probably too much work. "There's no need to drive down here," Stanley said, genial as always. "We understand one another. We've got a deal. There's no need to drive a hundred and twenty miles."

"Nonsense, Stanley," I replied. "You and Rosenblatt are Brooklyn Jewish ethnics, I'm a Chicago Irish Catholic ethnic. The only deals that really count are arrived at over a cup of coffee or a cup of tea and a doughnut or sweet roll in the middle of the morning. I'm driving down."

"That's pretty good street sociology," Stanley admitted with a laugh.

(In later years when junior colleagues would press me for an explanation of what I mean by "street smarts" I would reply that I mean the way Stanley got things done in the sociology department. "Discover a set of theoretical propositions based on Stan's leadership and you'll be the Max Weber of the *fin de siècle*," I would tell them. I would be surprised, however, if Stanley learned "how things work" in graduate school. Rather he brought the insights and instincts with him from the neighborhoods in which he grew up and didn't lose them in graduate school.)

The next day in warm and sunny Tucson, Stan, whom I'd known in Chicago, and Paul Rosenblatt, whom I'd met when I was being recruited in January by the University of Arizona and for whom I had already great respect, were sitting over our cups and doughnuts, working out our deal.

"Okay," Stanley said, "we want you on whatever terms we can get you. We understand your Chicago connection. Be here for a semester a year and you'll never hear any complaint from us. Do we have a deal?"

"We have a deal," I said, and the three of us shook hands on it. It could just as easily have been engraved in stone. I had become a faculty member of the University of Arizona.

I always said there were only three universities which would tempt me to leave Chicago—Harvard, because it was number one, the City University of New York, because of its distinguished faculty program and because it was in New York, and Arizona, because it was in the top ten and was in Arizona, which had already become one of my favorite places in the world. When Arizona approached me, through Stanley Lieberson, the head of the department, and Philip Hammond, the chairman of the recruitment committee, I really didn't believe the proposal was serious.

I suppose it shows the effects of my various traumas in Chicago that I could not believe one of the country's top departments would be interested in me. I had heard that Arizona was speaking to three sociologists and I assumed that, like all good departments, they had programmed their choices one, two, three and I was number three. However, I figured that a trip to Tucson in the middle of January, even for a ritualistic set of interviews, was worth the effort. It rained most of the time and I had pleasant chats with the members of the department and with John Schaeffer, the university president, with whom it developed I shared a strong interest in photography. But I didn't believe they were serious.

It t: ~ned out they were and that they were perfectly prepared to have me spend a semester at NORC in Chicago and a semester in Tucson. "You got a raw deal in Chicago," Stanley said. "If you don't mind my language, they screwed you. We think you're a superstar, and we want you here."

I left Chicago the January after the Papal election with mixed feelings. I still have those mixed feelings. I like the weather, the setting, the faculty, the students, the administration, the weekend parish where I do work, everything about Tucson except the fact that it isn't Chicago. My roots in Chicago are so deep and so profound that I can never really feel quite at home anywhere else. I became good friends with Stanley and Dudley Duncan, one of the greatest sociologists in America, and Dick Curtis, who succeeded Stanley as head of the department and, especially and characteristically, with the junior members of the department, in particular Mike Hout and Albert Bergesen. Also, I renewed friendships with two bright young political scientists I met when I had lectured for a Catholic group in Tucson, Dan O'Neil and Henry Kenski. I met Henry's wife Margaret (née Corgan) and their bright, lovely daughter Katie, and also Jim and Lucille Harkin, whom I'd known from lecturing at Syracuse, and their son Jeremy. In a couple of years I would find myself in St. Odilia's parish in Tucson, baptizing the new additions to the Harkin and Kenski families, Emilie Harkin and Carolyn Kenski. The latter nestles in my arms, bottle and dolly firmly in hand, on the cover picture of *Lord of the Dance*. Since then I have also baptized Carolyn's little sister, a certain Erin Noele Kenski, a little Hiberno-Slav, who is named after Noele Marie Brigid Farrell in *Lord of the Dance*, and who already shows signs of developing some of her namesake's tough-mindedness.

(The mother of the two little girls says she doesn't doubt the efficacy of my water pouring, but she has some questions about the success of my exorcisms!)

Monsignor Tom Cahalane (the proper Irish spelling of his surname is noted in the dedication of this book), the education director of the diocese in Tucson (well, he wasn't a monsignor then), a great smiling giant from West Cork (the Village of Glandore in the suppressed diocese of Ross near Skibereen—the Skibawn of the television version of *The Irish RM*), met me at the airport on my first arrival and announced, "Welcome home to Tucson, Andy."

The first Saturday evening I was there in my new house it was raining and I felt like a lonely exile. I went over to St. Odilia's parish, intending to participate in Mass on the laity's side of the altar rail and prepared to be skeptical, as I always am under those circumstances, on the quality of the sermon I would hear. Rarely have I been surprised under such circumstances. But St. Odilia was anything but what I expected. The church was new and well maintained; the choir was excellent; the liturgical services were carried out with éclat; and the young priest (I would later learn his name was Brian Bell) preached a wonderful sermon. I was taken with St. Odilia's and dreamed that night of the old days at Christ the King—images of people and events flooding back out of my unconscious. I called Cahalane on Monday and wondered if there was some way I might become part of the staff of St. Odilia's. "I'll have a word with the bishop," said your man from West Cork.

Next Saturday I said the five-thirty Mass.

I dedicated my book of Irish-American blessings to the priests and people of St. Odilia's: "I was homeless and you took me in." In Tucson, for the first time in many, many years, I had the experience of being wanted by both Church and university. Francis Green, the bishop of Tucson, sent me faculties of the diocese (permission to hear confessions and preach) by return mail when I informed him I was accepting the appointment at the university, and had me to dinner at his house the first week I was there (introducing me to the dangers of a margarita for the first time). Both he and President Schaeffer came to my first public lecture. Father Henry Miller, the pastor of St. Odilia's, was delighted to have me say Mass and preach and hang around in the back of church. The judgments made about me and my abilities by the University of Chicago and the Archdiocese of Chicago were categorically rejected by the University of Arizona and the Diocese of Tucson. I was an outsider, so I was welcome. Such, it is to be feared, is the nature of the human condition. "What do you expect?" Joe Bernardin said to me. "Chicago is your own country and your own people."

"But I'm no prophet," I insisted.

"Oh yes you are," he replied.

I believed him then—not that I'm a prophet, because I'm not, but that he thought I was.

It was, you will say, one more of my daft moves—thinking I could live in two worlds fifteen hundred miles apart, teaching and doing parish work in Tucson (activities I dearly love, which I could not do in Chicago) and maintaining my research base and my friendship network at home— Chicago always being home.

You would be correct: it was a daft Quixotish scheme and after many, many airplane flights back and forth between Chicago and Tucson— once in a while on the same day—I realized it was a daft idea. In fact, I am a marginal member of both Arizona and NORC, of both the Chicago community and the Tucson community.

My ambivalences did not decline with the passage of the years. I found myself more involved in Tucson and also more lonesome for Chicago. However, like a lot of other kinky moves which have caused me trouble of one sort or another, the Arizona appointment is something I would accept again if I had my life to live over. It provided me with powerful reassurance and morale reconstruction after hard times.

I enjoyed the classroom tremendously. My students divided into four separate categories: the Catholic kids who took the course because it was taught by a priest; the sociology students who thought I was a curiosity too good to miss; the critically minded left wing of the born-again Christians, for whom religious experience and faith were a help in getting through college but who didn't want to give up thinking (the born-again students were recruited for me by Bob Burns, a Dominican priest who was also the chairman of the Religious Study Committee, to which I was given a courtesy appointment at the university, and one of the finest priests it's ever been my pleasure to know); and returning students not in the seventeen-to-twenty-three-year-old college attendance window.

In this mixture one could not presume any sociological background and hence one could never fall back on jargon. Moreover, my method of instruction guaranteed a lively class period. I learned much from the

425

crossfire of discussion among these various groups of students and myself. It forced me to think through again my theories on the sociology of religion on which I was working with the Young Catholic Adult Study and led to my book *Religion: A Secular Theory* as well as *The Religious Imagination. Religion: A Secular Theory* is dedicated to my second class at the University of Arizona, because they used a manuscript version of the book as a text and one of the young women sociology students insisted that the least I could do in gratitude for their "dry run" on the manuscript was to dedicate it to them.

She was right.

My approach to the classroom is to assume that it is the student's time and money and it is the professor's obligation to maintain the student's attention. Therefore, I establish at the beginning of the quarter that while I have given them a reading list and subjects for discussion in each class, there is no such thing as required reading. As I say, it's their time and their money and I'm not going to try and make them do anything. Moreover, there are no course requirements. Since the university insists on some sort of proof of effort, they will at the end of the quarter either have to give me a paper or return on the final day of class a take-home exam. The paper can be on any subject they want in the field of the sociology of religion and I will read five pages of it. If they write more than five pages, they should circle the five pages they want me to read. If their stuff is really good they may even seduce me into reading more than five pages.

I then announce that having eliminated all the ritual and having discharged all our obligations to the academic game of material passing from the professor's notes to the student's notebook to the student's tests, we could go on to speak about the sociology of religion. Any questions?

They're silent for a moment and I say, "Hey, look, there's no point in my coming in and presenting canned lectures. If you want to know what I would say in canned lectures, just read my last book. It's your time and your money and I'm here to help you learn about the sociology of religion. So, what I will do is answer your questions on the subject for discussion today or any subject in the field of the sociology of religion. Sometimes I may even ask you some questions. If you don't have any questions, however, and I don't have any, then there's no reason for us to sit around."

I glance around the classroom expecting or seeming to expect a question. There isn't any, so I gather together my papers as though I'm about to leave and a hand goes up.

We've never had to adjourn a class early.

What about grades? I tell them early on that their class is to submit an advisory grade to me. They know how much reading they've done, how well they've participated in class, how hard they've worked, what sort of effort they've put into their papers, much better than I do. I reserve the right to lower or raise their grade but I want their advice. I also tell them that I assume that anybody intelligent enough to take my class probably rates minimally a B.

Only once have I lowered a grade and many times have I raised one, mostly for Protestant young women who find it hard to recommend an A for themselves even though they are at every class, participate in the discussions, read everything and do fine papers.

I use several gimmicks in the class. Notably, I show them Bob Fosse's film *All That Jazz*, because the film is a paradigm of my theory of the sociology of religion—a powerful grace experience which renews hope, an image retained in the memory from that experience which becomes a symbol and the story told to the rest of us in order to share that experience with us. *All That Jazz* is a remarkable film, and each time I see it with the students they catch something new that I've missed.

I also ask them how important they think ethnicity is in American society, and they tell me that it isn't important anymore, it's something no one pays any attention to. So then I pass around a sheet of paper which I announce constitutes a sudden surprise test (loud protests from the masses that I don't do that kind of thing). It is, in fact, a list of a hundred American names. I ask the students to identify the ethnic background of each name. Invariably the lowest proportion correct is somewhere around seventy-five. "Not sensitive to ethnicity, huh?" I ask them and we all laugh.

That trick I learned from Pete Rossi (with some modification). Another one I learned (also with some modifications) from Stan Lieberson.

I say, "Look, we all know that some people still have odd notions about members of other religious denominations. All of us in this classroom are mature and sophisticated and unprejudiced, but let's pretend for a moment that we're like those apes up at Tempe"—Arizona State, the Sun Devils, and our implacable enemies. "Let's put on the blackboard what they think in Sun Devil land about, let's say, Catholics. What are the things that Protestants kind of half-believe to be true about Catholics?" We put all the comments on the board amid much hilarity (you either laugh over such things or fight over them). Then we give Catholics an opportunity to respond, clarifying and defending where needed. The next step is to let the Catholics in the class say what their coreligionists at Tempe think about Protestants and give the Protestants their chance of replying (Catholics are firmly convinced that the children of Protestant ministers tend to be creepy and goody-goody, while Protestants are firmly convinced Catholic kids drink too much). Amazingly, all the old stereotypes persist, even though we know they're stereotypes and laugh about them. Amazingly, too, some of the stereotypes of both sides are exactly the same.

The feedback from the students and from the people at St. Odilia's (who pay me the compliment of calling the rectory to find out what time I'm going to say Mass) means a lot, as does the willingness of Bishop Green and Bishop Moreno to be seen in public with me, to let me take them to supper, and to commend my work.

So Arizona is wonderful for my morale and my self-confidence.

Tucson, then, has been and still is a healing experience. But it isn't home.

There was another healing experience going on in the summers at Grand Beach. The young man who was in charge of collecting water-skiers for me each morning showed up one day with a *girl*, a surprising phenomenon because by and large one did not expect Grand Beach teenage girls to be interested in skiing, and the girl's younger brother. She was a pretty high school sophomore with flashing brown eyes and a propensity to give detailed instructions to everyone. Her brother, a whimsical little (then) punk, was going into his freshman year and delighted in using (correctly, most of the time) elaborate words in his ordinary conversation (a couple of years later he would tell me that his girlfriend's mother had put the "quietus" on Katie's weekends with the Brennans at Grand Beach). Michele and Bob Brennan had entered my life and I think made up their minds, quite possibly that day, that they had come to stay. The next morning Michele showed up with two other girls, Kathleen Weber and Mary Carrol Murray.

"*Well*, Father Greeley, aren't we going to go water-skiing?"

428

Me: I didn't realize we had planned it for today, Michele.

Michele: (nodding vigorously) Yes, we did.

Me: Uh-uh.

Michele: (brooking no dissent) We *are* going skiing, aren't we, Father Greeley?

Me: I never argue with Irish women.

I once asked Michele, who is about half of Noele Marie Brigid Farrell in *Lord of the Dance,* if she ever lost an argument.

Michele: "Not *really.* Sometimes my Dad *thinks* that he wins arguments with me and I let him think that 'cause that is kinda good for him. Right?"

Bobby and Michele seemed, at first, much like any teenage boy and girl their ages, though there was a much closer and more caring relationship between the two of them than I've ever seen between an older sister and a younger (punk) brother, especially "Irish twins" born only a little more than twelve months apart. I was dragged off by the Irish twins to have supper at their house so that I could get to know their mother and father better. Until then, Bob and Jeanine were nodding acquaintances on the street. "My mother is a *terrible* cook," Michele confided to me, "but don't worry, I'll make the dessert!"

The Brennans were not typical Grand Beach people, not simply a commodities broker from River Forest, his gorgeous red-headed wife and their six children, for one of the six children, Tommy, was as badly handicapped a little boy as I've ever seen outside the hospital. Even at twelve, Tommy was no bigger than a baby and could do nothing for himself, probably not even see. The doctors were astonished that he lived more than a year and had often said it was just pure love from the other members of the family that kept him alive for so long. There was virtually everything imaginable wrong with the poor little fella. But what would have been a handicap or a burden or an unsupportable cross for many families became for the Brennans an extraordinary grace. Tommy, somehow or the other, held all the family together and intensified rather than weakened their love.

Their solution to the problem is not necessarily a solution for everyone, but it certainly was and is still a wonderful grace example for the people who know them both in Grand Beach and in River Forest. When Tommy died (Bobby found him dead in the bedroom at Grand Beach on Easter Monday) the family mourned him just as though he were another child in the family and it took a year for the mourning to come to an end. Michele, vigorous, outspoken, vivacious, seemed to miss him especially. She told me she could not remember ever in her life when she did not get up in the morning to wash him and clothe him and feed him. The mystery, first discovered on the ski boat, of why the Irish twins were so close to one another was explained: they were bound together by Tommy. And they still miss him. Jeanine said she could not possibly have done it without the help of all the children, especially Michele—a tough little five-year-old when Tommy came home from the hospital. The Brennans were a typical Irish upper-middle-class family who had reacted in an untypically graceful way to what, by any standards, was a family tragedy, with both astonishing and beneficial results for everyone involved. The inspiration in the Brennan clan was that they wore their bravery and generosity so lightly, without any apparent awareness of it. Such folks are a privilege to know. (My short story "Sionna Marie" is about the Brennans and Tommy.)

The conventional wisdom would say that a little girl burdened with responsibility for Tommy so young in life would be permanently affected by it. Permanently affected Michele certainly is, but not negatively. Twice in our water-skiing episodes, Bobby has saved up to buy a new super water-ski. Both times, the first day out after twelve unsuccessful efforts, he had given up and come back to the boat sulking, as only a teenage boy who has been thoroughly humiliated can sulk. Each time his sister blithely announced that she'd give it a try, dived off the boat and with her usual daffy nonchalance, popped out of the water and spun merrily back and forth across the wakes, ending up with a spectacular wipeout.

The first time this happened she swam back to the side of the boat with a big grin on her face.

"Not one word, young woman," I said. "Not one word!"

She grinned even more widely, dove under the water and came up with a perfectly serious face.

"Nice going, sis," Bob said heroically.

By the time we had returned to Grand Beach, however, Bob was prepared to announce to everyone who asked how the new ski worked, "Oh, I didn't get up. 'Course Shelly did it the first time!"

My friendship with the Brennans (acknowledged in the dedication of Lord of the Dance, "Friends in need") means much to me, especially because they came into my life after the final dissolution of my com-

430

munity, a trauma in which many of the members of my community said that I was incapable of sustained intense friendships. I wasn't sure they were wrong.

I ask myself occasionally what the Irish twins and the other Grand Beach young people like John Larkin, Julie Wallace, Lance and Heidi Hornaday, and Mike and Paul and Jenny Bolger are in my life, too young to be children, too old to be grandchildren. I think the answer is that they are my Hi Club. The parish priest can enjoy the fun of teenage enthusiasm and vitality without having to pay the various bills. Nonetheless they are a sacrament precisely because of the hope and promise such vitality represents. They reveal to us the energy and the superabundant life-sustaining grace of God.

There are teenagers in most of my novels—Lynnie's children in *Death in April*, Norine Cronin in *Thy Brother's Wife*, Maria's seminarian son, fast Eddie, in *Ascent into Hell*, Noele Farrell, teenager as protagonist in *Lord of the Dance*, and the various Ryan adolescents, Tim, Caitlin, O'Connor the Cat, Packy Mike and Packy Jack, Brigid, in my tales of that off-the-wall family.

A few reviewers thought Noele Farrell was an intolerable brat. Most, however, loved her, even as I do. (A creepy nun who claimed she worked with teenagers said Noele was "unrealistic." Geek.) However, she is certainly the kind of kid who would drive a sensible parent crazy, in part because her enthusiasm is not tempered by experience and in part because her hope is not tempered by cynicism. It is in the latter role that teenagers are sacraments and it is that role they play in my stories.

Later I would understand, as a few of the relationships in my small group church were patched together, that the charge I was incapable of friendship was another aspect of the projection mechanisms at work. Nonetheless, having been badly scarred in the process, I behaved warily in the first phases of my relationship with Bob and Jeanine and their kids. "It won't work," Jeanine said bluntly. "We'll never let you get away."

Admirable sentiments.

I think the only mistake one can make with such people is the mistake for which Michele intermittently gives boyfriends their walking papers— "He started taking me for granted. Can you imagine *that*, Father Greeley?"

No, I really can't imagine it, except it happens all the time. Fortunately for Michele, she was raised in a family where the father didn't take any of the women for granted—and would be in horrible trouble if he had!

The healing that occurred, both in Tucson and in Grand Beach, with the Brennans and with other new friends met there began before the pilfered-diary episode and made it possible for me to make it through that experience of being "torn down because he's successful" with a little bit more serenity. They also helped me to survive the outpouring of hatred that accompanied the publication and the success of *The Cardinal Sins*. "God," as my mother would have said, "shapes the back to fit the burden."

Meanwhile the ordinary work went on. The Knights of Columbus commissioned us to study young Catholics, and proved themselves excellent clients (save for the single matter of CCD pressure to cover up the finding of the success of Catholic schools) until the outburst over *The Cardinal Sins* led them to back away from me and the project.

The bad news in the Young Catholic Adult Study was that Catholics under thirty simply no longer took the Church's sexual ethic seriously. The good news, however, was that their images of God and Jesus and Mary and heaven were still powerfully and intensely Catholic and that their images also had a strong effect on their behavior, religious and social, a stronger effect than did their doctrinal orthodoxy. Moreover, we found in Catholics under twenty an emerging new religious sensibility heavily emphasizing the affectionate nature of one's relationship with God. Some of this sensibility was to be found in those over twenty too, but it seemed concentrated especially in the younger generation (campus ministers around the country are reporting the same phenomenon).

We also discovered that parish priests and husbands played a decisive role in the construction of this post-Vatican religious sensibility. "How do you implement an ecumenical council?" I asked in a phrase that Jean Jadot, the apostolic delegate, would frequently quote: "Through mothers, husbands and priests. How else?"

The Young Catholic Adult Study was rich in intriguing findings: a confidant relationship with a priest, for example, facilitated not only a woman's marital happiness, but her husband's too. Moreover, she and her husband were more likely than others of their generation to advocate both a celibate clergy and the ordination of women—perhaps feeling that men, too, would benefit from such confidant relationships.

There was a strong relationship, moreover, between the intensity of one's prayer life in the first decade of marriage and the intensity of one's sexual relationship. Favorable images of Mary correlated with sexual fulfillment in marriage. Sexual fulfillment during the last years of the first decade of marriage (a *Kramer vs. Kramer* phenomenon) was paralleled by, related to, and in part supported by a rebound in the intensity of their religious imagination. The most powerful influences on a young person's religious imagination were parents, friends, teachers, priests, and spouse —but only if the quality of the relationship was good. It didn't matter so much whether one had gone to a Catholic school or how many years one had attended, but how high one rated the quality of religious instruction. Moreover, it did not matter how active one was in the parish but rather how high one rated the quality of sermons. Finally, the higher the sexual fulfillment in marriage, the stronger the correlation of the religious imaginations between husband and wife. St. Paul was right. Marriage *is* the great sacrament.

My theory of the sociology of religion was complete. Religion is an utterly secular experience in that it begins, first of all, in the ordinary events of life which renew our hope, sometimes experiences as spectacular as the ecstasies of which William James wrote in *The Varieties of Religious Experience*, and at other times as simple and as ordinary as the touch of a friendly hand, reconciliation after a quarrel, the smile of a stranger on the street, a little kid toddling across the room, a glorious sunrise, the moon glowing on a winter lake at night, etc., etc., etc. Our religion is the result of those experiences in our life which renew our hope and give us a sense of purpose and direction in shaping the remaining events of our life and our religious symbol system is the memory of those hope-renewal experiences, normally expressed in terms of the overarching images of our tradition, which have been especially powerful hope-renewal experiences.

The paradigm was now clear: the hope-renewal experience (which one could call grace); the memory of that experience set aside in the special category of memories we call symbols because they give direction and purpose to our life (such symbols can be called sacraments because they reveal order and purpose to us); the stories by which we share hope-renewal experiences and images with others normally by trying to stir up in their imagination memories of experiences that parallel our own (stories are an attempt of imagination to communicate to other imagination, bypassing as best it can the barriers of cognitive proposition); and the community, which represents a group of people to whom we can tell our stories because they share our imagery, and whose images in turn shape our own further hope-renewal experiences and recollections.

To say that religion is story before it is theology is not to say it is make-believe or fictional or a "fairy" story unless one has a sophisticated under-standing that fairy stories also impose meaning on life. A story is a map, a paradigm, a template by which we impose order and meaning on the phenomena of our experience and attempt to shape and direct our future experience. To say that the resurrection of Jesus is a story is not to deny its historical truth but it is to say, rather, that its historical truth is less astonishing than its religious message, namely that life is stronger than death and that the God who raised Jesus from the dead will also raise us from the dead.

The questions about God, Jesus, Mary and heaven that we had used in the Young Catholic Adult Study proved fruitful. In 1983, with money from my book royalties, I commissioned NORC to add the God and Life After Death image questions to its General Social Survey. Unfortunately, the same items did not work quite so well in the General Social Survey. While in the Young Catholic Adult Study they had been administered in a do-it-yourself questionnaire, in the General Social Survey they were administered orally, and it turned out the respondents were likely to engage in a "yes-saying" phenomenon, i.e., they tended to agree enthu-siastically with all the images of God presented to them. Thus, at the suggestion of Tom Smith, the director of the General Social Survey project at NORC, in the 1984 GENSOC we gave our respondents a forced choice: they were to locate themselves on a seven-point scale between the images of God as Mother/Father, Master/Spouse, King/Friend, Lover/Judge, Liberator/Redeemer, Creator/Healer.

Two factors emerged: a Healer/Liberator factor and a Mother/Spouse/Friend/Lover factor. Those respondents who scored high on the latter factor were notably more likely to oppose capital punishment, to support government help for blacks to achieve equality, to approve of civil liberties for Communists, homosexuals and atheists, to support racial integration and not to vote for Ronald Reagan. Moreover, this "Grace Scale" con-tinued to be a powerful and significant predictor, even after the effects of education, sex, region, age and political and religious liberalism were taken into account. The evidence was that one could as well leave out in a survey these questions of religious imagery as one could leave out education or sex or region. Religion did matter after all: It was a major predictor variable, after all. Even within political ideology groups ("conservative," "liberal," "moderate") the religious imagination scale predicted a 15-percentage-point swing in the 1980 presidential election vote (as remembered in the spring of 1984) and in the 1984 vote as measured by Gallup the day after the election. (I must here acknowledge my gratitude to George Gallup for so quickly integrating our religious-image material into his regular survey.)

Any variable that can do that is sociologically exciting.

At last, after fifteen years of searching for it, we had a measure of the religious imagination that worked—one that strongly correlated with other attitudes and behaviors and that had considerable predictive power.

When my research assistant, Sean Durkin (nepotism, too, begins at home), presented me with the first table from the 1984 General Social Survey, it was a bit of a dramatic moment. Would we finally have a religion predictor variable that worked?

We did! I shouted enthusiastically. Finally, after all the years of trying, there was a religious variable that was as essential as the other standard analytic items in sociological research.

"How long did it take and how much did it cost to find it?" Sean, a young man with a comic flair, asked.

"Fifteen years," I said, "a couple of hundred thousand dollars of other people's money and, so far, forty thousand dollars of royalties."

Sean considered. "Yeah, it is worth shouting about!"

You bet your life.

The stage was set for my sister and me to sit down and do *How to Save the Catholic Church*.

The argument of the book, briefly, is that the Catholic experience is sacramental. It sees God disclosing Himself/Herself in the people, objects and events of ordinary life. Catholicism is not worried about too close an identification of God with world. It does not cause all that much concern to a "radical monotheism" which sharply disjoins God and world. It may be aware of some bitter experience of the danger of idolatry but it is not so preoccupied with this, as are fellow Yahwehists in Protestantism, Jewry and Islam, as to banish God from the world and make it a bleak and unsacred place. Moreover, the Catholic imagination is analogical: it sees God as similar to the people, objects, events and relationships of life. It would quickly add that God is different from all these, but Catholicism will still, in its first instincts, declare the similarity between God and world and only in its second instincts assert also a dissimilarity. Our fellow Yahwehistic religions proceed in the opposite direction, proclaiming dissimilarity and then, perhaps grudgingly, conceding similarity. We are likely to go over the extreme into superstition and have done so often in our history, but they are more likely to go to the extreme of totally separating God from the world and making the world a bleak and hollow and evil place. The quintessential Protestant says that the only sacrament we have is Jesus and Him crucified; the quintessential Catholic says that while the crucified and risen Savior is the central sacrament, everything else is or is capable of becoming a sacrament. "All is Grace."

The Catholic story is comic because it believes in the basic goodness of the world and the basic goodness of humankind (both sacramental, both analogical, that is to say both revealing of and metaphors for God). The Catholic instinct has always been to emphasize the basic and fundamental capacity of the world and its institutions and people for salvation—thus to believe in fresh starts, new beginnings and happy endings which are new beginnings. The Christmas story is the happy-ending story par excellence, and while the Catholic, in the midst of Christmas festivities, does not deny that the child who is born will die, it does nonetheless insist that it is the *birth* of a child which is what the story is about and not the death, because even the child who eventually dies on the cross only dies for a time and will be born again, as all of us are born again. The Holy Grail story that we know is a tragic story, a life-denying, flesh-denying tale, a Catholic might say a "Protestant" tale, for Lancelot gets neither Grail nor girl. But the more ancient and more pagan Celtic version of the story ends differently. The Irish Lancelot (my King Cormac MacDermot) finds the magic cup and gets the magic princess Belvacheem or Fair Breast, who in my story is Biddy, the girl down the street. Perhaps one should say, to be perfectly accurate, that Biddy gets him because she is no fainting, mid-Victorian gothic heroine but a vigorous worker of magic in her own right, and sometimes it appears that she pursues the King as hotly as he pursues her (a typical Irish woman, one might add). If Biddy represents the womanliness of God she also represents the Hound of Heaven.

So, according to some who study my novels, do all my heroines.

This flesh-affirming, life-affirming version of the Grail legend is Catholic; the life-denying, flesh-denying Arthur/Lancelot version is Manichean. Is comedy stronger than tragedy? The Catholic imagination says tragedy doesn't have the final word. That even when the ultimate tragedy of death comes, there is still something more to be said and that more will be the comedy of Bethlehem.

Finally, the Catholic community is organic. Catholic imagination does not picture society as a group of isolated individuals seeking their own purposes and goals, nor the religious society as a collectivity of isolated individuals relating to God. Rather, the world the Catholic sees is one of dense, complex interrelationships. We do not come into the world, live or die as isolated individuals, but rather as members of families, neighborhoods, local communities, friendship groups, work groups, all interconnecting and overlapping. The Church is nothing more than the local dense interactive organic community relating to God. We believe in organic community not as a matter of choice but, rather, once we make the commitment to a social order which, however defective, is nonetheless sacramental, we have no choice but to think of our Church as that sacramental, revelatory, potentially sacred social order actually turning to God. Human society may often turn corrupt as well as an organic human church but it is not basically corrupt, not intrinsically corrupt, so the Catholic imagination has always insisted.

How these different imaginations emerge is beyond the scope of this volume and beyond the scope of the book that Mary Jule and I wrote. Briefly, Catholicism was able to make its peace in an outburst of optimism after the resurrection, with all that was good and true and beautiful in paganism and in the pagan nature religions. None of the other great Yahwehistic world religions could so easily accept the pagan trappings.

How to Save the Catholic Church was written after several of my novels were published, but it comes out of the same matrix of intellectual and religious concerns that shape the novels. It carries essentially the same message: the most effective strategy for the Catholic Church today is to rediscover, reanalyze, reinterpret and renew its traditional imaginative heritage, its vast and rich repertoire of experience, symbol, story and community. That strategy seems so obvious one wonders why it would be necessary to argue it.

Some Catholic traditionalists advocate returning to the *status quo ante* 1960, as though that were possible and as though they remember accurately what it was like in the 1950s. Our strategy is to go back long before 1960, to Hopkins in the nineteenth century, Rubens in the sixteenth century, Michelangelo in the fifteenth, Aquinas and Dante in the thirteenth, Anselm and Bernard in the twelfth, etc., etc., etc. But so dry and arid and predigested was the Catholic tradition that was served up to most of us during our educational years, we don't realize there are great resources and riches in our own traditions. Therefore, we borrow from other people and from the current fads because we believe our own resources have been discredited and depleted. A Catholic neotraditionalist like Michael Novak can blithely say—and go unchallenged—that there is nothing in the Catholic tradition that justifies calling God a mother. Michael is up to his usual game of talking about something he has not studied, for there are many, many writers in the Catholic tradition who did call God a mother (and a lover and a brother and a sister and a nurse and all kinds of other relational opposites—based on the marvelous sacramental insight that all human relationships reveal something special to us about God's love).

The strategy Mary Jule and I advocate requires an exploration of the Catholic tradition. Our position, paraphrasing G. K. Chesterton, is not that such an exploration has been tried and found wanting, but that it has been found hard and not tried.

The Catholic heritage is too rich, too variegated, too ancient and too powerful to be ignored forever. Those who reject it either to leave the Church or to be swept along by passing enthusiasms inside it are a judgment on us for the shallow and superficial version of the heritage with which we indoctrinated young people not so long ago. That the heritage itself is still alive and well, if only in the experiential dimensions of the personality of the faithful, is evident from our research, which showed that Catholics were a third of a standard deviation higher than Protestants on a scale which measured the intimacy and affection of their images of God.

My years in Arizona, then, were a time of healing, of reorganization and reintegration of my own experience, of solid progress in understanding the religious imagination and of synthesizing much of my previous work into an organized and systematic program for the Catholic Church in its present crisis. My winters in Tucson (combined with the summers in Grand Beach) were a time of renewal and rededication. Once again without quite realizing it, I was crossing another rubicon in my life. My first two novels had disappeared. I had vowed I would continue to write fiction but was swept up in the Papal election study, the move to Arizona, the strains within my community, the conflicts in the Archdiocese (on Easter Sunday, the cardinal said I was a "damn liar"). Then there came an opportunity to work with Berney Geis, one of the great men of American fiction publishing.

I said to myself again: Shea and Tracy are writing about the theology of story; you are writing about the sociology of story; isn't it time that *someone* write stories? Are we not even more ready now for theological novels, for comedies of grace?

I had asked that question before I was caught up in the excitement of the Papal election research. I had to ask it again, more forcefully. My first two novels disappeared. Should I try again to write stories of God, comedies of grace?

If you don't, who will?

I hesitated. My convictions about the need for religious storytelling were still strong. Yet to work with Geis would require time, lots of it. The old fear returned. What if you fail utterly in telling stories? I asked myself. Look at all the time that would have gone down the drain—time perhaps better invested in the nonfiction that you know from experience you can write.

There was one question, however, that it never occurred to me to ask. The question was not "What if they fail?" The question was "What if they succeed?"

Anyway we saddled up Rosinante, said, "What the hell," and in the summer of 1979 I wrote *The Cardinal Sins*.

Then the one thing I never expected happened.

"Only one week on the *NYT* best-seller list," I said to Berney and Darlene Geis in New York on pub date in the spring of 1981. "I'll settle for one day."

Instead it was there for one year.

CHAPTER
23
Storyteller

LYNNIE

God-like
I made you
Out of dreamy stuff—
Apricot figment—
Human-like
You struggle free
Lusting for life
Of your own
Revealing

me
God-like
I now
Belong to you

"All right, Kevin, I'll say it and you'll have to mop up the tears on this hard floor of yours. I blamed the Church and God for things that were inside me and my family. I focused on all the ugly things and forgot about Father Conroy and Sister Caroline and First Communion and May Crownings and Hi Club dances, and Midnight Mass and all those wonderful things I loved so much. I gave them all up because I was angry. I blamed the Church for Tim's death. I loved him so much. I couldn't save him and I thought the Church should save him. Even when I was doing it, I knew I was wrong and that someday I'd be kneeling on the floor before you and pleading to be let back in."

"And now you have done it," I said, feeling a huge burden lift away and go spiraling off into space. "And the damn fool Church says, 'Ellen Foley Curran Strauss, we really didn't notice you were gone, because we never let you go.'"

This dialogue between Kevin and Ellen is the central moment in *The Cardinal Sins*. All my theology and my sociology and my pastoral experience and my life are crammed into the symbols and loves in those two paragraphs. Ken Prewitt, sometime director of NORC and now the president of the Social Science Research Council (and at this writing the new vice-president of the Rockefeller Foundation), says that he will read no more of my technical works, because all the sociology is in the stories and far more palatable there. It is the hard kernel of the book that these two chaste lovers pursue each other in God's service.

Many letter writers single this passage out, quite correctly, as the most moving in the book. Some tell me it has brought them, like Ellen, back to the Church.

I have never been asked about it by an interviewer. Only one book reviewer, not Catholic, has ever mentioned it.

How can it be missed? I wonder. How can readers be obsessed by the phony question of sex in a novel by a priest and miss the theme of the powerful sexual attraction between Kevin and Ellen, an attraction which is salvific for both?

The juxtaposition of stories about sex and celibate priests is enough to make many people quite incapable of paying attention to anything else. The startling nature of the *apparent* contrast priest/sex blinds them to what the story is *truly* about.

Add money to the sex-and-priest interaction and you have a surefire recipe for reviewer blindness.

442

I admit to being baffled about the obsession of critics with sex in my novels. As Archbishop Bernardin said to me in New York shortly before the publication of *The Cardinal Sins*, the sex in the book is mild in comparison with that in most modern novels. I suppose that for all too long the Church tried to present priests as men devoid of human feelings and emotions, perhaps persuading many Catholics and non-Catholics we were more like angels than humans. When a priest writes a novel in which there is an admission that passion is part of human life, it is so great a surprise that partly in real, partly in feigned shock many readers and critics can see nothing else.

The principal theme of *The Cardinal Sins*—obviously and self-evidently, I would have thought—is that God's love pursues the four main characters through their human loves for one another, sometimes licit, sometimes not, always with a sexual component, but never with the irresistible compulsion to sin.

It does not seem to me that it is such an original or daring theme. Nor one hard to perceive or recognize. That human passion is a sacrament and an instrument of divine passion is a notion as old as Yahwehism. It was used many times by the Catholic writers who flourished in the first half of this century, most notably Paul Claudel and Graham Greene. I would not have imagined it would be missed completely by so many of those who in one forum or another felt called upon to comment on the book.

The chagrin, the dismay, the outrage that a priest was using or trying to use this theme blocked the vision of many commentators. So great was their anger that the central theme itself was missed.

That is rotten theology of the priesthood because it separates a priest from the human condition. It is dangerously close to heresy. "Priests," a friendly ecclesiastic wrote me, "should not describe licentiousness."

But sex is not necessarily licentious. Nor is every description of sex that may be illicit necessarily a licentious one. We cannot hold the traditional Catholic position on the sacramentality of sex, we cannot commit ourselves to the theology of the Pope's audience talks and then think that sex is dirty.

"Why do you write about *sex?*" they ask. "Can't you find something more edifying or religious or important to write about?"

The answer, I think, is "no." Sex is edifying and religious and important. If that is offensive to some people, then there is nothing I can do about it. They do not understand that for those who believe human passion reveals divine passion, it is impossible to pretend for purposes of religious uplift that God made an artistic mistake in arranging the mechanics of procreation and that therefore we must tell our stories as though that mistake had not occurred.

All my novels are about God's love. They are stories of "epiphanies" of the "breaking in" of God to the ordinary events of human life. I think that is so obvious that I ought not to have to say it. If in fact I must say it repeatedly the reason is that many people have personal hang-ups that prevent them from seeing the obvious, and some people are sufficiently malicious as deliberately to deceive others about the subject matter of my stories.

Nora Cronin realizes that God is a loving mother. Hugh Donlon finally understands that Maria reveals a God who loves without love ever being merited. Noele Farrell, watching a sunbeam dance down Hoyne Avenue on a cloudy Palm Sunday, comprehends that while the powers of hell may hurt her again, they will not prevail against her. Catherine Collins sees that Nick Curran has been the Hound of Heaven relentlessly but respectfully pursuing her. Anne Reilly, emerging from a psychotic interlude surrounded by her "Angels of September" (Priest, Lover, Psychiatrist), knows that forgiveness is a reality that is as ever-present as the air she breathes. Red Kane is pursued by a "transcendental designated hitter" rather like his wife, Eileen. When Lisa Malone opens her eyes in the Olson Pavilion of Northwestern Hospital, Blackie Ryan realizes that it is both Halloween and Christmas and that the stars have never gone out. Sue Quinlan understands that her explosive passion for Larry Burke is an invitation to rebirth from a God who loves her even more than Larry does.

Why do so many in the national media miss these epiphanies around which I cluster enough pointers so that no one can doubt what they are supposed to mean?

Reviewers, interviewers and feature writers always need a cheap and easy lead. "Priest writes steamy novels" is a great lead even if it isn't true. When *The Cardinal Sins* was published, I found myself not so much explaining what my story meant as defending the notion that a priest might put sex in his stories. It was a weird experience. For the first few months after the novel's publication I was as close to Lewis Carroll's

Wonderland as anything I have experienced. The book went through ten printings and within the first year sold over three million copies. The mail I received was overwhelmingly favorable, the first time in my life that mail was not four or five to one against me. The letter writers understood I was writing a theological novel, a comedy of grace. On the other hand the Catholic reviews were as sustained an outpouring of hate and resentment as I had ever encountered. Perhaps half the secular reviews were favorable, some quite favorable, but virtually none seemed to have noticed the theological themes I had thought were self-evident and which my mail indicated many of the readers thought self-evident too.

"Why do people buy your books?"

My fellow priests had a ready answer, provided for them by Catholic reviewers: "Curiosity about steamy novels written by a priest."

The novels are not steamy, despite the frequent use of that smear word in the media, nor do most readers find them so (only 11 percent as we shall see). Curiosity about a novel written by a priest? Other priests have written novels, and one has promoted his book with a single theme: "Greeley writes garbage, I don't."

Books by and about priests don't automatically hit best-seller lists, not even books with sex in them, not even books with more sex than is in my stories. Part of the fascination with my early novels, I am sure, was that they were about priests, for priests are fascinating people—men standing halfway between heaven and earth, between God and humans. But *Lord of the Dance*, which was about a sixteen-year-old girl and the forty-year-old man she brought back from the dead, has been the most successful of all my novels, and priests play only a minor part in that story.

I sometimes wonder if there is not a statute of limitations on the "curiosity argument." Eight best-sellers in five years: I would think the Catholic reviewers would tire of such an explanation. Doubtless there was some curiosity at work in the sale of *The Cardinal Sins*, but with 80 percent of the readers saying they can hardly wait for the next book, it would seem by now that the curiosity factor is not all that influential.

The priest who promoted his book with the charge that mine was garbage has an explanation for the sales: my books have jacket covers which feature "naked women chewing crucifixes"—an inaccurate description of the jackets and probably an irrelevant one, given the fact that three-quarters of the readers of the books are women (women buy about two-thirds of all the novels sold in the country).

In the summer and autumn of 1981 while *The Cardinal Sins* was inexorably climbing the best-seller lists, I had no data. Yet there was no mystery in the publishing world about what was happening. The book had that most precious ingredient of all in the creation of a best-seller: word-of-mouth. Readers were telling other readers it was a good story, with vivid characters, and a religious message. This was exactly what I had hoped to accomplish. People liked the story and grasped its religious theme.

A frequent charge against *The Cardinal Sins* in Catholic circles is that while maybe it was a readable story, it was after all only trash. It was not "great literature" or a "literary novel." A Catholic woman reviewer tore the book apart on "literary" grounds (none of them pointing at its actual weaknesses, by the way) and then added as an afterthought, "I admit I couldn't put the book down."

So I had succeeded with her too. No greater compliment can be paid a storyteller. Better even than a Nobel Prize is a word-of-mouth that you couldn't put the book down.

The Cardinal Sins, like all books, had its faults and limitations. Generally the critics, whether friendly or hostile, paid no attention to these. It was a straight linear story. It had been overedited, so that the language was often as flat as an old telegraph message. There was a change in genre toward the end. Some of the characters did not have the complexity of texture they might have had. It moved almost too rapidly.

I agreed to much more editing than I would accept after *Thy Brother's Wife* because I was still learning the art of plot and narrative and did not understand what one should retain and what one should give up to an editor. Many of the faults mentioned above would have been mitigated if I had been more jealous in defense of my text. It was my first major effort in storytelling, however, and I wanted the story to be the strongest part of the book.

One of the more commonplace reactions from priests who would claim to be my friends was to say, "It's a great story, but..."

"But nothing," I would reply. "What I want here is a story. The rest comes later."

Without storytelling, what is the motive for fiction? There are doubtless some academic novelists writing for other academics who condemn story-telling on the grounds that ordinary readers like stories. Fine, if that's what you're into. If you want to write books for professors (whose praise that a book is "intelligent" often means they are quite sure nonprofessors won't like it), then by all means do so. But you should understand that for most of human history, it would have been incomprehensible that anyone would want to tell a story people would not enjoy listening to.

How did it all start?

Jim Miller, a political poll-taker in New York, and one of my closest friends, suggested that I find an agent in New York and referred me to his own agent, Hilda Lindley, the former advertising manager of the *New York Times Book Review*. Hilda, in her turn, introduced me to her good friend Berney Geis, a Jewish leprechaun in his early seventies who is one of the authentic geniuses of the American book-publishing industry (among other things, Berney invented the publicity tour, which has led me on some exhausted occasions to call down upon his curly white hair millions of ancient Celtic imprecations). Bernie thought that *The Magic Cup* and *Death in April* showed some storytelling talent and suggested the idea for the plot of *The Cardinal Sins*.

"It's been years since Henry Morton Robinson wrote *The Cardinal*. Could we have a story about two priests who grow up together, one becomes a cardinal and the other remains a simple priest? At the end the simple priest must save the cardinal from his own mistakes."

"We could call it *The Cardinal Sin*," said Darlene Geis.

Me: *Sins*.

A few days later, in the Beverly Wilshire hotel, on a promotion tour for *The Making of the Popes*, I rode up on the elevator for perhaps fifteen seconds with a petite, attractive blond woman in her early forties. That's my heroine, I thought, and Ellen Foley, God's most powerful sacrament in *The Cardinal Sins*, was born.

Six weeks later I submitted to Geis the first four or five chapters and he wrote back regretfully that I just didn't really seem to have narrative talent. I called him on the phone and demanded to know what was wrong with them. He spoke about the pace of the story, lack of action at the beginning, the absence of "hooks" at the end of each chapter, to draw the reader on to the next chapter.

"Is that all?" I demanded. "All right, I'll rewrite it."

Berney said that was up to me, and that he would pay the advance

447

he had promised but he didn't want to let me get my hopes too high.

Me: Hang the advance. I intend to write the story.

A month later he had the manuscript of *The Cardinal Sins* in his hands, and several months thereafter, in the wake of brilliant editorial work done by Judith Shafran, his vice-president and editorial director, Berney was ready to auction the novel to the twelve publishers to whom he normally submitted his "copublished" works.

Berney and other "copublishers" or "packagers" play a fascinating interstitial role in the world of New York book publishing. While packagers and agents overlap, they tend to have somewhat distinct roles, with the packager normally doing far more editorial work and exercising far more control over what happens in publication than an ordinary agent does.

Many novice writers resent the thought of an agent or a copublisher taking a cut of their profits. In both cases, however, what one purchases is wisdom and expertise. *The Magic Cup* sold seventy-five hundred copies, *The Cardinal Sins* sold three million copies. The quality of the story wasn't much different, if the craft in *The Cardinal Sins* was better. The difference was the agent and the packager.

The companies to which Berney offered *The Cardinal Sins* did not rush to snap it up. Only Warner Books, a relatively small but vigorously growing subsidiary of the Warner Communications giant, seemed interested. Howard Kaminsky, the witty, energetic young president of Warner (now, alas, translated to Random House, though ably replaced by Laurence Kirshbaum), respected Berney Geis's abilities at searching out storytellers and read the manuscript himself. As he said later to me, "It was a great story; I couldn't put it down."

He turned it over to his vice-president, Bernard Shir-Cliff, a shrewd veteran of the publishing business, and Shir-Cliff's independent reaction was the same: "Wonderful story!" They didn't buy the book because it was by a priest (they really didn't believe I *was* a priest, if the truth be told) or because it was about priests but because it was a good story.

Obviously I accepted their judgment, and just as obviously, so did the readers, but what makes my stories eminently readable is something I do not understand, probably will never understand, and I hope need not ever understand. Just the same, I have a committee of forty or so people in Chicago and around the country who read my books even before they go to my agent, Nat Sobel. If any of these folks tell me they don't enjoy the story, then I know I'm in serious trouble. Nat and his wife, Judith

Weber, and their associate, Marian Young, also read the book and give me their reactions. Only after I've integrated the reactions of the Sobel team and my review panel do we trust it to the editors at Warner. Then Warner's gifted editor in charge of me, Patrick O'Connor (for several earlier books the talented John Cox), goes over the book yet again, checking especially for effectiveness of story structure. The story isn't everything, but it is the essential thing; if the story doesn't work, then nothing else matters.

Hilda Lindley died of cancer between the auctioning of *The Cardinal Sins* and its publication, at the same time that my friends in Chicago demanded that I delete any references to them from the dedication of the book (without having read it). I learned that Hilda was dying, and *The Cardinal Sins* was dedicated to her. She died as she lived: quietly, efficiently, creating as little trouble or difficulty for others as she possibly could. We all thought she was in the hospital with the flu. Her husband asked me to stop in and see her and I was appalled to realize that, at the most, she had a couple of days to live. I went back to Berney Geis's office, ashen they told me, slumped down at a desk, and said to Berney and Judy Shafran, "We'll never see Hilda again in this world."

I suppose a word should be said here about the cover art on the books. The first time I visited the Warner Books office (wearing my Roman collar to reassure Howard Kaminsky and company that indeed I was a priest) the art director, Gene Light, showed me several possible designs for the jacket of *The Cardinal Sins*, none of which caught my fancy. At the bottom of the stack was the cover we actually used. "I know you won't like this one, Father Greeley," Gene said. (Having grown up in an almost entirely Catholic neighborhood in Brooklyn, Gene was the only one at Warner Books who insisted on calling me Father.)

I didn't know the background of the photograph when I looked at the cover, but it struck me instantly that it was a work of ingenious and sophisticated art, with clear allusions to the classics of American photography (like Callahan and Steiglitz and Westin, for example) and to older Greek antiquity. It was good art, an attractive picture which hinted at one of the themes of the book (God attracting us to Himself/Herself through our sexual attractions to others), and would demand attention on a paperback rack.

"Go with it," I said, much to everyone's astonishment. Later I would learn that my initial instincts were correct. It was one of a series of large-frame Polaroid self-portraits done by the young American feminist photographer Rena Small, with precisely the intent I saw in the picture: to celebrate in a nonexploitive way the erotic attraction of a womanly body. The photograph, along with others in the series, had hung in galleries and museums around the world (including the Center for Creative Photography at the University of Arizona) and had been featured in the highly reputable and serious *Camera Arts* magazine.

Are the covers designed to sell books? Of *course* they are. What other purpose except to present attractively the contents of the book? Are they exploitive? Obviously Ms. Small doesn't think so and neither do the galleries and magazines that have featured her work and neither do I. Those who complain about the obscenity of the jacket for *The Cardinal Sins* reveal more about themselves, their own prudery, and their own artistic ignorance than they do about the jacket. *Thy Brother's Wife* is a Holy Thursday story. The gold cross in the mouth of the red-haired woman on the cover represents the oral incorporation of God in the Eucharist. The *Ascent into Hell* cover is an allusion to Michelangelo's Creation, except that God, on this cover, wears fingernail polish and has breasts (more modestly covered than would be accomplished by most prom dresses or swimsuits) because one of the main themes of the story is the womanliness of God. Finally, on the cover of *Lord of the Dance* the reclining dancer, with her long red hair and a hint of enormous energy at rest, represents Noele Marie Brigid Farrell, the red-haired, green-eyed Christmas child who, in the story, symbolizes the Church. I sometimes think the people who moan about the covers of my books would only be happy if I chose the kind which would frighten readers away!

My novels are "stories of God." God is the principal character in all my novels, even making a brief walk-on in Nora Cronin's mystical experience in *Thy Brother's Wife* (in which Nora realizes that God is a Mother) and becoming a central character in *Patience of a Saint* as He wrestles, like the angel with Jacob, poor Redmond Peter Kane (and, like the angel, making up Her own rules as She goes along). They are not, I trust, moralistic stories. I don't try to persuade people to appropriately ethical behavior. Neither did the gifted storytellers who composed the David and Joseph stories in the Jewish scripture, nor did Jesus in His parables, which are singularly free (save in the theological commentaries evangelists add to them) of moralism for edification. God acts in my stories, as S/He does in the parables of Jesus: as someone working endlessly behind the scenes, pursuing us recklessly and relentlessly and passionately. It is perhaps awkward and embarrassing to have a God who behaves that way, but there is no escape from the image of such a God, either in the Jewish or the Christian scriptures.

I do not write, as the *Wall Street Journal* suggested, "to entertain so as to educate." Such an aim would pervert the storytelling enterprise. I rather write to captivate so as to illuminate, to capture the attention of the reader so that s/he will be open to the illumination of the "breaking in" of God in my stories. I do not intend so much to teach doctrinal truth as to illumine life with the explosive light of God's love.

When I began to write novels, I took as my model the so-called "Catholic novels" I had read as a young man and which my generation had to study in Catholic high schools and colleges—Graham Greene, Evelyn Waugh, François Mauriac, Georges Bernanos, men who wrote about sin and redemption, about death and resurrection, about old failures and new beginnings. To say that my goals are the same as theirs is not to say—as a Catholic questioner almost always asks, when I make this observation—that I have the same kind of talent as, for example, Graham Greene.

He is my favorite novelist. His book *The Power and the Glory* is the best book on the priesthood ever written (privately condemned by the Vatican, incidentally). He has been cheated out of his Nobel by cheap, tawdry Swedish academic politics. I make no claim to be in that league. Catholic reviewers are quick to insist to their readers that I am not a Greene or a Waugh or an Undset—or even, in *The National Catholic Reporter*, that I am not a Dante or a Michelangelo. Of *course* I'm not. I'm me and I'm not telling anyone else's stories but my own. While I admire Greene's work as that of the best Catholic novelist of our time, my vision of God is different from his, and my stories are much less morose because, I suppose, I have a much less morose temperament. I will yield his being an infinitely better writer, but I will also contend that my Catholic vision is more traditional than his because my books are much more likely to move toward a comic or happy ending. Blackie Ryan remarks at the end of *Virgin and Martyr*, "They will live happily ever after . . . they would have only three or four furious fights each week. . . . At least one day of the week they would not speak to each other . . . and on five days their life would be ordinary and routine. . . . But on the remaining day... ah, perhaps on that day would know the love which is reputed to reflect the Love that launched the universe in a vast *bang*.

"Maybe even a day and a half some weeks.

"Not much, perhaps. Only a little day—a little bit of light in the gloom, a little bit of life in the entropy, a little bit of love in the indifference.

"Maybe that is enough. Maybe, even, it is everything."

Not exactly a Hollywood happy ending!

"Are you writing literature or entertainment?" I am asked. "Do you think your novels will last? Are you aware that all you do is produce a good read and your works are without literary merit?"

These, I fear, are the questions that concern feature writers and college professors, but should not concern a writer, and certainly do not concern readers. When a reviewer or a questioner in an audience says that I don't write great literature, I usually ask who has produced great literature in this century. Faulkner, Joyce, Joseph Conrad, Graham Greene, D. H. Lawrence. Who else? Whoever sets out to write great literature will under ordinary circumstances write nothing or write a story few read. The producers of great literature are few and far between. They are occasional men or women of overwhelming talent, many of whom, by the way, like Charles Dickens, or William Shakespeare, were dismissed by the serious literary people of their own day. If you happen to have that kind of overwhelming vision then you will produce great literature without trying. If you don't, and it is ridiculous to assume you do, you'll still try to write great literature, but you'll end up writing junk, which is what many contemporary "serious" American novels are.

I am content at my age in life with my mission to write good stories. I reject completely the artificial distinction between a "good read" and serious literature. My stories are deadly serious. If they don't rate long reviews in *The New York Review of Books*, well, finally, so what? I am telling the kind of story I want to tell, the way I want to tell it, to people who like such stories, and that seems to me quite enough.

Will they last?

They might.

I'm not sure how many people currently publishing stories are going to be read even five years from now, much less twenty-five years. Obviously I hope my stories will last. I have the sneaking suspicion they

452

have more durability than many of my Catholic critics are willing to concede. This is based on my hunch that people will read them twenty-five or fifty or a hundred years from now for two reasons: they'll be good stories a hundred years from now just as they are now and, much more significant, people will read them to discover what it was like to be American and Catholic at the end of the twentieth century. In this respect, the overarching sociological framework of the novels—the two great transitions in American Catholicism—may give them more durability than those critics who dismiss them as "potboilers" might expect.

Perhaps it betrays a lack of "seriousness" on my part, however, that I don't much care whether people read them a century from now; I care whether they read them now. I write books for people, and if people like them, that's all I care about.

What kind of people? Well, the average age of the Literary Guild readers of *Lord of the Dance* was thirty-nine, their average number of years of education was fourteen (two years in college). A relatively small proportion of them (less than 20 percent) said their favorite books in the last year were "romances." Moreover, they had read, on average, fifteen books in the last three months. They are, as one might expect of Literary Guild members, readers who follow the *New York Times* hardback bestseller list through their Literary Guild membership, lower-middle-brow by the standards of the academic elites but still, given the number of books they read and their educational attainment, part of a tiny upper proportion of literate American readers. That I tell stories for those people that they like enough they can hardly wait for the next one is more than enough reward for my storytelling work.

The first three novels were about priests, and the plots were not, despite some complaint, the same plot. The first was about a man, Kevin Brennan, who like myself would never think of leaving the priesthood. The second was about a man, Sean Cronin, who seriously thought of leaving the priesthood but finally decided to stay, who discovered after many years as a priest that his vocation was authentic after all. The third was about Hugh Donlon, a man who, for sincere and well-intentioned reasons, became a priest even though he probably should not have, and ultimately left. It seems to me Kevin Brennan, Sean Cronin and Hugh Donlon represent the different patterns of response of priests to the changes in the Church in the years after the Second Vatican Council. In each case their responses were made with honesty, integrity and sincerity, and in each case they were made under the influence of God as mediated by a woman.

The second two of these novels, *Thy Brother's Wife* and *Ascent into Hell*, had Holy Week themes. The Holy Thursday liturgy celebrates the commitment of Christ and his followers to one another. Each year on Holy Thursday priests renew their commitment to the priesthood. So *Thy Brother's Wife* is about commitments, perhaps unwisely made, sometimes poorly kept but still kept nonetheless, and about the Eucharist which renews the strength of our commitment to one another and to the lifelong promises we have made. *Ascent into Hell* is a Good Friday story, the story of a man who must die a horrible death to his early dreams of what his life meant in order that he might rise out of the bottom of, as he puts it, the basement, the cold storage locker beneath the pit of hell, and climb back through hell to the beginning of a new life.

My fourth novel, *Lord of the Dance*, breaks completely with the clerical theme but not with the Holy Week theme. It is a a novel of resurrection, intimately linked to the Easter vigil liturgy and the mixing of fire and water, a sexual intercourse symbol tokening new life, the new life Jesus brought to us in his resurrection, which is offered to us in Jesus's name through the Church and which must happen repeatedly and endlessly in our own personal relationships. Noele Marie Brigid Farrell, a zany, bossy, plain-talking young woman who brings new life to all the members of her family at terrible personal cost, is a Church figure, conceived at Easter, born at Christmas and forcing all her family, sometimes much against their will, to go through their own personal deaths and resurrections. "Like, *totally!*" as Noele would say.

My next stories, six of them written at the time that I begin this memoir, are about three Chicago families in the "time between the stars"—between the 1933 and the 1992 World's Fair (represented by the fourth and eventual fifth star in the Chicago flag, although it looks now like the neopuritans who dominate the Chicago elites have sunk the 1992 fair). These families, the Ryans, the Collinses and the Caseys, represent the social and religious evolution of Chicago Catholics over the last half century. In particular it is the story of the Ryan family—Ned Ryan, the patriarch, a naval hero in World War II, a shrewd, gentle, kindly man, and his mercurial, passionate, splendid first wife, Kate Collins Ryan, and then, and especially, their children, Mary Kate Murphy, the psychiatrist,

Eileen Ryan Kane, the lawyer and eventual federal judge, and John Blackwood Ryan, Ph.D., eventually a monsignor and rector of the Cathedral of the Holy Name.

Blackie holds all the stories together and, while never the protagonist in any of the books, is nonetheless the central figure in the saga. Blackie Ryan is a character who has lurked in my imagination for a long, long time. While sometimes he speaks in my voice, he has an identity and integrity of his own. He is younger than I am, physically different, and has a degree in philosophy (albeit empirical philosophy) instead of sociology. Moreover, he is in much better stead with ecclesiastical authorities. Blackie has some of the characteristics of Chesterton's Father Brown, deliberately and consciously cultivated, according to the adolescent nieces and nephews in his family. His sister Mary Kate puts it a little better, perhaps: "The Punk was born with the persona; he developed the personality to fit it."

The world of the Ryan clan is endlessly evolving in my head. My decision not to arrange the novels in chronological order means I am always discovering new things about them, as I move back and forth through their history. Thus, it was only in the last couple of weeks that I discovered Blackie had done his doctorate on Alfred North Whitehead and that, at this moment, in addition to his duties as rector of the cathedral and as Cardinal Cronin's gray eminence and as a mystery-solving detective, he is preparing a major article on William James. His sister Nancy, I found out only last week, writes fantasy stories for children, and his sister Eileen, the wife of the columnist Redmond Peter Kane, has just been elevated to the federal bench.

As the various characters in the Ryan clan and their entourage of relatives and friends emerge from my imagination, I learn more about their world and about the years between the thirties and nineties which I share with them. The Ryans have become a matrix for my imagination, producing not only major novels but mystery novels and short stories. My editors have often pushed me to prepare a family tree, but I am not quite yet prepared to do that because I don't think I yet know all the Ryans well enough. Eventually, perhaps.

The first of the books, *Virgin and Martyr*, is about the dangers of religious enthusiasm, about the critically traumatic times of the late sixties in the Church and about God's grace, which, as John Shea has put it, "never gives up easily." The protagonist is a young woman who becomes a nun in the early 1960s, leaves the religious life in the late sixties and then goes to South America as a missionary and revolutionary.

The second story, *Angels of September,* is about guilt that becomes so powerful it finally seems to objectify and personify and obsess a woman and her art gallery. The third, *Patience of a Saint,* is about a down-at-the-heels Irish Catholic newspaper columnist named Redmond Peter Kane who, for no reasons he can discern, has been chosen by God, in his early fifties, to become a saint. An unpleasant and uncomfortable experience it seems to Redmond Peter Kane, who finally tries to throw a monkey wrench into the Lord God's schemes, only to discover, as Blackie Ryan says in his most memorable phrase, "Redmond Peter Kane, *never,* I repeat *never,* fuck with the Lord God!"

I want to put that on the frontispiece of the book but I don't think my editor will let me.

The fourth story, *Rite of Spring,* is about Brendan Ryan, a distant cousin of the clan and a man of extraordinary psychic capabilities who falls in love with a woman who may have never existed and then sets out on a quest to discover whether Ciara Kelly is real or not. It's the Holy Grail legend all over again, the story of the magic cup told in semicomic modern terms, with Blackie Ryan playing the Merlin role for all it is worth.

While priests lurk around all the members of the Ryan family, sometimes doing them harm, and sometimes good, none of the protagonists are priests. Catherine Collins in *Virgin and Martyr* is a nun who apparently dies as a Marxist revolutionary in Joseph Conrad's mythical South American country, Costaguana. Anne Marie O'Brien Reilly, the owner of the haunted art gallery (and in her early fifties, the most mature of my heroines), is a laywoman who has been savaged by the Church through much of her life—as many laywomen have. The two men who are the protagonists of *Patience of a Saint* and *Rite of Spring,* Redmond Peter Kane and Brendan Ryan, are both men who have been pushed around by the Church for much of their lives. Thus, in the four Ryan novels written so far, my protagonists are a nun, a laywoman and two laymen. Their sufferings with the Church during the two transitions that as I have said are the matrix of both my sociology and my novels are the raw material of the stories.

There is perhaps more comedy in the Ryan family stories than there is in either *The Cardinal Sins* or the Holy Week trilogy—though there

456

is a lot of comedy in the relationship between Noele Farrell and her cousin returned from the dead, Daniel Xavier Farrell. The Ryan clan and their relatives and friends tend to be outrageously larger than life and to respond with extravagant gestures to life's problems. Moreover, the people they attract, like Red Kane the columnist and Mike Casey the cop (the male lead in *Angels of September*) and Cindasoo McLeod, a redneck Coast Guard petty officer beloved by one of Mary Kate Ryan's sons, are colorful characters in their own right. Nonetheless, as some of those who have read the books in "time between the stars" have observed, they are angry novels, quite possibly more angry than *The Cardinal Sins*— furious at what ecclesiastical authority and inept, insensitive priests have done or tried to do to the Catholic laity in the last forty years. Blackie Ryan serves as a contrast to the shallow, selfish, insensitive, mediocre priests who abound in these stories. Blackie represents the priesthood at its best, the ideals in the priesthood that originally attracted me and that are still to be found in many if not most American priests—intelligence, pragmatism, zeal, wisdom and wit. Are there priests like Blackie Ryan? Well, perhaps relatively few who are quite as colorful as John Blackwood Ryan, but many who share his basic characteristics.

Unfortunately, not nearly enough.

"Blackie and Maria are Andy's vision of God," Bill Grogan insists (himself a Blackie-like priest appearing briefly in that role in *Death in April*). The passionately loving and implacably seductive Maria and the ingenious, determined mystery-solving Blackie. "And Noele, the fair bride, violated but inviolable, is his Church."

Only God is even better, more lovely than Maria, more comic and resourceful than Blackie. And more deviously determined than Noele.

The Ryans and their relatives are also a symbol for the Church, loyal, faithful, zany, tender, resolute. When they decide they are going to adopt someone who needs their help, they do not even bother to ask. Their niece Catherine, their distant cousin Brendan, Mike Casey, Nick Curran, Lisa Malone, are gathered into the clan with affection, persistence, and ingenuity. The Church has a long way to go before it comes close to that model.

With the publication of *Lord of the Dance* the fury of ecclesiastical reaction to my novels abated somewhat. It was as if the reviewers and the editorial writers and the letter writers and the columnists and the clergy realized the books had become part of the environment, and their anger and vehement attack would not drive them out of existence.

If I had realized the books were going to be so successful I would have anticipated the violent outburst of anger against them. Not realizing it, however, I was momentarily stunned by the vehemence of the assault occasioned by *The Cardinal Sins* (and most of the assault was from the liberal and left end of the Church, not the conservative or right). There was nothing planned or coordinated about the attack; it didn't have to be. A few smear words were picked up—"steamy," "soft-core porn," "salacious," "washing the Church's dirty linen in public," "playing into the hands of the Church's enemies," "paranoia," etc., etc., etc. I could not reasonably object if the criticisms were about taste or literary structure, but such issues were swept aside in personal assaults on my motivation and my character and in monumental distortions of the novel's obvious storylines and themes.

Some of the assaults were just plain false. The most typical, though not the most malicious, was the charge that I put all the "dirty" scenes in italics in order to attract attention to them, a story that became absolute truth for most priests. In fact, the italic scenes represent those parts of the book which are not told from the point of view of the narrator, Kevin Brennan. There is much in them that is not erotic and there are some erotic passages in the nonitalicized segments of the novel.

A priest reviewer announced triumphantly that my priests never prayed, as though that said something about them and me. The cry promptly echoed around the country.

If my priests didn't pray, it was possible that prayer did not fit the storyline. One is not, after all, presenting a videotape replay of a day in the life of the priest.

However, Kevin Brennan actually prays twenty-two times in the course of *The Cardinal Sins*.

The story was simply untrue, which did not prevent it from being repeated time and time again.

It was also asserted with serene confidence that the book was based on my conflict with Cardinal Cody. No one who knew anything about Chicago could possibly think that Pat Donahue, my cardinal, had anything in common with Cardinal Cody, besides the red hat. Yet the story continues to flourish.

The worst experience at the time of the publication of *The Cardinal Sins* was with my deteriorating small group church. Somehow they came to believe, without reading the manuscript of *The Cardinal Sins*, that I was being exploited by "New York Jews." They are not normally given to anti-Semitism, but at that stage of our relationship, any stereotype seemed licit so long as it was aimed at me. I found the anti-Semitism offensive nonetheless and was also angered by the implications that (1) I was not alert enough to know if I was being exploited and (2) I was not capable of writing a book which would have any other goal than exploitation.

Their problem was that it was absolutely intolerable that they should be put in the position of having to defend my novels and having to deny that they were any of the people in the stories.

I had dedicated the book to the children of the community. A woman member phoned me in Tucson to say that the others were afraid to tell me the truth: no one wanted his or her children's names associated with the book. It was her duty to tell me to protect their children from identification with it. None of them had shown any interest in reading the manuscript, despite my offers, but they didn't need to read it to know they didn't want to have their children suffer the burden of the dedication.

Later others denied she was speaking for them, but I'm not sure whether that was true. In any event I promised to change the dedication. Then she wrote me what was perhaps the most cruel and vicious letter I have ever received, denouncing me for embarrassing them with my foolish new "hobby." I should stop my ridiculous stunts and settle down to enjoy the fruit of my work—whatever that might have been—instead of pursuing crazy new schemes.

She and her husband were the first teenagers I had met at Christ the King. I had officiated at their marriage, baptized their children, stood by them in rough times. Now she wanted me, in effect, to die.

Her outburst revealed more about her own angers and frustrations than it did about me or my novel. That did not, alas, make it hurt any less. I'm not certain of the extent to which *The Cardinal Sins* contributed to the final death throes of the community. If I had to guess, I'd say it was an occasion rather than a cause, an excuse rather than a real problem. However, I do accept the fact that many of them were simply fed up with having to defend me.

It was only after the hardbound edition of my third book, *Ascent into Hell*, that it dawned on me that I could do research on my readers and thus objectively evaluate the impact of my stories. Till then I was bemused by the stark contrast between the popularity of the books and the violent and angry attacks in the Catholic community, more violent and angry on the left (in the *National Catholic Reporter* and the *Commonweal*) than on the right (*The National Catholic Register* and *The Wanderer*).

If it had not been for the outpouring of mail from readers, I might have hesitated. Everything else that I had written occasioned an approximate ten to one in unfavorable mail: it is an iron law of writing, especially controversial writing, that the complainers set pen to paper (or impulse to disk these days) and the admirers do not. But from *The Cardinal Sins* the ratio of favorable to unfavorable mail runs about twelve to one.

(I mentioned this in one of my columns and some two hundred people signed a letter saying that they did not like my books and they were writing me to cancel the effect of the favorable mail. Thoughtfully, they sent a copy of their letter to the cardinal, the delegate, and the Pope. I didn't feel constrained to count them, however, because the petition admitted that most of them had not read the books. You don't read, you don't get the franchise. Alas, as I will note in the next chapter, my cardinal gives the nonreaders not less but more votes.)

Mark Harris, in preparing his profile about me for the *New York Times*, plowed through thousands of these letters and drew the conclusion which I quote at the beginning of this book—my parish is in my mail box.

In the next chapter I'll describe the formal research that, with my sociologist's hat on, I did on my readers. To put some flesh on the statistical bones and to respond to those critics who say that "it is hard to imagine" any positive effect, here are a few quotes from the mail:

"It is possible for goodness to survive without mistakes, for commitments to continue despite falls—how good to see those concepts so deftly woven into human frailities." (Minnesota)

"I have taken instructions and am ready to receive Confirmation in the Catholic Church." (Massachusetts)

"I have heard and dealt in criticism of you. . . . I now believe much of that criticism is based on envy . . . the wonder of your faith shines through all of the pages of *Lord of the Dance*." (Illinois)

"As a Catholic freshman in a non-Catholic college your book helped to deepen and strengthen my faith." (Minnesota)

"After thirty-five years, I have returned to the Church. I am weeping for joy as I write these words." (Arizona)

Andrew M. Greeley

"Made me realize the continuing vitality of the Church—the evergreening of it that kept and keeps my hope alive." (Illinois)

"Your perceptions of God have strengthened me, broken my heart again, and made my walk with Him closer and more thrilling." (Mississippi)

"As a Protestant living in Northern Ireland, I found your books full of humanity." (Belfast)

"As a Lutheran I learned much about the Roman Catholic Church . . . you wiped away many of the prejudices I was taught in Confirmation class." (Florida)

"I am one of those 50's Catholic kids who has fallen in love with her faith and her God because of the things you write." (Texas)

"There are thousands who have for years read your magnificent work and look to you as part of what we hold to our Catholic faith for." (Oregon)

"You are showing that it is a living, breathing, and growing Church." (Australia)

"I want to let you know that you have influenced me, touched me, aided me, provided intellectual justification for holding on to a heritage." (Pennsylvania)

"I did not feel your book would condone sin, but I felt maybe God in his infinite mercy would spare a little bit of forgiveness for a sinner. . . . Not being able to find a priest in my own parish willing to have just a little bit of compassion, without the obvious lectures, I thank you." (New York)

"It is as deeply Christian (I believe) as anything I've read for some time." (York, England)

And finally from a seminarian whose precise location will be nameless lest he suffer reprisal.

"I wanted to thank you for your considerable contribution to the field of Gospel literature. Your books do literally proclaim the Good News of the love of God for his poor creatures . . . an honesty and a dedication which is so needed today for Catholic students and especially for those thinking of pursuing the priesthood. It gives me the much needed impetus to remain open to the Church and to her people."

I have received more reactions like those to my novels than to all my other work in the priesthood put together and multiplied by ten or even twenty. I quote them to establish that the novels do have a positive effect on people against those who deny the possibility of such

461

an effect. More than any other reason, those letters compel me to continue to write as long as God gives me the ability to do so.

Mark Harris saw the letters as a parish in the mail box. I gave the same collection to Cardinal Bernardin. They did not move him in the least to modify his demand (about which more in the next chapter) that I abandon the stories if I want to do weekend parish work in the Archdiocese. Apparently he saw in thousands of such letters no merit at all over against the complaints of those who had not read my stories.

What can I tell you?

I must be candid: I am dismayed that a religious leader, so as to appease complainers, can cavalierly write off thousands of people who report these results of reading my stories.

(Lady Wisdom: "Dismayed" are you? How long have you known bishops? It is religion you expect of them, is it now?)

Has storytelling, especially successful storytelling, changed my life, other than by reducing my purgatory obligations with book promotion tours?

Not really. I now have some extra money to fund research (including research on the Catholic Church in Ireland) and to add a swimming pool to swim my daily mile when the lake is too cold or too rough—an exercise for which I have no intention of apologizing—at Grand Beach and to hire my sister to write theology books. I also find myself much more preoccupied by storytelling than I would have been in the past (though thus far not to the extent of shutting down my sociological imagination). I read fiction now not merely for enjoyment (though for that too) but also to study technique and craft. Without much in the way of conscious effort I find myself watching people, listening to conversations, poking around environments, looking not quite so much for story as for raw materials that might later fit into stories.

While storytelling is fun, my principal reason for writing novels is the same as my reason for preaching a sermon on Sunday—novels are a means of spreading the good news that God loves us. Anyone who denies that such is my principal motive for storytelling is not telling the truth.

I feel I have found a new parish, even if as Mark Harris said it is in my mailbox.

Are there any spiritual payoffs in storytelling?

I can think of two. First of all it has made me much more sensitive and sympathetic to other human beings. The creation of characters, getting inside them and discovering what makes them tick, has taught me much about human nature and made me have far greater feelings of poignancy and pain for my fellow humans than I ever had before— so much so that sometimes I must flee rather impersonal scenes in the airport or railroad stations or even walking down Michigan Avenue to avoid tears. Creating the romance between Marie and Hugh Donlon in *Ascent into Hell,* for example, forced me to be much less impatient than I had been with my fellow priests who had left the ministry.

Second, I think I know a little bit more about how it feels to be God. For like God, a storyteller creates people, sets them in motion, outlines a scenario for them, falls in love with them and then is not really able to control what they do, sometimes for weal, sometimes for woe. One of the most striking examples of a character acting up for weal is Melissa Jean Ryan in *Rite of Spring.* In my original plan she was designed to be a spoiled brat, a pushy, noisy little bitch, much like the daughter in *Angels of September.* But, while the *Angels* daughter fit the suburban, upper-middle-class bitch persona I had designed for her, Jeannie Ryan wasn't having any and became a different character than I originally intended. My initial plan had been to send Blackie Ryan along with Brendan on the quest in Ireland for Ciara Kelly. Then I hesitated—perhaps instead of Blackie, it would be more interesting to send Jean. Finally, it was almost as though Jean settled the issue for me. *She* would go to Ireland and play Watson to her father's Holmes—except on the scene she became Holmes to his Watson.

I'm sure many of the things we do disturb the God who created us and loves us. I wonder, though, whether God, too, sometimes has the pleasure of being surprised when we turn out better than He had intended us to.

Finally, I know I have the courage of my convictions when I preach. I *always* tell a story, not as an introduction to the sermon, but as the sermon itself. For an example, consult in the coda of this book my (admittedly outrageous) adaptation of Jack Shea's "king of Crete" story.

What about the result of storytelling that I will now apparently forever be rejected by the Archdiocese of Chicago?

I am sitting in Eason's bookstore on O'Connell Street in Dublin, feeling like a monkey in a zoo as I sign books (having fended off an attack from the Legion of Mary, of all people). Even though the per

463

capita consumption of my books by the Irish (God love them!) is greater than by Americans, I still am bored and look silly. I begin to flirt with a young woman sacrament person who has the prettiest blue eyes in all Ireland. (I would not exaggerate on a matter of this importance.) She is at the flirtatious age, between eighteen and twenty-four (*months,* *that is*), and makes faces back at me. Her parents ask if I will sign a book for Ciara so that when she grows up she will have her very own copy. They look a little less than prosperous, so I reach for the paperback of *The Cardinal Sins.*

"Ah, no," says her mother. "We have that one already and we loved it. We want the new one for Ciara."

So someday, long after I've gone to the Land of Promise in the West—to be Irish about it—there will be a young woman who will tell her own children about the crazy Yank priest who flirted with her and signed her book with the dedication that she had the prettiest blue eyes in all of Ireland.

For that I'll gladly be a square peg.

Image and Metaphor (or Fear and Loathing) in Chicago

The pure, anguished notes of a Mahler posthorn
As they tumble round a mountain top
Gossamer rainbow wings on fragile breezes born
Ecstatic pleasure I pray will never stop.
With a cleansing gust of wind the front arrives
The hull tilts, sails flap, I duck the swinging boom
The soggy gray clouds gone, my soul revives
Ballooning spinnakers briskly tug for home.
Mists coalescing create a familiar smile
Shrewd, cheerful, only lightly touched by age
Forty years seem but a little while
Recaptured blue eyes turn another page.

A melody, changing wind, a remembered face
Metaphoric gifts that need not be but are
Mystery, wonder, marvel, amazing grace
Seducing comic hints sent from afar
Of eternal surprise a tempting trace
For my dark night journey a newborn star.

Reaction to my novels has been overwhelmingly favorable from readers, mixed from priests and book reviewers, and unfavorable from my archbishop, who has made it clear that I will not be welcome in the Archdiocese until I stop writing novels.

He doesn't tell me to stop writing. Rather he tells me that he wishes I would give up my fiction and that if I want to do weekend parish work in Chicago I will have to give it up.

Sometimes I think there are two novelists named Andrew Greeley. One is the fellow who writes the novels I write. The other is the one who writes the books that are reviewed by some critics, especially Catholics, and who is roundly condemned by priests, literary experts, bishops, and other folks who mostly haven't opened them. I've read reviews and listened to discussions of my novels that are utterly unrelated to anything I have written. There is an image about the books which has nothing to do with the reality of them but which is nonetheless firmly believed.

"It's not just Catholics," Carol Nie tells me. "Norman and I argue with people we know who haven't read your books either and are outraged that a priest should write about human passion."

Ingrid Shafer has made the same observation; after discovering my books in a university bookstore, she read them with interest:

> Clearly his works responded to a profound human need to find meaning in life. It seemed that Greeley's sensitivity to the tragic possibilities of human existence had engendered their own negation, the assurance of hope and grace revealed against the dark shadows of sin and despair. Above and beyond the chaotic jungle of errant human passions and the Church as a human institution corrupted by authoritarianism, envy, and lust for power, his words conjured up a bright, warm image of God as passionate, caring and sustaining Presence and the "real" Church as a community of equals, a genuine mother whose nurturing love enfolds every last one of her children within her warm embrace.
>
> My scholarly curiosity had been aroused, and I began to survey critical responses to the novels. Surprise turned to dismay and, finally, utter consternation. While most of the reviews I read were favorable, far too many seemed oblivious to the rich symbolic tapestry presented in the works. References to the liturgical cycles, the grand themes of the Mass, and the Christian year, carefully chosen poetry and hymns, the generally metaphorical nature of the stories were universally disregarded. . . . Instead far too many reviewers focused on

the titillating morsel of a celibate priest actually describing moments of physical intimacy and, horror of horrors, daring to use erotic imagery to convey theological insights.

In their eyes and minds works which Greeley considers "comedies of grace" were reflected as blasphemous, steamy sleaze, deserving of a plain brown wrapper, and his readers were curtly dismissed as ignorant soap-opera addicts whose brains could barely grasp the contents of the the *National Enquirer*.

Could I have been wrong? I reread the novels. The religious symbolism and theological themes seemed even more powerful the second time around. . . . Why is it, I wondered, that Greeley's spiritual message appears obvious to me as well as thousands, perhaps millions of average . . . readers, while so many reviewers miss the point completely? Can the same surface be transparent to some while remaining totally opaque to others?

Professor Shafer thinks she has found the explanation:

> The problem is not only, or even primarily, the fact that Greeley employs highly charged and often erotic religious symbols, nor the fact that reviewers know he is a priest. The "blinding effect" occurs at the juncture of sexual imagery with the author's special status as a celibate priest, particularly a priest who is successful in financial terms, a bona fide priest actually portraying moments of sexual encounter! Red lights start flashing! . . . Blasphemy! Pornography! Filth! Judgment has been passed before the first page of the book is read. . . . Never mind that the . . . erotic scenes are depicted with sensitivity, taste, and tenderness and are understood as such by most nonclerical readers. The mere fact that they were hatched in the mind of a priest warrants their condemnation. To add insult to injury, the works have been commercially successful and thus, claim the critics, must have been written for the appallingly un-Christlike reason of acquiring wealth. . . . Greeley's fiction functioned as a literary Rorschach test of metaphoric multicolored inkblots designed to elicit stock responses from the Catholic elite's unconscious.

Professor Shafer performed an interesting experiment to test her hypotheses. She mailed questionnaires which contained sixteen sexual passages from contemporary novelists to college professors and book review editors. One batch of questionnaires merely said that each passage was from the works of a "well-known living author"; the second batch added the parenthetical phrase "such as Andrew Greeley." The third batch gave the names of the authors of each passage (writers like Saul Bellow, John Updike, David Lodge, Robertson Davies, Irving Wallace, Edna O'Brien, Joyce Carol Oates, Harold Robbins, Robert Penn Warren, and Erica Jong).

I will leave to Professor Shafer the exposition of her findings, but three seem especially important here:

1. My passages were highly rated both in quality and "inoffensiveness" as long as the respondent didn't know they were written by me. If my name was attached to the passages, however, the rating plummeted dramatically.

2. The very mention of my name in the parenthetical phrase caused the average rating of *all* the passages to decline by three quarters of a standard deviation. The correlation between my name at the head of a questionnaire and lower rating for all passages was .44, meaning that more than a fifth of the variation in responses could be accounted for by the hint that I might be involved. The strongest negative impact, however, was not on one of my passages but on a quote from Robertson Davies, poor man!

3. The correlation between low ratings for all passages and my name at the top of the questionnaire was .66 for Catholic respondents: my name accounted for almost half the variation among Catholic professors and book review editors.

4. When the sixteen passages from all the authors were evaluated anonymously, four of my passages took the top four positions. But when the respondents knew the names of the authors, my passages fell from the top of the heap to the bottom—two tied for eighth place and two for thirteenth. The passages of the famous authors (Bellow, Updike, Styron) jumped from the bottom of the nameless list to the top of the named list.

The clerical culture cliché that I am a poor writer is valid, then, when critics and professors know that I've written a passage. But when they don't know it the quality of my writing improves enormously and receives a very high rating. Indeed in Professor Shafer's research the top rating. So maybe I do have some literary skills as well as popular appeal, but the former only when the critics don't know that the writer is me!

Professor Shafer made her point: the name of the game is prejudice, prejudging in the strict sense of the word.

(Lady Wisdom: Ah, she's a tricky one, that Professor Shafer, isn't she?

And why wouldn't reviewers be prejudiced against a priest? Would you be after thinking the species has already reached the Omega Point?)

Can the myth about my novels be evaluated empirically? I asked myself that question after the publication of *Thy Brother's Wife*. Do the readers think they are steamy novels written by a priest to make money? Do they read them only out of curiosity about trash written by a priest?

I figured that it was time to put on my sociological hat and find out what the readers thought. Warner Books agreed to put twenty-five thousand business-reply card research questionnaires in the paperback edition of *Ascent into Hell*.

Ascent into Hell is about a priest who falls in love with a nun, impregnates her and leaves the priesthood to marry her. On the theological level it is a parable of the contest between grace and justice, with Maria, the childhood sweetheart (not the nun), representing God's implacable grace.

Who are the readers? Sixty-five percent are Catholic, as opposed to 25 percent Catholic in the population, thus confirming my first assumption about a Catholic reading audience. Their average age is thirty-nine. Half of them do not attend church regularly. Three-quarters pray every day. Seventy-five percent of them are women. Eighty percent have read the previous novels. (The age and sex may be overestimates. Older people and women are more likely to cooperate with surveys.)

And how do they react to the novel? First of all, how much harm is done to the priesthood and the Church? Almost two-thirds say the book caused them to have greater respect for the priesthood. Only 6 percent say it made them feel contemptuous of priests, so my theology of the humanity of the priesthood—lifted from the Epistle to the Hebrews—works despite the clerical murmurantes. Twelve percent say the book caused them to have less respect for the Church. Six percent feel it is a disgrace to the Church and the priesthood. Sixty percent, however, say that the book has helped them to better understand the Catholic Church.

What do the readers think of the story itself and its religious impact? Eight percent agree that the author should be ashamed of writing such trash. Ten percent say it was written merely to make money. Only 6 percent agree with the bishop of Orlando that it would be a threat to the faith of young people.

On the other hand, 70 percent report that the novel made them think seriously about religious problems, 60 percent agree it was a novel with a deep spiritual message in the form of a fascinating story, 45 percent say it helped them to understand the meaning of God's love, and 38 percent acknowledge it helped them to understand better the relationship between religion and sex. Finally, 26 percent report that the story deepened their religious faith.

More than half of the Catholics who are not regular church attenders testify that the book brought them closer to their Church. Eighty percent of the non-Catholics say that *Ascent* gave them a better understanding of the Church, and 72 percent of them said it increased their admiration for the priesthood. Only 11 percent said it caused them to have less respect for the Church and only 5 percent said it made them feel contemptuous of the priesthood. Let him whose evangelization net spreads farther cast the first stone.

What about the sex scenes? Do the readers find them as vertiginous (you can always tell a college English instructor by her vocabulary) as did the *America* reviewer?

In order:

Human	86%
Sensitive	80%
Tasteful	72%
Sympathetic	70%
Delicate	62%
Mild	58%
Inspiring	58%
Compelling	48%
Unreal	12%
Steamy	11%
Racy	8%
Trash	7%
Obscene	5%

Undoubtedly, there are Catholics who are angered and shocked by my novels, some of whom have read them. There is no reason to think any of these folk are going to leave the Church or change their religious practice because of the books. And they do not have to read them.

"Do these data reassure the Vatican and American bishops?" I was asked after a presentation at the annual meetings of the MLA. Certainly not. The ecclesiastical power elite is not interested in data or truth or what the faithful really think or even in religion. It cares rather about preserving its own power and the myths which support that power. The myth says the laity have to be shocked by my stories and therefore it must be true, data to the contrary notwithstanding.

In one of my research analyses, I observed that 20 percent of the readers of the paperback edition of *Ascent into Hell* were new ones who had read none of my previous books. Half indicated they had now become members of the more or less permanent audience. How did they differ from those new readers who were not so enthusiastic?

Three variables seem to account for three-quarters of the variance between the two groups: agreement that the book had made them think seriously about religious questions, agreement that the book helped them to understand the relationship between religion and sex, and agreement that the book was a mixture of fascinating story and religious message.

So where sex, religion and story intersect, one finds an explanation of why a casual reader (80 percent had bought the book because they saw it on the rack) becomes a committed member of the audience. Fair enough, it seems to me. The explanation is plausible, it seems to fit the data, and it certainly is congruent with my intention in writing the novels in the first place.

In subsequent research on readers of *Happy Are the Meek* I found that the proportion of readers who say that this mystery story helped them to understand the nature of God's love and the relationship between religion and sex had increased to one half.

What impact does reading one of my novels have on the religious imagination of those who say the book helped them understand the relationship between religion and sex and those who say it improved their understanding of God's love?

I cross-tabulated the four religious-imagination items mentioned in the previous chapter with those two questions. Those who said *Lord of the Dance* helped them to better understand the relationship between religion and sex are 6 percentage points more likely to picture God as a "mother," 15 percentage points more likely to imagine Him as "spouse," 22 percentage points more likely to picture Him as "lover" and 12 percentage points more likely to think of Her as "friend."

Those who say the book improved their understanding of God's love are 8 points more likely to say "mother," 12 points more likely to respond "lover," and 11 points more likely to pick "friend." On five of the eight comparisons the differences are statistically significant. Moreover, the effect concentrated among those readers who found the sex in the stories either "compelling" or "sensitive." The sexual elements in my stories are sacramental—as I intended them to be.

There are two possible conclusions one can draw from the data. The first is that those who find more understanding of God's love and of the relationship between religion and sex in an explicitly religious/symbolic novel do undergo a development in their religious imagination in the direction of a high score on the grace scale.

The second explanation is that those who already have high scores on the grace scale have a tendency, after reading a book such as *Lord of the Dance,* to feel they better understand God's love.

There is little reason to choose between one or the other explanation and not much need either. Both imply a relationship between the novel and the religious imagination. Even the second, a greater feeling of understanding for those who have high scores on the grace scale, would not be unacceptable to an author interested in affecting the religious imagination of his readers in a graceful and gracious direction.

So most readers find the sexual scenes in my books to be "mild," "tasteful," "sensitive" and "delicate" and "compelling." And it is precisely those who find the sexual scenes effective who are most likely to have their image of God moved in the direction of more powerful love. The use of the sexual metaphor—God's passion for us compared to human passion—is a powerful and efficacious way of telling stories of God.

This finding is critical to my rationale for storytelling and for using the sexual metaphor as well as my defense against those who attack my stories as "inappropriate" for a priest: it is precisely the sexual metaphor in my stories which produces the religious impact; the image of human love as a sacrament of divine love has an effect on how readers imagine God. This assertion is no longer a theoretical postulate, but an empirically demonstrated fact (and in research on three novels).

Which St. Paul knew long ago, as did Hosea, and the Lord Yahweh in Genesis, and those who put the spring fertility ritual of candle and water in the liturgy of the Roman rite.

My relationship with the official Archdiocese of Chicago, as I have indicated in previous chapters, has not changed since Cardinal Bernardin replaced Cardinal Cody. In some ways the relationship is worse; Cardinal

Cody never seriously tried to persuade me to give up my storytelling. The present cardinal has made it a condition for "reconciliation" with the Archdiocese.

It is almost impossible not to like Bernardin. Most of what you read about him in the newspapers and magazines does not describe adequately the skills and warmth of his personality. He is the most interpersonally sensitive man I've ever met—he recognizes suffering quickly and is strongly moved to heal it if he possibly can. He is by principle and personality a collegialist: he rules by building consensus rather than by issuing commands. He can absorb more abuse than most of us and not lose his temper, not even be threatened by it. (I once shouted at him on the phone for a solid hour and he spoke not a single angry word in return. The next day I called to apologize, not for the substance of my complaints, on which I continued to stand, but for my ill temper, and to praise him for his astonishing forbearance. "That's what bishops are for," he replied.)

He is a quintessential American, a pragmatist, an empiricist, a pluralist in the sense that William James would define these terms. He is eager to learn, flexible in his thinking, and feels no need to insist that as a bishop he knows everything that needs to be known. He is a master juggler, keeping in balanced movement a large number of very hot potatoes. Yet, for all his low-key, undramatic pragmatism, he is a man of deep and powerful passions. (I sometimes wonder what it would be like to be around when he finally explodes. I doubt that anyone will ever see it.) Unlike many of his fellow bishops, he does not have to fake a respect for and an enjoyment of his fellow humans in all their rich and fascinating diversity, including women, whom he finds charming and easily charms.

In a way he came to Chicago both too late and too early—too late because most of the harm his predecessor could do had already been done and too early because the Archdiocese is not ready yet for an environment in which the archbishop is not expected to be the only visionary.

Just as some of the men who came before him might have been ideal bishops in the nineteenth century, so Bernardin might be an ideal bishop for the authentically post-Conciliar Church of the twenty-first century— a church in which the Curia and its capricious exercise of raw power need no longer be feared and an archbishop is no longer charged with being the solitary visionary in his diocese.

In the present situation, however, a Catholic leader is expected to be both the only visionary and forfender of Curially created disasters.

Role conflict with a vengeance!

Role conflict, moreover, which puts an eccentric, off-the-reservation square peg like me particularly at risk.

He is certainly the best archbishop Chicago was likely to get and one of the most effective Church leaders in the world. However, he is not an easy man with whom to deal because his style changes unpredictably. On one occasion, he is a warm, friendly, sensitive fellow priest. On another he is an evasive, formally canonical, Curial bureaucrat, in whom one must search intently to find a trace of candor. The former person, I believe, is the real man; the latter is the mask he often feels constrained to wear to keep happy the power centers in the ecclesiastical structure, especially the Vatican. I can if necessary cope with men who have one or the other personality, but I find it difficult to deal with a man who seems to have both. Nor am I the only one with this problem; it is now widely acknowledged in the Archdiocese.

I have defended him in the past and will continue to defend him against the charge of habitual dishonesty—"as dishonest as Cody," a bitter Chicago cleric remarked. He is rather a sensitive priest caught in a position where the demands of keeping as many people as possible happy are sometimes almost unsupportable, like that of a dean or provost in a university some of whose top-level officials are lunatics.

I would not be surprised if he often feels that I am one of the nearly intolerable burdens he must carry. As his friend Jean Jadot wrote to me, "I feel sorry for our friend Joe. It would not be easy to be your bishop."

Perhaps so. The cardinal told a journalist in 1983 that he was under national pressure on three issues—abortion, nuclear weapons and me. I think this gives me too much importance, as the Irish would say, "altogether."

(Lady Wisdom: Ah, sure you're not worth that much trouble, 't all, 't all.)

Cardinal Bernardin would never dream, save on direct orders from Rome, of attempting to revoke my present set of permissions. He knows full well that there would be an enormous outcry if he did and that he would end up by losing a good deal of his carefully cultivated media image. Moreover, to give him his due, in principle he believes priests ought to feel free to write, and would be most reluctant to infringe on anyone's freedom.

However, unlike Meyer, who encouraged me and expanded my permission to write, and unlike Cardinal Cody, who, despite himself, confirmed that permission, Cardinal Bernardin has not confirmed my permission to write, but he has not retracted it either. He has made it clear repeatedly, however, that I will be a "nonperson" in the Archdiocese of Chicago until I stop writing my novels "or take the sex out of them."

Which means taking human beings out of them.

It may seem even bizarre to try, however indirectly, to silence a writer whose novels are having a considerable religious impact. Yet in the strange economy of the Archdiocese of Chicago at the present time, millions of satisfied readers count for nothing and a handful of angry letter writers (many of whom have not read the books) stand for everything.

Once since he has been archbishop of Chicago has Bernardin publicly acknowledged that I exist—an exchange on WBBM in May of 1985 with John Madigan, an archreactionary radio journalist.

Madigan: Cardinal Bernardin, I'd be stoned in the streets if I let this program end, and we have a few more minutes, without asking you about the status of Father Greeley, the best-known priest in Chicago. He's unanchored and he's still canonically assigned here at St. Ambrose parish although he's there infrequently if at all. What is his status?

Bernardin: His status is the same as it was before, before I came. He's a priest of the Archdiocese, but he is engaged primarily in research, teaching, writing, and so he does not have an assignment in the Archdiocese. But he is a priest of the Archdiocese.

Madigan: And you approve his present status?

Bernardin: This is the status he has had for some time. We have a number of priests who are in special work.

Madigan: You don't intend to change him?

Bernardin: At the moment I have no plans for that.

It was those other three cardinals, fellas, I'm not responsible for him!

(Lady Wisdom: Ah, your eminence, I know how you feel. Sometimes I try to blame him on other Gods too!)

Some time before the Madigan interview, one of the cardinal's staff visited me to inform me that I would be given an honored role in the Archdiocese again if I was willing to do penance and apologize to all those I had offended by writing my novels. I cited my research on the overwhelming positive reaction of the readers.

"It's not those who read the novels," he said, "it's those who don't read them, but are shocked that you wrote them."

Think about that, guys.

I could not believe that the cardinal would actually take such an astonishing position. How can an author be responsible for the image of his books formed by people who don't read them? No one would make such an absurd demand.

In the summer of 1985, feeling that our estrangement had too long violated the Gospel demand for reconciliation, I attempted a new "dialogue" with the cardinal. He was most charming. We had a long and friendly conversation. He insisted that the functionary had not come on his instructions and that there was certainly no demand for public penance. My freedom to write was not in question.

But the message of the functionary?

It was the cardinal's position too: if I wanted to be "normalized," if I wanted to be part of the Church in Chicago again—do weekend parish work—I would have to give up writing fiction with sex in it.

Was that not equivalently public penance?

Some might think so.

Why did he want me to give up writing novels?

Because people had complained. There was shock and scandal that a priest would write about sex. Especially damaging was the image of the novels among those who had not read them but were offended that I had written them.

You can't mean that!

But he could. I found myself in a strange never-never land, part Franz Kafka's Castle, part Lewis Carroll's Wonderland and part Joseph Heller's Catch-22—a world in which you received no credit for the substance of your books and were held responsible for the image of them among nonreaders (some nonreaders—it was never made clear how many but I had the impression that even a few dozen were enough to cause the cardinal grave concern).

I argued vigorously that in an era when a fifth of the priests in the country leave to get married, when cardinals die in whorehouses, when bishops are arrested for solicitation, when priests are convicted of pederasty, when the Vatican bank wastes billions, when 80 percent of the laity reject the Church's teaching on birth control and premarital sex, when there are financial scandals all over the American Church (in-

476

cluding Chicago), it was a little hard to think my novels were going to shock anyone.

(I did not add that the only event which had really shocked the laity was the birth-control encyclical.)

But, the cardinal responded, he had a dilemma. Some people did not understand why I wrote the novels.

Would there not be scandal if I announced that I would no longer write them at his request?

No, only some initial disappointment.

Obviously he had little respect for either their value or their effect on those who claimed that my stories had brought them back to Church. They were entertainment, nothing more. And, horror of horrors, offensive to those who had not read them, but were shocked that I wrote them. Indeed the opposition to them was strong, very strong.

Besides, they had been translated into other languages, had they not?

At first I did not notice the suspicious tone in his voice. I thought he would be proud that a priest of his Archdiocese was being translated.

Yes, into French, Spanish, Portuguese, Dutch, Turkish, Finnish, German and Italian. And there was a British edition which was especially popular in Ireland—more books sold per capita than in the United States.

Pride comes before a fall.

He shook his head in dismay. He could well believe that they were successful in Ireland. But, you see, he received complaints from bishops in other countries (by implication especially Irish bishops). They were troubled by the shock that the image of the books had produced in their people.

Had the bishops read any of the novels? Or had they been content with reports or with passages torn out of context?

That was not the point. They had complained about the *image* of the books.

The Irish reviews were generally more favorable than not, no small accomplishment in Irish reviews. And the letters from Ireland were even more favorable than those from America.

Yes, but the image among those who complained was one of shock.

Image, image, image. Cardinal Meyer had dismissed the complainers. Cardinal Bernardin was siding with them. "Many" thought the books were inappropriate for a priest because of excessive and sometimes questionable sexual explicitness.

I told him about Professor Shafer's book soon to be published by Loyola University Press.

Is it unfavorable? Again in a tone of voice that assumed the study would be unfavorable and that it would be one more problem for him.

No, it is quite favorable, as a matter of fact.

Then, though I only appreciated this fact later, *Eros and the Womanliness of God* dropped off of his agenda. As an unfavorable book it might have been very important. As a sympathetic critique it became irrelevant.

Did I understand his problem? Did I see he was caught in a dilemma?

So I argued my case—thousands of letters from readers praising the religious impact of the books on their lives, the data from my research on the readership, a stack of reviews (about three-quarters of the reviews are favorable), Professor Shafer's study, comments from other scholars (Michael and Madonna Marsden, Charles Scribner, Sister Hester Valentine, Wendy O'Flaherty).

All in vain. There were, you see, still complainers, especially the complainers who had not read the books.

I was back in CK and the complainer was doing in Max and Lem and Erich. I didn't like the pastor and I did like Joe, but I had grown up. I told him that I intended to be a priest for the rest of my life and a writer for the rest of my life.

He admitted graciously that he never doubted either.

I was aware as the conversation went on that my stomach was churning, my heart was pounding, my nerves were fraying. I felt shattered. After all, I am a product of a seminary training and an experience of the priesthood in which the word of a cardinal, especially a good and holy cardinal, was almost as good as the word of God. The cardinal was dismissing a work into which I had poured much of my life energies as so unimportant that its termination would produce only mild disappointment. What if he was right? What if the sexual passages were "excessive" and "inappropriate for a priest"?

In my head I remembered the data, the letters, the favorable reviews, the personal comments, the results of Professor Shafer's research and analysis, the theories on which my stories were based. But my emotions were deeply shaken by a man of his importance suggesting that the work of years was not merely worthless but dangerous.

There was something else that was terrifying about the conversation, though I could not put my finger on it at the moment. Only later, after long reflection on our conversation, did I finally comprehend that it was in effect the same conversation I had with Cardinal Cody when I had brought him copies of *The Education of Catholic Americans* twenty years before. Cardinal Cody had heard complaints that I wrote too much. Cardinal Bernardin had heard complaints that the "steamy" sex in my stories was shocking those who had not read the books.

That's all either cared about. Nothing had changed.

Cardinal Bernardin was friendly, patient, kind. Cardinal Cody was unfriendly, manic, and crazy. But the substance was the same.

(Lady Wisdom: Faith, you must have gone round the bend altogether if you expect respect from an archbishop.

Me: He claimed to be my friend.

Herself: And you were idjit enough to believe that?)

I found a number of aspects of this exchange disturbing:

1. The complainers, especially those who complained without reading the books, were being given absolute veto power just as they had been by the pastor at CK, thus reducing creative work (by anyone) to the lowest common denominator imposed by pharisaical scandal.

2. There was no evidence—social research, literary criticism, praise from those who like my books—that could be given any weight in the face of the complaints.

3. The Cardinal was so encapsulated in the clerical culture that he was concerned only about the tiny minority, 10 percent at the most, who might claim to be shocked and not troubled by the 90 percent of American Catholics who reject core doctrines of the Church's sexual ethic. The acknowledged leader of the liberal wing of the hierarchy is not searching desperately for ways to reestablish contact with those who have turned off the Church on sex (and the evidence that my novels do that for many, many people is persuasive), but rather worrying only about offending the complainers.

4. For a man who takes brave stands on war and justice, his treatment of me seemed a little less than courageous. Protest the closing of steel mills, visit Daniel Ortega, campaign against gang wars, but when one of your priests is under assault by crank letter writers, the best you can do is to tell John Madigan that you have no plans "at the moment" to discipline him. When he thinks that the serious work of careful scholars on the substance of a writer's books is of no importance and complaints

from nonreaders about the image of the books is all-important, does he not run the risk of looking like a hollow man—all appearance and image without conviction or substance? It does not sound exactly like Albert Meyer, does it?

5. The Cardinal is an outspoken foe of prejudice. Yet does he not, when he gives those who haven't read my novels or who systematically misunderstand them the final word over those scholars who have studied them carefully and the vast majority of readers who do understand them, yield power to those who prejudge, to the prejudiced in other words? In caving into such pressures is he not aiding and abetting prejudice against one of his priests who has the right to be defended against prejudice? Moreover, when he attempts to manipulate my enthusiasm for parish work to persuade me to stop writing is he acting any differently from Cardinal Cody? Cardinal Bernardin is an attractive man, but this is not very attractive behavior.

6. Finally, despite his own intense personal piety, religion—the human relationship to God—did not seem to fit into the cardinal's calculus. There can be no reasonable doubt that my fiction had caused many readers to understand better the nature of God's love for us. But that did not matter, not if there were "complaints." Somehow God's love was less important than balancing political pressures within the ecclesiastical institution. A bishop's role, it would seem, is to be a politician; he fends off complaints within the Church and takes stands on controversial issues outside the Church. But when one of his priests uses the traditional sexual metaphor in stories about God's love—effective stories, according to studies of the readers—a bishop does not celebrate the fact that God's love is being preached. Rather he does his best in public to pretend that the priest does not exist and warns him in private that if he wants to return to weekend parish work, he'll have to take the sexual metaphor out of his novels.

Cardinals Stritch and Meyer both affirmed that the Church needed priest writers; Cardinal Cody wished and Cardinal Bernardin wishes that this particular priest did not write (or did not write novels in which the sexual metaphor for God's love appears) and that they could find some way to prevent him from writing without risking harm to their images in public controversy. Perhaps the Second Vatican Council never happened.

Some of those who have read the first drafts of this story find it incredible that Cardinal Bernardin would insist that I stop writing novels and, in effect,

480

do some form of public penance because of the harm done by my novels to those who have not read them but are shocked that I wrote them.

"That's crazy!" is the usual reaction.

What can I tell you?

I should be grateful for two things:

1. I have not been condemned or put on the Index (which doesn't exist anymore, although as is obvious from this part of my story the mentality still exists) or forbidden to write.

2. The cardinal didn't use thumbscrews.

(I showed these and some other pages to the cardinal to give him an opportunity to challenge any factual inaccuracies he might find; I have deleted some passages where his recollection of the facts is different from mine. He did not, however, deny his deep concern about the scandal created by the image of my books among those who had not read them but were shocked that I had written them. It may be that Chicago Chancery Office spokespersons—whose concern for truth has historically been the same as their Kremlin counterparts—will deny such concern after publication of this book. All I can say is that it is entirely too weird a position for me to make up.)

The most fundamental difference between me and the cardinal, I suppose, is that we have different models of human nature. I take it that humankind is more powerfully motivated by metaphor than by any other form of communication (and the research on my readers certainly supports that assumption). The cardinal believes, I think, that since most people are unable to articulate a theory of metaphor they won't be affected by it; rather they will be shocked by metaphors which are new or unusual and which they don't understand.

A story has its illuminating effect to the extent that it is able to insinuate itself subtly into the personality of the one who hears it or reads it, blast open the perceptive structure of the personality with an explosion of dazzling light and then, through the power of such radiant illumination, modify the way the person sees his/her existence, perhaps ever so slightly, and thus the trajectories and the templates of the person's life. As Paul Ricoeur remarks in a persuasive analysis of Proust, "Marcel's" failure to recognize Gilberte, his childhood sweetheart, followed by his recognition of her daughter, is the turning point in the story. Time is lost, but paradoxically it can be regained, at least in story. "Time regained...is time lost eternalized by metaphor."

I recognized my Gilberte instantly, but that's another matter.

"The idea of Time was of value to me for yet another reason: it was a spur, it told me that it was time to begin if I wished to attain to what I had sometimes perceived in the course of my life, in brief lightning-flashes . . . at those moments of perception which made me think that life was worth living. How much more worth living did it appear to me now, now that I had seemed to see that this life we live in half-darkness can be illumined, this life that at every moment we distort can be restored to its true pristine shape, that a life, in short, can be realized within the confines of a book."

So Proust wrote a story about this story in his life, an intolerably long story perhaps, but one that is nonetheless designed to open up the personality of the readers to the possibility of sharing his metaphor and the truth incarnated in the metaphor: the past is not lost. It can be eternalized in story. Life is stronger than death. Mademoiselle de St. Loup's youthful vitality is a better metaphor of the meaning of life (my interpretation and I think Ricoeur's and possibly even Proust's) than Gilberte's decline.

We shall all be young again. We shall all laugh again.

This subtle operation of metaphor as contained in story on the consciousness of the reader need not be explicitly described by the reader, nor even understood. Stories do their work without the need for the process to be described by nonfiction in every case—a point which is hard for most priests, trained in an emotionally and poetically barren hyper-cognitive approach to reality, to comprehend.

Frank McConnell describes how story works:

> You are the hero of your own life-story. The kind of story you want to tell yourself about yourself has a lot to do with the kind of person you are and can become. You can listen to (or read in books or watch in films) stories about other people. But that is only because you know, at some basic level, that you are—or could be—the hero of those stories too. You are Ahab in *Moby Dick*, you are Michael Corleone in *The Godfather*, you are Rick or Ilsa in *Casablanca*, Jim in *Lord Jim*, or the tramp in *City Lights*. And out of these make-believe selves, all of them versions of your own self-in-the-making, you learn, if you are lucky and canny enough, to invent a better you than you could have before the story was told.

As Wendy O'Flaherty says in the quote at the beginning of this book, I am retelling the (Irish) Catholic myth of passionate redeeming grace,

482

I did not invent the myth. I simply retell it. "A myth is a story that many people have found meaningful for a long time... the myth is always in style, even before one updates its hemline to fashionable length." The power of the myth, as Professor O'Flaherty remarks, is that readers both have it and want more of it.

What surprises me about the analysis I have been able to do of my readers is not that for many of them this process works, but that far more of them than I would have thought are fully aware of what is happening.

A reader of a story must have a certain docility of character and flexibility of personality to be captivated and thus illuminated. S/he must be "open" to the possibility, to use Ricoeur's terminology, of being "refigured" by the "configuration" of the story—of "seeing" new possibilities in his/her own life in the radiance the narrative metaphor sheds on reality.

Just as some people cannot "get" a joke, so some people are incapable of seeing the "point" of a metaphor. They are so caught up by the use of the feminine pronoun for God or scatological expletives or a description of sexual desire or a priest committing sin that they can perceive nothing else. For reasons which may not be their own fault they are so witless in their personality, so inflexible in their character, so rigid in their perceptiveness that they literally cannot see the metaphor. That which is an affront to their sensibility blinds them to the light of metaphor.

Two illustrations. In reviewing *Thy Brother's Wife* a conservative Catholic layman could not go beyond the "vile and filthy" image of the consecrated hands of a priest which every morning touch the sacred body of Christ profaning themselves by touching the body of a woman. A liberal Catholic layman could not go beyond the injustice of a rich, sinful woman (Nora Cronin) escaping death as a punishment for her sins. Since she did not die as she should have—and as Kristin Lavransdatter did—the story was devoid of theological content.

Both reviewers missed completely the metaphor of Nora's womanly passion reflecting the maternal passion of God, a metaphor which for most readers was self-evident. They missed it in part because of ignorance. The conservative was unaware that the hands of married priests of the Eastern churches touch the bodies of their wives and the body of the Lord every day, that St. Peter was a married man (and one hopes, for the sake of Mrs. Peter, skillful in the use of his hands to excite married love), and finally that the body of woman is sacred too, a revelation of God's life-giving, life-nurturing, life-healing love. The liberal was unaware that there are other theologies besides that of divine wrath for the rich. But their ignorance was secondary to their rigidity—personality needs constrained them to fixate on that which was irrelevant to the metaphor and thus blind themselves to the metaphor.

If some people do not "get" the sexual metaphor, ought I not refrain from using it? Indeed, to pursue Cardinal Bernardin's point, ought not I protect the easily shocked by taking sex out of my novels, by not using the sexual metaphor for God's love?

The answers to this objection come to the heart of the power of story to captivate so as to illuminate:

1. The objection is the same as if one argued that jokes ought not to be told lest one embarrass those who routinely do not "get" jokes: one gives veto power to the witless.

2. The research shows that it is precisely the sexual metaphor which accounts for the religious effectiveness of my stories—those who find the sexual scenes "compelling" are the ones on whose religious imagination the stories have the greatest impact.

3. If one throws out the metaphors some personalities cannot absorb, one quickly loses all metaphors and hence all story. One has made the lowest common denominator of sensibility and sensitivity the norm and hence has nothing to say. Or to rephrase this response, the two reviewers I cited a few paragraphs back would have been affronted and fixated at any metaphor because they approached the story of Sean and Nora Cronin with preconceived opinions and needs which precluded their being illumined by the metaphor of Nora Cronin as sacrament of God.

4. Finally, a Catholicism without the sexual metaphor is an incomplete Catholicism. The metaphor abounds in both the Jewish and Christian scriptures, in the liturgy (the Easter vigil) and in the tradition. To demand that it be excluded from my stories is to try to make them not more Catholic but not Catholic. My sister Mary Jule contends that Cardinal Bernardin fails the "shocked faithful" not by refraining from a condemnation, but rather by refraining from an insistence that the sexual metaphor is essential to the Catholic tradition. He is dodging, she contends, his responsibility to defend the integrity of the Catholic imaginative heritage because he knows that the integrity of the heritage will offend those who complain to him. He is failing in a responsibility that is his *ex officio* as bishop.

Metaphor works with those who are able or willing to permit it to work, those whose personalities are sufficiently open that the metaphor can insinuate itself, then turn on its blazing lights and compel them to exclaim, "Oh! God loves as Nora does!" and then perhaps to recognize a new or renewed direction for their lives.

It is for such that one tells stories, not for those who will not or cannot allow the light of metaphor inside themselves.

The ones who chose not to get the point of Jesus's stories, who refused to be either captivated or illuminated, were not the ordinary people but the scribes and Pharisees. Hypocrites.

If you reduce metaphor to that which all readers will permit to work, then you will use no metaphor and will tell no stories. You will turn on no dazzling lights because you have thrown away your electricity. You will not illuminate because you have deprived yourself of the power to captivate.

There are two components to a metaphor, two aspects of reality that correlate and are capable of illumining one another. Thus Shakespeare has Romeo comparing Juliet to the sun. That image illumines Juliet for us. She is not only a tizzy teenager but also the source of light and heat and warmth and life. But the sun too is illumined. It is like Juliet and hence we see that medium-sized star as we had not seen it before, playful, gracious, loving.

We need not process this "correlation" in rational propositions. We do not have to understand the literary theory behind metaphor. We do not even have to know that what we have heard is a metaphor. The mere juxtaposition of the two images—the girl and the sun—slips into our imagination and our personality and does its subtle and powerful work.

Is that what I claim happens in my novels?

The data from the research I cited earlier in this chapter confirm that is precisely what happens—those who find the sexual imagery "compelling" or "sensitive" among those who say that the book has helped them to understand better the nature of God's love are precisely the people who are more likely to have warm and intimate images of God. The theory of the "illuminating" effect of metaphor is neatly confirmed.

My 1987 novel *Patience of a Saint* illustrates neatly how the sexual metaphor achieves its purpose of "correlating" human and divine love. Perhaps the most erotic of my novels (and it will not offend the complainers any less that the eroticism is all between a man and his wife), it is the story of a man who falls in love again with his wife, perhaps the most intensely pleasurable experience humans can have. He realizes that the two loves illuminate one another—that God is like Eileen and Eileen is like God. The reader who knows the intensity of sexual passion in his life realizes (unless he has completely closed himself to the illuminating power of the metaphor) that God's passion for us is even stronger than that very strong human passion. He also realizes that his human lover (should there be one) is a hint of God, a sacrament of God, a way to God. Human love is a sacrament of divine love and a participation in it.

Three passages (all rated highly by Professor Shafer's respondents who did not know they were mine and rated poorly by those who did) demonstrate my explicit linkage of human and divine passion:

> Light, heat, fire, overwhelming, invading, possessing love; dazzling truth, beauty and goodness; confidence, hope, joy, the promise that all would be well; a love so unspeakably powerful that, in the instant it possessed Red, he knew that he could never escape from it. Nor would it ever permit him and Eileen to escape from one another. When its joy seemed so intense that he knew he would die, the operator of this transcendental Concorde jet turned on the afterburners and Red thought he had died and was in heaven, a golden city whose ivory walls were his wife's breasts.

Now, gentle reader, does that passage seem "steamy"? Does it seem "excessive" or "questionably explicit" or "inappropriate for a priest"—to use the cardinal's words? Can you understand my astonishment at the myth which says that this kind of writing makes me a clerical Harold Robbins?

Right there, attentive friend, is the core of the problem. Priests are not supposed to notice that women have breasts, much less refer to that fact in their writing, and even much less than that to compare them to the heavenly Jerusalem.

It's 1950 again and the cardinal is the Jesuit spiritual director warning us about Janet Leigh.

(Lady Wisdom: I'm rather impressed with the ingenuity that went into the design of the breast, to tell you the truth. But then I'm not a bishop.)

Or another passage—one which achieved the highest rating of all sixteen (including passages from Bellow, Oates, Updike, Styron, Penn Warren) in Professor Shafer's study (39 percent of the respondents rated it as best or second best in the sample in which the names of the authors were not known; the rating fell to 14 percent when my name was attached to the quote):

> "I have evil designs on you, green-eyed witch," he said softly. His hands brushed lightly and quickly from her shoulders to her thighs, then made their return journey more slowly and forcefully.
>
> "No, that's not what I want today. Let me do it to you." She smiled shyly. "A way of saying thanks for all the support during the trial."
>
> Eileen, creature of light, was blessed with the lightest fingers and the lightest lips, the most radiant smile and the most happy laughter in the world. Her subtle body was wind and air and, alternately, moonlight and sunlight, gentle waves and lazy surf, spring zephyr and winter wind.
>
> Then, as she guided him, drenched in poignant sweetness and healed of all his hurts and regrets, slowly and skillfully to the shining mountain tops of their lovemaking, he knew that he had finally unlocked the secret of his magic, green-eyed wife just as she had unlocked the secret of healing his accumulated pain.

Again, learned colleague, does that seem "excessive" or "inappropriate"? Or would you vote with four-fifths of my readers that the passage is "delicate," "compelling," "sensitive" and "tasteful"?

And do you wonder as I often do what all the complaining is about?

I'll tell you why that passage would upset the cardinal and those who hassle him with complaints: a priest ought not to know about love play. Especially he ought not to know that sometimes a woman may take the lead in love play and work wondrous and delightful healing for her man. And if he knows that such things happen, he ought not to acknowledge that he knows. And he certainly should not compare foreplay in which a *woman* heals her man to God's healing forgiveness. He most definitely ought not to encourage married lovers to that kind of self-indulgent behavior on the grounds that it can be "sacramental" (revelatory) of God's love.

What kind of a man is it that would yield his masculinity to such an extent that he permits that sort of fondling from someone who is, after all, a bag of vomit and ordure, to quote the ineffable St. Bonaventure?

Sex is only for procreation anyway, isn't it?

That's the problem, you see. The Church is now prepared to admit that marital sex and even marital sex play is "all right" and may also give some hint of what God is like. But it doesn't want priests suggesting either of those facts too vividly. The laity might enjoy sex "too much." Or to be more precise, men might enjoy women "too much," glory be to God!

(Lady Wisdom: Thank you. To tell the truth, I think I did a pretty good job designing women to be delicious. Men too as far as that goes. I sometimes wonder why the amadons—radical feminists and bishops—think I put sexual differentiation into the world. Why should they feel that people are supposed to ignore it instead of enjoying it?)

What can I tell you?

Precisely because it consists of an unexpected and surprising juxtaposition of images, metaphor tends to shatter old perspectives and, in its essential role of illumining, to offer the possibility of new perspectives. Life does not have to be lived the way I have lived it till now in a world in which Juliet is the sun and the towers of the heavenly city are like the breasts of a rediscovered wife. In such a world, illuminated by a sudden, surprising flash of light, new possibilities and new challenges appear. Not everyone sees the possibilities and challenges in the light of every metaphor, but the point is that for those who are open to the possibility, metaphor has the capability of offering change and possibly inducing it, a possibility that prose propositions usually lack.

Consider another illustration from Professor Shafer's list of passages which are highly regarded until respondents know that I wrote them, a passage which is more explicitly metaphorical and somewhat more explicitly sexual:

Cathy Collins has fought her way back to health after being brutalized in a South American prison. Her psychiatrist thinks she's ready again for love, but Cathy is afraid that her experiences have spoiled her for men. Fragile, frightened, ready to run, Cathy invites her faithful but perennially hesitant sweetheart Nick Curran into her apartment. Just as Eileen Kane is the healing grail for Red, so Nick Curran is Cathy's grail. He is uneasy and frightened by his responsibility.

> She was wearing a rosary around her neck, the crucifix hanging between lace-covered breasts. . . . I drew her head against my chest and unfastened her bra, kissing her back and pathetically thin shoulder blades. I chose a small area on one of her shoulder blades and caressed it with my index finger, carefully and slowly as if I were healing all of her through that one spot. She sighed peacefully.

Then I moved her lightly away, disposed of the flimsy bra and captured each breast, caressing it gently and pushing it against her ribs.

God, I said to myself, I hope I'm not going too fast.

"You're the only man in the world who would do this for me."

"The pleasure is mine," I said as I began to kiss and nibble at my twin captives, feeling confident that the Person watching me from her rosary did not mind sharing her and had indeed always intended to share her with me.

I'm doing all right, I told Him, but don't desert me now.

Now, gentle reader, I ask you, does that carefully described and cautiously executed tenderness seem trashy or steamy or sleazy? Does it read like "softcore porn"? Do you think it "dirty"? Does it seem excessive or questionably explicit or inappropriate? Or do the men and women who use those adjectives to describe it tell you more about themselves than they do about either *Virgin and Martyr* or its author?

Gentle reader: That's not how my priest described your writing. If that's the way you write about sex, I don't understand why there's so much fuss.

Me: Tell me about it.

(This passage was ranked first or second by 30 percent of Professor Shafer's respondents who did not know that I had written it. The percentage fell to 15 percent among those who knew I had written it. The previous passage and this one won first and second place in the section of eight passages in the Shafer study. Among those who didn't know that I was the author, these two passages ranked ahead in quality of quotes from Joyce Carol Oates, Robert Penn Warren, Saul Bellow and William Styron. However, among those who knew the names of the authors, the two passages were sixth and seventh out of eight, only a little higher in quality than a quote from Jacqueline Susann! Do I think I am a better writer than Oates, Bellow, Penn Warren and Styron? Course not. The point is that the respondents—book critics and professors—thought that these two passages of mine were better written than quotes from them *until they knew the names of the writers.* Do I think on the basis of the Shafer study that I write better than a lot of critics would admit? What do you think?)

A final quote from the Shafer study in which the violence of sexual passion and hunger is explicitly related to the violence of the mutual hunger between God and us—a passage which topped Professor Shafer's list among those who did not know I was the author, and which won seventh place, ahead only of a quote from Harold Robbins, among those who knew the authors.

> Our love was not the sensitive, tender affection we had known the last time together in her anonymous room in the Chestnut Plaza. It was angry demonic love, our bodies yelling their protest against so long a separation. I had the top of her dress and her bra off within ten seconds and my head buried between her legs in ten more. Ciara's response was as violent as my attack. For a few minutes of wild passion and headlong, heedless pleasure we existed only for each other.
>
> In the dank little room with its musty smell and the sound of a combo somewhere in the hotel playing early Beatles, I knew that she was indeed my holy grail, my life, my purpose, my destiny. I might live without her, but it wouldn't be much of a life. God put me in the world for Ciara Kelly.

Brendan Ryan's passion for Ciara Kelly (or vice versa) is inadequate as a metaphor of God's love for us only by defect: it is less violent than God's passion. God's passion is much more violent, demanding, consuming than Brendan's and our need much more vehemently responsive than Ciara's (or vice versa).

There are doubtless some people who "freeze" at the juxtaposition of the images of "priest" and "breast" or of "breast" and "cross" or of "priest" and the metaphor of kissing the loins of a lover as a symbol of God's demanding passion and are incapable of illumination by the metaphor— for reasons of education or personality or character. I sympathize with such folk, but they do not have to read my books and they violate my rights and the rights of others when they attempt to prevent me from using such metaphors. They do not have the right to impose their own sensibility on everyone else.

Am I angry at Cardinal Bernardin because he thinks uninformed complaints more important than the demonstrated positive effects of my work and because he dismisses my efforts with what is in effect contempt?

No, not angry. Disappointed. Hurt because I thought he was a friend. And frustrated because what I must do to satisfy him is eliminate all complaints, patently an impossible task unless I am prepared either to die or never write another word.

The myth is falsehood, and those who are intimidated by it are servants of falsehood. But the myth also goes with the territory. If a priest writes novels, particularly successful novels, in which sexual differentiation and the resulting passion is described as a metaphor of God's love, he will certainly be victimized by myth, regardless of the fact that his readers think the sexual scenes in his books are tasteful and sensitive and delicate.

Ideally a bishop, presented with accurate research on the impact of his priest's books, should defend him from such false mythology, but we do not live in an ideal world.

Bishop Bill McManus, visiting me in Tucson, tells me that I am far better off in my present status. "You're as free as a retired bishop!"

I suppose so, but as a believer in community and a loyal member of the community I still would like to belong. And I'll beat Herself to it, I know it is unreasonable to expect to have your cake and eat it too.

So I will continue to be a square peg in Chicago. And maybe better off because of that.

(Lady Wisdom: Haven't I been after telling you that all along?

Me: Do you ever make a mistake?

Herself: Course not!

Me: And you get the last word always?

Herself: Am I not the first Word too?)

CHAPTER
25
The End of Volume One

With her springtime smile
In gentle and warming hands
Mary holds the world

Four models shape the story I have tried to tell—three of them suggested to me one way or another while the story was in progress (in addition to the semifacetious, half-fun and full-earnest, as my mother would have said, Quixote model and the somewhat ironic "square peg" model). From Erika Fromm I discovered the importance of the lake, from Ernest Hartmann I learned about thin boundaries, from Jack Shea in a passing remark during a phone conversation I took the image of "Paradise Lost" and "Paradise Found" and from Ingrid Shafer I drew the notion of the pursuit of the Grail, the magic cup and the magic princess.

All are finally the same metaphor. I search for the God of the lake, the tender loving affectionate God of childhood happiness to be re-discovered through exploration of the world beyond the boundaries of the self. And within the internal boundaries of the self, I search for the paradise (the park, the garden, as Elizabeth Moynihan reminds us in her study of Persian gardens in India). In this journey from Para-dise Lost (the First Naiveté) to Paradise Regained (the Second Naiveté) I have come a long way, not all the way yet, but a long way still.

It is about this pilgrimage I write my novels and tell my stories.

The pilgrimage, on which we all go, one way or another, each with his or her own set of models/metaphors/stories, is finally a quest for union, among the dimensions of the self and between creature and Creator, being and Being.

As I work on this chapter I have had a perfectly splendid nightmare which ties all four models together. I am on a ship, part QEII, part SS Milwaukee Clipper, on which there have been hidden explosives. I must find them. I also must warn Paul and Erika Fromm, who are on the deck beneath me. I despair of uncovering the bombs and run down the stairs to the next deck. Just as I arrive there, the explosive goes off; the ship tilts forward and sinks rapidly. I leap over the side and swim fran-tically. But the suction of the sinking ship grips my feet. I struggle with it and I wake.

Now there are two options. One is to force myself to stay awake and remember the details for this chapter. The other is to go back to sleep and will an end to the dream in which, I suppose, I will not only break free of the sinking ship, but also rescue the Fromms and probably everyone else too (when Greels is a hero he is Solemn High Hero). Obviously I chose the first option. Interestingly, once this option was exercised, it was hard to go back to sleep, as though I had done some violence to the ordinary course of events. Somehow I *should* have finished the nightmare in the usual way.

I suspect most of my colleagues in the priesthood and others in the Catholic elite will not like my metaphors; they are not relevant enough, not moral enough, not authoritative enough. Once again, they will say, it is proved that I am not Merton or Berrigan (or a host of other folk, for the most recent list of which see the latest issue of *The National Catholic Reporter*) and that there is no theological merit, no compassionate insight in my imagery.

That's too bad. Just as in the Father's kingdom there are many mansions, so on the pilgrimage to that kingdom there are many paths. It is the essence of the genius of Catholicism that it celebrates the diversity of ways home. Those who find only one or two sets of metaphors/models/ stories acceptable and are not interested in deviant stories do violence to that Catholic tradition.

Moreover, I think my set of models traces the path the Church and the priesthood will follow in the next century or two. I'm not offering my life as an exemplar, only as a rough trajectory. Both the Church and the priesthood will almost certainly rediscover the riches of the Catholic heritage, especially its imaginative riches. The themes and images of my novels will shape the future, not because they are in my novels, but because they are the essential *archetypes* for any resurgence of the Catholic imagination.

The Church today is hung up on morality and authority to the exclusion of all else. For the left it is the morality (generally loveless) of secular relevance and for the right the morality (generally loveless) of sexual irrelevance. Both appeal to authority to support their position. Curiously, the left, which ignores Church authority on sexual issues, invokes that authority on matters of poverty and nuclear weapons, while the right, which pays small attention to social concerns, invokes authority to support rigid sexual morality.

The mass media take both seriously.

The laity take neither seriously.

In all this struggle between two moral, not to say moralistic, systems

495

which provide simple answers to everything each group thinks is crucial to human life, there is little attention paid to God, to life and death, good and evil, love and hatred.

The institutional Church is presided over by men who have fibbed and finessed, dissembled and deceived so often that even those who are not psychopaths often have a hard time distinguishing between what is true and what isn't.

Father Leo Mahon insists he has never known anyone who loves the Church or the priesthood more than I do. He wants me to end this story by showing the "progression by which grace transforms hurt into acceptance and then into wisdom and freedom." I'm flattered by his compliment and I do indeed love both the Church and the priesthood. But I don't believe that acceptance is what I feel or what I ought to feel.

Should I end my comments on the current state of the priesthood with "compassion, grace and forgiveness"? Okay, Leo, I forgive the myth-makers, I have compassion for them, I pray for them.

But I won't let them get behind my back. Nor will I go into a dark room with them.

One trusts one's fellows in the clergy about as much as a century and a quarter ago here in Arizona one trusted a band of marauding Apache.

An angry conclusion?

Only about clergy, not about priests, in Ed McKenna's distinction. Priests are wonderful, the salt of the earth, the kind of men to whom I dedicate this book. Clergy are the envious passive/aggressive murmurantes and naysayers who dominate clerical culture.

It has not always been such and it will not always be. The Church and the priesthood, composed of humans, will always be less than perfect, but a religionless Church and a priesthood devoid of generosity and loyalty are historical aberrations. Envy and moralism will always be part of any religious organization, but they need not be, have not been, will not always be quite so characteristic of Catholicism in the United States as they are today.

Anyone who knows any history can be certain of that.

Thus the first part of my story, Volume One, comes to an end.

It is only Volume One, an account of my life so far. Whether I ever write subsequent volumes is in the hands of God, as is the tomorrow of all of our lives. I looked up the other day in the *Statistical Abstract* my life expectancy. Remarkably, it is somewhere between twenty and twenty-five more years.

The genes in our family are erratic. Some of my ancestors have lived to ripe and vigorous old ages. Some die young. If I live to be sixty-one I will have passed all the males in my parental and grandparental generation. But I drink lightly and smoke not and swim a mile every day and sleep eight hours every night and stay under a hundred and seventy-five pounds and live in a time of antibiotics.

Vain speculation. Marty Phee, my M.D., says I've lucked out on the genes and that I should provide for retirement. After I've paid off my grants to the university and the seminary, I'll do that. It would be foolish not to. Having thus exercised ordinary prudence, I will leave the question of whether there will be material or opportunity for Volume Two (or Three or Four) to Other Parties.

With whom it is impossible to argue.

I am under no illusion that life need continue to be relatively peaceful. We are all fragile. We can be easily hurt by chance and/or by the malevolence of those who don't like us. I learned during the late seventies and early eighties that Murphy's law is fundamentally sound: anything can go wrong anytime. To put one's security anywhere but in God's love is absurd.

Nonetheless at the present moment there is some peace. For that I give thanks and take stock.

Perhaps the main reason for my still tentative peace is that storytelling has paid an unexpected bonus: it has become an exploration in self-understanding. As I said early in this book, I write novels first of all for myself and for the road map through the realities of self and world and God that the stories provide.

Wisdom, I think, is what these road maps might be called. The first tiny smidgen of it.

In frustration agonized engines moan
Spinning tires strain against the frozen slush
Caught in a cosmic traffic jam, each alone,
While the universe reverts to primal mush
Life a brutal mess wreathed in tailpipe gas
Emptiness crudely packaged by random chance
Our kind, in a blizzard trapped, a struggling mass
Blind while gross, angry snowflakes madly dance.

In the distance through the swirling mist
A warming glow, an incandescent window pane
Where laughing tender grace may still exist
To end with a single touch confusion's reign
We glimpse through the snowdrifts of chaos dense
In a soothing love's brief flare, some hint of sense.

I accept, however regretfully, the loss of the promise of the golden moments after the Council. For the Renewed Church to have risen, Venuslike, all dewy and young in the middle and late sixties would have been too easy. It might have happened if enough of us had been faithful enough to the *xairos* of that time. We weren't, we blew it, and that's that. It will now be a long time before the benefits of the present renewal era are harvested. The action now and perhaps for decades will not be in the institution. The Vatican, the National Conference, the Chancery are talking only to themselves. Blessedly, the paying customers show no signs of walking out. That gives us time. Enough time? Please God, yes. But that's beyond my control. I will write my stories and pray. The early sixties were times of great possibility, of *xairos*, to use the Greek word for "special times." I think that was finished by the end of 1968. Or in this country maybe even with the death of Albert Meyer.

If there is a *xairos* now it is in the tradition and the community, both of which have survived the end of the Counter-Reformation with surprising vitality. The intellectual, artistic, devotional and ethical ferment in the grassroots of the Church—unaided and usually unrecognized by the leadership—is the most promising sign of the times currently available to be read.

Mircea Eliade, a sympathetic and sensitive outsider, puts his finger on the most likely developments in Catholicism in the years to come: "It seems to me that this crisis is bound to be creative and that once the trials and controversies are over, other, more interesting, more living and more meaningful things may emerge."

But I can't do much to affect that possibility, other than to tell my stories and write my social science. We are now settling down for the long haul.

Decades, centuries.

In St. Peter's First Epistle, with an allusion to the prophet Hosea, the Church is said to be both a fair bride and a whore, a position which will doubtless be offensive to the Vatican. I offered my life to the Church as institution and discovered that at the present time in its history the institution is, to use words that will keep June Rosner happy, not yet completely the fair bride.

Fortunately for me, the fair bride is alive and well in the community and the heritage.

I have come to a vision of Church as loving mother who cares for us regardless of whether we want to be cared for, a Church which is represented in my novels by the ubiquitous, zany, ingenious and implacable Ryan family. Is the Church as loving and supportive as Ned Ryan's clan? Surely not. Can it be?

Why not?

And a God who is like Maria and Blackie and Blackie's sibling Eileen.

On the margins of the institution not as it might easily be, but as it in fact is now, I am nonetheless in the center of the community, beginning to acquire my first smidgen of wisdom in pursuit of the Lord/Lady of the Dance.

If, as I suggested at the beginning of this book, the quest for the Grail is the quest for the total self as sacrament of the total God, then my own quest has been greatly accelerated by writing novels. The women in my stories have brought me into closer contact with the tender dimension of my personality than anything else in my spiritual pilgrimage. The poem to Lynnie, the "apricot figment" in *Death in April*, which appears at the beginning of Chapter 23, hints at the scary experience of discovering a lot about yourself from the characters you create.

Now all I have to do is permit that dimension of my selfhood to flourish more serenely and more confidently in my life.

That should keep me busy.

There have been three turning points so far in my life as a priest. The first was in the early sixties when I took the Sunday Night Group at its word and embraced the ideal of professional competence over against clerical mediocrity. The second was in the middle seventies when my socioreligious reflections led to a paradigm which emphasizes the imaginative, the poetic, the communal, the traditional, the nonpropositional aspects of religion. The third was in the late seventies when, impelled by the momentum of the first two turning points, I began to try to write stories of God. I resolved to be the best I possibly could at what I was doing, I studied the response not only of the intellect but of the whole personality to religion, I told contemporary parables. All three were unexceptionable activities, until they were marked with the tainted word "successful."

Each of the turning points brought me farther down the road. It is impossible to go back, even if I wanted to.

But it'll be a cold day in hell when I leave.

I wrote, perhaps too militantly, in a previous chapter that my terms are acceptance and freedom. Realistically, I don't expect acceptance. Realistically too I don't expect freedom unless I'm prepared to fight for it whenever someone tries to mess with me.

Could it ever be otherwise? I don't see how, but as I said in the beginning of this story, I don't believe in burning bridges.

It ought not to be this way. As Jack Shea remarked at supper the other night, any priest who does anything will be in trouble with his fellow clergy. No priest should have to endure from his fellow priests what those of us who try to do something today have to endure. Okay, I survived, but that's no thanks to the clergy.

The Church cannot continue to permit the priesthood to impose on its members the lowest common denominator of envy-ridden, passive/aggressive mediocrity. The Church will not be able to respond to the challenges and the opportunities of the years ahead without a sophisticated, professionally trained, mutually supportive, enthusiastic clergy.

That too, I fear, is for the decades, the centuries.

So, Greels, Quixots, have you found the Grail and the princess?

Not yet.

But now I think I know where they are.

(Lady Wisdom: 'Tis about time you found them!)

CODA: A Return to CK

Saguaro Blossoms
Detonate in spring bouquet.
Time that I go home.

In December of 1985 I returned for a Sunday Mass at St. Praxides. It was the year of the fiftieth anniversary of the parish and all the former associates (once curates) were invited back. In the same year that I was writing this book and rediscovering the friends and loves of St. Ursula, I went back twenty-one years to my second parish.

Like St. Ursula, CK came alive again in my life. The experience was pure joy.

I preached on the king of Kerry, a story I had first heard from Jack Shea in a much shorter form as the king of Crete. You must imagine it being told with a thick if quite phony brogue.

Once upon a time, long, long ago, there was a great king in the Kingdom of Kerry in the West of Ireland named Fergus MacDiarmud UiDonal (McDermot O'Donnell, if you wish). He was a great and good and wise and brave king and he ruled his people justly and wisely. There was peace and prosperity in the whole Kingdom of Kerry during the half-century he ruled and all called him Fergus the Good.

But at last he grew old as we all must and his health failed and he knew he was going to die. So he summoned his councilors and his warriors and his poets and his priests and ordered his servants to carry him out to the meadow in front of his ring fort. There he said a tearful goodbye to his wife of fifty years and his children and his grandchildren and even his little great-granddaughter, a blond-haired toddler about three years old looking just like that little girl in the second row.

That's right, just like *you!*

Then as life was slipping away he looked up at the green hills and the blue sky and the golden fields and the silver lakes of the Kingdom of Kerry and loved all the kingdom and all its people. Finally, just as he commended his soul to God, he scooped up in his right hand a clump of thick, rich Kerry turf.

Well, the next thing he knew he was at the gates of a big city with great ivory walls and a big gold-and-silver gate. In front of the gate was a man, dressed in white robes and wearing a triple crown, sitting at an IBM PC AT computer, with a fishing rod next to it.

"And who would you be," says your man Simon Peter, alias Pope Peter I, "and what would you be wanting from us?"

"Well," says the king, respectful, but not afraid, "I'm King Fergus

MacDiarmud UiDonal, king of Kerry, and if it's all the same to you I wouldn't mind if you let me into that city."

All the time the king was holding the clump of Kerry turf behind his back.

"UiDonal, is it? Well, now, let me see." Your man called up his Lotus 1-2-3 and punched in an entry. He made a mistake—infallibility does not apply to operating a PC—corrected it, and touched the ENTER key. "Ah, yes, your majesty, we have a long record on you here in our data base. And most of it's good, very good indeed. A few wild moments when you were young, but, sure, Himself forgave them long before you did. To tell you the truth, me bucko, there's no purgatory at all, at all for you."

"Well, I'm grateful to you for that, God knows," King Fergus said with a great west of Ireland sigh.

The Pope punched in an escape sequence and, pretty as you please, the great silver-and-gold gates began to swing open.

"Ah, just a minute now, your majesty," your man says as King Fergus slipped by him. "What's that you're holding in your hand?"

"'Tis nothing at all."

"'Tis too." Peter punched a Control C and the gate stopped swinging. "What have you got there?"

"Sure, 'tis nothing but a wee bit of Kerry turf, to remind me of home, if you take my meaning."

"I take your meaning, all right, but you can't have it. Against the rules. No one enters the kingdom of heaven save with empty hands."

"Well, your reverence, if that's the lay of the land"—King Fergus was not the kind of man you'd want to fool with when his back was up— "I'd just as soon not go in, if I can't bring me piece of Kerry turf with me."

"Rules is rules," your man insists.

"Then I'll just wait out here."

The Pope put in a hurry-up call, murmured discreetly into the phone, listened, said "Aye," and hung up.

A minute later the big silver-and-gold gates swung open and out strode the Lord God Himself. He's ten feet tall and has long blond hair and looks like a linebacker for the Chicago Bears. He embraced the king, slapped him on the back, and boomed out in a rich baritone voice,

"Faith, it's good to see you, Fergus me boy; we've been waiting up for a long time for you. Come on right in, we'll have a wee talk about how difficult it is to be a king. Just toss aside that little bit of Kerry turf and come on in. There'll be the singing and the dancing and the telling of tales all night long."

Your man Fergus MacDiarmud UiDonal was moved by this warm greeting, but not moved enough. Like I say, when he got his back up, he could be a difficult man.

"Saving your reverence," the King says, "I'll not be coming in unless I can bring me little handful of Kerry turf. Sure it won't do any harm at all, at all."

Well, the Lord God seemed greatly disappointed. "Faith, we can't let you do that, Fergus me friend. Rules is rules. You can't come into the kingdom of heaven save with empty hands. I don't make the rules, you know. Well, actually I do, but that's one we just can't change, if you take my meaning."

"I can wait," the king says, real stubborn-like.

So the Lord God sighed a great west of Ireland sigh and walked slowly back into the city.

And the great silver-and-gold gates clanked shut.

"You might go around to the back and see if Herself will let you in," says your man Simon Peter. "Sure, She gets a lot of folk in that way, and Herself having a lot of clout. But that's one rule even She won't bend."

"If it's all the same to you," the king said, still real stubborn, "I'll wait here in the rain."

Didn't I tell you it was raining outside of the heavenly city? Well, course it was.

The Lord God is devious and will stop at nothing to get us into the heavenly city. So He disguised Himself as an Irish countryman—you know, the gray suit which hasn't been cleaned or pressed for forty years, the old brown sweater, the dirty tie, the big galoshes, the cap pulled down over his head—and put a big Havana cigar in his mouth. Then He slipped out of the gates and stood next to King Fergus MacDiarmud UiDonal, watching in silence as the mists rose up over the bogs.

"Have one," says the Lord God, offering a cigar to the king. "They don't hurt you up here."

"Aye, don't mind if I do," says King Fergus.

"'Tis a bad night."

"'Tis."

"'Tis warm and comfy inside."

"Is it now?"

"'Tis."

They both sighed together.

"We have some fine Jameson's and the best Guinness in the cosmos inside. They don't hurt you up here either."

"Is that true?"

"'Tis."

They sighed again.

"You could come in and have a drop of Jameson's by the fire, if only you will get rid of that handful of dirt you've got there."

"I know who you are," King Fergus explodes. "You're no countryman, you're the Lord God. And You ought to be ashamed of Yourself with all them tricks. I'll not come in without me Kerry turf."

"Ah, but we can't allow that, don't you see. Sure, no one comes into the kingdom of heaven..."

"Save with empty hands," the king finishes for him.

So the Lord God, dejected-like, walked back into the heavenly city.

And the big silver-and-gold gates clanked shut.

The next trick the Lord God pulled was to disguise Himself as a wee blond colleen, with a few freckles on her nose, looking just like the king's great-granddaughter or like yourself out there in the second row. Right, she looked just like you.

And the colleen who was really the Lord God slipped up to King Fergus MacDiarmud UiDonal and says to him, "O King Fergus, they're having a wonderful party inside for all the little kids, but I can't go unless I can find a grown-up to take me. Would you ever think of being me grown-up?"

Well, the king was moved, let me tell you. "You can't find another grown-up?"

"Not at all, at all."

"Well..."

"Just put down that silly old turf and we can both go to the party."

"I'll not be taken in by your tricks," the king shouted. "I know who

505

You are, You're not a wee lass, You're the Lord God in disguise. And I won't come in without me Kerry turf, and don't repeat the rules, I know them by heart..."

So King Fergus and the Lord God and your man Simon Peter all said together, "No one enters the kingdom of heaven save with empty hands."

And, with tears in her eyes, the little blond colleen with the freckles on her nose went back into the heavenly city.

And the big silver-and-gold gates clanked shut.

Well, the night got darker and the rain colder and the Kerry turf more crumbly. And King Fergus began to think about it.

Sure, Fergus, he says to himself, a prize amadon you are. This isn't Kerry, it's the kingdom of heaven. They make their own laws here and they're not going to change them for you, even if you wait till all eternity. You've been counting on sneaking through those gates since you were a wee lad. Isn't it time you'd be after coming to your senses?

So with the loudest sigh all day, doesn't he stroll over to St. Peter's desk and toss the turf on the ground.

"Begging your reverence's pardon, but there's no sense in fighting the Lord God, is there now?"

"Not at all, at all," says your man Simon Peter happily. He punched in the escape code, making no mistake this time. The big silver-and-gold gates of heaven clanked open. "There's no one goes through those gates save with empty hands."

"Aye," says the king, feeling like he was pretty much the fool, if you take my meaning, but still mourning for his lost Kerry turf.

And so he walked through the big silver-and-gold gates. And do you know what he found inside?

Do you?

Ah, you don't.

Sure you do.

Well, I'll tell you. Inside, waiting for King Fergus MacDiarmud UiDonal was... what?

The green hills and the blue skies and the golden fields and the silver lakes and the whole Kingdom of Kerry!

They applauded after the sermon, sang "Lord of the Dance" at Communion, and then applauded again after the blessing. Indeed heaven must be like this. In the parish hall afterwards, many of the beloved faces of the past, none the worse for wear, reappeared. The years at CK had been worth it after all.

I could have this all back for the asking. The cardinal would be so grateful to me for easing his burden of worry about the poor folk who had not read my books but were shocked that I wrote them that he would give me almost any assignment that I wanted.

Of course, that kind of compromise would be infidelity—to St. Angela, to CK, to my mailbox parish. To Herself.

(Lady Wisdom: You bet your life it would be.)

The Ryan clan was there of course, en masse. And Noele Farrell too— she led the singing of "Lord of the Dance." I was the only one that could see them because they exist on a different level of being. What would they say if I betrayed them?

Blackie, Mary Kate, Eileen, Packy?

As Mary Kate would say, I wouldn't dare.

And Noele would warn me that it would be, like, *totally* geeky.

CK will always be with me—waiting like the blue skies and the green grass and the golden fields and the silver lakes of Kerry. So will St. Angela.

That is enough.

The blessing I gave at the end of Mass is prayer for myself and for all of us.

AVRAN

May the tunes of angels echo in your brain
May heaven's rhythms tap your twitching feet
May you sing along with Mary's sweet refrain
And may you sway to the Lord's demanding beat
Dance with all the lovers He has taught your song
And, sure, spin with Him at every chance
Whenever He invites you all night long
Never say "no" to the Lord of the Dance!

ABOUT THE AUTHOR

Andrew M. Greeley is the author of seven best-selling novels including *Angels of September*, *Virgin and Martyr*, *Lord of the Dance*, and many more, as well as a regular contributor to such publications as *The New York Times*, *TV Guide*, and the *Chicago Sun-Times*. Father Greeley has also written countless nonfiction works on religion, sociology, Catholic education; books of meditation and catechism; and devotional books. These include *The Making of the Popes*, *The Jesus Myth*, *The Hesitant Pilgrim*, *The American Catholic*, and *The Mary Myth*. He is a priest of the archdiocese of Chicago and professor of sociology at the University of Arizona in Tucson, where he does weekend work in three parishes.